ENTREPRENEURSHIP

AF810948

Dr. Achut P. Pednekar

Ph.D., M.Com., B.Ed., DBM,
Assistant Professor, D.M.'s College of
Arts, Science, Commerce, Management Studies & Technology,
Assagao, Bardez – Goa.

Himalaya Publishing House

ISO 9001:2015 CERTIFIED

First Edition : 2012
Reprint : 2016
Reprint : 2019
Reprint : 2021
Reprint : 2024

Published by : Mrs. Meena Pandey
for **HIMALAYA PUBLISHING HOUSE PVT. LTD.,**
"Ramdoot", Dr. Bhalerao Marg, Girgaon, Mumbai - 400 004.
Phone: 022-23860170, 23863863; **Fax:** 022-23877178
E-mail: himpub@bharatmail.co.in; **Website:** www.himpub.com

Branch Offices :

New Delhi : "Pooja Apartments", 4-B, Murari Lal Street, Ansari Road, Darya Ganj, New Delhi - 110 002. Phone: 011-23270392, 23278631; Fax: 011-23256286

Nagpur : Kundanlal Chandak Industrial Estate, Ghat Road, Nagpur - 440 018. Phone: 0712-2721215, 2721216

Bengaluru : Plot No. 91-33, 2nd Main Road, Seshadripuram, Behind Nataraja Theatre, Bengaluru - 560 020. Phone: 080-41138821; Mobile: 09379847017, 09379847005

Hyderabad : No. 3-4-184, Lingampally, Besides Raghavendra Swamy Matham, Kachiguda, Hyderabad - 500 027. Phone: 040-27560041, 27550139

Chennai : No. 34/44, Motilal Street, T. Nagar, Chennai - 600 017. Mobile: 09380460419

Pune : "Laksha" Apartment, First Floor, No. 527, Mehunpura, Shaniwarpeth (Near Prabhat Theatre), Pune - 411 030. Phone: 020-24496323, 24496333; Mobile: 09370579333

Cuttack : Plot No 5F-755/4, Sector-9, CDA Markat Nagar, Cuttack - 753 014, Odisha. Mobile: 09338746007

Kolkata : 3, S.M. Bose Road, Near Gate No. 5, Agarpara Railway Station, North 24 Parganas, West Bengal - 700109. Mobile: 9674536325

DTP by : Harshali

Printed at : Geetanjali Press Pvt. Ltd., Nagpur. On behalf of HPH (P).

Dedicated to

My Offsprings
Partha
and
Yash

Preface

Varying techno-economic state of affairs and globalization of markets have posed many challenges and also changed the way the business is being run irrespective of diverse factors. The practice of administration/management is dependent on the different socio-economic, political, and legal environment factors in which the business is in commission. He must make decisions, plan, organize and implement and control the activities in the ecological perspective.

The book is written keeping in mind the requirements of various categories of scholars and their curriculum requirements. It may acts as a useful reference for B.A., B.Com., B.Sc., B.B.A and M.Com. courses.

Planning of the Book

Keeping in mind the curriculum requirements of Universities, the book is organized into twenty-four chapters. Each part is dealt with satisfactory detail.

Special Features of the Book

- A perfect guide for entrepreneurial teachers and instructors.
- A means of infomation on entrepreneurs, entrepreneurship, schemes, projects and linked issues.
- The subject matter is presented in such a simple and lucid style that the prospective students can grasp it easily and quickly.
- It would also prove to be of immense help to students opting for business as their career.
- Case studies are included to understand the depthness of the subject matter.
- Useful references are included area wise to help the students, who need the greater details.

Dr. Achut P. Pednekar

Acknowledgements

It gives me immense pleasure to present this book on Entrepreneurship, planned to support entrepreneurs to grab a distinctive prospect and make a gainful profession through self-employment.

I have been extremely gratified by the acceptance and usage of my book Entrepreneurship Management Semester-V and Semester-VI, acknowledging with sincere thanks the enriching feedback from the experts and readers. If the books impulsively stimulate the attention of the students, entrepreneurs, faculty members of entrepreneurship studies, policymakers and researchers, the credit logically goes to all the teachers teaching the subject.

In writing this book, I have benefited considerably from the works of a number of scholars and authors. While preparing this book, I have collected the relevant material from Government publications, books and newspapers. My teachers, colleagues and friends offered me valuable suggestions in the preparation of the manuscript. My sincere thanks are due to all of them. I am also grateful to those who have helped me in compiling the matter for this book.

I do not make any claim to originality or comprehensiveness, rather, I have honestly attempted to bring together the scattered text on the subject. However, the arrangement of the chapters is my own creation.

The academic encouragement received from my Principal Dr. D.B. Arolkar, management, librarian, teachers, colleagues and students in preparing this book is acknowledged with very high praise.

I feel great pleasure in expressing my profound gratitude to my respected teachers late Professor Dr. C.N. Sontakki, Ph.D guide and late Professor Shekhar H. Kulkarni, the former HoD of Commerce, D.M's College Assagao, Bardez — Goa.

I am deeply indebted to my publishers M/s. Himalaya Publishing House, Mumbai, for their wholehearted support and cooperation at all stages of the preparation of the book.

Lastly, no words can effectively articulate my debt of appreciation to my father, late Shri Pundalik L. Pednekar, and mother, Smt. Pramilabai P. Pednekar, for generating in me a perpetual interest in higher studies. I will be failing in my obligation if I do not mention here the incredible co-operation, I received from my wife Mrs. Reshma A. Pednekar in the completion of this voluminous work, in particular, whose endurance, support, backup, sympathy and love helped to bring this effort to final result.

Finally, I welcome suggestions and criticisms regarding the contents of this book, which will enable me to make the book more useful to our readers.

Dr. Achut P. Pednekar

Contents

1 INTRODUCTION

Introduction, What is Entrepreneurship? Who is an Entrepreneur? Qualities of an Entrepreneur, Skills of an Entrepreneur, Functions of an Entrepreneur, Summing Up.

Introduction

A general impression of entrepreneurship can be made by at first tracing the origin of entrepreneurship. The origin of entrepreneurship in the form of its concept or theory dates back to over more than four centuries. 'The entrepreneur' said the French economist **J.B. Say**, around 1800, as a 'shift in economic resources out of an area of lower and into an area of higher productivity and greater yield'. But **Say's** definition does not tell us who this 'entrepreneur' is. And since **Say** coined it almost two hundred years ago, there has been total confusion over the definitions of **'entrepreneur'** and **'entrepreneurship.'**

What is Entrepreneurship?

Entrepreneurship, it is commonly believed, is enormously risky. And, indeed, in such highly visible areas of innovation as high-tech microcomputers, for instance, or biogenetics–the casualty rate is high and the chances of success or even of survival seem to be quite low. Entrepreneurship is 'risky' mainly because few of the so-called entrepreneurs know what they are doing. They lack the methodology. They violate elementary and well known rules. This is particularly true of high-tech entrepreneurs.

Entrepreneurship is the purposeful activity of an individual or a group of associated individuals, undertaken to initiate, maintain or exaggerate profit by production or distribution of economic goods and services. Entrepreneurship is very often associated with adventurism, risk bearing, innovating creativity, etc. It is concerned with making dynamic changes in the process of production, innovation in production, new usage for materials, etc. It is a mental attitude to take calculated risks with a view to attain certain objectives. It also means doing something in a new and better manner.

Who is an Entrepreneur?

*The word 'entrepreneur' first, appeared in the French language, verb 'enterprendre' means "between-taker" or "go-between" or "to do something" or "to undertake" and was applied to leaders of military expeditions in the beginning of the sixteenth Century. By the 16th century, the noun entrepreneur, had emerged to refer to someone who undertake a business venture. The first academic usage of the term was by economist **Richard Cantillon** in 1730. For **Cantillon**, the bearing of risk engaging in business without an assurance of the profits that will be derived is the distinguishing features of an entrepreneur.*

After 1700, it was applied to other types of adventures, mainly civil engineering like the construction of roads, bridges, harbors and buildings.

The term entrepreneur was further popularized by economist **Jean Baptiste Say**, who in the early **1800s**, used the term to refer to individuals who create value in an economy by moving resources out of areas of low productivity and into areas of higher productivity and greater yield.

J. B. Say developed the concept little wider. According to him an entrepreneur is an important agent of production who gets together other factors of production. His definition reads as follows:

'The entrepreneur is the economic agent who unites all the means of production...the labour of the one, the capital or the land of the other and who finds in the value of products which result from their employment, reconstitution of the entire capital that he utilizes and the value of the wages, the interest and the rent which he pays as well as profits belonging to himself.'

McClelland views, 'an entrepreneur as a producer and controller'. He remarks by paying that an entrepreneur is someone who has some control over the means of production and produces more than he consumes in order to sell or exchange it for income.

J. A. Schumpeter, defined entrepreneur as an individual who carries out new combines of means of production by which these occurs disequilibrium.

According to **Schumpeter,** an entrepreneur is an innovator, who introduces something new in the economy. Innovation may be:

(1) Introduction of the new product;
(2) Introduction of new methods of production;
(3) Making changes in the organization and management.

Innovation, indeed, creates a resource. There is no such thing as 'resource' until man finds a use for something in nature and, thus, endows it with economic value. There is no greater resource in an economy than 'Purchasing Power.' But purchasing power is the creation of the innovating entrepreneur.

Peter F. Drucker, in his book '*Innovative Entrepreneur*' defines entrepreneur as innovator. According to him 'Innovation is the specific tool of entrepreneur, the means by which they exploit changes as an opportunity for a different business or a different service'.

In the **United States**, the entrepreneur is often defined as one who starts his own, new and small business. Entrepreneurs create wealth and employment. They are innovators who evoke demand and they are job-givers instead of job-seekers. As an entrepreneur, one is not only realizing the goal in his life but is also a source of livelihood for so many. The entrepreneur always searches for change, responds to it, and exploits it as an opportunity.

Oxford English Dictionary (1933), defined entrepreneur as 'One who undertakes an enterprise, especially a contractor, acting as intermediary between capital and labour.' Undertaking of an enterprise involves combining capital and labour for the purpose of production. Anyone who undertakes this task is an entrepreneur. The entrepreneurial class is an 'employing class' as it creates jobs.

Generally speaking any individual possessing an entrepreneurial spirit and who is actively involved in the field of entrepreneurship can be called or referred to as an 'Entrepreneur'. Nowadays, it is very often associated with "risk-taking", "innovating", "adventurism", "thrill seeking" and "creativity".

Qualities of an Entrepreneur

Several research studies have been carried out to recognise traits of a true entrepreneur. The true entrepreneur is one who is endowed with more than average capacities in the task of organizing and coordinating the various other factors of production. He should be a pioneer, a captain of industry. The supply of such entrepreneurship is however quite limited and all are not endowed with such talent. The modern entrepreneur is one who detects and evaluates a new situation in his environment and directs the making of such adjustments in the economic systems as he deems necessary. He conceives a new industrial enterprise, displays considerable initiative, grit and determination in bringing his project to fruition. Successful entrepreneurs, whatever their individual motivation— be it money, power, curiosity or the desire for fame and recognition— try to create value and to make a contribution, still, successful entrepreneurs aim high. They are not content simply to improve on what already exists, or to modify it. They try to create new and different values and new and different satisfactions, to convert a 'material' into a 'resource' or to combine existing resources in a new and more productive configuration.

In order to make the business a success, an entrepreneur should possess the following trait:

(I) ***Willingness to Assume Risk:*** 'No risk, no business' or 'no risk, no gains.' There is an element of risk in every business; hence, an entrepreneur should be prepared to accept failure as a challenge and opportunity. **Richard Cantillon**, an Irish man living in France, defined entrepreneur as an agent who buys factors of production at certain prices in order to combine them into a product with a view to selling it at uncertain prices in future. **Knight** also described entrepreneur to be a specialized group of persons who bear uncertainty. People who need certainty are unlikely to make good entrepreneurs. But such people are unlikely to do well in a host of other activities as well in politics, for instance, or in command positions in a military service, or as the captain of an ocean liner. In all such pursuits decisions have to be made, and the essence of any decision is uncertainty.

(II) ***Leadership:*** An entrepreneur leads entire industrial activities and all divisions. He leads and provides direction to managers, supervisors, engineers, technical staff, group leaders, etc. Through, this he generates frankness, wide acceptance and trustworthy environment. As leader of industry he encourages good performance. He creates trust, keeps individual contacts. He listens everybody calmly, clarifies priority. **Robert D. H.,** opines that the person, who strives for establishing business successfully, is a leader with great foresight. He also dreams big entrepreneurship also includes leadership. He is who amplifies growth. When you wish to have tomato, you buy seeds, which grow in fertile land, you carefully water them. Thus, you are not producing tomatoes but you are growing them.

(III) ***Decisiveness:*** An entrepreneur has to take various decisions when establishing an enterprise. He also has to plan properly to apply these decisions. The decision making activity is the work of a manager performs to arrive at the conclusions and judgments necessary for people to act. The main decisions related with establishment of an enterprise:

(1) Decide about product to manufacture;
(2) Decide how to manufacture and by what means;
(3) Ownership of production facility;
(4) Source of finance;
(5) Location of enterprise;
(6) Choice of technology;
(7) Aids, subsidy encouragement provided by govt; and
(8) Production cost, price, sell, profit and the opportunities for production and selling of the products and problems related.

To apply business decisions, he has to take important managerial decisions. For this he has to plan for production, finance, market, arrangement of means, etc. He has to plan production, finance, to purchase raw material, to arrange sells, etc., and more of such managerial decisions.

Arthur H. Kaul, describes him as a person taking comprehensive decisions which affect everywhere. According to **Arthur,** an entrepreneur sets business objectives and changes them if necessary or decides beneficial, need–based objectives.

(IV) ***Creative Thinking:*** An entrepreneur should basically be creative and imaginative. He should have a killer instinct to perform and to do something beyond average in the market, society or business. He develops new thoughts, concepts and approach by grabbing original viewpoint or from business environment. **Joseph Schumpeter,** has given concept of five types of initiations which is directly connected with creativity:

(1) New product;
(2) Newer production system;
(3) Explore new market;
(4) Search for new source of raw material or semi–finished material;
(5) To arrange new management or administration system.

(V) ***Confidence in Project:*** Setting up a new business enterprise is a very challenging and rewarding task. Several problems are involved in this task. Right from the conception of a business idea up to the start of production, numerous decisions have to be taken. In order to succeed in this task, an entrepreneur must correctly perceive the nature and intensity of problems to be faced and prepare and implement appropriate plans. The delay will definitely cause problems and affect production which in turn affects the profitability.

(VI) ***Technical Knowledge:*** The entrepreneur should have in-depth knowledge about the technical aspects of the project. He should be well conversant with the manufacturing and trading process and also know about the economic aspects of the technology including costs and benefits. Technical knowledge implies the ability to devise and use new and better ways of producing and marketing goods and services. Complex and confusing technical know-how is not preferable in the initial stage. Generally, the technology which is indigenous or available locally and should be easy to use is preferable. A good entrepreneur is one who is interested in changing the pattern of production to suite the available resources, market conditions and quality of output.

(VII) ***Flexibility:*** Most successful people after weighing the pros and cons of a decision, tend to change if the situation so demands. They do not hesitate in revising their decisions. Successful entrepreneurs are persons with open minds, not rigid.

(VIII) ***Ability to Marshal Resources:*** An entrepreneur should possess the ability to mobilize necessary resources in the best possible manner for achieving the business goal. He should be able to minimize the cost of production without reducing the quality of the product or service. In order to do this, an entrepreneur needs sound judgment, accurate forecasting vision and knowledge of the global business. He should be able to break up old traditions and develop new ones. He should have high ambitions, the will to conquer, the impulse to fight and succeed and prove superior to others.

(IX) ***Market Orientation:*** The liberalization and globalization process made free entry of business enterprises into our country. World has become a small village because of technological development. Hence, the need arise for every entrepreneur to know about the market, the substitutes available, its price, quality, special features and about the customers and their taste. He should have flexible policy to change anything according to the need of the customers to bring satisfaction to them. The above information should be collected up to dates and necessary modification should be made whenever and wherever necessary.

(X) ***Determination, Courage and Perseverance:*** Entrepreneurs have drive and high energy levels, they are achievement-oriented and they are tireless in the pursuit of their goals. They devote their energy to completing the tasks immediately before them. **Dwight Eisenhower** quoted as saying, 'No matter what the weather looks like, and we have to go ahead now. Waiting any longer could be even more dangerous. So, let us move it." The point here is that people who can judge when a decision needs to be made and make it, are for more likely to succeed in entrepreneurial ventures. To achieve a goal he has got to be a gambler, he has got to be certain that he can do it. There are the words of entrepreneurship, dreams, determination and willingness to take risks. **J. B. Say** observed, that an entrepreneur must possess the following qualities: "He must have judgments, perseverance and the knowledge of world as well as of business. He is called upon to estimate, with tolerable accuracy the importance of specific product, the probable amount of demand and the means of its production at another, buy or order the raw material, collect labour, find consumer and give at all times a rigid attention to order and economy in a world, he must possess the art of superintendence and administration."

(XI) ***Honesty:*** This again is the most important factor which plays a major role in the successful operation of the business. If a businessman is not honest, he cannot stand long in the market.

(XII) ***Drive to Achieve and Grow:*** The entrepreneurs have a strong desire to achieve high goals in business. This high achievement motive strengthened them to surmount the obstacles, suppress anxieties, repair misfortunes and devise expedients and only set up and run a successful business.

(XIII) ***Low Need for Status and Power:*** An entrepreneur reviews consequences of every task in reference to inspiration and need of authority. He is very much self-confident, which makes him to trust others. He behaves like a director to carry out his job. If such entrepreneur works only for power and self-interest, he jeopardizes entire organisation to avoid this. An entrepreneur should work with balance and awakening. He should assign some of his assignments and treat people to make them work for him and to act accordingly.

Skills of an Entrepreneurs

Many people believe that entrepreneur possess innate, genetic talents and needs intuition, creative thinking and innovative ability among other skills, on the other hand, an entrepreneur depends more on human relations and conceptual abilities. However, experts generally agree that most entrepreneurs were not born; they learned to become entrepreneurs. Organisation successfully managed various training programmes for entrepreneurs– developed and proved that people of any class can own a business and respectfully earn their livelihood. Organisation holds skills based development for the rising demand of training in the fields like rural market capacity; unit-wise finance distribution, in-house financial management in NGOs, etc. An entrepreneur can create self-employment by a very tiny industry or 'Kutir Udyog' to employ himself and his family. To run his industry, he needs skilled, semi-skilled, and unskilled labourers, technicians, engineers, managers, etc.

Let us see some of the important skills required for entrepreneur.

(1) ***Conceptual:*** Entrepreneur possesses the ability to identify relationships quickly in the midst of complex situations. They identify problems and begin working in their solution faster than other people. They are not troubled by ambiguity and uncertainty because they are used to solving problems. Entrepreneurs are natural leaders and are usually the first to identify a problem to overcome. If it is pointed out to them that their solution to a problem will not work for some valid reason, they will quickly identify an alternative problem-solving approach.

(2) ***Technical :*** Technological change is an important factor in the process of economic development of every country. Invention and innovations have improved the global economy. A good entrepreneur should have the interest in introducing changes in the pattern of production, to suit the available resources, market conditions and quality of output. He should have interest to explore new ideas, new technology, new production method, etc. The entrepreneur must have a reasonable level of technical knowledge. An entrepreneur who lacks this technical skill cannot improve his business in this modern market.

(3) ***Human Relation:*** The most important entrepreneurial skill contributing to his success are emotional stability, personal relations, consideration and tactfulness. In other words, maintenance of public relations or human relation most often makes the difference between success and failure of an entrepreneur. An entrepreneur must have good relations with his customers in order to gain their continued patronage and win their confidence in his product. He must also maintain good relations with his employees, if he is to motivate them to higher levels of efficiency.

As the business grows and assumes an organizational structure, entrepreneur goes through a classic management crisis. Their strong direct approach induces them to seek information directly from its source, by passing the structural chains of authority and responsibility. Entrepreneur with good interpersonal skills will be able to adjust and survive as their organisation grows and becomes more structured.

(4) *Communication:* The 'gift of the gab' is a must for a successful entrepreneur. Good communication also means that the entrepreneur has the ability to put his point across effectively and with clarity. Communication must be to the point, crisp and convincing. Communication ability is the secret of the success of most entrepreneurs.

(5) *Diagnostic:* Diagnosis is used to measure risk. It guides in choice of segments and attack strategy. It gives an initial idea of how to go about planning, development, because it justifies the order in which the entrepreneur attack the segments. There are two distinct part of it: technical diagnosis and commercial diagnosis.

Technical diagnosis consists of evaluating two different dimensions of risk: technology-related risk and risks related to the technological environment. Whereas, commercial diagnosis consists of assessing two dimensions of the risk involved: company advantages and shortcomings and market appeal and constraints.

Managing groups in organisation is difficult. An entrepreneur must have the skill to develop group into a productive unit by nurturing its activities, encourage open communication and trust among the people, stimulate discussion on important issues, provide task related information at appropriate times and analyze external factors such as competition and external threats and opportunities.

An entrepreneur must always remember that the achievement of goals often increases the cohesiveness of a group because people are proud to be identified with a winner and to the thought of as a competent and successful team, 'Success breeds success'.

(6) *Decision Making:* Running a business requires taking a numbers of decisions. Decision making means the ability to choose the correct alternative from a number of alternatives. The entrepreneur has to take decision himself even without the support of his staff or any statistical fast figures. An entrepreneur should take the risk of decision making whether it is right or wrong because taking no decision at all is bad than taking wrong decision. Hence, an entrepreneur should have the capacity to analyze the various aspects of the business for arriving at a decision.

(7) *Managerial:* The entrepreneur must have the skill to manage the men and other factors of production and able to harvest to the best of his organisation. He must have the ability to select, train and maintain the persons composing of labour force. The entrepreneur combines in him managerial functions, though they are strictly different than the standard entrepreneurial duties. The entrepreneur thus has a multifaceted personality when he undertakes managerial functions.

(8) *Project Development:* The entrepreneur should select a suitable, proper and appropriate project which gives him reasonable profit. If the project is selected properly half of the work is over. According to **Albert O. Hirschman**, "The development project connects purposefulness, something qualitatively new, and the expectation that a sequence of further development moves will be set in motion. Development projects are privileged particles of the development process." If the project has been selected without due care, it cannot achieve the objects.

(9) ***Marketing:*** The success of a project depends on how it is able to sell the product/service in the market. This is because marketing is the only activity which produces revenue while all other activities incur expenditure. If the new venture does not have a market focus from the very beginning, all it is likely to create is the market for a competitor. The greatest danger for the new venture is to 'know better' than the customer what the product or service is or should be, how it should be bought, and what it should be used for. They are paid to satisfy customers.

(10) ***Time/Process Management:*** Time Management is the act or process of exercising conscious control over the amount of time spent on specific activities, especially to increase efficiency or productivity. Time management may be aided by a range of skills, tools, and techniques used to manage time when accomplishing specific tasks, projects and goals. This set encompasses a wide scope of activities, and these include planning, allocating, setting goals, delegation, analysis of time spent, monitoring, organizing, scheduling, and prioritizing. Initially, time management referred to just business or work activities, but eventually the term broadened to include personal activities as well. A time management system is a designed combination of processes, tools, techniques, and methods. Usually time management is a necessity in any project development as it determines the project completion time and scope. Entrepreneur must possess this skill to manage the time.

(11) ***Stress Management:*** It is the amelioration of stress and especially chronic stress often for the purpose of improving everyday functioning. Stress produces numerous symptoms which vary according to persons, situations, and severity. These can include physical health decline as well as depression. According to the **St. Louis** Psychologists and Counseling Information and Referral, the process of stress management is one of the keys to a happy and successful life in modern society. Entrepreneur may come across numerous stressful demands that can prove difficult to handle, stress management is the best way to manage anxiety and maintain overall well-being. Entrepreneur must able adopt or design various mechanism to control the level of stress. Meditation can be one of the ways of minimizing the impact of stress.

(12) ***Anger Management:*** Entrepreneur during course of his/her business activities may come across a variety of problems. Problems if not tackle in advance, it will turn into chronic. Accumulated problems if not tackle stage-wise, may build up anger. In anger, entrepreneur may take wrong decision which in turn ruins the business. Possible that in annoyance he/she may reveal business secrets which may benefit the rivals. Hence, the best alternative is to control the anger with the help of meditation, self realization, apprehension, and understanding.

(13) ***Personality and Individual:*** Impressive personality and individual skill help to develop entrepreneurship. In absence of them entrepreneurship withers up. These qualities require for entrepreneurs since they have to work with officers, managers, engineers, labours, customers, investors, Govt. officers, ministers, social, economic, industrial organizations, trust, etc.

(14) ***Analytical:*** Entrepreneurs are realistic; they have a matter of fact approach about business undertakings. They are not likely to let personal likes and dislikes stand in their way. When they require assistance, they select experts rather than friends and relatives to help them. They generally do not take an emotional attitude towards their business or a problem.

(15) ***Pioneering:*** Entrepreneurs are people who have the skill to explore, or venture into new opportunities. They always like to create or discover new methods of production, new markets. They are thus pioneers in their own field.

(16) ***Unification and Organization:*** An entrepreneur comes in contact with many unions and organizations. He has to deal with them regularly. He has to gather or arrange many things in many ways and to unite all of them for a common goal. So he must have the qualities of unification and organizational skills.

(17) ***Problem–solving:*** Entrepreneur is not creating problems but solves them. He should have spontaneity and skill to solve any complex problem.

(18) ***Computer Knowledge:*** Whatever may be the business, odds are that it could be significantly improved by having a computer. From basic letters to client billing to presentations and fliers, how entrepreneurs today survive without one is a mystery, and especially if they are young and in business they better have e-mail. As a young entrepreneur, computer knowhow is supposed to be part of their birthright. Entrepreneur who is computer literate can use the computer and software to perform different aspects of their jobs. Computer is a helpful tool for decision making. Some important applications of the internet are e-mail, file transfer protocol, usenet, telnet, acquiring software and world-wide web.

Functions of an Entrepreneur

There has been a great deal of confusion and contradiction in literature on entrepreneurial functions. Classical economists, considered the entrepreneur as the owner of the business enterprise to which he supplied capital. No distinction was made between the entrepreneur and the capitalist and as a result profits and interest were lumped together. But in the modern corporation ownership is separated from control. Ownership of business lies with shareholders who bear risks but do not exercise control. Control lies with a small group of insiders known as Board of Directors. This group bears little risk and receives a large remuneration even when no through dividend is paid to the shareholders, i.e., the nominal owners. Thus, the classical theory of enterprise fails in a large public company. A new theory of firm is required which should take into account the income of an entrepreneur when he is not owner of business.

The functions of an entrepreneur have been given in different ways by different authors. The authors like **Knight**, **Cantillon** and **J.B. Say** emphasized, that risk bearing is the main function of an entrepreneur. **Marshall** and **J. B. Say** also stated, that the function includes coordination, supervision and management. But according to **Schumpeter**, the main function of an entrepreneur is innovation.

The present day modern economists say that an entrepreneur has to perform a number of functions for the successful conduct of his business. **Robinson** stated, the functions as provision of capital, risk-bearing, administration and technical management. Thus, whatever may be the organizational set up or the technological advancements, the functions we shall analyze are detailed below:

(1) ***Innovation:*** The entrepreneur is one who should always think of new ideas and innovations. It does not mean that he should do research all the time, but it means that he should find out ways and means of doing a job at minimum cost and get maximum profits. Innovation means finding out new methods, new areas of operation, new products, etc.

Schumpeter, visualized entrepreneur as an innovator. He considers that innovation can take the following forms:

- Introduction of a new product;
- Introduction of a new improved technology for the production of an existing product;
- Opening of a new market into which a specific product has not entered so far;
- Discovery of new source of supply of raw material; and
- Carrying out a new form of organisation.

Peter Drucker, considers three important conditions to be fulfilled while carrying out innovations; They are:

- Innovation require knowledge and ingenuity. It is a demanding process by which a purposeful focus is given by persistence, commitment and hard work;
- Innovation must be built on one's own strength; and
- Innovation always has to be close to the market, focused on the market, indeed it should be market-driven.

(2) *Planning the Project:* Planning is one of the first and foremost principles of management and yet, it doesn't take long to find oneself in an inescapable disarray with no plan or map in sight. Schedules, targets and projects can go haywire in no time if the course is not charted out and reviewed from time to time. Planning is a strategy that needs to be revisited by employees and managers alike as often as required.

"Planning' and 'Making Plans' are two different things in organizations. Planning is about weaving sales, operations, recruitment, market intelligence with the thread of native intelligence and backing it up with execution. Planning is often the key to success – it helps define and make a shared vision of the success that the organization wishes to achieve.

Planning on the size of the unit, choice of the product, production cycle, quality, quantity, area of operation, investment, costing, profitability, etc., i.e., a project preparation is must, failing which the unit will become sick and the entrepreneur will lose his venture and confidence.

Total involvement, close follow-up of each stage of the project's progress, production schedule, orders and supplies quality and quantity maintenance, etc., are various functions of an entrepreneur while the project is launched and implemented. His agility, honesty and integrity will project him as a potential leader to his men at work.

(3) *Risk Taking and Uncertainty Bearing:* The future is unpredictable. The entrepreneur has to take risks in these circumstances. If the venture succeeds, the entrepreneur profits; if it does not, losses occur. Thus, taking risks forms an important entrepreneurial function. Risks are of two types—insurable and non-insurable. Non-insurable risks are the possibility of changes in the tastes and preferences of the consumer, techniques of production and so on. These non-insurable risks are called uncertainties. Uncertainty bearing is thus an integral part of the entrepreneurial function. The entrepreneur makes use of his initiative, skill and good judgment to reduce the uncertainties of business.

(4) *Procurement and Mobilization of Resources:* Entrepreneurship development is a human resource development task, a process which deals with human motivation, skills, competencies, social and economical risks and investment of financial and physical resources of the individual and the state. Most of the functions have human focus and it vary from person– to-person, time-to-time and place-to-place. **J. B. Say,** opines that an entrepreneur is an economic agent who assembles means of production.

(5) *Taking Business Decisions:* All decisions concerning business are taken by the entrepreneur. Once the entrepreneur is convinced that a particular line of production offers large prospects of profit, he decides to enter it. He has to formulate an action plan regarding the product and the quality of the product to be produced. He has to evolve the best possible method of production which would earn him a sizeable profit. Suitable changes in the size of the business have to be effected by him. Employment of personnel, choosing the location for the production unit and everything that is needed for the development of the business has to be decided by him.

(6) *Organizing:* According to **J. B. Say**, an entrepreneur is one who coordinates and organizes the resources and oversees the activities of the enterprise to produce the required goods and services. **Alfred Marshall,** recognized organisation and management of the enterprise as the main function of an entrepreneur. It implies bringing together the various factors of production. In the initial stage of the establishment of an enterprise the entrepreneur may talk all decisions by himself. But as the enterprise grows and the work of decision making becomes more complex, the entrepreneur delegates authority to subordinates executives. However, the central function of the entrepreneur remains the same. Thus, organisation and management function includes–

(a) Planning of an enterprise;
(b) Coordination, administration and control; and
(c) Routine type of supervision.

A person may own capital, land or labour but ownership alone does not make him an entrepreneur. What is required is organizing ability for assembling these factors of production in the right proportion to obtain the best results.

(7) ***Perception of Market Opportunities:*** **Peter Drucker,** defines an entrepreneur as one who always searches for changes, responds to the changes occurring and exploits them into opportunities. If the product has nationwide market, the analysis for the demand and supply should be done accordingly. Existing and potential demand in the domestic and export markets, consumption trends, nature of competition, competitor's market shares, availability of substitutes, barriers and possibility of entry of substitutes and technological developments taking place in the industry product all should be assured and evaluated by the entrepreneur. A detailed market analysis should be conducted covering market opportunity and strategy for converting the opportunity into a reality.

(8) ***Marketing of Products and Responding to the Competition:*** Production is meaningless without market. Therefore, the very purpose of an entrepreneur is to produce what the customer will buy. Notwithstanding, there are few main reasons conditioning the marketing of products produced. These are:

(i) Unable to face competition in respect of quality, cost and standardization of the product;
(ii) Lack of boosting the role of marketing; and
(iii) Dearth in marketing personnel.

Consumer knows best what he wants and the habit/tastes which are going to be popular in the near future. Contact with prospective customers can also reveal the features that should be built into a product and service. Market research can find out what customers buy, how they buy, what constitutes value for them.

Entrepreneur who are running a new venture need to spend time outside in the marketplace, with customers and with their own salesmen, looking at customers, listening to them and exploring their values. The new venture needs to build in systematic practices to remind it that a 'Product' or a 'Service' is defined by the customer, not by the producer. If needs to work continuously on challenging itself in respect to the utility and value that its products or services contribute to customers. The disadvantages of a competitive market can be cancelled, to some extent, by improvement in transportation system facilitating the movement of raw materials and finished goods and increasing the demand for producer goods. Germany and Japan as the prime examples, where rapid improvement in market was followed by rapid entrepreneurial appearance.

(9) ***Financial Management:*** Financial management is the conscious effort to formulate long-term policies relating to major aspects of financing investment and dividend decisions with a view to accomplishing the objectives of the firm. The strategic decisions about the different finance functions, which go far beyond the traditional concept of procurement of funds, have to take into consideration, the growth strategies and marketing policies, all of which must ultimately become interacting and interdependent parts of same whole.

The financial management practices of a firm are likely to affect the capital structure of the firm, the total investments in fixed and current assets, sales growth and profitability.

(10) ***Upgrading Process and Product Quality:*** The modern world of business is full of complexities and needs a constant attention and efforts to face the problem. In the time, when a tough competition is creating a lot of problems, it is necessary for every entrepreneur to understand the competition situation. In facts may be a matter of business life and death. India has a highly price sensitive as well as quality sensitive markets. In the case of many products, the household and institutional markets may have altogether different type of competition. Development and dissemination of appropriate technology to improve productivity and quality could be given more stress. Research and development efforts could be enhanced. An entrepreneur should realize that buyer's perception of quality is a major arbiter of value/ price. No matter what the entrepreneur thinks, it is the perceived quality that determines the desirability of the product and it is the entrepreneur's job to understand the buyer's decision process.

(11) ***Fulfilling Social Obligations:*** Business and society are meant and exist for each other. Without the help of society, business cannot be operated. Business is required to meet the varied needs of the society. It can exist only if it fulfills its responsibility towards the society in the socially acceptable manner. Social interest is a desire on the part of the people to establish social relations and to make use of goods and services for better social interaction. Hence, fulfilling social the responsibility towards the society is social responsibility. **Koontz** and **O Donnel** observed that, *'Social responsibility is an interpersonal relationship that exists when people are continuously dependent upon one another in both organized and unorganized way." According to* ***Keith Davis*** *and* ***Robert L. Blomstorm,*** *''Social responsibility refers to the obligations of decision makers to take actions which produce and improve the welfare of society as a whole, along with their own interests."*

In simple words social responsibility means an intelligent and objective concern for the welfare of society that limits or prevents individual and corporate behaviour from ultimately positive contributions, wherever feasible, to the betterment of human resources in different ways as desired by society. Social responsibility indicates personal obligation of people as they act in their own interest to ensure that the rights and legitimate interests of others are not sacrificed by their behaviour and action.

Every entrepreneur seeks an enhanced public image so that it can gain more customers, better employees and other benefits. It can be possible by assuming social responsibilities beyond the commercial and legal obligations.

Summing Up

A general feeling of entrepreneurship can be made by at first tracing the starting point of entrepreneurship. The beginning of entrepreneurship in the form of its notion or theory dates back to over more than four centuries.

What is Entrepreneurship?

Entrepreneurship is the purposeful activity of an individual or a group of associated individuals, undertaken to initiate, maintain or exaggerate profit by production or distribution of economic goods and services.

Who is an Entrepreneur?

The word 'entrepreneur' first, appeared in the French language, verb 'enterprendre' means "between-taker" or "go-between" or "to do something" or "to undertake" and was applied to leaders of military expeditions in the beginning of the sixteenth Century.

The first academic usage of the term was by economist ***Richard Cantillon,*** *in 1730. For* ***Cantillon,*** *the bearing of risk engaging in business without an assurance of the profits that will be derived is the distinguishing features of an entrepreneur. After 1700, it was applied to other types of adventures, mainly civil engineering like the construction of roads, bridges, harbors and buildings.*

J. B. Say, developed the concept of little wider. According to him an entrepreneur is an important agent of production who gets together other factors of production. His definition reads as follows:

'The entrepreneur is the economic agent who unites all the means of production...the labour of the one, the capital or the land of the other and who finds in the value of products which result from their employment, reconstitution of the entire capital that he utilizes and the value of the wages, the interest and the rent which he pays as well as profits belonging to himself.'

McClelland views 'an entrepreneur as a producer and controller'.

J. A. Schumpeter defined entrepreneur as an individual who carries out new combines of means of production by which these occurs disequilibrium. According to Schumpeter an entrepreneur is an innovator, who introduces something new in the economy. Innovation may be:

(1) Introduction of the new product;

(2) Introduction of new methods of production; and

(3) Making changes in the organization and management.

Peter F. Drucker, in his book *'Innovative Entrepreneur'* defines entrepreneur as innovator.

In the **United States**, the entrepreneur is often defined as one who starts his own, new and small business.

Oxford English Dictionary (1933), defined entrepreneur as 'One who undertakes an enterprise, especially a contractor- acting as intermediary between capital and labour.' Undertaking of an enterprise involves combining capital and labour for the purpose of production. Anyone who undertakes this task is an entrepreneur. The entrepreneurial class is an 'employing class' as it creates jobs.

Qualities of an Entrepreneur

Several research studies have been carried out to traits of a true entrepreneur. The true entrepreneur is one who is endowed with more than average capacities in the task of organizing and coordinating the various other factors of production.

In order to make the business a success, an entrepreneur should possess the following trait: Willingness to Assume Risk; Leadership; Decisiveness; Thinking; Confidence in Project; Technical Knowledge; Flexibility; Ability to Marshall Resources; Market Orientation; Determination, Courage and Perseverance; to Achieve and Grow; Need for Status and Power.

Skills of an Entrepreneur

Many people believe that entrepreneur possess innate, genetic talents and needs intuition, creative thinking and innovative ability among other skills on the other hand, an entrepreneur depends more on human relations and conceptual abilities. An entrepreneur can create self-employment by a very tiny industry or 'Kutir Udyog' to employ himself and his family. To run his industry he needs skilled, semi–skilled, and unskilled, labourers, technicians, engineers, managers, etc. The following are some of the important skills required for entrepreneur: Conceptual; Technical; Human Relation; Communication; Diagnostic; Decision Making; Managerial; Project Development; Marketing, Time/Process Management; Stress Management; Anger Management; Personality and Individual; Analytical; Pioneering; Unification and Organization; Problem–solving and Computer Knowledge.

Functions of an Entrepreneur

There has been a great deal of confusion and contradiction in literature on entrepreneurial functions. Classical economists, considered the entrepreneur as the owner of the business enterprise to which he supplied capital. The classical theory of enterprise fails in a large public company. A new theory of firm is required which should take into account the income of an entrepreneur when he is not owner of business.

Thus, whatever may be the organizational set-up or the technological advancements, **the functions detailed as below:** Planning the Project; Risk Taking and Uncertainty Bearing; Procurement and Mobilization of Resources; Taking Business Decisions; Organizing; Perception of Market Opportunities; Marketing of Products and Responding to the Competition; Financial Management; Upgrading Process and Product Quality; and Fulfilling Social Obligations.

2 EVOLUTION, THEORIES AND TYPES OF ENTREPRENEUR

The Evolution of Entrepreneur Definitions

Introduction

An entrepreneur is one of the important segments of socio-economic change. An entrepreneur has the initiative, skill for innovation and who looks for high achievements. He is in also search for new opportunities, new techniques, new lines of production, new products and co-ordinates all other activities. He is a catalytic agent of change and works for the good of people. The development of the theory of entrepreneurship parallels to a great extent the development of the term itself.

Earliest Period

An early example of the earliest definition of an entrepreneur as a go-between is Marco Polo, who attempted to establish trade routes to the Far East. As a go-between, Marco Polo would sign a contract with a money person to sell his goods. A common contract during this time provided a loan to the merchant-adventurer took the active role in trading, bearing all the physical and emotional risks. When the merchant-adventurer successfully sold the goods and completed the trip, the profits were divided between the capitalist and the merchant-adventurer in the ratio 3:1.

Middle Ages

In the middle Ages, the term entrepreneur was used to describe both an actor and a person who managed large production projects. In such large production projects, this individual did not take any risks but merely managed the project using the resources provided, usually by the Government of the Country. **Oxford English Dictionary** (1897) defined an entrepreneur as "the director or a manager of a public musical institution, one who 'sets-up' entertainment, especially musical performance".

13th Century

The earliest definition was found from the 13th century. The origin of the French verb enterprendre means to do something or to undertake.

16th Century

In the early 16th century, the Frenchman who organized and led military expeditions were referred to as "entrepreneurs".

17th century

In the 17th century, the word 'entrepreneur' was applied to other types of adventurers, mainly Civil Engineering activities such as construction and fortification. By the seventeenth century, the term was associated with risk bearing, with the entrepreneur being "a person who entered into a contractual relationship with the government for the performance of a service or the supply of goods. The price at which the contract was valued was fixed and the entrepreneur bore the risks of profit and loss from the bargaining.

Richard Cantillon, an Irishman living in France, and author in the 1700s, image of an entrepreneur as a bearer of non-insurable risk. According to him, entrepreneur carry on production and exchange of goods at some risk, facing the possibility of bankruptcy, when the demand for their products is weakened. **Richard Cantillon**, in 1725, associate entrepreneur with risk-bearing, **Francois Quesnay**, an entrepreneur was simply a tenant farmer who rents property at a fixed rate and produces at given output with given factors at given price.

18th Century

In the 18th century, the person with capital was differentiated from the one who needed capital. The entrepreneur was distinguished from entrepreneurs and venture capitalists. Many of the inventions developed during this time were reactions to the changing world. The hospital, in its modern form a social innovation of the enlightenment of the eighteenth century, has had greater impact on health care than many advances in medicine. Management, that is, the 'useful knowledge' that enables man for the first time to render productive people of different skills and knowledge working together in an 'organization', is an innovation of this century. Eighteenth century economists are **Richard Cantillon, Robert Jacques Turgot** and **Francois Quesnay**.

19th Century and 20th Century

During the 19th century the "ability to take calculated risks" was added to the definition. One of the great achievements of this century was the 'invention of invention'. In the middle of the 20th century, the notion of an entrepreneur is an innovator. 'Invention' had become 'research', a systematic, purposeful activity, which is planned and organized with high predictability both of the results aimed at and likely to be achieved.

Theories of Entrepreneurship

Entrepreneurship is the combination of many skills and traits. It is the mental inclination to achieve pre-determined business or industrial objectives by taking calculated risks. While entrepreneurial skills can be imparted by training, the entrepreneurial traits are either in-born or developed out of social and cultural conditioning. Entrepreneurs have played and are playing a crucial role in the socio-economic development. The importance of presence of entrepreneurs for the progress of a society is well brought by **Zin Kin's** statement, 'No entrepreneur, No development'. The phenomenon of entrepreneurship development has been viewed, explained and interpreted differently by social scientists. Among those who have stressed on the psychological aspects as contributing to entrepreneurial success are **Joseph**

Schumpeter, McClelland,Hagen and **Kunkal.** Entrepreneurship is inhibited by the social system, which denies opportunities for creative facilities. The forces of custom, the rigidity of status and the distinct new ideas and of the excuse of intellectual curiosity, combine to create an atmosphere inimical to experiment and innovation. The theories of **Weber** and **Cochran** in this context are mainly sociological in nature. An analysis of the entrepreneurial theories propounded by different experts provides and interesting study and will help understand the complex nature of entrepreneurship.

The concept of entrepreneurship and its theory have been evolved over a period of more than two centuries.

Opinions on this can be classified on three topics:

(a) The Economists view.

(b) The Sociologists view.

(c) The Psychologists view.

(a) ***Economic Theory:*** In economic analysis, entrepreneurial functions are supposed to be directed towards the materialistic objective of maximization though its foundation may be of a high order such as social, patriotic, spiritual or psychological. **Mark Casson**, in his book "***The Entrepreneur-An Economic Theory***" presented a functional definition of the entrepreneur and considered why the entrepreneur function is so valuable. He emphasized that the demand for entrepreneurship stems from the need to adjust to change and that the scarcity of the requisite personal qualities, and secondly, by the difficulty of identifying them when they are available. According to **G. F. Papanek** and **J. R. Harris**, economic activities are the main drive for the entrepreneurial activities. In some cases, it is not so evident, but the person's inner drives have always been associated with economic gains. These incentives and gains are therefore regarded as sufficient conditions for emergence of industrial entrepreneurship. There is lacking of entrepreneurship due to various kinds of imperfections in market and inefficient economic policies. When an individual recognizes that the market for a product or service is out of equilibrium, he may purchase or produce at the prevailing price and sell to those who are prepared to buy at the highest price. They are not 'risk–focused'; but 'opportunity–focused.'

(b) ***Sociological Theory:*** Sociologists argue that entrepreneurship is most likely to emerge under a specific social culture. According to them, social sanctions, cultural values and role expectations are responsible for the emergence of entrepreneurship. Sociologists consider the entrepreneur as a role performer corresponding to the role expected by the society.

According to **Cochran** the entrepreneur represents society's model personality. His performance depends upon his own attitudes towards his occupation, the role expectations of sanctioning groups and the occupational requirements of the job. Society's values are the most important determinant of the attitudes and role expectations.

According to **Horelitz**, culturally marginal groups promote entrepreneurship and economic development. Such groups, because of their ambiguous position are peculiarly suited to make creative adjustments and thereby develop genuine innovations.

According to **Derossi**, Co-ordination at every stage-inception, maintenance and expansion is the function of an entrepreneur.

Flaria thinks that entrepreneur needs two qualities:

(1) ***Optimistic outlook:*** There is a possibility of change, the environment can be mastered and he himself can introduce the required change. He finds difficulties, challenging and stimulating; he thrives on them.

(2) ***Dynamic:*** In a share as dynamic industry, new problems are seized upon as opportunities for testing one's own capabilities.

(c) *Psychological Theory:* Among psychologists, **Frank Young** describe an entrepreneur as a change–agent. According to the advocates of this theory, entrepreneurship is most likely to emerge when a society has sufficient supply of individuals possessing particular psychological characteristics.

K. L. Sharma maintains that entrepreneurs are men with qualities of leadership in solving persistent professional problems; but those persons likewise demonstrate eagerness to seize unusual opportunities.

Uday Pareek and **T.V. Rao** describe entrepreneurship as creative and innovative response to environment. The entrepreneur is goal–oriented rather than means-oriented.

Schumpeter believes that entrepreneurs are primarily motivated by an atavistic will to power, will to found a private kingdom or will to conquer.

Individual with higher achievement motive tend to take keen interest in situations of high risk, desire for responsibility and a desire for a concrete measure of task performance.

Integrated Theory

Development in any walk of life has always depended, to some degree, on individual qualities of entrepreneurship. Every theorist has looked at the entrepreneur and entrepreneurship on the basis of this perception, and therefore, can, at best, provide only a limited view of entrepreneurial phenomenon. No view is right or wrong, or more or less; in fact, the various factors which cause the emergence of entrepreneurship are interlocking mutually dependent and usually reinforcing. Entrepreneurship is influenced by a multitude of factors and therefore, no single factor by itself can generate entrepreneurship. Entrepreneurship is the outcome of a complex and varying combination of social-economic, psychological and other factors. It can be noticed from figure below that economic, political and legal factors can be quickly manipulated to make the environment conducive to the emergence of entrepreneurship. On the other hand, sociological and psychological factors take sufficiently long time to change. It is the ambition that electrifies man's action. The common saying—aimless life is a goalless game—emphasizes the importance of ambition in life.

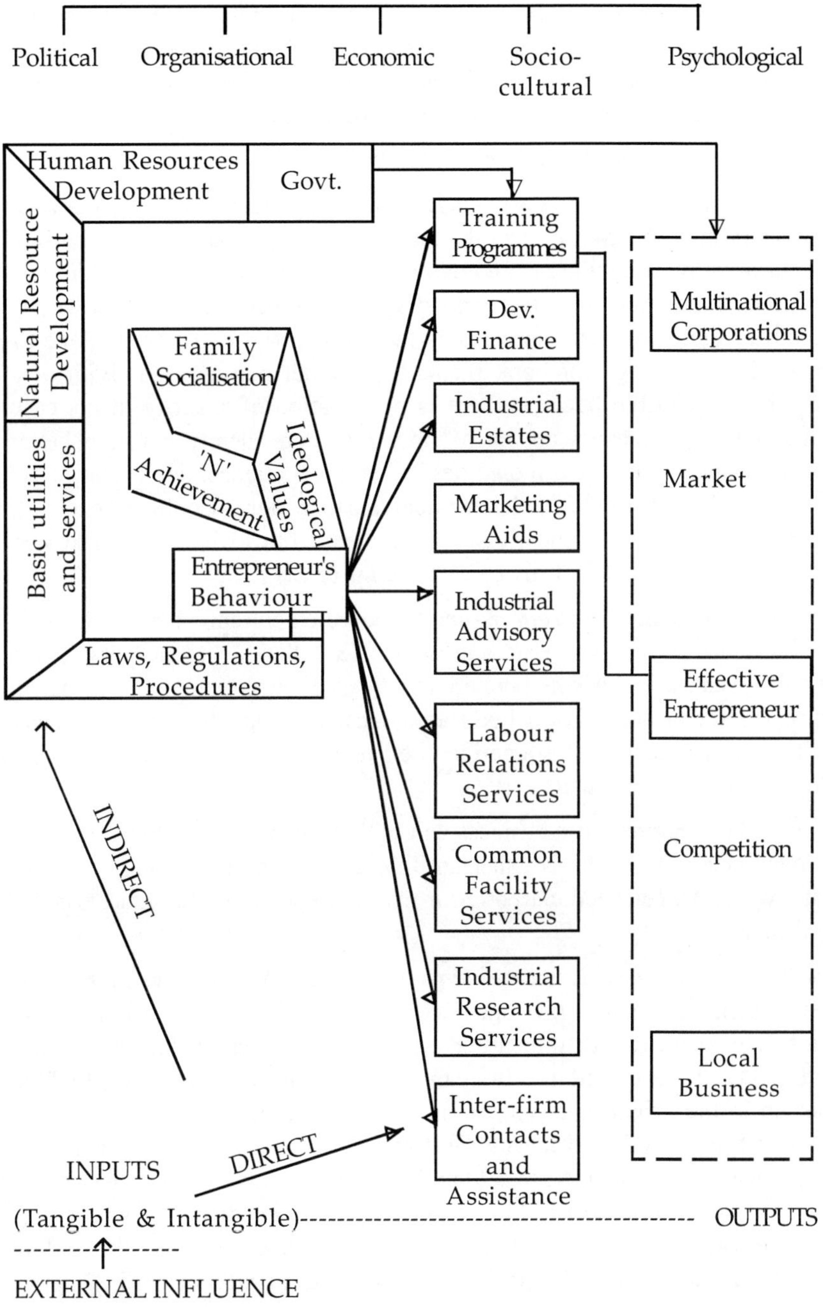

Fig. 2.1: Integrated Contextual Model

Types of Entrepreneurs

Schumpeter, made the entrepreneur the adventurous innovator who acting on his own account, introduces changes that others do not dare to experiment with. **Arthur H. Cole,** distinguishes between empirical, rational and cognitive entrepreneurs. The empirical entrepreneur hardly introduces anything revolutionary and follows the principle of rule of thumb. The rational entrepreneur is well informed about the general economic conditions and introduces changes that look more revolutionary. The cognitive entrepreneur is well informed, draws upon the advice and services of experts and introduces changes that reflect complete break from the existing scheme of things.

The entrepreneurs have been briefly classified below:

(1) *Gender (Man/Woman Entrepreneur)*: From the olden days man is supposed to organize for everything, i.e., work to get money, protect the family and also organize the welfare of the family, i.e., arranging for education of the children, finding out accommodation, etc. In business also we find that man has been dominating right from the early days and women were not allowed to do any sort of business. The advantage of man entrepreneur is that he can run about from place-to-place to secure orders for his business, arrange for bank finance, carry out marketing activities by travelling long distances, etc. This is possible because there is no question of security in his case. But a woman entrepreneur if given proper security and chance to work independently can show better results than the man entrepreneur because of the inborn qualities in her, i.e., patience, perseverance, tolerance, etc. She has the ability to organize the people, leadership qualities to lead the people and energy to shoulder heavy responsibility. She should have the imitating or inventive qualities which will make her more prominent in the business world. **(for more details refer to chapter 3.)**

(2) *Educated/Uneducated Entrepreneur*: An educated entrepreneur is one who has receives the basic education at least, i.e., he can read and write. He is thus a literate person who has undergone school and/or college education. Again there are two types of education, one is formal education and the other is the specialized education. Formal education means any faculty, i.e., arts, science or commerce. Special education means technical education, i.e., degree or diploma in engineering, technology, computerization or physics, chemistry, etc.

An uneducated entrepreneur run business unit with the help of their knowledge and experience. An uneducated entrepreneur is one who is either an illiterate person or a person who even does not know how to read and write. An educated entrepreneur may have some formal education, but he may not be technically qualified.

(3) *Location (Urban/Rural Entrepreneur)*: Urban entrepreneurs are those who work in the city areas. They set up their units in the cities due to certain location advantages. For example, if the product is sold in the urban areas we find that the urban entrepreneur sets up his factory in the urban area. Items like Refrigerator, T.V., etc., are used mostly by the urban people and, hence, we find that these factories are usually set up in the urban or city areas and not in the rural areas. This is because the urban entrepreneur comes from the urban place and he does not like to work in the rural place as he is not used to rural life. Moreover, if the products are sold in the city areas only, the factories are put up in the urban areas so that the transportation cost is less. The rural entrepreneur is one who comes from the rural areas, i.e., from the villages. This type of entrepreneur is not used to urban life and, hence, he puts up his factory in the rural area only. His products are also agro-based items, i.e., agricultural products, poultry products, milk products, etc.

(4) *Local/Indian/Foreign Entrepreneur*: Entrepreneurs can play an important role as the suppliers of various commodities for satisfying the 'local demand'. Satisfaction of the demand at the local level with the help of the local entrepreneurs is advantages for various reasons. They are considered as the 'Sons of the soil'. The local entrepreneurs are able to have better understanding of the nature of the products demanded. They also know the typical local condition and the reasons as a result of which the demand is created. Sometimes, the local demands are temporary. They are either seasonal or are sporadic. In such cases, the commodities that are required for satisfying the demand are not manufactured on a very large-scale. The local entrepreneurs are satisfying their demand. Local entrepreneurs are in a position to establish good relations with their customers. The local entrepreneurs use the locally available raw materials for satisfying the local needs. They help the producers of the raw materials because they are able to mount their products near to their places and can get better prices for their products.

An Indian entrepreneur is one who is born in India and sets up his business on traditional approach. He either carries on the business of his forefathers in the similar ways as was done years back or brings about changes in the business by introducing new methods and techniques if he is qualified and has undergone suitable training in business entrepreneurship. Hence, an Indian entrepreneur has all the qualities and if trained properly can show the best results. But in India we find that the Indian entrepreneurs do not get chance to acquire knownledge and experience due to shortage of educational and training institutions in India which impart training in entrepreneurship especially in the rural areas.

A foreign entrepreneur is one who sets up his unit in India with his skill and ability. He is the citizen of another country who sets up his unit in India. He comes to India with a new product as an idea and sometimes has collaboration/agreement with an Indian entrepreneur for conducting the business jointly. But due to various restrictions on the foreign entrepreneur, such entrepreneur are not found in plenty in India.

A foreign entrepreneur has certain qualities which he tries to utilize in the Indian industry. This helps the Indian entrepreneur to learn from their experience the new methods, techniques, etc. The foreign entrepreneur also has the advantage of investing more capital.

(5) *Innovative Entrepreneur*: An innovative entrepreneur is one who introduces new goods, finds out new methods of production, discovers new markets and makes necessary changes in the working of the enterprise. Such type of entrepreneur can work only when the business has already been developed. It means that these entrepreneurs like to find new ideas ways and means of production, of doing the jobs, etc., Hence they are not interested in the formation of the company, but are interested in the product, marketing, finance, etc., which come afterwards.

(6) *Imitative Entrepreneur*: An imitative entrepreneur is one who is ready for important the idea which is found out by the innovative entrepreneur. It often involves what has aptly been called subjective innovation. By western standards an imitative entrepreneur may be a pedestrian figure, an adopter and imitator rather than a true innovator. Imitative entrepreneurs do not invent themselves, but they imitate the techniques and methods, technology and inventions made by other entrepreneurs. Such entrepreneurs are found in the underdeveloped areas where they copy or imitate the ideas learnt from the developed regions.

(7) *Fabian Entrepreneur*: Fabian entrepreneurs are shy and docile who are generally found in the underdeveloped countries. These persons avoid risks and undertake only those works where success is sure. They take all care and caution before making any change in their work schedule. These entrepreneurs are of lazy characters and are satisfied in working more. If they want to introduce new things or take important decisions, they consider all factors, pros and cons and think twice before introducing a new idea or taking any decision. They are influenced by old traditions, customs and superstitions. They do not deal in items of liade which according to their customs are not allowed. In India, Fabian entrepreneurs have not done any business in certain items though there was much scope and availability of natural resources. For example, dealing in poultry was considered to be a business not of a certain class of people.

The Fabian entrepreneurs like to continue their own ways of business and do not like to change their old methods and practices. This does not allow them to have progress. Fabian entrepreneurs always have negative attitude and, hence, modern methods and techniques of production cannot be applied because of which the costs cannot be reduced. Hence, the demand for their products does not increase. The only way a Fabian entrepreneur adopts is that he takes advantage of the opportunity which comes in his ways and not through any special efforts.

(8) *Drone Entrepreneur*: These entrepreneurs like to do routine jobs. They too do not like to go in for sophisticated production methods. They are satisfied with their old methods, policies and procedures. Hence, they are not interested in knowing what the new technology is, new management methods are, new cost saving devices are, etc. These types of entrepreneurs are therefore a peculiar type who do not consider change for better, but are satisfied with what they have. They are, in short, afraid of any change, i.e., change in product, change in organisation or change in the methods and techniques of production.

(9) *Individual and Institutional Entrepreneurs*: In the small-scale sector individual entrepreneurs are dominant. Small enterprises outnumber the large ones in every country. Such entrepreneurs have the advantages of flexibility, quick decision making and state patronage. But a single individual can establish, operate and control an organisation up to limit. Thereafter, it becomes necessary to institutionalize entrepreneurship. The business will have to acquire a number of new entrepreneurial skills through a corporate body. A group of entrepreneurs has to develop to handle the increasingly complex network of decision making. The central function of the entrepreneur remains the same but the basic decisions like the line of business, the amount of capital employed, etc., are taken collectively by the group of promoters at the helm of affairs. Thus, individual entrepreneur and institutional entrepreneurs coexist and support each other. Corporate sector is the symbol of institutionalized entrepreneurship.

(10) *Entrepreneurs by Inheritance*: A time, people become entrepreneurs when they inherit the family business. In India, there are a large number of family-controlled business houses. Firms in these houses are passed from one generation to another.

(11) *Technologist Entrepreneurs*: With the decline of the joint family business and the rise of scientific and technical institutions, technically qualified persons have entered the field of business. These entrepreneurs may enter business to commercially exploit their inventions and discoveries. Their main asset is technical expertise. They raise the necessary capital and employ experts in financial, legal, marketing and other areas of business. Their success depends upon how fast they start production on the acceptance of their products in the market.

(12) *Forced Entrepreneurs*: Many persons become entrepreneurs on account of the circumstances. The moneylenders of yesteryears enter into business due to decline of money lending business with the growth of banking and government legislation. Neo-rich Indians returning from abroad (NRIs) and educated unemployed seeking self-employment may also be described as forced entrepreneurs. In some cases newly married bridegrooms start business with the financial support of their in-laws. This class of entrepreneurs accounts for the maximum number of failures because there is no proper screening of misfits. Failure of this type of entrepreneurs can be reduced with proper training.

(13) *Based on Decision Making:* An Appealing Entrepreneur is an entrepreneur who tends to be highly energetic and outgoing person. He is quick in taking initiatives and in exploiting opportunities. Such entrepreneur shows high emotional involvement with the aspirations and needs of his followers, argues their enthusiasm and inspires them to be loyal and committed. Entrepreneur strives to gain their full confidence and influences them in such a way that they will do whatever he wants. He mostly depends on his personality for getting things done. Domineering Entrepreneur does not give sub-ordinate's the freedom to influence his thinking, decision or behaviour. All decision making power is centralized and does allow at all, his subordinates in the decision making process. Employee Oriented Entrepreneur allows the subordinates to take active part in the decision making process. He is more adaptive and responsive. Due importance is given to the needs, motives and feelings of the subordinates.

Summing Up

The Evolution of Entrepreneur Definitions

The development of the theory of entrepreneurship parallels to a great extent the development of the term itself.

Earliest Period

An early example of the earliest definition of an entrepreneur as a go-between is Marco Polo, who attempted to establish trade routes to the Far East. As a go-between, Marco Polo would sign a contract with a money person to sell his goods. A common contract during this time provided a loan to the merchant-adventurer took the active role in trading, bearing all the physical and emotional risks. When the merchant-adventurer successfully sold the goods and completed the trip, the profits were divided between the capitalist and the merchant-adventurer in the ratio 3:1.

Middle Ages

In the middle Ages, the term entrepreneur was used to describe both an actor and a person who managed large production projects.

13th Century

The earliest definition was found from the 13th century. The origin of the French verb enterprendre means to do something or to undertake.

16th Century

In the early 16th century, the Frenchman who organized and led military expeditions were referred to as "entrepreneurs".

17th Century

In the 17th century, the word 'entrepreneur' was applied to other types of adventurers, mainly Civil Engineering activities such as construction and fortification.

18th Century

In the 18th century, the person with capital was differentiated from the one who needed capital. The entrepreneur was distinguished from entrepreneurs and venture capitalists. Eighteenth century economists are Richard Cantillon, Robert Jacques Turgot, and Francois Quesnay.

19th Century and 20th Century

During the 19th century the "ability to take calculated risks" was added to the definition. One of the great achievements of this century was the 'invention of invention'. In the middle of the 20th century, the notion of an entrepreneur is an innovator. 'Invention' had become 'research', a systematic, purposeful activity, which is planned and organized with high predictability both of the results aimed at and likely to be achieved.

Theories of Entrepreneurship

Entrepreneurship is the combination of many skills and traits. It is the mental inclination to achieve pre-determined business or industrial objectives by taking calculated risks. The importance of presence of entrepreneurs for the progress of a society is well brought by **Zin Kin's** statement, 'No entrepreneur, No development". An analysis of the entrepreneurial theories propounded by different experts provides and interesting study and will help understand the complex nature of entrepreneurship.

The theories of entrepreneurship enunciated by the social scientists from time-to-time are: Economic Theory; Sociological Theory; Psychological Theory and Integrated Theories of Entrepreneurship

Types of Entrepreneurs

Schumpeter made the entrepreneur the adventurous innovator who acting on his own account, introduces changes that others do not dare to experiment with. **Arthur H. Cole** distinguishes between empirical, rational and cognitive entrepreneurs. The empirical entrepreneur hardly introduces anything revolutionary and follows the principle of rule of thumb. The rational entrepreneur is well informed about the general economic conditions and introduces changes that look more revolutionary. The cognitive entrepreneur is well informed, draws upon the advice and services of experts and introduces changes that reflect complete break from the existing scheme of things.

The entrepreneurs have been briefly classified as

Gender (Man/Woman Entrepreneur); Educated/Uneducated Entrepreneur, location (Urban/Rural Entrepreneur); Local/Indian/Foreign Entrepreneur; Innovative Entrepreneur; Imitative Entrepreneur; Fabian Entrepreneur; Drone entrepreneur; Institutional Entrepreneurs; Entrepreneurs by Inheritance; Technologist Entrepreneurs; Forced Entrepreneurs; and Based on Decision Making.

3 WOMEN ENTREPRENEURSHIP

Introduction, Concept, Definition, Economic Empowerment and Entrepreneurship, Functions of Women Entrepreneurs, Growth and Development of Women Entrepreneurship, Areas for Development of Women Entrepreneur, Problems of Women Entrepreneurs, Summing up, Case Study.

Introduction

Women constitute around half of the total world population. Women account for 48 per cent of the total population in the country and in the available social structure, they, in general, are discriminated lot not only economically but also socially. Considering the size of women population in the world, and recognizing that enough has not been done to channelise the 'women power', countries around the world are looking at ways and means to empower them. India is no exception to this. National Policy for the Empowerment of Women' stated in their reports that "Since women comprise the majority of the population below the poverty line and are very often in situations of extreme poverty, given the harsh realities of intra-household and social discrimination, macro-economic policies and poverty eradication programmes will specifically address the needs and problems of such women. That a vast majority of poor women are based in rural areas is revealed by the observation of the said Policy when it said: "Consequently, the access of women particularly those belonging to weaker sections including Scheduled Castes/Scheduled Tribes/Other Backward Classes and Minorities, majority of whom are in the rural areas and in the informal, unorganized sector – to education, health and productive resources, among others, is inadequate. Therefore, they remain largely marginalized, poor and socially excluded." Rural and urban poor apart, the better off sections of women population do also need support to make more meaningful contribution to the economy. This segment of women comprise educated, experienced and economically better off and socially empowered than the former. The available institutional structure for promoting and protecting the cause of women basically comprise a **Ministry of Women and Child Development** (carved out as separate Ministry in 2006) and the **National Women Commission**, established as statutory body in 1992. The **Self-Employed Women's Association Bank** was established in 1974, as the first separate bank for poor, self-employed women workers. That includes hawkers, vendors and home-based workers such as weavers, potters, incense makers and papad rollers. The bank's objective is to provide credit to self-employed women with a view to empower them and minimize the uncertainty of available credit at exorbitant interest rates.

Concept

The prospective role of women entrepreneur in India has been realized since a long time. India history reveals that there have been several women like **Rajia Sultan**, **Rani Laxmi Bai**, **Nur Jahan**, and **Rani Padmini** who has successfully rules their kingdom. In modern, India also several women leaders and administrators like **Sarojini Naidu**, **Indira Gandhi**, **Vijay Laxmi Pandit** who have succeeded in their statesmanship. All these prove that Indian women are in no way inferior to men in all walks of life and they can be good entrepreneurs as men in the country.

Entrepreneurship growth is slow in India and Women's entrepreneurship is still slower due to the discouraging social factors. It is only during last 10 to 15 years women have started becoming entrepreneurs and started industries and business. Women entrepreneurship in India is still just at the infancy level in our country.

Definition of Women Entrepreneur

*The **Government of India** has defined a women entrepreneur as "an enterprise owned and controlled by a women having a minimum financial interest of 51 per cent of the capital and giving at least 51 per cent of the employment generated in the enterprise to women."* The above definition has come in for severe criticism on the condition of employing more than 50 per cent of women entrepreneurs. Hence women entrepreneurs are expected to take the first step in organizing and co-ordinating the business activities, and at the same time they are also expected to innovate, imitate or adopt an economic activity to be called "women entrepreneurs".

Women entrepreneurs may be defined as the women or a group of women who initiate, organize and operate a business enterprise. The common dimension in the definition of empowerment is power: power to influence one's own life, power to make one's own choices and the power to act upon these choices.

Economic Empowerment and Entrepreneurship

Empowering women does not mean merely ensuring jobs and a place in political system for a few of them, though this is a welcome step, but going beyond this. The uneducated/undereducated, poor and deprived women really need empowerment. Economic improvement of women population not only would help the family but also the economy at large. While solutions to women on social front do boost their confidence, the economic empowerment would not only raise their confidence levels but would also enable them to become part of mainstream economy. While poverty alleviation programmes such as **National Rural Employment Guarantee Schemes (NREG),** ensuring minimum calories' intake through subsidized supply of food items, etc. can address the problem largely but there is a fear that these would make them dependents and may also encourage corruption at implementation level. The ultimate objective of a welfare programme should be to make the beneficiary self-dependent and economically independent, so that she makes economic contribution, rather than just be a dependent. Economic empowerment would also enable them to access better education, medical care/facilities, etc., and thus, climb a step ahead on the social ladder.

Being empowered is important to the health and well-being of women. Empowerment has use as a concept to encourage and authorized workers to take the initiative to improve operations, reduce costs and improve product quality and customer service. The process of empowerment aims to increase women's ability to act as well as give them power over their own lives. They are regarded as the better half of the society. In traditional societies, they were confined to the four walls of houses performing household activities. In modern societies they have out of the four walls to participate in all sorts of activities. The global evidences buttress that women have been performing exceeding well in different sphere of activities. It is a great boost to women, whereby the women on their own can work towards the betterment of their status and on the status of their family. The women can be self-dependent. The study reveals that women are prompt, honest and regular in the payment of the installment. One would commonly find a woman-owned/managed retail trade, tailoring (women), vegetable vending, beauty parlours, etc., shops around the country.

Functions of Women Entrepreneurs

The women entrepreneur has to react to new ideas, demand and exploit the opportunities and thereby contribute to technical progress. A women entrepreneur is expected to perform the following functions:

(a) ***Risks*****:** The women entrepreneur has to take risks in the form of changes in tastes of consumers, techniques of production and new innovations. Such risks can be minimized if women take earlier initiative, use skill and judgment.

(b) ***Decision making*****:** The women entrepreneur has to decide the nature of type of products to be produced. She enters a particular industry which offers her the best prospects and products and produces those goods which she thinks will pay her the most and employees those methods of production which seems to her the most profitable. She effects suitable changes in the size of the business, its location, techniques of production and does everything that is needed for the development of her business.

(c) ***Innovation*****:** The women entrepreneur conceives the idea for the improvement in the quality of product line. She considers the economic viability and technological feasibility in bringing about improved quality.

(d) ***Managerial function*****:** She formulates production plans, arranges finance, purchase raw materials, provides production amenities, organizes the sales and also undertake the task of personnel management. She undertakes a venture, assumes risk and earns profit. She is a woman who has a strong motivation to achieve success.

Growth and Development of Women Entrepreneurship

According to **Ministry of Micro, Small and Medium Enterprises** women-owned enterprises accounted for just 10 per cent of the total 10.5 million enterprises in the country in 2001-02. It is, however, important to know that more than 85 per cent women entrepreneurs were operating as unregistered entities and apparently based in rural areas, perhaps an indication that they are income-generating activity for self/family. Women enterprises were concentrated in sectors with particular ease of entry and low returns. This does not mean that women entrepreneurs are not in to quality products/services, but their number would be relatively small. This is borne out of the fact that the average investment in a MSE was only ₹ 1.47 lakh, as revealed by the Third Census of Small-scale Industries. Some category of woman informally takes up business activities like academic and non-academic coaching, fabric painting, making dresses, tailoring, etc., as part-time activities as well as to supplement family income.

The forgoing observations about the constraints faced by women entrepreneurs pose many challenges to policy makers in improving the business environment for them.

The policy approach, however, has to make a distinction between 'survivalist enterprises' (poverty alleviation) and commercial ventures owned and proposed by 'better off' sections of women, since each require a specific treatment. In case of the former category, they have to strengthen so that they can continue to generate income for self/family on long-term basis, and, if possible, graduate to commercial venture level. Moreover, in respect of the other category, they need support in establishing and successfully managing/operating their enterprises, besides coping up with the fall-outs of globalization.

To help women take active participation in the economy via enterprises, both the categories need firstly improved access to finance. Although MSEs are part of priority sector lending, women entrepreneurs do not get any special facility. Policy makers can consider stipulating certain percentage of MSE lending to women-owned ones as is now available for tiny &cottage units and units with investment below a certain level to ease the problem. Commercial banks also need to be impressed upon to be more considerate towards women entrepreneurs to build their confidence and make them more communicative. Further, Banks should consider adopting liberal attitude in extending loans to small service and trading enterprises as a vast majority of women entrepreneurs are apparently in these activities. As much as 50.09 lakh SHGs had savings of ₹ 3,785 crore with banks as on 31st, March, 2008, across the country, 80 per cent of which were exclusively women groups.

Areas for Development of Women Entrepreneur

Today we find women in different types of industries, traditional as well as non-traditional, such as electronics, engineering, jewellery, stitching and tailoring, fashion designing, agarbatti, candles and soaps manufacturing, rexin bags manufacturing, soft toys manufacturing, various masala making, cooking and catering, computer education, beauticians' course, boys fiber molding, decorative wax art, creative painting, embroidery, knitting, crochet etc.

Although the list of successful women entrepreneurs is quite long, selected representatives of women entrepreneurs are mentioned below:

Sarada Ramani: At an age when women are supposed to be fighting middle-age crisis, **Sarada Ramani** began her career. After 14 years of marriage and a 12-year-old daughter, **Sarada** returned to books when she was 35 years old. Having acquired a post-graduate degree in computer applications, she went in search of a job as an IT programmer, only to be told that she was too old! Undaunted, she thought of her own enterprise and launched 'Computer International', a small computer education unit, in 1996. Beginning with just six employees, today her firm has transformed into an outsourced product development company that employs 150 people.

Along with success came awards that were constant morale boosters. She won the 'National Award for Small-scale Entrepreneur-2003' and 'Best Women Entrepreneur of the Country-2004'—certainly a huge leap from 'rejected' status.

Apart from her love for programming, **Sarada** believes relationship building is her strength, which has contributed immensely in making her company grow. "My company is my third child and I have nourished it in a befitting manner," she says.

Her quest for achievement seems insatiable as she now aspires for a Ph.D in entrepreneurship after having acquired an MBA degree recently.

At the same time, she says she feels no different than the housewife next door. "Entrepreneurship requires no great degrees, no solid financial back-up, but just determination to face all the challenges," she says. A simple truth!

Ishita Khanna: We start in a mountain desert where people were sent to exile in early times because of its harsh living conditions. That's where **Ishita Khanna** decided to start her company.

Ecosphere, a not-for-profit organization, is located in the trans-Himalayan valley of Spits, which translates as "the middle land" in Tibetan. It has swiftly grown into a social enterprise working on issues ranging from climate change and women's empowerment to responsible travel and energy efficiency. Khanna's objective is to hand over the running of the organization entirely to the locals in the coming five years.

Earlier this year, Ecosphere received India's first Green Energy and Green Livelihoods Achievement Award from The Sierra Club, the oldest and largest grass roots environmental organization in the U.S. "Spits' extreme winter and dusty environs of a rugged back country make for a beautiful setting but a hard working environment," says **Khanna**, whose vision is redefining the way environmental conservation is practiced in India. "Spits' geographical isolation and poor communication infrastructure has been one of the major hurdles. What would otherwise be achieved in a day or two in the city would take weeks and sometimes even months in Spits."

Shahnaz Husain: **Shahnaz Husain**, who started India's first professional herbal salon in the balcony of her house in Delhi in 1971, now reigns over an Ayurvedic beauty care empire. Husain, who has worked with eminent names such as **Helena Rubinstein, Christine Valmy, Swarzkopf and Lancôme,** realized early on how much damage chemical cosmetics can cause. Her customized beauty care based on the concept of "herbal care and cure" found instant appreciation, and the enterprise grew.

She spares nothing—fruits, vegetables, gold and even diamond dust all have found a place in her organic concoctions. "The ancient Indian system of Ayurveda is the oldest and most organized system of herbal healing in the world. I was convinced that it could offer ideal answers to modern cosmetic care," she says. "Armed only with complete faith in my concept, I entered highly competitive international markets, without commercial advertising or fancy packaging." The brand—which has hundreds of franchises throughout the country—supplies to Harrods in London, Galleries Lafayette in Paris, the Seibu chain in Japan, La Renascent in Milan and El Crete Ingles in Spain, and the list continues to grow.

Vandana Shiva: Among the most enterprising women putting India on the world map is **Vandana Shiva**, Ph.D. The globally known scientist and environmentalist described the idea behind her organization: "I started Navdanya because of two reasons. In 1984 the violence in Punjab and the Bhopal tragedy compelled me to study why agriculture had become like war." She wrote the book "The Violence of Green Revolution" for the United Nations as part of that investigation.

In 1987, because of her work on Green Revolution, she was invited to a meeting on biotechnology in Geneva. There, she says, "the big chemical industries laid out their plans on how they wanted to patent every seed and genetically modify our food and how they are going to use the Uruguay Round of GATT to impose this dictatorship over life and food on the world." Says Shiva, "I felt compelled to defend freedom and took inspiration from Gandhi's spinning wheel to start saving patent-free, GMO-free seed. That is how Navdanya was born in 1987."

Over the course of this journey, **Shiva** has faced corporate policies and governmental laws supporting farming and agricultural models that are unsustainable. Now, two decades later, Navdanya has 46 organic seed banks across the country. Navdanya's efforts are spreading not only awareness about the importance of organically grown food but also supplying organic food grown at its farms in the Uttaranchal region of the Himalayas. She adds, "The message I would give to women entrepreneurs is that they must change the model of business from one based on greed and exploitation to one based on sharing and conservation."

Jyoti Jeevan Naik: "Nothing is impossible. Women, especially who hail from rural areas, should aspire to join together to imitate a small-scale business of their own. They can generate fantastic results if they pool their resources and strengthen their bonds with one another". These are the golden words quoted by Late **Jyoti Naik**, the former President of Shri Mahila Griha Udyog Lijjat Papad, an Indian women's co-operative based in Mumbai. Lijjat Papad is a household name today and leading an organisation comprising of 42,000 members in no mean task. In this context, **Jyoti Naik** is an epitome of what a hard-working self made lady can achieve in the male-dominated social milieu.

Shri Mahila Griha Udyog Lijjat Papad, popularly known as Lijjat, is an Indian women's co-operative involved in manufacturing of various fast moving consumer goods. The organization's main objective is empowerment of women by providing them employment opportunities. Started in the year 1959 with a seed capital of ₹ 80, Lijjat has an annual turnover of around ₹ 650 crore, with ₹ 29 crore in exports. Lijjat is headquartered in Mumbai and has 67 branches and 35 divisions all over India. It is one of the last repositories of Sarvodaya Model of collective ownership.

Jyoti Naik was associated with the brand for over four decades. She joined Lijjat at the age of 12 to assist her mother in rolling papads. In 1973, she started the work of packing at Sahakar Bazaar branch, Bandra and later on, became the Sanchalika of the Wadala Branch. She became the president of the organization in 1999 and continued till her death in 2009. From 1999 to 2009, the sales figures have doubled and exports have trebled. Lijjat has also ventured successfully into khakhra, masala, wadi, detergent powder and cakes and bakery products.

Business volumes notwithstanding, the barometer for measuring the real strength of this community enterprise is its social capital. How many organizations can boast of a ₹ 650 crore top line with 42,000 semi-literate women at the helm of the affairs?

Jyoti Naik was the face of these women for years and she has been awarded by numerous agencies/organizations for her leadership. Lijjat received the *'Best Village Industries Institution'* award from KVIC for the period 1998-99 to 2000-01. In 2002, the *'Businesswoman of the Year'* award was given to the *"The Women behind Lijjat Papad"* at the Economic Times Awards for Corporate Excellence. Her economic background and lack of educational qualifications couldn't deter her from being at the fore-front of an empowering movement. she continues to serve as an inspiration for thousands of women.

Pia Singh: Steering from the bounty of nature to the luxury of lifestyle, DLF India is the country's largest real estate company in terms of revenue, earnings, market capitalization and developable area. Spearheaded by its director, **Pia Singh**, the company is becoming synonymous with luxurious entertainment around the country. *Avante-garde* shopping malls, modern residential and commercial spaces, and the introduction of international luxury brands such as Gucci, Bulgaria and Louis Vuitton under one roof are just a few of the projects the graduate from Wharton Business School has executed.

Apart from the revenue DLF generates from these properties, it holds regular exhibitions and significant events on its properties, such as India Fashion Week. A low-key visionary who also studied film-making at New York University, Singh is always behind the scenes and always directing the company forward.

It's interesting to note that none of these ladies discussed the hurdles that crossed their paths while they were realizing their dreams. It seemed as though they didn't want to waste time dwelling on what's done. As **Khanna** says, "There are numerous doubts that plague one before one takes the plunge. However, the more one thinks about it, the plunge seems more difficult. Hence, while I strongly believe that one must plan an initiative thoroughly, if you are passionate about what you want to do, that is half the battle won already."

Problems of Women Entrepreneurs

The basic problem of a women entrepreneur is that she is a woman. This is because of her dual responsibility towards family and workplace. The attitude of society towards her and the constraints in which she has to live and work are hostile. With joint families breaking up many women simply don't have the support of elders. However, in rural India joint families are still the order of the day. Women have to face resistance not only from men but also from elderly woman who are ingrained with this attitude of inequality. This attitude of reservation creates difficulties and problems at all levels, i.e. family support, banking, marketing, training, licensing etc. The main problems faced by women entrepreneurs can be analyzed as:

(i) ***Family involvement:*** Most of her time is devoted in the upliftment of the children and other members of the family. Married women entrepreneurs have to strike a balance between the home and business. Her success to a great extent is dependable on the support extended by her husband and other members of her family.

(ii) ***Male dominance:*** Equal treatment to men and women is absent at all levels in the society as well as at business level. There exists a male superiority ego complex with creates an obstacle in the road to success.

(iii) ***Social attitude:*** In a male dominated society women do not get equal treatment inspite of the constitutional and legal equality, in practice the attitude of men is not only tradition-bound but even of those who are responsible for decision making and research is not of equality. It is not that women do not have skills or capacity but they are not properly trained because it is felt that if a skill is imparted it is felt that it is imparted to a girl, because when she gets married she takes away the skill with her.

(iv) ***Lack of education:*** The literacy rate among women in India is quite low. Due to this lack of education women are unaware of the latest developments taking place in different areas of knowledge e.g., finance, marketing, accounts, competitors, etc.

(v) ***Non-availability of finance:*** Women entrepreneurs suffer from inadequate financial resources and working capital. Banks are reluctant to provide assistance to women because banks feel that these women may at any time leave their business and become housewives again.

(vi) ***Shortage of raw materials:*** Scarcity of raw materials and other inputs is one of the main reasons for the failure of the enterprise run by women. These women lack the capability to take the advantage of the market when the prices are low due to shortage of working capital. Moreover, they are also unable to avail the attractive discounts offered by their suppliers.

(vii) ***Severe competition:*** Women entrepreneurs' faces severe competition severe competition for their products from male dominated industries. The organizational set-up is poor which is unable to pump the required funds at right time. Moreover a lot of capital is required for regular advertisement of the product to withstand in the market.

(viii) ***No risk bearing capacity:*** The most important pre-requisite for success in entrepreneurship is the risk bearing capacity. All throughout her life-time she has led protected life dominated by the family members namely her parents, elder members in the family and after marriage her husband and in-laws. Hence at no time has she faced the risk of life alone. She therefore lacks the risk-bearing capacity and without the risk-bearing she cannot become a successful entrepreneur.

(ix) ***Too much dependence on middlemen:*** The women entrepreneurs are mostly dependent on middlemen who take the major share of the profits. It may be possible for the women to eliminate these intermediaries, but then it will necessitate a lot of running about, which may be difficult for the women entrepreneurs.

Summing Up

Introduction

Women constitute around half of the total world population. Women account for 48 per cent of the total population in the country and in the available social structure, they, in general, are discriminated lot not only economically but also socially. Considering the size of women population in the world, and recognizing that enough has not been done to channelize the 'women power', countries around the world are looking at ways and means to empower them.

Concept

The prospective role of women entrepreneur in India has been realized since a long time. India history reveals that there have been several women like **Rajia Sultan**, **Rani Laxmi Bai**, **Nur Jahan**, and **Rani Padmini** who has successfully rules their kingdom. In modern, India also several women leaders and administrators like **Sarojini Naidu**, **Indira Gandhi**, **Vijay Laxmi Pandit** who have succeeded in their statesmanship. All these prove that Indian women are in no way inferior to men in all walks of life and they can be good entrepreneurs as men in the country.

Definition of Women Entrepreneur

*The **Government of India** has defined a women entrepreneur as "an enterprise owned and controlled by a women having a minimum financial interest of 51 per cent of the capital and giving at least 51 per cent of the employment generated in the enterprise to women."* The above definition has come in for severe criticism on the condition of employing more than 50 per cent of women entrepreneurs.

Women entrepreneurs may be defined as the women or a group of women who initiate, organize and operate a business enterprise.

The common dimension in the definition of empowerment is power: power to influence one's own life, power to make one's own choices and the power to act upon these choices.

Economic Empowerment and Entrepreneurship

Empowering women does not mean merely ensuring jobs and a place in political system for a few of them, though this is a welcome step, but going beyond this. While solutions to women on social front do boost their confidence, the economic empowerment would not only raise their confidence levels but would also enable them to become part of mainstream economy. The ultimate objective of a welfare programme should be to make the beneficiary self-dependent and economically independent, so that she makes economic contribution, rather than just be a dependent. Economic empowerment would also enable them to access better education, medical care/facilities, etc., and thus, climb a step ahead on the social ladder.

Functions of Women Entrepreneurs

The women entrepreneur has to react to new ideas, demand and exploit the opportunities and thereby contribute to technical progress. A women entrepreneur is expected to perform the following functions: Risks; Decision making; Innovation; and Managerial function.

Growth and Development of Women Entrepreneurship

According to **Ministry of Micro, Small and Medium Enterprises** women-owned enterprises accounted for just 10 per cent of the total 10.5 million enterprises in the country in 2001-02.It is, however, important to know that more than 85 per cent women entrepreneurs were operating as unregistered entities and apparently based in rural areas, perhaps an indication that they are income-generating activity for self/family. The forgoing observations about the constraints faced by women entrepreneurs pose many challenges to policy makers in improving the business environment for them. Policy makers can consider stipulating certain percentage of MSE lending to women-owned ones as is now available for tiny &cottage units and units with investment below a certain level to ease the problem. Commercial banks also need to be impressed upon to be more considerate towards women entrepreneurs to build their confidence and make them more communicative. Further, Banks should consider adopting liberal attitude in extending loans to small service and trading enterprises as a vast majority of women entrepreneurs are apparently in these activities. As much as 50.09 lakh SHGs had savings of ₹ 3,785 crore with banks as on 31st, March, 2008, across the country, 80 per cent of which were exclusively women groups.

Areas for Development of Women Entrepreneur

Today we find women in different types of industries, traditional as well as non-traditional, such as electronics, engineering, jewellery, stitching and tailoring, fashion designing, agarbatti, candles and soaps manufacturing, rexin bags manufacturing, soft toys manufacturing, various masala making, cooking and catering, computer education, beauticians' course, boys fiber molding, decorative wax art, creative painting, embroidery, knitting, crochet etc.

Although the list of successful women entrepreneurs is quite long, selected representatives of women entrepreneurs are **Ramani, Ishita Khanna, Shahnaz Husain, Vandana Shiva, Jyoti Naik, and Pia Singh.**

Problems of Women Entrepreneurs

The basic problem of a women entrepreneur is that she is a woman. This is because of her dual responsibility towards family and workplace. The attitude of society towards her and the constraints in which she has to live and work are hostile. With joint families breaking up many women simply don't have the support of elders. However, in rural India joint families are still the order of the day. Women have to face resistance not only from men but also from elderly woman who are ingrained with this attitude of inequality. This attitude of reservation creates difficulties and problems at all levels, i.e. family support, banking, marketing, training, licensing etc. The main problems faced by women entrepreneurs can be analyzed as: Family involvement; Male dominance; Social attitude; Lack of education; Non-availability of finance; Shortage of raw materials; Severe competition; No risk bearing capacity; and too much dependence on middlemen.

Case 1- Analysis of Trends in Growth and Development of Entrepreneurship in Goa

Background

Entrepreneurship is a human universal. All over the world, and throughout history, people have shaped businesses. Yet, although women make up more than 50 per cent of the world population, they own and manage appreciably fewer businesses than men. Venture type and management styles very across genders as well. Women entrepreneurship presents quite a lot of distinctive characteristics that differentiate it from men entrepreneurship. All over the world, female entrepreneurship has become an important component of academic and policy conversations around entrepreneurship. Still, there is much gaps, and encourage scholars to push the frontier of knowledge in this further are the goals of this work.

Goa though a tiny state on the west coast of the country, it possess the distinction of achieving high levels of both economic and social development. The economy of the State has shown a growth of 10 per cent per annum. The social indicators of the state like literacy, birth rate, death rate, infant mortality rate etc. are impressive and many of these are comparable with the developed nations in the world. The state has reached the level of replacement in population growth more than a decade ago.

The size of the population is 13,47,668 as per census 2001. Women constitute a significant proportion of the total population of our state (Population of Goa 1.3 million according to the 2001 Census). Out of the total migrants in the state, 64.76 per cent are migrants within the state, 34.07 per cent are migrants from other states within the country and 1.17 per cent is migrants from other countries. Data reveals 70 per cent migrants from within the state. (Economic *Survey*, 2008-09)

In the state of Goa, as per the revised estimates (2004-2005) of the planning commission, 13.8 per cent of the population lives below poverty line, of which 21.3 per cent in urban areas and 5.4 per cent in rural areas.

Activities Respondents' Occupation

Exhibit I Activities Respondents' Occupation

Activities	M	%	F	%
Spare parts shop	19	1.23	02	0.48
General stores	121	7.81	88	21.05
Cold drink house and ice cream parlour/fruit juice and other products	10	0.65	03	0.72
Medical stores	11	0.71	04	0.96
Bakery	09	0.58	04	0.96
Catering unit/restaurant	26	1.68	11	2.63
Photo/video studio/multimedia projector	16	1.03	03	0.72
Xerox centre	06	0.39	04	0.96
Communication centre	08	0.52	04	0.96
Cyber cafe and computer related works/tally accounting unit/computer training centre	24	1.55	10	2.39
Travel and tourism/passenger training centre	08	0.52	02	0.48

Readymade garments and fashion boutique	17	1.10	52	12.44
Beauty parlour	01	0.07	12	2.87
Tailoring unit	08	0.52	86	20.57
Hair cutting saloon	06	0.39	–	–
Fabrication/engineering workshop/turning job	45	2.90	–	–
Repairs sales and services/servicing centre/jewellery unit	44	2.84	11	2.63
Manufacturing unit	28	1.81	09	2.15
Flour and masala mill	04	0.26	07	1.68
Papad/pickle making unit	04	0.26	05	1.20
Screen printing/printing press	05	0.32	04	0.96
Cantering plates	04	0.26	–	–
Wholesale trading	86	5.55	46	11.00
Fishing unit/acquisition of fishing canoe	36	2.32	01	0.24
Sound system and D.J. music/musical band	34	2.19	04	0.96
Hardware/electrical goods	20	1.29	05	1.20
Dental/ayurvedic/homeopathic clinic/medical clinic/ occupational health laboratory	10	0.65	05	1.20
Hiring of Pandal/lighting/decoration/catering items/plastic chairs etc.	26	1.68	10	2.39
Footwear shop	01	0.07	01	0.24
Tourist taxi	109	7.03	01	0.24
Goods carrier	280	18.07	–	–
Yellow/black taxi	160	10.32	04	0.96
Yellow/black motorcycle	222	14.32	–	–
Yellow/black auto rickshaw	77	4.97	02	0.48
Others	65	4.19	18	4.31
Total	1550	100	418	100

Source: Economic Development Corporation, Panaji-Goa.

Note: Compilation of data

Govt has introduced 37 activities in the year 2010, 418 female and 1550 male have registered in the year 2008 whereas, 522 female and 2292 male registered in the year 2010. Percentage-wise the figure may be not as much of (18.55%) but number-wise it is shows high potential.

If we analyses the influx of male and female in the business as a profession, the male strength shows the maximum but if it is analysed on the basis of the percentage it is known that the female strength shows the maximum. For instance, 121 male opted for general store scoring percentage at 7.81 whereas 88 female opted for general stores securing 21.05 percentages. Male gender prefers tourist taxi, goods carrier, yellow/black taxi, yellow/black motorcycle business as the most prominent business for them to carry on, whereas, female prefer general stores, readymade garment, tailoring whole trading as the business of prior consideration.

Govt has reduced the rate of interest from 8% to 6% to the female entrepreneurs in-between. This probably may be the rationale to increase the number of female beneficiary.

Self-help Groups (SHGs)

The idea of Self-help Group had started first in Canacona, in the year 1999. The main aim of this idea was to bring about socio-economic development and to provide opportunities for poor women to come together and to improve their economic and social status, and to meet the credit needs of the poor for economic activities.

Presently, there are in about 84 SHGs under the Below Poverty Line, which are interspersed in the different village panchayats of the Canacona taluka. A study showed that Gaondongrem has 17 SHGs, Cotigao -19, Khola houses 19, Agonda is home to 9 SHGs, Poinguinnim - 6, Shristhal -13, and Loliem-Polem has one self-help group operating from its jurisdiction. Incidentally, Cotigao, Khola and Gaondongrem have a sizeable numbers, because, there are more BPL families living in these areas. Source reveals that there are about 1800 families living Below the Poverty Line (BPL) in the talukas.

The women, once they gain experience in dealing with small collection of savings, issue of small loans to members in need, follow up of the repayment of these small loans, maintaining group records, etc., feel confident to deal with bigger and larger loan facilities from commercial banks. With these loans, they carry out agricultural activities, initiate repairs of their houses and the houses of their group members, use the funds for the educational purposes of their children, get into vegetable cultivation, go out and get medical treatment and attention if required and on overall improvement of their economic and social status. The women keep themselves occupied through various activities, like selling the products they make, which are often domestic, and other allied activities, including stitching of clothes, preparation of sweets and pickles, handicraft items, etc. the profits gained from sales is then divided among the members of the group.Swarnajayanti Gram SwarozgarYojana(SGSY) Scheme had introduced to facilitate the women to acquire Business loans amounting to ₹ 50,000/- @ 12.50 per cent subsidies per head.Until now, 440 entrepreneurs have registered under SGSY schemes. A group loan, which can be availed by the SHG, is about ₹ 5 lakh, which has a subsidy benefit of 25 per cent. It known from the source that if loan is taken by a group of 10 members, when divided among them, each member gets ₹ 50,000 each, from which each member has to pay back ₹ 40,000, thereby profiting by ₹ 10,000 each. The source says that annually, the RDA organises inter-state exhibitions entitled, 'SARAS' where the SHGs from various states come together and sell their products. This is a sort of ready-made market for them to sell their goods, also gives them an opportunity to expose their products to buyers from other states and provides them fresh and new ideas on how to run their SHG and what new activities to take up. The SHG can also avail the benefits of another scheme meant for them under the Social Welfare Department, wherein they can avail a sum of ₹ 25,000 as loan amount for upgrading their existing business or activities. In order to avail this, any SHG registered with the co-operative societies can avail the same, provided the group exists for a period of at least two years. If the SHG is not registered, then the bank account or statement of the last two years can serve as proof to avail the scheme.

The source says that women had entered in the field of entrepreneurship by acquiring loan for purchase of power tiller for horticulture activities, selling coconuts, vegetables, fruit, making of sweets and pickles, papad and the activity of salt fish or dry fish.

Each year, the Institute of Rural Development and Administration (GIRDA), Ela hold orientation-training programme to the BPL SHG groups, Old Goa on the topic like how to maintain accounts, how to write the minutes, how to market the products, etc. Agnel Vocational Training Institute at Verna has also trained nearly 40 members of different SHGs in a two months course in catering till know.

Statistics of SHGs Linkage Group in North and South Goa

Exhibit – II Statistics of SHGs linkage group in north and south Goa

BANKS	SHGs(N)	SHGs(S)	TOTAL	%
SBI	42	51	93	11.63
SBM	0	0	0	0
SBT	0	0	0	0
BOB	30	31	61	7.63
BOI	140	18	158	19.75
BOM	17	0	17	2.13
CAN	131	75	206	25.75
CBI	11	0	11	1.38
CORPBK	23	07	30	3.75
DENABK	17	8	25	3.13
INDIANBK	0	0	0	0
IOB	149	0	149	18.63
OBC	0	0	0	0
SYNDBK	09	04	13	1.63
UCOBK	12	0	12	1.5
UNIONBK	15	09	24	03
VIJBK	01	0	01	0.13
IDBIBK	0	0	0	0
INDUSINDBK	0	0	0	0
TOTAL CBs	597	203	800	100
GSCB	719	148	867	99.20
GOAUCB	0	0	0	0
MAPUSAUCB	07	0	07	0.88
TOTAL COOPS	726	148	874	100
GR. TOTAL	1323	351	1674	

Source: Nabard Goa branch

Note: Compilation of data

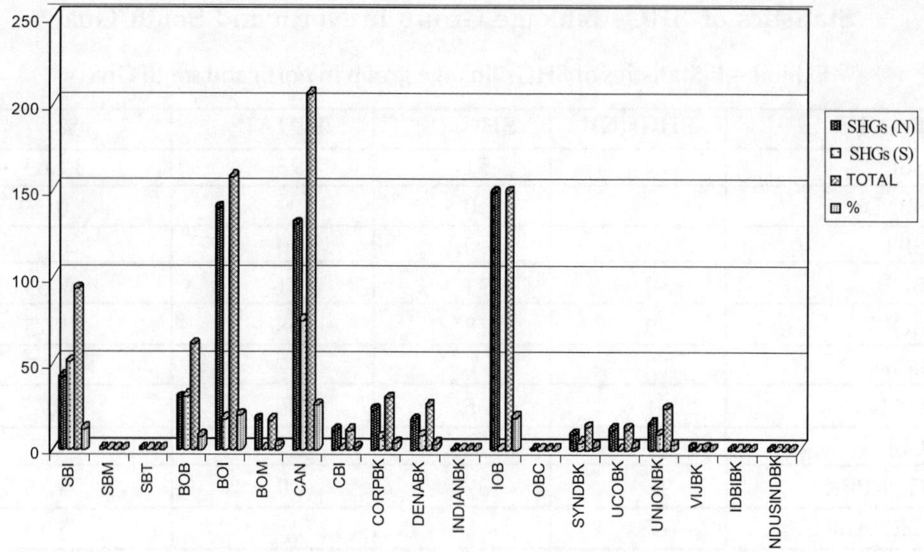

Fig - II SHGs linkage group in north and south Goa

For effective implementation of government sponsored schemes/programmes; the role of the banks cannot be sideline. The role of the banks in economic development is to remove the deficiency of capital by stimulating savings and investment. The bank encourages the habit of saving among the people and enable small savings to be accumulated into large funds thus available for investments.

The study reveals that north district of goa state has registered maximum number of SHG group in total. The figure reproduce concerning 1323 numbers in north while, 351 in south Goa almost certainly due to the inventiveness and encouraging outlook of the recovering officer and the staff. About 25.75 per cent of the women entrepreneur has taken the benefits of SHG Linkage Programme with the help of Canara Bank, 19.75 per cent from Bank of India and 18.625 per cent Indian Overseas Bank.

The study reveals that 47.79 per cent of SHGs has secured loan from Central bank whereas, 52.21 per cent from Co-operative Banks. The overall answer of study put forward that financial help launch by these Banks has really enhanced the right of entry to financial services to the women and had well thought-out positive impact on the socio-economic conditions and the lessening of poverty of SHG female members and their households.

It is acknowledged from the reading that entrepreneur have more intricate time obtaining loans from the bank. Credit is available to entrepreneurs from banks under the CMRY schemes. As the loan procedure in commercial banks is lengthy and wearisome, the bank officials do not show interest in doling out such small loan. The entrepreneurs shared that they were apprehensive to approach banks as the loan amount are small and the documents required be very complicated added to which was the contrary attitude of banks for sanctioning the loan. The route of making the credit line available to the entrepreneurs can be made user-friendly and be available with minimum documents to be submitted. Low level of education resulted in entrepreneurs undertaking activities related to their existing skills. The lack of professional skill also slowed down their competence of forthcoming banks for financial backing.

Skills Preferred by Respondents

Exhibit - III Skills Preferred by Respondents

SKILLS	BENEFICIARIES	%
Stitching and tailoring	80	17.35
Fashion designing	25	5.42
Agarbatti, candles and soaps manufacturing	82	17.79
Rexin bags manufacturing	45	9.76
Soft toys manufacturing	45	9.76
Various masala making	20	4.34
Cooking and catering	45	9.76
Computer education	23	4.99
Beauticians' course	05	1.08
Boys Fibre moulding	24	5.21
Decorative wax art	26	5.64
Creative painting	21	4.56
Embroidery, knitting , crochet	20	4.34
TOTAL	461	100

Source: Mineral Foundation of Goa, Panaji-Goa.

Note: Compilation of data

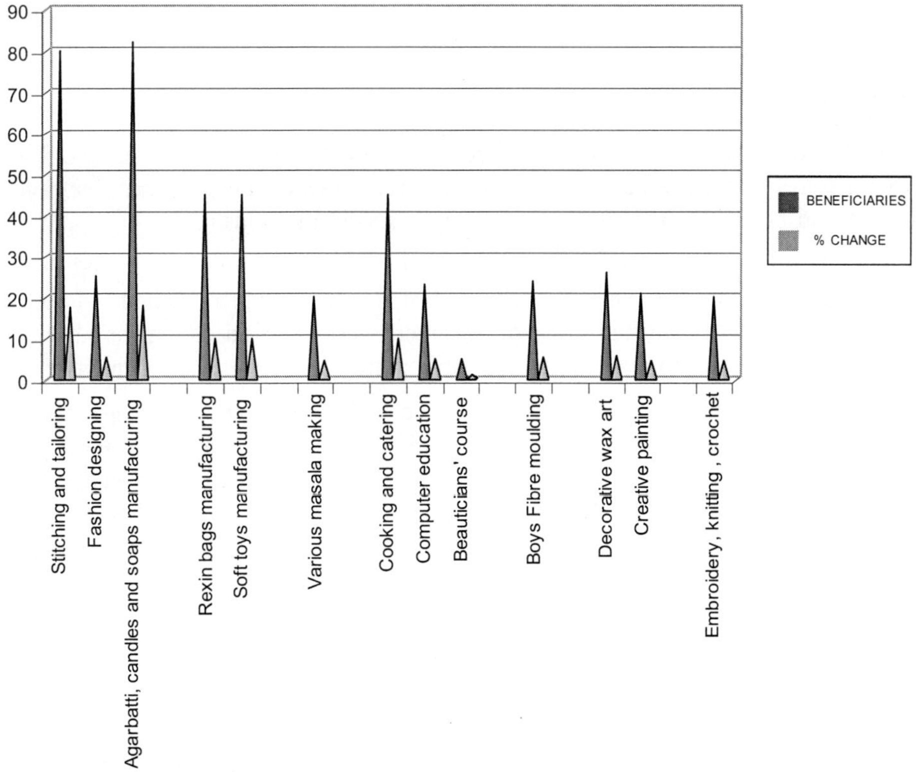

Fig - III Activities preferred by Respondents

It is a known fact that selling of Agarbatti, candles and soaps manufacturing is a leading business activities along with stitching and tailoring among the mass section of the population. Cooking and catering which assumes to be the back-borne of the mass section of the female population indicates only 9.76 per cent of the total 461 (100%). Influx of females is notices more in the business of stitching and tailoring, Agarbatti, candles and soap manufacturing rather than other skills.

The rural women are out of action due to various reasons, such as; most of them are socially backward, illiterate, with low motivation and poor economic base. Individually, a rural woman is not only weak in socio-economic term but also lacks access to the knowledge and information, which are the most important components of today's development process. However, in a group, they are empowered to conquer many of these weaknesses.

Governments has been playing a role of launch pad, and are target-oriented and also aggravated to widen the agenda of SHGs. Government has been providing funds to plausible NGOs for capacity building of the primary and secondary stakeholders. Funds are made available for examine, testing, and encouragement. Govt felt a need for decentralized aptitude building and support services in order for the SHG movement to blossom. For every 5-10 SHGs, there must be a mentor that emerges from the movement itself. There is a need for unremitting innovation to promote growth and ensure sustainability. With the dawn of technology, SHGs could take on several go-betweens that benefit their members. There is a great potential if the movement is supported with an idea and tactic.

In order to engender entrepreneurship opportunity and to ensure achievement of government sponsored schemes, banks have formed 4205 SHGs & linked 2328 SHGs as on 31st March 2009. There is sturdy evolution in the formation and linkage of SHGs. As per the statistics available from the District Co-operative Central Banks reveals that the bank have shaped 4811 SHGs & linked 2610 SHGs as on 31st, March, 2010.

Conclusions

The speedily varying economy has affected to endeavor out as entrepreneurs. The entrepreneurial activity for some gender is an economic need; while for others, a pure business endeavours though their numbers would be small, each, however, require a specific treatment.

Only a small fraction of entrepreneurs, who is in to relatively high-end products, and those registered can avail of such support, while a vast majority of them remain without any assistance. Efforts should be made to bring unregistered enterprises into fold of registered ones so that a large section of entrepreneurs can avail of the available policy concessions and benefits.

In order to formulate development unbiased and momentous, it is imperative that every plan, proposal or policy be based on a clear understanding of the possible impact these would have on the status of women. Researcher and policymakers need to develop a gender-sensitive insight into the developmental models that are currently practiced.

4 THE ENTREPRENEURIAL PERSPECTIVE

Nature and Development of Entrepreneurship, External Factors influencing the growth of Entrepreneurship, Entrepreneur's Role towards Regional Development & Industries, Role of Entrepreneurs in the Present Milieu, Ways and Means to Promote Entrepreneurship, Summing Up.

Nature and Development of Entrepreneurship

Entrepreneurs have played an important role in the economic development of the developed countries for example, America, Russia and Japan tends to support the fact that the economy is an effect for which entrepreneurship is the cause. The people in the underdeveloped countries are also becoming more and more aware of the significance of entrepreneurial development in the process of their economic development. Now, people have begun to realize that for achieving the goal of economic development, it is necessary to increase entrepreneurship both qualitatively and quantitatively in the country. It is only active and enthusiastic entrepreneurs who fully explore the potentialities of the country's available resources—labour, technology and capital. **Schumpeter,** visualized the entrepreneurs as the key figure in economic development because of his role in introducing innovations. **Peter Drucker**, has aptly described the relationship between an 'entrepreneur ' and 'changes'. He says, "Entrepreneurs see changes as the norm and as healthy. Usually, they do not bring about the changes themselves. But the entrepreneur always searches for change, responds to it and exploits it as an opportunity."

David McClelland has introduced a new dimension to the importance of entrepreneurship in economic development. He says that the development of entrepreneurship depends on human motivation to achieve or need for achievement. **McClelland's** hypothesis is that society with a generally high level of achievement will produce more energetic entrepreneurs, who in turn would accelerate the process of economic development. That is why there is a steady stream of entrepreneurs in the developed countries where the motivation to achieve is very high. Similarly, in the underdeveloped regions this motivation is either lacking or low, causing a short supply of entrepreneurs.

The following factors may be considered as the developing and determining factors which help to achieve the entrepreneurial development. The factors by itself reflect the aspects of growth of entrepreneurs towards development:

(1) ***Efficiency and economy:*** According to **Prof. Lewis**, the economical and optimum use of the factors of production is necessary for producing maximum output with the minimum cost of production. In order to do this, new advanced production technique should be used. New experiments should be made with different techniques of production. It is necessary to increase the geographical and occupational mobility of factors of production. Efficiency and technical skill should be utilized for maximum efficiency and optimum use of resources.

(2) ***Availability of resources:*** For achieving entrepreneurial development it is necessary that the human and natural material resources are available in adequate quantities, e.g., water, forest, land, mineral and capital equipment should be made available in large quantities.

(3) ***Manpower or human resources:*** Manpower or human resources means the quantity as well as the quality of population. The number of labourers available depends on the population growth. High productivity and efficiency would depend on their skill enterprise knowledge, imagination and good health. Efficient manpower in ample quantity is necessary for economic growth.

Quality of population can be improved by educating and training the masses. According to Prof. Drucker, the people should be willing to accept new economic challenges and search for new opportunities for development and progress. For accepting challenges for economic development, qualities such as honesty, integrity efficiency and leadership are necessary. The number of people possessing these qualities should be large. However, the rate of growth of population should not be more than the rate of growth of national income because it would reduce the per capita income of the society and this would lead to a lower standard of living.

(4) ***Creation of capital assets or capital formation:*** Capital formation means the creation of permanent capital assets like means of transport, machinery, tools and equipment factories, water and power resources, irrigation projects, etc. This capital formation is the basis of entrepreneurial development. Capital formation is the result of savings, i.e., national income minus consumption. When capital, made available out of savings, is invited in productive channels, it leads to production in agriculture and industry. For achieving economic growth, the ratio of capital and investment to output must be increased. The proportion of investment in capital goods industries to investment in consumption goods industries should also increased. Real savings, their investment in productive channels through intermediary institutions and the use of resources lead to capital formation.

(5) ***External resources:*** If domestic resources are not adequately available, then progress of enterprise can be achieved with the help of resources, like capital and technical know-how from foreign countries. These resources may be borrowed, or they may be secured as foreign aid. Foreign resources should be used till the underdeveloped economy reaches the take-off stage, i.e., the stage of self-reliant growth. External resources are used only to meet temporary difficulties.

(6) ***Technological advancement:*** Entrepreneurial progress in modern times cannot be achieved without using advanced technology. Advanced technology necessitates the use of up to date techniques of production and the most modern and highly sophisticated machinery. The chief advantage of modern technology is that, it increases the tempo of production and improves the quality of the output. An underdeveloped economy cannot take advantage of advanced technology in the initial stages of economic growth because technological advancement does not take place. Till the underdeveloped economy develops its own technology, it has to import advanced technology from foreign countries. Technological advancement depends on investment of capital research, in production techniques and, also in human resources. Capital, when invested in research and education of labours, leads to the advancement of knowledge and technology. Savings and science lead to technological progress. As a result, methods of production are revolutionized, modern techniques and tools can be used, and therefore, there is a saving in time, labour and money costs. Technological advancement leads to improvement in capital assets which is the basis of economic growth.

(7) ***Suitable investment pattern:*** For achieving economic progress in an enterprise, resources should not remain idle, and at the same time they should not be wasted. They should be used in the most economical manner. This necessitates the proper selection of the investment pattern. Investment of resources in various sectors like agriculture, small and large-scale industries, transport, consumer goods and capital goods industries should be balanced. It is necessary to determine a suitable pattern or priority for investment on the basis of the importance of the various sectors in the economy, e.g., in an agricultural economy, investment priority and method of production would be decided first for agriculture and then for other sectors.

External Factors influencing the growth of Entrepreneurship

There are various factors of external environments which surround the business enterprise. Each of these environments is discussed as below:

(i) ***Cultural Environment:*** The belief of the working force, their readiness to recognize the changes and behavioural habits depend upon the culture of the country. In any country the small savings of common man generate big investment. But the rate of saving and investment depends upon the cultural beliefs of the people. Some jobs and business are well thought-out to be higher standard according to the cultural environment. Traditional businesses enjoy a far above the ground status. From this point of view the elder people in the family or the other members of the society try to dishearten the new venture.

(ii) ***Social Environment:*** Caste system, traditional businesses, joint family system, religious matters are the factors of social environment. If the society is against innovation, or making new ventures, the entrepreneurs would not have much chance to make progress. A society accepting the new ideas can raise its living standards of living and economic growth. Therefore, growth of entrepreneurship is dependent on the behaviour of the society with the entrepreneurs.

(iii) ***Political Environment:*** The government favours the atmosphere of the industries and gives confidence the new entrepreneurs in the country with the help of taxation policies, price fixation and territorial restrictions. The government may formulate the first move to new schemes for the entrepreneurship. It may launch educational and training courses for them. The government can take steps in providing the needed finance through various financial institutions.

(iv) ***Business and Economic Environment:*** The entrepreneurship builds up faster in a favourable business climate. The necessities of the entrepreneur, other than finance are raw-materials, power supply, transport facilities etc. These requirements are fulfilled with the help of favourable business climate. Business climate is unfavourable due to natural factors, and smooth interactions of economic forces. When the business environment is not suitable, the entrepreneurs are obligatory to face a greater amount of uncertainty, problems of scarcity of labour and raw material due to which, many of them get disheartened and drop the project. This slow down the rate of economic growth.

Entrepreneur's Role Towards Regional Development and Industries

Regional development leads to an equitable distribution of employment opportunities which remain no more confined to a few states leading to a wide disparity in the per capita income among different regions. If industrial development in the country is to proceed rapidly and regularly in a balanced manners, then increasingly greater attention will have to be paid to the development of those states and regions which have so far remained backward.

Regional development also helps in the attainment of certain social objectives like avoidance of emigration of labour, prevention of the occurrence of depressed areas and equalization of the per capita income in different parts of the country.

Balanced regional development of the different parts of the country, extension of the benefits of economic progress to the less developed regions and widespread diffusion of industry are among the major aims of the planned development.

Industrial sector in India, as in any other part of the world, comprises large, medium and small-scale units. In addition, we have a large sized, village and cottage industries sector, consisting mainly of artisans and households, where industrial activities are carried out at some either or full-time or part-time basis. These are all interdependent activities and this interdependence should be explicitly recognized while solving a development strategy for the industrial sector as a whole.

To realize the plan objectives of the balanced regional development, various fiscal and financial incentives are offered to entrepreneurs, to set up their units in specified backward region. The financial institution introduced in 1970, the scheme of concessional assistance to projects set up in backward areas. The concessions were in the form of lower promoter's contribution, lower interest rate, longer moratorium and amortization period, flexible debt equity ratio, reduction in the underwriting commission and in commitment charges on undrawn balance.

The Central Government's investment policy can be one of the effective tools to correct the regional imbalances in development of backward regions and to promote entrepreneurship in the country.

From the very beginning of planning in India, the development of entrepreneurship in backward regions has been adopted as a basic strategy for economic development of the country. In backward regions, the entrepreneurs, most of whom are first generation entrepreneurs, face several problems such as lack of finance, shortage of raw materials, lack of market coverage, lack of technical and managerial skills, improper project planning, shortage of power, etc. Entrepreneurship among rural people is lacking mainly due to lack of risk-taking ability, lack of business experience, lack of technical know-how, ignorance of various facilities and incentives available for setting up industries, lack of aptitude and necessary motivation. Lack of infrastructural facilities is the main hurdle in the growth of entrepreneurship in backward regions; a dynamic organizational infrastructure to coordinate the activities of entrepreneurial development in such areas is a basic prerequisite. Such an organisation can bridge the gap of knowledge, lack of expertise, training and aptitude. It can face problems of finance, raw materials marketing, transportation, etc.

Role of Entrepreneurs in the Present Milieu

The following are some of the important roles performs by an entrepreneur in such hyper competitive and aggressive market:

(1) *Catalytic Agent:* As a catalytic agent the entrepreneur has to change the approach of the workers so that the latter accepts essential changes in system arrangement and process which the organization is consider introducing in order to fight with the rivals. Entrepreneur should able to change the viewpoint and norms established and accepted by workers.

(2) *Developer:* Entrepreneur has to play a pivotal role in developing among the employees requisite knowledge, skills and suitable attitudes and improve their performance.

(3) *Facilitator:* Role of entrepreneur will be to promote a refreshing climate of mutual trust and confidence between the organization and workers through a high degree of empowerment and recognition, openness, faithfulness, internal and external fairness and team work. This will evidently direct to behavioral changes in the right direction.

(4) *Input Completer:* Input completion involves making available inputs that improve the efficiency of existing productions methods or facilitate the introduction of new ones. The role of the entrepreneur is to improve the flow of information in the market.

(5) *Organizer:* Entrepreneur as an organizer is one who combines the various factors of production related to the business by performing his organizing function. He generally avoids involving in risks and prefers to stay in secure positions. Since they are basically promoters of business, they promote their business by combining the various factors of production.

(6) ***Manager:*** Entrepreneur in the capacity of a manager involves himself with the management activity of an organisation. He gets the work done from his subordinates in the best possible manner by performing his managerial functions. His scope of operation particularly relates to planning, co-ordinating and guiding.

(7) ***Innovator:*** An entrepreneur is regarded as an innovator of new ideas, new products and new procedures. He understands what are the needs of the customers and try to give them new products as early as possible and tries to satisfy them.

(8) ***Imitator:*** The entrepreneurs will have to play the role of imitating entrepreneurs who will have to imitate the technics and technology of their counterpart in advance countries and then use them profitably in our country.

(9) ***Era of Liberalization, Privatization and Globalization:*** The entrepreneur will have to strive hard in setting a goal to make India a develop nation. Since, India has to keep pace with the developments which are taking place in UK. USA, JAPAN and other industrially advanced countries.

(10) ***Incubator:*** Entrepreneur as incubator supports the revolution of business with high potential, into self-sufficient, rising and gainful enterprise. By reducing the risks of business formation, entrepreneur is planned to contribute to economic growth through sustaining new enterprises. As an incubator, Entrepreneur provides affordable space, shared office services and business development assistance in an environment conducive to new venture, survival, growth, diversification and modification.

Ways and Means to Promote Entrepreneurship

Several steps can be taken to promote entrepreneurship in backward areas. Proper atmosphere and coordination must be created between the concerned authorities and the likely entrepreneur. They should have adequate technical staff for selecting and guiding genuine investors. The officials of these agencies must be motivated for honest and sincere approach. An orientation in their outlook and approach is necessary. Before the loan is released, proper techno-economic viability of the proposal should be carried out and cost-benefit study should be conducted. Proper infrastructural facilities should be developed in these areas. The planners and policymakers should be fully familiar with the problems and priorities of these areas. Drawbacks and obstructs in the institutional framework and various schemes of assistance should be removed. Emphasis should be on industries based on local resources. The agencies should monitor the progress of assisted units. Their officials should frequently visit the entrepreneurs to ensure that the facilities are being availed of suitably.

In India, government agencies and financial institutions often provide essential infrastructural facilities like land, power, raw materials and finance at concessional rates to entrepreneurs in backward areas. Technical guidance, training, marketing assistance, subsidies and tax exemptions are also available. But there is often lack of coordination among the different agencies like banks, state financial corporations and the government. For example, the financing agencies insist on a license before granting finance. But licensing authorities grant permit only after the vehicle is acquired. Officers of various agencies lack requisite knowledge to guide the entrepreneurs. In some cases, the officers harass the entrepreneur who ultimately loose their interest.

To summarize, an integrated and multidimensional approach is required for the growth of entrepreneurship in backward areas and for identifying opportunities that have growth prospects based on local resources. It is necessary to provide the technology, finance and other assistance which the small-scale entrepreneurs need very acutely, by the various government authorities and institutions.

Summing Up

Nature and Development of Entrepreneurship

Entrepreneurs have played an important role in the economic development of the developed countries for example, developed countries tends to support the fact that the economy is an effect for which entrepreneurship is the cause. The people in the underdeveloped countries are also becoming more and more aware of the significance of entrepreneurial development in the process of their economic development.

Schumpeter, visualized the entrepreneurs as the key figure in economic development because of his role in introducing innovations.

Peter Drucker, has aptly described the relationship between an 'entrepreneur ' and 'changes'.

David McClelland, has introduced a new dimension to the importance of entrepreneurship in economic development. He says that the development of entrepreneurship depends on human motivation to achieve or need for achievement.

McClelland's, hypothesis is that society with a generally high level of achievement will produce more energetic entrepreneurs, who in turn would accelerate the process of economic development.

The following factors may be considered as the developing and determining factors which help to achieve the entrepreneurial development: Efficiency and economy; Availability of resources; Manpower or human resources; Creation of capital assets or capital formation; External resources; Technological advancement; and Suitable investment pattern.

External Factors influencing the growth of Entrepreneurship

There are various factors of external environments which surround the business enterprise viz. Cultural Environment; Social Environment; Political Environment; and Business and Economic Environment.

Entrepreneur's Role towards Regional Development and Industries

Regional development leads to an equitable distribution of employment opportunities which remain no more confined to a few states leading to a wide disparity in the per capita income among different regions. Balanced regional development of the different parts of the country, extension of the benefits of economic progress to the less developed regions and widespread diffusion of industry are among the major aims of the planned development.

The Central Government's investment policy can be one of the effective tools to correct the regional imbalances in development of backward regions and to promote entrepreneurship in the country.

In backward regions, the entrepreneurs, most of whom are first generation entrepreneurs, face several problems such as lack of finance, shortage of raw materials, lack of market coverage, lack of technical and managerial skills, improper project planning, shortage of power, etc. Lack of infrastructural facilities is the main hurdle in the growth of entrepreneurship in backward regions; a dynamic organizational infrastructure to coordinate the activities of entrepreneurial development in such areas is a basic prerequisite.

Role of Entrepreneurs in the Present Milieu

The following are some of the important roles performs by an entrepreneur in such hyper competitive and aggressive market: Catalytic Agent; Developer; Facilitator; Input Completer; Organizer; Manager; Innovator; Imitator; Era of Liberalization, Privatization and Globalization; and Incubator.

Ways and Means to Promote Entrepreneurship

Several steps can be taken to promote entrepreneurship in backward areas:

(1) Proper atmosphere and coordination must be created between the concerned authorities and the likely entrepreneur.

(2) They should have adequate technical staff for selecting and guiding genuine investors.

(3) The officials of these agencies must be motivated for honest and sincere approach. An orientation in their outlook and approach is necessary.

(4) Before the loan is released, proper techno-economic viability of the proposal should be carried out and cost-benefit study should be conducted. Proper infrastructural facilities should be developed in these areas.

(5) The planners and policymakers should be fully familiar with the problems and priorities of these areas.

5 INTRAPRENEURS – AN EMERGING CLASS

Intrapreneurs — the New Entrepreneur, Entrepreneur v/s Intrapreneur, Summing Up.

Intrapreneurs — The New Entrepreneur

The Indian economy has seen a rise in the number of entrepreneurs in recent years and many young professionals prefer to be independent. Millions proudly claim the title of entrepreneur on one hand, but on the other hand, a title that hasn't had the attention it deserves is that of an 'Intrapreneur'.

An employee who is given the financial support and resources to create new products, services and systems, is called an Intrapreneur. Some of the greatest business leaders of the past made their early mark in business as Intrapreneurs. Former General Electric Chairman **Jack Welch** made a name for himself by building GE's engineering plastics business as if he were starting his own company. **Lew Lehr**, former Chairman of 3M, similarly but his career on his intrapreneurial pursuit of 3M's expansion into the health care industry. "With the information age making its way into corporations, the business expanding in many different ways, it is realized that the command and control policy that was earlier the foundation on which the organizations thrived, was slowly crumbling. And with it, it was taking the very soul of the company–the employees, have emerged as the differentiating factor for the success of organizations,' says **Anand Pillai**, Senior VP and global head, talent transformation, intrapreneurship development and EFCS transformation initiatives, HCL.

Most progressive organizations view intrapreneurship as a way to develop and retain the best manpower they have and provide an entrepreneurial atmosphere within the organization itself. The competitive nature of the business drives the intrapreneurial culture and the pace of business has multiplied as well with growth opportunities available and a market size that is expanding. Also, Indian companies have started empowering people in the lower levels where true innovation can occur," says **Anurag Jain**, VP, services delivery, Dell Services. Three-dimensions thinking persistence, good communication skills, team management and networking abilities are key traits, says **Jain**.

The term 'Intrapreneur' was coined in America in the late seventies. Several senior executives of big corporations in America left their jobs to start their own small business because the top bosses in these corporations were not receptive to innovative ideas. These executives turned entrepreneurs achieved phenomenal success in their new ventures. What is more that they are causing a threat to the organizations they left? Such Intrapreneurs breed the innovative entrepreneurs who inaugurate new products.

Intrapreneurs introduce new products services and processes which enabled the company to grow and succeed in a changing environment. **Pinchot**, suggested the creation of a system which will provide selected executives a status within the corporation similar to that of an entrepreneur in the society. Such people are 'Intra-corporate entrepreneurs' or 'Intrapreneurs'.

Let us have the points of difference between the two terms:

Entrepreneur v/s Intrapreneur

Difference	Entrepreneur	Intrapreneur
(1) Dependency	An entrepreneur is an independent businessman.	Whereas, an Intrapreneur is semi-independent businessman
(2) Risk	An entrepreneur bears full risk involved in the business.	A Intrapreneur does not fully bear the risk of the business he develops and operates.
(3) Operation	An entrepreneur operates from outside an organisation.	On the contrary, an Intrapreneur operates from within the organisation itself.
(4) Raising of capital	The entrepreneur himself raises the recovery capital from various sources.	On the other hand, the Intrapreneur does not raise the capital himself.
(5) Guarantee of returns	Guarantees the return to people who give him finance.	Does not guarantee any return to the supplier of capital.
(6) Characteristics	The entrepreneur is an innovator.	Whereas, the Intrapreneur is a creator or inventor.

Summing Up

The term 'Intrapreneur' was coined in America in the late seventies. Several senior executives of big corporations in America left their jobs to start their own small business because the top bosses in these corporations were not receptive to innovative ideas. These executives turned entrepreneurs achieved phenomenal success in their new ventures. What is more that they are causing a threat to the organizations they left? Such Intrapreneurs breed the innovative entrepreneurs who inaugurate new products.

Pinchot, suggested the creation of a system which will provide selected executives a status within the corporation similar to that of an entrepreneur in the society. Such people are 'Intra-corporate entrepreneurs' or 'Intrapreneurs'.

6 BUSINESS ENVIRONMENT ANALYSIS

Introduction, Environmental Analysis Process, What is Environmental Scanning? Need for Environmental Scanning, Features of Environmental Scanning, Significance of Environmental Scanning, Factors Governing the Choice of Environment Forces, Techniques of Environmental Search, The Process of Scenario Building, What is SWOT analysis? Summing Up, Case Studies.

Introduction

Environmental analysis is a systematic process that starts from identification of environmental factors, assessing their nature and impact, auditing them to find their impact on the business, and making various profiles for positioning.

Environmental Analysis Process

A business manager should be able to analyze the environment to grasp opportunities or face the threats. Organizations need to build strength and repair their weakness available in the business environment. Therefore, this process consist not only a single step but a process of various steps. Environmental analysis comprises scanning, monitoring, analyzing and forecasting the business situation.

Scanning is to get the relevant information from the information overload. It is to focus on the most relevant information.

Monitoring is to check the nature of the environmental factors.

Analyzing requires data collection and use of different required tools and techniques. Forecasting is to find the future possibilities based on the past results and present scenario.

Environmental analysis process is not static but a dynamic process. It may differ depending on the situation. However, a general process with few common steps can be identified as the process of environmental analysis these are

(a) Monitoring or identifying environmental factors;
(b) Scanning and selecting the relevant factors and grouping them;
(c) Defining variables for analysis;
(d) Using different methods, tools and techniques for analysis;
(e) Analyzing environmental factors and forecasting;
(f) Designing profiles; and
(g) Strategic positioning and writing a report.

Brief discussion is made on each of the step of this environmental analysis process:

(a) ***Identifying Environmental Factors:*** First of all a strategist should identify all the relevant factors that might affect his or her business. In this process, one should first know what the internal areas of the business are. This includes all the systems, internal structure, strategies followed, and culture of the organization. All these areas can be covered into the five functional areas in classical approach. Similarly, a business daily interacts with the close environmental components outside the business such as customer, competitor and supplier. It might cover all other stakeholders such as trade union, media, and pressure group. Furthermore, general such business environment factors as political, legal, economic, socio cultural and technological factors are to be identified.

(b) ***Scanning and Selecting Relevant Key Factors:*** Out of all the business environmental factors, a strategist should focus only on the relevant factors for further analysis. All the factors are not equally important and affecting the business. In this context, a strategist has to scan the environmental trend to select only the most affecting environmental factors from the information overload. This step paves the way of environment analysis and forecasting.

(c) ***Defining Variables for Analysis:*** Selected environmental factors are to be further specified into the variables. A concept can be interpreted into different variables. For example, political situation can be measured using few variables such as instability, reliability, and long-term effect. Economic environment might cover many variables such as Per Capita, GDP, and Economic policies that can be further classified into many other variables. Variables are the basis of measurement in environmental analysis process. Variables can be compared, grouped, correlated, and predicted to find a clearer picture of the broader concept. It is, therefore, necessary to define the variables first in any kind of analysis including the environmental analysis.

(d) ***Using Different Methods, Techniques and Tools:*** Different types of methods, tools, and techniques are used for analysis. Some of the major methods of analysis can be Scenario Building, Benchmarking, and Network methods. Scenario presents overall picture of its total system with affecting factors. Benchmarking is to find the best standard in an industry and to compare one's strengths and weakness with the standard. Network method is to assess organizational systems and its outside environment to find the strength and weakness, opportunity and threats of an organization.

Some of the techniques of primary information collection can be Delphi, Brainstorming, Survey, and Historical enquiry. Delphi technique collects independent information from the experts without mixing them. Brainstorming is information collection technique being open minded without criticizing others. Survey is to design questions and ask the participants whereas, the historical enquiry is a kind of case analysis of past period.

Analysis tools can be statistical such as general descriptive tools as mean, median, mode, frequency. Tools can be inferential as ANOVA, correlation, regression, factor, cluster and multiple regression analysis. There are many tools of analyzing functional areas. Finance and accounting mostly use profitability, leverage, fund flow and other similar accounting and financial tools for analysis. Human resources use employee turnover, training, satisfaction and many others as the basis of evaluating strength and weakness. Production area is assessed using quality control, productivity, breakdown and many others. Similarly, marketing effectiveness is judged from the sales volume and market coverage. Research and development is perceived successful, if it can really develop the strength in an organization.

(e) ***Forecasting Environmental Factors:*** Collecting relevant information from the selected areas and to identify the variables in such areas are the basics of analysis. Analyzing the past information to predict the future is the main objective of this step. It is, therefore, a comprehensive process that analyzes collected information using different tools and techniques.

(f) *Designing Profiles:* After analyzing the environmental factors they are recorded into the profiles. Such profiles record each component or variables into left side and their positive, negative or neutral indicators including their statement in the right side. Internal areas are recorded in Strategic Advantages Profile (SAP) and external areas are recorded in Environmental Threat and Opportunity Profile (ETOP). Strength, Weakness, Opportunity, and Threat (SWOT) profile can be designed combining both of these two profiles into one. There are varieties of reporting formats or profiles used for external and internal business environment analysis. Environmental Threat and Opportunity Profile (ETOP) is commonly used to report the external environmental situation whereas Strategic Advantages Profile (SAP) report the internal environmental situation. Both of these profiles can be merged into Strength-Weakness-Opportunity-Threat (SWOT) profile. David used External Factor Evaluation (EFE) Matrix to present weighted score of external environmental factors. Similarly, he used Internal Factor Evaluation (IFE) Matrix to make the reporting of internal environmental audit. Environmental threats and opportunities profile (ETOP) is a commonly used profile related to external business environment. Strategic Advantages Profile (SAP) is related to internal business environment. Nowadays, Strength and Weakness and Opportunities and Threats (SWOT) profile has become very popular. Present writing pursued the approach of reporting external and internal business environment using the same approach.

Preparing ETOP

Environmental threat and opportunity profile is referred as ETOP profile. It identifies the relevant environmental factors. Such factors might be general environmental factors and task environment factors. Thereafter, it is necessary to identify their nature. Some factors are positive to the organization whereas others are negative. Therefore, it is necessary to find out their impact to the organization. Positive, neutral, and negative sign in ETOP denotes the relevant impact of environmental factors.

Preparing SAP

Strategic advantage profile is known as SAP. It shows strength and weakness of an organization. Preparation of SAP is very similar process to the ETOP. There are generally five functional areas in most of the organizations. These areas are Production or Operation, Finance or Accounting, Marketing or Distribution, Human Resource and Corporate Planning, and Research and Development. These functional areas are listed to identify their relative strength and weakness in SAP. Very similar to the ETOP, positive, neutral, and negative signs are denoted and brief description is written in SAP profile. Each functional area is very broad having many components inside. All these above described profiles provide a clear picture to understand the strategic position of an organization.

(g) *Strategic Position and Report Writing:* After analysis of business environment, a strategist knows the actual situation and can make some future forecasting based on the environmental analysis. After preparing the profiles strategists prepare formal report that describes the business environment. The report might present issues and best strengths of business environment in a systematic process.

What is Environmental Scanning?

Environment scanning is that exercise that involves continuous process of monitoring the dynamic interplay of all those forces namely, economic, competitive, technological, socio-cultural, demographic and political forces to determine the opportunities. In the words of *L.R. Jauch and W.F. Glueck, "environmental analysis is the process by which strategists monitor the environmental factors to determine opportunities for and threats to their firms"*. Environmental diagnosis consists of managerial decisions made by assessing the significance of the data of the environmental decisions made by assessing the significance of the data of the environmental analysis. Thus, environmental scanning is both a mental task of analyzing and synthesizing. Analyzing, in that it decides the whole into small and meaning parts for its microscopic close-up details and synthesizing, in that it is correlating and matching the parts into single whole. Thus, it projects both bird's eye view and the fish-eye view of the forces operating in the environment.

Need for Environmental Scanning

The question arises as to why environmental scanning is resorted to? There must be some reasons for going in for environmental scanning. Based on the experience of companies of America and England, the reasons for environment scanning are:

(1) ***It Imprints the Image of Existing Environment:*** Environment scanning provides a clear-cut picture about the existing competitors, suppliers, government, consumers, employees, technological, innovations and their stands, policies movements all speaks a lot. A perfect knowledge of each component of external environment will go a long way in that each factor has its effects on the organisation. The knowledge and exposure helps in making an appropriate strategy which matches most in keeping the organisation to environmental requirements. The company is better placed to choose the most viable strategy.

(2) ***It Makes Possible to Have Effective Strategist:*** The strategists are decisionmakers which make the very fortune of a company. Environmental scanning gives the thread-based microscopic information consisting of facts. Any sound decision which is taken is worthwhile, if it is based on facts. One should remember that the position of a strategist is such that he is a slave of external environment and its forces force him to be proactive rather than reactive. He has to take things as they come from the external environment. Even the proactive strategies are based on the external forces which are given by the external environment. When the strategists get detailed and updated data in every sphere of the environment, consumers reactions, competition, stand, government policies, employees stance, social and cultural impacts, all are not independent but interdependent. As a result the strategists are placed at the commanding height to monitor and act accordingly.

(3) ***The External Environment Throws Open the Opportunities and Threats:*** Environmental scanning is to see what opportunities are open to the firm. What is important to rate is that every opportunity comes with challenging threats. Opportunities are the chances that help the firm to achieve its present goals and objectives. On the other hand, threats are blockades to achieving these goals and objectives. Much depends on the strategists. It is a challenging, thrilling and rewarding job in case the opportunities are identified in their proper perspectives and the threats are met with. It is a matter of overcoming the threats to enjoy the cream of opportunities.

(4) ***It Helps In Reading The Future:*** What we know about future is that it is certainly uncertain. Each one of us knows that one day or other, we are going to die. However, we do not know when we will die? How we die? With all this uncertainty of life, human's race lives or aspires to live on the fond 'hope' that "tomorrow is ours". Humans are optimistic. Similarly, every business house is keen on knowing what future holds for it. Environmental scanning has that ability which reduces the uncertainty to the minimum; the invisibles become more visible. With the given strengths and weaknesses, one is able to plan well as to how best to capitalize on opportunities and dismantling the threats. **Dr. P. F. Drucker, the modern Guru of management**, says anticipating future is important that challenges the human skill. He warned the managers of tomorrow that they are to be "anticipative" than "reactive" as they are dealing with turbulent water.

Features of Environmental Scanning

The features that come to the surface when probes the very significant that speaks of the nature of environmental scanning or analysis or appraisal. These are:

(1) ***It is Holistic Exercise:*** That is environmental scanning is not partial study but the total study of all environmental components. It is different that while explaining, these factors have been divided into specific components at general and industry level. Since it is imperative to know opportunities and threats, there is need for analyzing these factors or components together. These components are not independent but interdependent. In case we take one by one, it would be futile exercise because particular components might speak of only threats or opportunities. Hence, there is need for overall study together in order to trace the opportunities and threats.

(2) ***It is an Exploratory Process:*** What is more important is that this process is exploratory or 'heuristic' as some experts put it. The monitoring of environment or environmental search is related with not only the present developments or details of components but most strategic part is concerned with exploring the unknown future. It is a process of moving from the known to the unknown. Everybody knows about future is that it is uncertain rather unknown. "What you are?" is not that important. What is more important is "What you will be?" The crux of the problem is what could happen and not what will happen *per se*. That is the strategist should think of many alternative situations where step by step will be able to state clearly the postulations of the future, speculating not gambling scientifically of alternative outcomes, assessing probabilities and finally crystallizing the rational conclusions. Thus, it is a mental process involving sound judgment and juggling of impringing variables based on fertile imagination. It is an exercise of "nine-dot" puzzle.

(3) ***It is Continuous Process:*** Environmental scanning is a continuous process that never ends. It is not 'stop and go' but going on forever. A continuous scanning helps to pick new signals or triggers in the overall pattern of intertwined trends. This calls for detailed and meticulous studies to have 'close-up' or 'fish-eye' view on the moving target. The track events are continuously compared and analyzed and set aside. It is like playing with different colours and finding the impact of each colour giving different shades, hues and combination meant for future reference.

(4) ***It is Indispensable:*** Environment scanning is so basic and strategic that strategic management swears by environment scanning. Without environmental scanning, it is almost impossible for the organisation to trace the opportunities and associated threats and the strategy formulation and implementation which speaks of future. The task of strategic management is to develop the alternative solutions of which the best one is to be implemented. To choose, the strategist has huge stock of possible alternative solutions this generation of maximum possible alternatives; one has to depend on environmental scanning at length. Once there are exhaustive stocks of alternatives, the chooser has the best choice and rest can be avoided. Hence, environmental scanning is almost indispensable because a strategist cannot just proceed without environment scanning.

Significance of Environmental Scanning

One cannot underestimate the role of environmental scanning because it is indispensable and crucial. **Mr. Ian Wilson**, in his write-up 'The Benefits of Environmental Analysis' edited by **Kenneth J. Albert** the title "*The Strategic Management Handbook*," published by McGraw Hill N. Y. 1993 pp. 9.6-9.7, has compared the role of environmental analysis with the function of radar. He says "If a ship is sailing on a sea of uncertainty, there are two essential requirements to a successful voyage. There has to be star to steer the ship. Secondly, there must be radar to signal the existence of rocks, reefs and clear water in the unchartered sea. Similarly, a business firm operating in an uncertain environment must have a vision of the business (a guiding star) and a system of environmental analysis (radar). In fact, empirical studies have proved beyond doubt that those firms that undertake systematic environmental scanning have fared well than those who did not. In case of companies that are right on top—say H.P., LG, HLC,

Compaq, Asian Paints, Bharat Petroleum, Reliance, Infosys, ICICI, and the like have proved that environmental scanning has been responsible for the highest growth in Indian corporate sector. The crucial role of environmental scanning can be explained under following heads:

(1) ***It helps in Converting Threats into Opportunities:*** Environmental scanning allows the strategists to anticipate opportunities and plan design optional or alternative responses to these opportunities. This is somewhat easy. When opportunities exist, selection is not a problem. What is important is that environmental scanning, if done scientifically, helps in preventing the threats or develop strategies that can turn the threats to opportunities for the benefit of the organisation. Both these opportunities and threats are first traced and then threats are reduced to opportunities. However, one cannot take for granted that threats can be converted into opportunities. This requires a tenacity and endurance to develop the ability to scan the environment. If all the companies were able to do that, then every company would have earned good profits, growth and reputation.

(2) ***Changing Colour of Environment:*** The business environment changes are not only quick but constantly taking place. These changes create an imbalance in the organisation have to be traced by the strategists as to what causes are at work that create an imbalance in the environment, and therefore, the imbalance forced upon the organisation so what new opportunities are thrown upon by the changed environment along with the threats. It enables the firms to develop those strategies which will help in encashing on opportunities and converting the threats into opportunities. The changes in package of opportunities and threats are to be accepted and worked upon under the broad spectrum of organizational objectives. Even it can call for changes or amendment of strategies with a view to attain the basic objectives of the organisation.

(3) ***Narrowing Down the Alternatives:*** An in-depth and meaningful environmental scanning assists the strategists to reduce the range of available alternatives and eliminate options that are totaling inconsistent with forecast opportunities or threats. Environmental scanning is an exercise that makes available good number of alternatives to deal with opportunities and threats. Of these alternatives and options, which is the most viable and promising has to be traced out. It is strategists who are to work on this, based on the managerial skills and experience. This is needed because the valuable time which is more than money can be saved and same can be better utilized for more money can be saved and same can be better utilized for more pressing and important alternatives.

(4) ***Strategic Management starts with Environmental Scanning:*** Environmental scanning is the starting point of strategic management strategy formulation and strategy implementation are the outcome of environment scanning. What the environment has done for the organisation in terms of opportunities and the threats caused by changes in the environment. To implement the strategy, the first thing is formulation of strategy. Again this strategy formulation is based on what impact the environment has on organisation in terms of opportunities and threats. Only when the strategists trace the opportunities and threats can they proceed to develop the right strategy to encash on opportunities or converting threats into opportunities. Thus, the surfing the changing environment and tracing the opportunities and threats is the very preface to the tall task of strategy formulation and implementation.

I. Environment Search

The first aspect of environment scanning is environment search or monitoring the environment. Stated simply, environmental search is to do with collection of information from the relevant environment. It means and includes two things namely, “what to search?" and "where to search?" The first aspect deals with the type of environmental factors to be analyzed and the second aspect with the sources of information about these environmental factors.

The Type of Environmental Factors to be Scanned

That way, there are countless environmental factors that influence the operation of business system of an economy. There is no need to take into all these factors because, as seen from the angle of a particular form, not all are relevant. That is why the organisation in question is to concentrate only on relevant factors of environment. The relevance of a factor will depend on the answers to two very pertinent questions. These questions are:

(1) Whether a particular factor has an impact on the organisation?

(2) If so, what is the degree of impact?

The answers to two questions will generate different degrees of impact as the business or organisation and the probability of impact. A matrix can be structured, showing two variables namely the impact on business and the probability impact, to identify the 'high priority' environment factors. A matrix of this kind can configure as under:

Probability of Impact		Degree of Impact on Business	
	High	Medium	Low
High	Critical	High priority	Low priority
Medium	High priority	High priority	Low priority
Low	To be watched	Low priority	Low priority

The matrix indicates as what to do with a given factor or factors. Thus, those factors that fall under the category of 'critical' and 'high priority' should be analyzed. If the factors fall under the category of high priority but the probability of that impact is low, it is to be kept under watch and so on.

Factors Governing the Choice of Environment Forces

The determination of the degree of impact or the probability of impact is qualitative where personal judgment plays an predominant role. This subjective determination makes each firm or organisation to have differing readings as visualized by the strategist involved. There are some factors that determine the choice of forces for analysis. These are:

(1) *Nature of Environment:* It is the exact nature of environment that has impact on selection of environmental factors for analysis. That differs from case to case:

(1) In case the organizational factors are homogeneous and stable, there is lesser need for environmental search because the organizational adaptability takes care.

(2) In case the environmental factors are homogeneous changing, the organisation is to watch these changes for which it needs information. Here also one need not worry as the factors are homogeneous which can be easily identified.

(3) In case the factors are heterogeneous stable, the strategist is expected to identify the heterogeneous factors and the way in which they influence the organisation. Once this is done, the organizational spotlight becomes brighter as these factors do not change rapidly.

(4) In case the environmental factors are both heterogeneous and dynamic, the work of environmental search is increased. That is what these factors are and how they are affecting is a must.

(2) *Managerial Philosophy:* Generally the managerial philosophy determines the actions that managers will take in connection with different factors that influence their decisions. The managerial philosophy covers the manager's attitudes, reactions to the situations, and the way they look at the variables. If the managers are positive and forward looking they are long-sighted and are interested in future. Accordingly they take active interest in collecting more and varied information about future happenings keeping in mind the present happenings. It is this positive frame of mind which gives much importance to environmental scanning as they need much more information. It is these people who strongly believe in **"Opportunities knock at your door once"**. That is opportunities once missed are missed forever. It is the main reason why they need more information in framing their strategies for the future. These are the managers who are not very bold and are happy keeping themselves in day to day management. There are managers who are not bothered as to what is going to happen in future. Such people hardly need information of environmental changes as they believe in "take care of present, future takes care itself."

(3) ***Age of the Organisation:*** Many times, it is the age of organisation that determines the type of information that is needed. The aged organisation has little information about environment as its managers are already swimming in the organizational changes caused by environmental changes. They are seasoned and know what is what and what level of impact of each force is. These managers are able to distinguish between relevant and irrelevant from the angle of their firm. On the contrary an organisation is young, and its managers are also hot blooded, they need cooling down of their blood and collect more and more information and later they decide what is relevant and what is not.

(4) ***Type of the Business:*** The type of the business the organisation is engaged is a matter that decides the length of information required. When we talk of the type of business, we talk of the way in which the business is defined. In case an organisation has defined business in narrow terms, then the focus of that organisation will be narrow as far as environment is concerned. On the other hand, if it is broadly defined, definitely the information needed is much more broad and varied. In case of a business with only one line of activity, the information needed is much lesser as opposed to a concern which is highly diversified.

(5) ***Size and Power of the Organisation:*** It has two points namely size and power. It is noticed that under normal circumstances, larger the size the more intense interaction it has with its environment. Again, it is the relative power of the organisation which plays significant role as to what is the extent of information needed. That is, to what extent an organisation can influence the environment and get influenced by environmental forces. The findings in this connection are:

(1) The more powerful is the organisation relative to its competitors, the less it will focus on the competitive sector of the environment. The living example is that of public sector undertakings in India.

(2) The less dependent the organisation is on the government for subsides and other facilities, less it will emphasize the environmental analysis on the political aspect of the environment.

(3) The lesser is the dependence of the organisation on one or a few suppliers, the less it will focus its attention on the supplier aspect of the environment.

(4) The geographic dimensions of the organisation affect the type of interaction which the organisation has with its environment. More the geographical spread more will be the information needed as each geographical place differs. It is clear that local organization required little information as compared to multinationals.

Techniques of Environmental Search

Once the organizational factors are identified for analysis, the organisation goes in for searching the relevant facts about these factors. These are techniques which range simple information collection through verbal source to highly complex forecasting techniques. The organisation has to choose any technique which is more suited to its requirements. These techniques are:

(1) ***Verbal Information:*** It is through verbal information that managers can learn about environment. The sources of verbal information are:

(a) Employees may be superiors or subordinates or peers.

(b) Outside sources like customers, wholesalers, retailers, broken suppliers, competitors and their employees, financiers, academicians and government authorities. These inside and outside sources are important because they observe the environment as they like it from their angle. Generally, higher the levels of persons involved, more reliable is the information about environmental changes.

(2) ***Spying:*** Here spying is to collect the information indirectly. Thus, if the organisation is to collect information about competitors, the information is collected from the clients, customers, dealers and other persons and institutions dealing with the competitors. Another way of spying is to collect information through disguised research by outsiders, say consultants. Unless you resort to these, you will not get the information.

(3) ***Company Records:*** It is the corporate planning departments which collect relevant information. The planning department acts as advisor to strategic planners. The department of corporate planning is to collect relevant information as a matter of routine.

(4) ***Publications:*** If strategists can get good deal of information from various publications, may be monthlies, fortnightlies or weeklies, quarterlies, bimonthlies. Though most of the publications are dealing in socio-economic and political environmental factors, it is quite possible to get information on technology, ecology, demography and so on. What is important is the search for information.

(5) ***Forecasting:*** A forecast is a prediction of future events. Forecasting is the prediction of future with certain amount of accuracy. In other words, forecasting means estimation of types, quantity and quality of future work say, sales, and, therefore production. It is that exercise that gives rise to plans for dealing with future. It is a systematic attempt to predict the future with the greatest possible accuracy based on the past or known events.

The forecasting techniques are broadly classified into three categories as:

1. Qualitative, 2. Time-series, and 3. Causal

The Qualitative methods are:

(1) Grass roots.
(2) Market research.
(3) Panel consensus.
(4) Historical analysis.
(5) Delphi-method.

The Time-Series analysis techniques are:

(1) Simple moving average.
(2) Weighted moving average.
(3) Exponential smoothening.
(4) Regression analysis.
(5) Box Jankins Technique.
(6) Time series.
(7) Trend series.

The Causal techniques are:

(1) Regression analysis.
(2) Economic models.
(3) Input/output models.
(4) Leading indicators.
(5) End-use method.

(6) Leading indicator method.

(7) Econometric models.

The strategists get good deal of information through these forecasting where the future behaviour of environmental forces is made available.

(6) ***Alternative Scenarios:*** 'Scenario' or 'alternative scenario' technique is used to explore the likelihood of possible future developments and changes and to identify interactions of uncertain future trends and events. In the words of **Thomas S. Mandel**; in a write-up "Future scenarios and their uses in corporate strategy" in "*The Strategic Management Handbook*" edited by Mr. **Kenneth, J. Albert** and published by McGraw Hill 1993 pp. 10-11, "Scenarios constitute an effective device for sensing, interpreting, organizing and bringing to bear diverse information about future in planning and strategic decision making." Different matching, possible scenarios are generated by experts in the field which are in qualitative form and present their findings as "this is the way it will be; this is what is going to happen, this is what the situation will be at the future time." These are all "aha" statements which come from the bottom of the heart. In fact, they are brain child of these great visualizers.

The Process of Scenario Building

Scenario building is a process and involves certain steps. These steps are:

(1) ***Preparing Background:*** Just as an edifice needs a foundation, the scenario building needs preparing an essential background on which scenario may be developed. This preparatory work involves assessing the overall environmental factors relevant for the industry sector. A preliminary model for environmental analysis is prepared, indicating different industry trends, at this stage.

(2) ***Selecting Critical Indicators:*** Of the various environmental trends identified under step one; the critical indicators for the industry sector are selected. That is a search is made about the future potential events which are likely to affect these trends. At this stage Delphi Panel is nominated. Such panel is essential because it is the panel of experts whose opinion is considered as credit in evaluating the industry future.

(3) ***Establishing Past Behaviour Indicators:*** This is a step that involves three sub steps. That is analysis of past behaviour of each major indicator is made on the basis of available data; reasons for past behaviour are identified; interview schedule for Delphi Panel is prepared.

(4) ***Verifying the Potential Future Events:*** Verifications of potential future events influencing the trend, is made on the basis of Delphi Panel's expert advice which may be in the form of:

(a) Evaluation of part trends;

(b) Assessment of potential impact of future events;

(c) Assessment of the probability of future events;

(d) Forecasting of future events;

(e) Assumptions for forecasts; and

(f) Rationale for projected values.

(5) ***Forecasting the Indicators:*** Once the opinion of the Delphi Panel is collected, forecast of each major indicator is made on the basis of additional literature that is available. Trend Impact Analysis (TIA) and Cross Impact Analysis (CIA) are made for this purpose. TIA is the analysis of relevant events affecting the major trends and CIA builds into the analysis the recognition of the events that impact upon one another and they do not occur independently of each other.

(6) ***Writing of Scenarios:*** In this terminal step, scenarios are writtern. Usually, there may be more than one scenario as this is done in the context of fluid future environment. These alternative scenarios are taken into account for establishing environmental opportunities and threats.

II. Environmental Diagnosis

The second part is environmental diagnosis. Environmental diagnosis is the assessment of environmental factors in terms of opportunity or threat and the importance of their impact. Environmental diagnosis is comparable to diagnosis of a patient in medical science where it is used to identify the disease and its criticality. This environmental diagnosis as a part of strategic management identifies both threats and opportunities. That is both negative and positive effects are reckoned with. Once the data are collected for relevant environmental factors and analyzed, the process of determining the impact of these factors–either positively or negatively-and the degree of impact is undertaken. This exercise involves expression of opinions which help in the organisation to arrive at a decision as to whether to react to, or ignore, or anticipate the opportunities or threats discovered.

Preparation of ETOP

ETOP is the Environmental Threat and Opportunities Profile—a summarized projection of the environmental factors and their likely impact on the organisation when the environmental scanning is undertaken on a formal and systematic way, it is essential that the results are structured. ETOP is the most useful way of structuring the results of environmental scanning. An ETOP preparation involves four logical steps:

(1) ***Identification of Different Components of Relevant Environment:*** As an ETOP is the depiction of environmental scanning, this process follows that of environmental scanning. That is, the starting point is the identification of different components of relevant environment. Generally, each major component is divided into subcomponents as is done in the case of environmental scanning. For instance, the economic environment is divided into subcomponents like General Economic Conditions, Economic Systems, Economic Policies, Economic Growth, Interest Rates, and Exchange Rates. Similarly, competitive environment is sub-divided into subcomponents as Risk of Entry by Potential Competitors, Rivalry among Established Companies, Bargaining Power of Buyers, Bargaining Power of Suppliers, Threat of Close Substitutes and so on.

(2) ***Assessing Significance of Environmental Factors:*** Significance of environmental factors is assessed at this stage. The degree of significance can be in qualitative terms like high, medium, low or it can be qualified 6, -4, -2. The noteworthy point is that all the environmental variables, including relevant ones, will not have same degree of significance.

(3) ***Assessing Impact Factor:*** An environmental factor which is relevant may either present threats or opportunities depending upon the exact nature of environmental factors and their behaviour. Positive impact of a factor is an opportunity and negative impact is threat. Impact factor may also be quantified.

(4) ***Combining Significance and Impact Factor:*** Combination of significance and impact factor can give a clear picture of the industry sector. In case both the variables are quantified, these can be combined by multiplication. Quantified figures can be useful in comparing the different industry segments or different industries.

Let us take the case of Gujarat Industrial Trucks Limited.

ETOP- Gujarat Industrial Trucks Limited

Environmental component	The Impact (opportunity/threat)
I. Socio-economic	Domestic and foreign market (+) Resource constraints (-) The production is technically superior (+)
II. Technological	Updated production facilities (+)

III. Legal/Political	Liberalization for technology import (+)
IV. Competitive	Exemption in excise (+) High employee turnover (-) placing second fiddle after Rexello–the market leader (-)
V. Suppliers	Merger of small units for getting inputs (-)
VI. Customers	Distribution and logistic management is not catching up (-)

Note: + = an Opportunity

— = A threat

What is SWOT Analysis?

SWOT analysis is a simple framework for generating strategic alternatives from a situation analysis. It is applicable to either the corporate level or the business unit level and frequently appears in marketing plans. SWOT stands for Strengths, Weaknesses, Opportunities and Threats. The SWOT framework was described in the late 1960s by **Edmund P. Learned**, **C. Roland Christiansen**, **Kenneth Andrews** and **William D. Guth** in *Business Policy, Text and Cases*. The General Electric Growth Council used this form of analysis in the 1980s.

SWOT means analysis and assessment of competitive strengths and weaknesses of a firm in relation to competitor; and environmental opportunities and threats which a company may likely face. SWOT analysis is as such, a systematic study and identification of those aspects and strategy that best suit the individual company's position in a given situation. It should be based on logic and rational thinking such that a proper strategy improves on organization's business strengths and opportunities and at the same time reduce the attached weaknesses and threats that are thrown open by external environment.

What are Strengths?

Strength is a power and excellence with resources, skills and advantages in relation to competition and requirement of the community of a firm serves or plans to serve the same. Strength is a distinct or clear-cut technical superiority with best technical know-how, financial resources and the skills of the people who make the organization's goodwill and image in the markets for products and services, labour, finance, firm's access to best distribution network or the supply-chain. The discipline, morale, attitude and the culture of the employees at all lends with a sense of belonging. Thus, it refers to the competitive advantage which a firm can exert in market for finance, labour, and products and services.

What are Weaknesses?

A weakness is the incapacity, deficiency or laxity in resources including limitation such as technical, financial manpower, skills, brand image, distribution pattern etc. In other words, it refers to all sorts of constraints or obstacles which deter or check movement or progress in a certain direction and may also inhibit an organisation in gaining a distinct competitive advantage. Firm's strengths and weaknesses are a matter of interpretation and how the resources can be best utilized to achieve the best results as compared to other similar competitive organizations. These are purely internal forces and factors required to be studied and assessed from time-to-time. Since more and more competitive organisation with the state-of-the-art technology and resources are entering in the market and competitive forces are heated up making them more intensified.

What are Opportunities?

An opportunity is the external factor or force in the business environment that changes because of external forces such as governmental policy, industrial policy, monetary policies, and political situation at local, state, national and international levels. Formation of trade blocks, trade barriers including changes in social, legal and cultural improvement in the business work. That is, opportunities are created out of sudden or deliberate changes on which a wise, creative business units harp or encash. An opportunity is a major favourable advantage to a firm, provided the same can be availed strategically. Proper analysis of environment and identifications of a new market, new and improved consumer group with better product substitute or supplier's relationship could represent opportunities for a concern. Thus, in EXIM policy may bring opportunities to some export houses, an amendment of MRTP Act. FERA (FEMA), excise sales tax, customs duties, corporate taxes might bring opportunities. Policies of W.T.O. as members may avail opportunities, the policies of liberalization, privatization and globalization have given ample opportunities for those who are serious of exploiting them. Iraq war that devastated the normal life, is having good many opportunities to rebuild it. The terrorist groups and their activities have encouraged warfare goods and resources. Even simple case of making helmet compulsory for rider and pillion rider has boosted both standard and spurious productions of helmets.

What are Threats?

A threat or environmental threat is a challenge by an unavoidable trend or a development that leads to erosion of the company's position in absence of purposeful action. Threat is always an unfavorable environment for a firm, say slow market growth entrance of resourceful multinationals or transnationals, increased bargaining power of buyers or suppliers because of large number of options, quick rate of obsolescence due to hyper technology change, adverse situation because of change in climatic conditions, government policies, rules and regulations natural calamities. All these put the organizations in a helpless and forlorn position putting in disadvantageous or handicapped situation posing a serious threat to the smooth sailing of an organisation. The year 2001, a year of new millennium, 2002 SAARS, 2003 maximum earthquakes, 2004 a year of Olympic; Euro 2004 Football; 2008 a year of BIRD FLU; 2009 a year of SWINE FLU in India and Kubhamelas that have brought in opportunities.

Strengths and Weaknesses

STRENGTHS	WEAKNESSES
Marketing	
Strong brand image	Poor brand image
Strong distribution network	Weak distribution
Deep product mix	Narrow product mix
Efficient and motivated sales force	Poor salesforce
High quality product	Poor product quality
Production	
Economies of scale	High cost due to small size
State-of-the-art technology	Obsolete technology
Efficient input sourcing	Inefficient input sourcing
Efficient inventory management	Poor inventory management
Strong R&D support	No R&D support

Finance	
Comfortable debt-equity ratio	Lop sided capital structure
Large internal accruals	Very high interest payment
High dividends and market capitalisation	Poor reserves
High credit rating	Low credit rating
Human Resources Management	
Qualified and experienced human resource	Redundant human resource
Motivated Human resources	Excess manpower
Good industrial relations	Poor morale
Good human resource management	Poor industrial relations
	Poor human resource management
Efficient Board of Directors	Inefficient Board of Directors Unhealthy conflict between members of the board
Efficient and motivated managers	Conflict between members of the Board and top managers Inefficient managers

Opportunities and Threats

OPPORTUNITIES	THREATS
Regulatory/Political	
Delicensing	Delicensing
Dereservations	Dereservation
MRTPA relaxations	MRTPA relaxation
Import liberalisation	Import liberalisation
Price decontrol	
Liberalisation of foreign investment	liberalisation of foreign investment
Technology policy	Technology policy
Capital market reforms Boom	Political instability Recession
Economics	
Steady and fast increase in income	Economic instability
Social/Demographic	
Favourable change in consumer attitude	Unfavourable change in consumer attitude
Increasing population	stagnating/declining population
Change in age composition of population	Change in age composition of population
Growth of consumerism	Growth of consumerism
Growth of environmentalism	Growth of environmentalism

In Table above, several common factors figure under opportunities as well as threats. This is because what is an opportunity for firms is a threat for some others. For example, delicensing is an opportunity for many firms to enter new business or to expand existing business but it poses a threat to existing firms who were enjoying the benefits of a protected market. Similarly, while import liberalization is a threat to import competing industries, it is an opportunity for some other firms to obtain materials/ technology cheaply.

Summing Up

Introduction

Environmental analysis is a systematic process that starts from identification of environmental factors, assessing their nature and impact, auditing them to find their impact to the business, and making various profiles for positioning. A common process of environmental analysis or scanning is discussed in the following section.

Environmental Analysis Process

Environmental analysis comprises scanning, monitoring, analyzing, and forecasting the business situation.

Environmental analysis process is not static but a dynamic process. It may differ depending on the situation. However, a general process with few common steps can be identified as the process of environmental analysis these are:

(a) Monitoring or identifying environmental factors,
(b) Scanning and selecting the relevant factors and grouping them,
(c) Defining variables for analysis,
(d) Using different methods, tools, and techniques for analysis,
(e) Analyzing environmental factors and forecasting,
(f) Designing profiles, and
(g) Strategic positioning and writing a report.

What is Environmental Scanning?

Environment scanning is that exercise that involves continuous process of monitoring the dynamic interplay of all those forces namely, economic, competitive, technological, socio-cultural, demographic and political forces to determine the opportunities. In the words of L. R. Jauch and W. F. Glueck, "environmental analysis is the process by which strategists monitor the environmental factors to determine opportunities and threats to their firms.

Need for Environmental Scanning

The question arises as to why environmental scanning is resorted to? There must be some reasons for going in for environmental scanning. Based on the experience of companies of America and England, the reasons for environment scanning are:

It Imprints the image of existing environment; It makes possible to have effective strategist; The external environment throws open the opportunities and threats; It helps in reading the future.

Features of Environmental Scanning

The features that come to the surface when probes the very significant that speaks of the nature of environmental scanning or analysis or appraisal. These are: Holistic Exercise; Exploratory Process; Continuous Process and Indispensible.

Significance of Environmental Scanning

One cannot underestimate the role of environmental scanning because it is indispensable and crucial. **Mr. Ian Wilson**, in his write-up 'The Benefits of Environmental Analysis' edited by **Kenneth J.**

Albert the title "*The Strategic Management Handbook*", published by McGraw Hill N. Y. 1993 pp. 9.6-9.7, has compared the role of environmental analysis with the function of radar. He says "If a ship is sailing on a sea of uncertainty, there are two essential requirements to successful voyage. There has to be star to steer the ship. Secondly, there must be radar to signal the existence of rocks, reefs and clear water in the unchartered sea. Similarly, a business firm operating in an uncertain environment, must have a vision of the business (a guiding star) and a system of environmental analysis (radar).

The crucial role of environmental scanning can be explained under following heads:

It helps in Converting Threats into Opportunities; Changing Colour of Environment; Narrowing down the Alternatives; and Strategic Management starts with Environmental Scanning

I. Environment Search

The first aspect of environment scanning is environment search or monitoring the environment. Stated simply environmental search is to do with collection of information from the relevant environment. It means and includes two things namely, "what to search?" and "where to search?" The first aspect deals with the type of environmental factors to be analyzed and the second aspect with the sources of information about these environmental factors.

The Type of Environmental Factors to be Scanned

That way, there are countless environmental factors that influence the operation of business system of an economy. There is no need to take into all these factors because, as seen from the angle of a particular form, not all are relevant. That is why the organisation in question is to concentrate only on relevant factors of environment. The relevance of a factor will depend on the answers to two very pertinent questions. These questions are:

(1) Whether a particular factor has an impact on the organisation?

(2) If so, what is the degree of impact?

The answers to two questions will generate different degrees of impact on the business or organisation and the probability of impact.

Factors Governing the Choice of Environment Forces

The determination of the degree of impact or the probability of impact is qualitative where personal judgment plays an predominant role. This subjective determination makes each firm or organisation to have differing readings as visualized by the strategist involved.

There are some factors that determine the choice of forces for analysis. These are:

Nature of Environment; Managerial Philosophy; Age of the Organisation; Type of the Business; Size and Power of the Organization; and Geographic Dimensions.

Techniques of Environmental Search

Once the organizational factors are identified for analysis, the organisation goes in for searching the relevant facts about these factors. These are techniques which range from imple information collection through verbal source to highly complex forecasting techniques.

The organisation has to choose any technique which is more suited to its requirements. These techniques are:

Verbal Information; Spying; Company Records; Publications; Forecasting; and Alternative Scenarios.

The Process of Scenario Building

Scenario building is a process and involves certain steps. These steps are:

Preparing Background; Selecting Critical Indicators; Establishing past Behaviour Indicators; Verifying the Potential Future Events; Forecasting the Indicators; and Writing of Scenarios.

II. Environmental Diagnosis

The second part is environmental diagnosis. Environmental diagnosis is the assessment of environmental factors in terms of opportunity or threat and the importance of their impact. Environmental diagnosis is comparable to diagnosis of a patient in medical science where it is used to identify the disease and its criticality. This environmental diagnosis as a part of strategic management identifies both threats and opportunities. That is both negative and positive effects are reckoned with. Once the data are collected for relevant environmental factors and analyzed, the process of determining the impact of these factors–either positively or negatively–and the degree of impact is undertaken. This exercise involves expression of opinions which help in the organisation to arrive at a decision as to whether to react to, or ignore, or anticipate the opportunities or threats discovered.

Preparation of ETOP

ETOP is the environmental Threat and Opportunities Profile–a summarized projection of the environmental factors and their likely impact on the organisation when the environmental scanning is undertaken on a formal and systematic way, it is essential that the results are structured. ETOP is the most useful way of structuring the results of environmental scanning.

An ETOP preparation involves four logical steps: Identification of Different Components of Relevant Environment; Assessing Significance of Environmental Factors; Assessing Impact Factor; and Combining Significance and Impact Factor.

What is SWOT Analysis?

SWOT analysis is a simple framework for generating strategic alternatives from a situation analysis. It is applicable to either the corporate level or the business unit level and frequently appears in marketing plans. SWOT stands for Strengths, Weaknesses, Opportunities and Threats.

Case 2- SWOT Analysis of Modi Xerox

A SWOT analysis of the Modi Xerox, made in the early 1990s is given below. The company has repositioned itself from just a copier company to a document company and reformulated its corporate mission statement as "to develop, manufacture, service and finance a complete range of document processing products and services to help our customers to make their office more productive".

SWOT ANALYSIS OF MODI XEROX

STRENGTHS	WEAKNESSES
Strong brand name Strong market presence access to technology Quality of trained and skilled manpower Motivated salesforce and excellent market coverage	More expensive than the competitors Small product range low productivity (International STD.) Inadequate investment on information Software systems and debase
OPPORTUNITIES	**THREATS**
Large and growing market easy access Technology Advantage of synergy in the product range	Fierce international competition (expected) to the Xerox Price down cost up High personnel attrition rates

Case 3- SWOT Analysis of Tata Motors

The following analysis deals only with strengths, weaknesses, opportunities and threats:

SWOT Analysis

Strengths

- The internationalization strategy so far has been to keep local managers in new acquisitions and to only transplant a couple of senior manager from India in to the new market. The benefit is that Tata has been able to exchange expertise. For example, after the Daewoo acquisition the Indian company learn work discipline and how to get the final product 'right first time'.
- The company has a strategy in place for the next stage of its expansion. Not only it is focusing upon new products and acquisitions but it also has a programme of intensive management development in place in order to establish its leader for tomorrow.
- The company has had a successful alliance with Italian mass producer Fiat since 2006. This has enhanced the product portfolio for Tata and Fiat in terms of production and knowledge exchange. for example, the Fiat Palio style was launched by Tata in 2007 and the companies have an agreement to build a pickup targeted at central and south America.

Weaknesses

- The company's passenger car products are based upon 3rd and 4th generation platforms which put Tata Motors Limited at a disadvantage with competing car manufacturers.
- Despite buying the Jaguar and Land Rover brands; Tata has not got a foothold in the luxury car segment in its domestic, Indian market. Its the brand associated with commercial vehicles and low-cost passenger cars to the extent that it has isolated itself from lucrative segments in a more aspiring India?
- One weakness which is often not recognized is that in English the word Tata means rubbish. Would the brand sensitive British consumer ever buy into such a brand? May be not, but they would buy into Fiat, Jaguar and Land Rover.

Opportunities

- In the summer of 2008, Tata Motor's announced that it has successfully purchased the Land Rover and Jaguar brands from Ford Motors for UK 2.3 million pound. Two of the World's luxury car brand have been added to its portfolio of brands, and will undoubtedly off the company the chance to market vehicles in the luxury segments.
- Tata Motors Limited acquired Daewoo Motor's Commercial vehicle business in 2004, for around USD $16 million.
- Nano is the cheapest car in the world retailing at little more than a motorbike. Whilst the World is getting ready for greener alternatives to gas-guzzlers, is the Nano the answer in terms of concept or brand? Incidentally, the new Land Rover and Jaguar models will cost up to 85 times more than a standard Nano!
- The new global track platform is about to be launched from its Korean. The answer is that new and emerging nations such as India, South Korea and China will have a thirst for low-cost passenger and commercial vehicles. These are the opportunities. However the company has put in place a very proactive Corporate Social Responsibility (CSR) committee to address potential strategies that will make operations more sustainable.
- The range of super Milo fuel efficient buses are powered by super-efficient eco-friendly engines. The bus has optional organic clutch with booster assist and better air intakes that will reduce fuel consumption by up to 10 per cent.

Threats

- Other competing car manufactures have been in the passenger car business for 40, 50 or more years .Therefore Tata Motors Limited has to catch up in terms of quality and lean production
- Sustainability and environmentalism could mean extra costs for this low-cost producer. This could impact its underpinning competitive advantage. Obviously, as Tata globalizes and buys into other brands this problem could be alleviated.
- Since the company has focused upon the commercial and small vehicle segments, it has left itself open to competition from overseas companies for the emerging Indian luxury segments. For example ICICI bank and DaimlerChrysler have invested in a new Pune-based plant which will build 5000 new Mercedes-Benz per annum. Other players developing luxury car targeted at the Indian market include Ford, Honday and Toyota. In fact the entire Indian market has become a target for other global competitors including Maruti Udyog, General Motors, Ford and others.
- Rising prices in the global economy could pose a threat to Tata Motors Limited on couple of fronts. The price of steel and aluminum increasing is putting pressure on the costs of production. Many of Tata's products run on diesel fuel which is becoming expensive globally and within its traditional home market.

Case 4- SWOT Analysis of Pepsi Cola

The following analysis deals only with strengths, weaknesses, opportunities and threats:

SWOT Analysis

Strengths

- Coca-Cola has been a complex part of American culture for over a century. The Products' image is loaded with over-romanticizing, and this is an image many people have taken deeply to heart. The Coca -Cola image is displayed on T-shirts, hats and collectible memorabilia. This extremely recognizable branding is one of Coca-Cola's greatest strengths. "Enjoyed more than 685 million times a day around the World Coca-Cola stands as a simple, yet powerful symbol of quality and enjoyment".
- Additionally, according to **Bettman**, Coca-Cola bottling system is one of their greatest strengths. It allows them to conduct business on a global scale while at the same time maintain a local approach. The bottling companies are locally owned and operated by independent business people who are authorized to sell products of the Coca Cola Company. Because Coke does not have ownership of its bottling network, its main source of revenue is the sale of concentrate to its bottlers.

Weaknesses

Although domestic business as well as many international markets is thriving, Coca-Cola has recently reported some "declines in unit case volumes in Indonesia and Thailand due to reduced consumer purchasing power". According to the article in Fortune magazine, "Japan, unit case sales fell 3 per cent in the second quarter of 1998, this seems to be strange because while Japan generates around 5 per cent of worldwide volume, it contributes three times as much to profits. Latin America, Southeast Asia, and Japan account for about 35 per cent of Coke's volume and none of these markets are performing to expectation.

Coca-Cola on the other side has effects on the teeth's which is an issue for health care. It also has got sugar which continuous drinking of Coca-Cola may cause health problems. Being addicted to Coca-Cola also is a health problem, because drinking of Coca-Cola daily has an effect on our body after few years.

Opportunities

Brand recognition is the significant factor affecting Coke's competitive position. Coca-Cola's brand name is known well throughout 94 per cent of the world today. The primary concern over the past few years has been to get this name brand to be even better known. Packaging changes have also affected sales and industry positioning, but in general, the public has tended not to be affected by new products.

Coca-Cola's bottling system also allows the company to take advantage of infinite growth opportunities around the world. This strategy gives Coke the opportunity to service a large geographic, diverse area.

Threats

Currently, the threat of new viable competitors in the carbonated soft drink industry is not very substantial. The threat of substitute, however, is a very real threat. The soft drink industry is very strong, but consumers are not necessarily married to it. Possible substitutes that continuously put pressure on both Pepsi and Coke include tea, coffee, juices, milk, and hot chocolate.

Even though Coca-Cola and Pepsi control 40 per cent of the entire beverage market, the changing health consciousness of the market could have a serious affect. Of course, both Coke and Pepsi have already diversified into these markets, allowing them to have further significant market shares and offset any losses incurred due to fluctuations in the market.

Consumer buying power also represents a key threat in the industry. The rivalry between Pepsi and Coke has produce a very slow moving industry in which management must continuously respond to the changing attitudes and demands of their consumers or face losing market share to the competition. Furthermore, consumers can easily switch to other beverages with little cost or consequence.

7 CREATING AND STARTING THE VENTURE

Defining "Opportunity", Identifying a Business Opportunity, Sources of Ideas, Steps in Idea Processing and Selection, Establishment of an Enterprise, Summing Up.

Defining "Opportunity"

In simple terms, *opportunity may be defined as an attractive project idea which an entrepreneur accepts as a basis for his investment decision.*

A mere "possibility" is to be distinguished from business "opportunity". Good business ideas must be capable of being converted into feasible projects.

Therefore, two major ingredients of a business opportunity needs to be highlighted:

(1) good market scope, i.e., gap between present or likely demand and supply; and

(2) an attractive/acceptable return on investment.

Apart from these two criteria's, a business opportunity needs to be analyzed from other view points for its viability such as technical, production, commercial and managerial. These criteria's are interlinked and a decision about one, affects others.

According to **Peter F. Drucker**, **opportunities are of three kinds: addictive, complementary and breakthrough.** Addictive opportunity is concerned with utilizing the existing resources without making any change. Complementary opportunities results in introduction of new ideas and involves change. Breakthrough involves drastic and fundamental change in the existing business. Risk is least in additive opportunities, greater in complementary and greatest in breakthrough opportunities. Bearing in mind these factors and expecting a fair return on investment, the entrepreneur has to choose a project.

An entrepreneur is said to be an opportunity seeker. For the potential entrepreneur his/her first task is to identify, explore and then select an attractive business opportunity.

Identifying a Business Opportunity

Project identification is a difficult task faced by an entrepreneur. He comes across several investment opportunities. In the first instance he has to select a few projects which have been subjected to preliminary evaluation. *"Project is concerned with collection, complication and analysis of economic data for the eventual purpose of locating possible opportunities for investment and with the development of the characteristics of such opportunities"*

An entrepreneur should explore for proper opportunities while establishing a new enterprise or business. He has to start his new enterprise by selecting a proper opportunity out of available options.

Hence, it becomes very important for entrepreneur to identify proper opportunity, to analyze it and to find out which is the best for him. In a nutshell, to identify a project is main task of an entrepreneur while establishing a new enterprise. If he succeeds to grab the best opportunity, he can become a successful entrepreneur. But if he fails to do so, if he diverts himself from best opportunity, he has to undergo a number of hindrances coming in his way.

Generally we believe that there are number of opportunities for an entrepreneur to select a project. We call opportunities to available options for project. He can establish various kinds of projects. But it he is not capable or it he is not going to do it, hence, he has to select the best opportunity after analyzing available options.

When he analyzes various opportunities, he scrutinizes every matter with reference to project, service, market, technology, instruments, quantity and standard of production, location of production, time of period, encouragements, profitability, etc. Out of this analysis he finds the best project and commences his activity. But it is not easy to recognize the best opportunity out of various options.

Various government agencies and ministries came out with publications containing latest information, various government schemes, encouragements, benefits, administrative process, etc., The govt.'s commerce ministry publishes detailed exports information for agricultural products through nodal agencies. Gujarat Agro-Industries Corporation also provides information about how to establish and develop agricultural industries. Gujarat Industrial Technical Consultancy Organisation Ltd., prepares project profiles about many products and information about foundation and development of enterprises. District industry centre also provides such informations in every district. Central Govt Five-Year Plans documents, as well as economic survey before Central budget and budget documents also provide information useful for industries and govt. policy about industries. Document of population census also give many important information.

Through these and many other sources, an entrepreneur gathers information containing many options for starting a new enterprise. He analyses this information. He keeps some standards and parameters which can be known as standard for project selection.

While selecting a project an entrepreneur keeps given standards in his mind:

(1) ***Amount of Capital Investment:*** A professional manager has worked in a multinational company or a big Indian company with big investment. However, it should be from 3 lakh to 5 crore rupees because it is essential in current age of global competition. If he opts for the investment less than ₹ 2 crore, he will have to access many financial institutes, whereas he can gather finance for the project worth ₹ 4-5 crore through equity or a big industrial finance corporation.

(2) ***Selection of Location for Enterprise:*** A new entrepreneur generally will establish his industry in his district, state or any nearby centers. If he does it in backward area, he gets certain additional benefits including tax benefit, etc. He can find such backward area in his own district, state or nearby locations. He should select the location where he can attract high level managers. Besides this, the facility and availability of raw materials, labourers, infrastructural facilities, land, water, govt. offices and administration.

(3) ***Technology and Technical Know-how:*** An entrepreneur starting an enterprise for the first time would not prefer to use complex or imported technology. Complex and confusing technical know-how is not preferable in the initial stage. Generally, the technology which is indigenous or available locally and should be easy to use is preferable.

(4) ***Parts, Machinery and Means of Production:*** An entrepreneur should follow the instruction of experienced experts while selecting spares machinery and means of production. He should not compromise against quality. He should emphasize on quality, effectiveness, utility rather than cost. He should think in long-term benefits and not short-term while planning for purchase of spares, machines and means of production.

(5) ***Market Availability:*** Market availability should also be thought while selecting product or location. He should think that he doesn't have to face cut-throat competition in initial stages. If there are limited number of customers and manufacturers in the market, the market-related problems can be solved easily.

(6) ***Adoption and Selection of the Best Business Concepts:*** An entrepreneur should select ideas which are the best for his product and entire project. It is necessary to make the project profitable, capable and socially acceptable. He should see to it that he is self-dependent. He should gather opinions for probable products from every possible source. These can be found from customers, competitors, distributors, agents research analysts, etc.

(7) ***Analysis of Opportunities and Selection of Project:*** After gathering detailed information about project, it is checked and analyzed. Past demand supply condition should be checked for the product to be manufactured probably. Decision for the project can be taken from the current trend, for the future demand. If the product has nationwide market, the analysis for the demand and supply should be done accordingly. But if the market is limited, the analysis should be done referring concerned states only. Sometimes, some industries work as ancillary unit to main industries. In this situation, it is required to think about demand of main industries.

When there is no materialistic product to be manufactured but workshop or service station project is on hand, the selection of such project should be done only after scrutinizing the respective demand. In this reference business environment, quantity of job orders, local competition, etc., should be kept in notice.

If the product to be manufactured is currently being imported, present import subscription policy of government and future probability should also be checked simultaneously. Govt import policy, import duty, import controls etc., matters need to be noticed. Prices of imported product, quality, demand, and current trend also require checking.

Before assuming future prospects for the demand and supply of the product it is advisable to check production capacity of existing units, number of units, industries, and permission for use of production capacity, import-export capacity of the product, etc.

Detailed study of available opportunities regarding project should be done. Demand supply market, trends of competition, income expense profitability and all other concerned facts should be evaluated.

Sources of Ideas

The sources from which an entrepreneur can obtain business ideas are numerous and some of them are given below:

(1) ***Market Characteristics:*** The supply and demand conditions of various products will give an idea about unfulfilled demand. Demand for new products should also be analyzed. The success of "Maggie" noodles is an example of unsatisfied demand for fast foods. "Surf" catered to the upper segment of the market. Later "Nirma" entered to satisfy the lower strata of the market. The acceptance of "SINTEX" water tanks is another example.

(2) ***Product Profile:*** An analytical study of the end products and by-products can throw light on new project ideas. For example, mini steel plants have been started using steel scrap which was discarded as waste. Again small firms can supply components or parts to large firms.

(3) ***Imports and Exports:*** The Government of India is now encouraging exports. There is now great scope for import substitution and export of various items. AVT group of companies are successfully exporting tissue culture plants.

(4) ***Emerging Technologies:*** Commercial exploitation of indigenous or imported technologies is another source of project ideas. One best example, is Xerox. Till Xerox Corporation adopted the idea in 1960, it remained as an unexploited invention.

(5) ***Social and Economic Trend:*** Social and economic status of people are always subject to change and offer vast opportunities. An entrepreneur should observe these changes. For example, there is now a shift towards ready-made garments, possessing consumer durables on hire purchase basis, etc.

(6) ***Changes in Consumption Pattern:*** Changes in consumption pattern of the people in home country and foreign countries also require the entrepreneur's attention. Nescafe introduced granulated coffee in India as consumers abroad preferred granulated coffee to powdered instant coffee.

(7) ***Revival of Sick Units:*** A sick unit gives ample investment opportunities in the hands of a dynamic entrepreneur. He can revitalize and turn a sick unit into a profitable one.

(8) ***Chance Factors:*** An entrepreneur may come across a sheer chance which may turn out to be a good project idea. Imported mixes were not suitable to the ingredients used in Indian cookery. Satya Prakash Mathur's wife complained to him about the non-suitability of imported mixies and Mathur manufactured "Sumeet" mixies to suit Indian conditions.

(9) ***Trade Fairs:*** Trade fairs are often organized under the auspices of the Industries Department of the Central and State Governments and Trade Organizations. International and national trade fairs and exhibitions are held at Pragathi Maidan in New Delhi. Machinery and tools for the small-scale units and ancillary products required by the major industries are displayed at the national, state and district level fairs. An inquisitive and dynamic entrepreneur can get lots of ideas by visiting these fairs.

(10) ***Electronic Commerce:*** E-Commerce is increasingly used by existing corporations to extend their marketing and sales channels, as well as being the basis for some new venture. An entrepreneur starting an Internet commerce venture needs to address the same strategic and tactical questions as any other entrepreneur. Use of websites can facilitate the entrepreneurs to find information about the products and services that a company offers over the Internet.

(11) **Trade and professional journals/magazines:** Trade and professional journals/magazines are also sources of ideas. These journals/magazines give information relating to products manufactured and spares/components required by various industrial units belonging to a particular trade.

Steps in Idea Processing and Selection

(1) ***Preliminary Evaluation and Testing of Ideas:*** Once business ideas are discovered, screening and testing of these ideas is done. The following considerations are significant in the evaluation and testing of business ideas.

(a) ***Technical feasibility:*** It refers to the possibility of producing the product. Technical feasibility of an idea is judged in terms of availability of necessary technology, machinery and equipment, labour skills and raw materials. The advice and assistance of technical experts may be necessary to judge the technical feasibility of various business ideas.

(b) ***Commercial viability:*** A cost-benefit analysis is required to ascertain the profitability of the ideas. An elaborate study of market conditions and prevailing situation is made to assess the viability and prospects of the proposed projects. This is known as feasibility study of the project. A number of calculations have to be made about the likely demand, expected sales volume, selling price, cost of production, break-even point, etc. The services of market analysts and financial experts may be necessary for this purpose.

There is a difference between a business idea and a business opportunity. While the idea for a product or service may be workable (technically feasible), the proposed business built on this may not profitable. It is normal for an entrepreneur to have several ideas for business that have to be rejected before finding one that is not only workable but worthwhile. In order to judge the workability and profitability of the proposed business, feasibility analysis has to be conducted.

(2) *Detailed Analysis:* After preliminary evaluation of the idea, the promising idea is subjected to a thorough analysis from all angles. Full investigation is carried out in the technical feasibility and economic viability of the proposed project. Financial and managerial feasibility of the idea are tested. At this stage a lot of information is required. Consultations with experts in various areas of the industry may be necessary to carry out the detailed analysis. Due care should be exercised at this stage because the idea is finally accepted or rejected at this stage.

After the evaluation of a business idea is completed, the findings are presented in the form of a report known as 'feasibility report' or 'project report'. This report helps in the final selection of a project. It is also useful for procuring licenses, finance, etc., from government agencies.

(3) *Idea selection:* The feasibility report is analyzed to finally choose the most promising idea. Generally, the following considerations influence the selection of idea for a product or service:

(a) Products whose imports are banned or restricted by the government;
(b) Products which can be exported easily and profitably;
(c) Products whose demands exceed their supply so that there exists ready demand;
(d) Products in which the entrepreneur has manufacturing and/or marketing experience;
(e) Parent ancillary relationships, i.e., the product are to be manufactured for a parent company;
(f) Products which showed high profitability;
(g) Products based on the expansion or diversification plans of existing firms of the family/friends/relatives;
(h) Products which ensured specific advantages. The advantages might accrue because of the scale of the industry or the locations of the factory or technology of manufacture;
(i) Products favoured by the countries, industrial/licensing policy, e.g., delicensed industries;
(j) Products for which incentives and subsidies are available.

While considering these various factors–market, own experience, policy and incentives–an entrepreneur would generally come across a mix of some encouraging and some discouraging factors with reference to every product. It therefore, became necessary to analyze and compare the pros and cons. A selection matrix may be prepared for this purpose. In the selection matrix given in table below a comparison is made between Project A and Project B.

Entrepreneurial Selection Matrix

Sr. No.	Data	Project A	Project B
1.	Product	Priority industry	Reserved for small industry
2.	Raw materials required	Imported	Indigenous
3.	Machinery	Imported	Indigenous
4.	Market	Defence ministry	Local
5.	Technical Know-how	Foreign trained personnel	Indigenous
6.	Locations	Free trade zone	Backward area
7.	Profitability	High	Low

Many more items can be added for such comparison. The matrix indicates the type of diverse data that needs to be collected for each project. It also throws light on how each item can hold out some encouraging and some discouraging factors. The entrepreneurial selection needs to take all these factors into account.

(4) ***Input Requirements:*** Once the promoter is convinced of the feasibility and profitability of the project, he assembles the necessary resources to launch the enterprise. He has to choose partners/collaborators, collect the required finances and acquire land and buildings, plant and machinery, furniture and fixtures, patents, employees, etc., discussion have to be made about the size, location, layout, etc., of the enterprise, the form of ownership organization has to be selected. According to **Subin**, the firm is located by assembling and organizing the physical facilities, developing operation and production processing, advertising its product and initializing its sales promotion campaign, recruiting labour and accumulating inventories.

Assembling state is an important landmark in the entrepreneur's journey to establishment of an enterprise. The main inputs required for launching an enterprise are as follows:

(1) ***Information and Intelligence:*** In the turbulent business environment, information and intelligence have become the key input in the entrepreneurial success. An entrepreneur requires relevant data on the following aspects:

(a) Size and nature of demand for the product or service;
(b) Volume and sources of supply;
(c) Price cost volume relationship;
(d) Sources of raw materials;
(e) Type and supplier of technology, machinery and equipment;
(f) Number and type of personnel required and their sources;
(g) Amounts and sources of funds required for the enterprise;
(h) Nature and degree of competition;
(i) Governing policies and regulation concerning industry;
(j) Export import condition for the product/services every entrepreneur has to develop a sound system for regular, collection, procuring and dissemination of the required information. Such a system is called management information system. A sound system supplies the right amount of information at the right time to the right person. The use of computer helps to improve the effectiveness of management information system.

(2) ***Finance:*** Finance is the lifeblood of the business and it serves as the lubricant for the wheels of business machinery. A business enterprise requires finance for the fixed assets (fixed capital) as well for the current assets (working capital), there are two main methods for estimating the funds required for an enterprise.

(i) ***Cost theory:*** Under this method, financial requirements of an enterprise are the aggregate of fixed assets, current assets, intangible assets like goodwill, cost of promoting and establishing the business. The total outlay incurred on these items constitutes the capitalization of enterprise. This method is relatively simple and convenient for a new enterprise. But it may fail to reflect the earning power of the enterprise. Problems of over-capitalization and undercapitalization may arise.

(ii) ***Earnings theory:*** In this method, the capitalization of a company is equal to the capitalization value of its estimated earnings. If the average annual net profits of a company are estimated to be ₹ 50 lakh, and the return on the investment in the concerned industry is 25 per cent, the amount of funds to be raised would be ₹ 200 lakh. (50 lakh × 100 over 25). This theory provides a more realistic basis but there are problems in correct estimation of future earnings particularly for a new enterprise.

Once the amount of funds required are estimated, the entrepreneur has to identify the sources from which the funds are to be raised from different sources (e.g., shares, debentures, loans, et.). This decision is known as the capital structure. It is a very crucial decision because it influences the real worth of the enterprise and the returns to the owners.

After deciding the capital structure, the funds are raised. System is created for the efficient management and control of working capital and earnings.

(3) *Personnel:* People are the most valuable asset of an enterprise and this asset does not depreciate. An enterprise has to make the following decision concerning the personnel:

(i) Number of personnel required for management, technical and other positions in the enterprise;
(ii) Qualification and experience required by the personnel to perform the jobs effectively;
(iii) Sources of recruitment from which the need staff will be procured;
(iv) Procedure and methods of selecting the best candidates;
(v) Methods of orientation and training to be employed for the selected personnel;
(vi) System and criteria for evaluating the performance of employees;
(vii) Policies and procedures for the transfer and promotion of staff;
(viii) Policies and methods for remunerating the personnel;
(ix) Facilities to be provided for the safety, health, welfare of the personel;
(x) Participation of personnel in the management of the enterprise.

Establishment of an Enterprise

Introduction

This is a very significant matter. Success or failure of enterprise depends on this decision. Business success depends on which industry, where and how he establishes. He has to give heed on scientific and proper planning for the establishment of the enterprise. He needs to take many decisions. Which product to manufacture? Where and how much to produce? How to arrange finance? What should be the price of product? How to sell? Etc. These are the questions an entrepreneur has to ask while doing this process.

Important Decisions Related with Establishment of an Enterprise

An entrepreneur has to take various decisions while establishing an enterprise. He also has to plan properly to apply these decisions. Following are the main decisions related with establishment of an enterprise:

(1) First of all an entrepreneur has to decide about which product to manufacture. He will land on this decision after studying many facts. He manufactures the product having good demand and availability of raw materials. For this matter he consults experts. Rather than manufacturing conventional product he opts for the product having new look, new formation and different use. He examines and tests that product. He checks the marketability of the product. After such process he selects the product.

(2) After deciding about which product to manufacture he has to decide how to manufacture and by which means? This is also called factor planning means of production, i.e., land, building, plant, machinery, raw materials, technology, labourers, etc., are to be arranged. What should be the required quantity and from where to gather these means, are to be decided and to be arranged by the entrepreneur.

(3) After this, an entrepreneur has to take important decisions about the ownership of production facility. To make entire arrangement for the factors of production, how to shape the enterprise/ company etc., are the things to be decided. It is to be decided, whether to set up individually owned company, partnership firm or joint stock company. Joint stock company type of formation is essential to do business with large base and huge investment. Small–scale business can be carried out in individual or partnership firm.

(4) After deciding formation, an entrepreneur has to decide on source of finance. He has to finalize source and quantity of required finance. Industrial finance corporation, shares, debentures, bond, public loan, fixed deposits, internal sources, nationalized-private-cooperative foreign banks are the sources out of which an entrepreneur has to decide about the source and quantity to raise fund.

(5) An entrepreneur has to decide location of enterprise after product and formation. This is an important question. **Weber, Florence** and other scholars have given concepts about selecting location in industrial economics. Easy availability of raw material, labourers, etc., helps to prefer the location. This can be an ideal location for establishing enterprise. Moreover, central, state and local self-government also provide certain facility to establish or to develop an enterprise which is also considered while setting up a company.

(6) After solution of above, the question comes in front is technology selection for production, because present is an age of technology, hence, it is given sizable importance to decide about production. It needs to decide about production. It needs to decide about type of machinery, with modern and automatic production process.

(7) An entrepreneur has to think about the aids, subsidy, encouragements provided by the government. Because there are certain conditions and process are required to fulfill for financial, fiscal, structural, and administrative and market-related encouragement. Hence, effective planning with proper decision is required to avail such benefits.

(8) What will be the production cost? What should be the price? How to sell? What will be the profit? What are the opportunities for production and selling of the products? And what are the related problems? These are the questions need to be studied. Future prospects, problems and industrial development are the factors being planned out.

Thus, while setting up an enterprise, many decisions require heed. Business planning is being done keeping many things in notice while establishing an enterprise.

Summing Up

Defining "Opportunity"

In simple terms, opportunity may be defined as an attractive project idea which an entrepreneur accepts as a basis for his investment decision.

While selecting a project an entrepreneur keeps given standards in this mind: Amount of Capital Investment; Selection of location for enterprise; Technology and Technical know-how; Parts, Machinery and means of Production; Market Availability; Adoption and Selection of the Best Business Concepts; and Analysis of Opportunities and Selection of Project.

According to **Peter F. Drucker**, **opportunities are of three kinds: addictive, complementary and breakthrough.** Addictive opportunity is concerned with utilizing the existing resources without making any change. Complementary opportunities results in introduction of new ideas and involves change. Breakthrough involves drastic and fundamental change in the existing business. Risk is least in additive opportunities, greater in complementary and greatest in breakthrough opportunities. Bearing in mind these factors and expecting a fair return on investment, the entrepreneur has to choose a project.

An entrepreneur is said to be an opportunity seeker. For the potential entrepreneur his/her first task is to identify, explore and then select an attractive business opportunity.

Identifying a Business Opportunity

Project identification is a difficult task faced by an entrepreneur. He comes across several investment opportunities. In the first instance he has to select a few projects which have been subjected to preliminary evaluation. *"Project is concerned with collection, complication and analysis of economic data for the eventual purpose of locating possible opportunities for investment and with the development of the characteristics of such opportunities"*

Sources of Ideas

The sources from which an entrepreneur can obtain business ideas are numerous and some of them are given below:

Market Characteristics; Product Profile; Imports and Exports; Emerging Technologies; Social and Economic Trend; Changes in Consumption Pattern; Revival of Sick Units; Chance Factors; Trade Fairs; and Electronic Commerce; and Trade and Professional Journals/Magazines.

Steps in Idea Processing and Selection

Preliminary Evaluation and Testing of Ideas; Detailed Analysis; Idea Selection; and Input Requirements.

Establishment of an Enterprise

An entrepreneur has to take various decisions while establishing an enterprise. He also has to plan properly to apply these decisions. Following are the main decisions related with establishment of enterprise.

(1) First of all an entrepreneur has to decide about which product to manufacture.
(2) After deciding about which product to manufacture he has to decide how to manufacture and by which means?
(3) After this an entrepreneur has to take important decisions about the ownership of production facility.
(4) After deciding formation, an entrepreneur has to decide on source of finance.
(5) An entrepreneur has to decide location of enterprise after product and formation.
(6) After solution of above, the question comes in front is technology selection for production, because present is an age of technology, hence, it is given sizable importance to decide about production.
(7) An entrepreneur has to think about the aids, subsidy, encouragements provided by the government.
(8) What will be the production cost? What should be the price? How to sell? What Will be the profit? What are the opportunities for production and selling of the products? And what are the related problems? These are the questions need to be studied. Future prospects, problems and industrial development are the factors being planned out.

8 PROJECT MANAGEMENT

Introduction, Concept of Project Formulation, Need for Project Formulation, Significance of Project Formulation, Elements of Project Formulation, Break-even Analysis, What is a Project?, What is Project Report?, Contents of a Project Report, Significance of Project Report, Importance of a Project Report, Summing Up, Annexure

Introduction

Project Management is used extensively by various organizations to accomplish their pre-determined goal and objectives. Various models, formulae, and charts have been developed to help upcoming entrepreneur to manage their projects effectively. *The Project Management Institute defines Project Management as 'the application of knowledge, skills, tools, and techniques to project activities to meet project requirements.'*

Concept of Project Formulation

Project formulation is the systematic development of a project idea for the eventual objective of arriving at an investment decision. It has the built-in mechanism of ringing the danger bell at the earliest possible stage of resource utilization. Project formulation involves a step by step investigation and development of project idea. And it provides a controlled mechanism for restricting expenditure on project development. One stage of the exercise leads to the other. In case, a weakness is observed at any stage of investigation, the entrepreneur can exercise his discretion of calling off the exercise, if the facts so warrant. It enables him to take decisions in a scientific way of providing a concrete set of facts.

Project formulation is a process involving the joint efforts of a team expert. Each member of the team should be familiar with the board strategy, objectives and other ingredients of the project. Besides being an expert in his area of specialization, he should be able to play his role in the overall scheme of things. The government official who deals with the project's final clearance has to be treated as forming part of the team. He should be well informed about the project. A well formulated feasibility report provides a medium which cuts across scientific, social and positional prejudice and provides a common meeting ground for all those who have a contribution to make in successful implementation of a project.

Project team should consist of experts in major substantive fields of the project. Depending on the situations any large project should comprise the following team members:

(a) One industrial economist;
(b) One market analyst;
(c) One or more technologist/engineer specializing in the appropriate industry;

(d) One mechanical and/or industrial expert;
(e) One civil engineer, if needed; and
(f) One management accounting expert.

Need for Project Formulation

The entrepreneur in the developing country has to encounter a number of problems while establishing a new project. These problem cause greater concern to many enthusiastic entrepreneur. However, they could be saved to a greater extent by undertaking a project formulation exercise at the appropriate time.

(1) ***Selection of Appropriate Technology:*** The first problem faced by an entrepreneur is in the matter of selection of appropriate technology for his enterprise. Modern technology developed in the highly industrialized countries may not be suitable for adoption in the developing countries as the conditions prevalent differ from country to country. For example, the optimal size of plants recommended for a highly industrialized country may be too big for acceptance in a developing country owing to the factors such as limited market for the products and limited availability and skilled labour. Hence, the entrepreneur has to examine the project idea thoroughly as regards its design, production, marketing, after sales services, etc.

(2) ***Influence of External Economics:*** The second problem relates to the absence or non-availability of external economics. No project can function in isolation in any economy. It has to depend on other industries for the supply of raw materials, power, tools, spare parts, or on ancillary enterprise which can provide technical, financial and managerial services or on a complex network of communication and transport facilities or an intricate system of business practices. The entrepreneur in developing countries has, therefore, to consider not only the basics costs of the project but also the ancillary costs which in industrially advanced countries would have been contributed by the external economics.

(3) ***Dearth of Technically Qualified Personnel:*** The third problem is the non-availability of technically qualified and appropriate personnel. Modern technology calls for a certain minimum supply of various skills that are generally lacking in developing countries.

(4) ***Resources Mobilization:*** The fourth problem is resources mobilization. In the context of present day development of the magnitude and size of project, it would be very difficult for an entrepreneur to provide the entire development capital that a project may need.

(5) ***Knowledge about Government Regulations:*** Besides these problems the entrepreneur has to comprehend a number of government directives, import and export policies, price controls, etc., the difficulty is to be familiar with all these regulations, for they are not available in a consolidated and detailed form in most of the developing countries. However, in India, a compendium entitled 'Guidelines for Industries' has been published by the Ministry of Industrial Development. It provides information regarding the industrial policy, licensing procedures, guidelines for foreign collaboration, import and export control order and foreign exchange orders. It also has information regarding the present status of capacities and possibilities of future development in various industrial fields like metallurgical industries, electronics equipment industries, transportation industries and the like.

These problems make the entrepreneur to undergo a lot of harassment, disappointment and despair. However, a project formulation exercise undertaken at the right time mitigates the severity as well as magnitude of these problems.

Significance of Project Formulation

A well-formulated project is the best passport for obtaining the required assistance from financial institutions. When there is a situation of resource constraint and the available resources are allocated to various project based on their importance and viability, a well formulated project formulation is the best way of selling a project idea to a financing agency.

Project formulation will also be of great assistance for obtaining necessary government clearance and in meeting the hurdles of procedural formalities. It will pinpoint the matters for which government sanctions have to be obtained and also provide an independent assessment of the feasibility of obtaining these sanctions based on the existing government policies. The project report submitted by the entrepreneur will establish his bonafides in the eyes of the bureaucracy and obtain due government sanctions without much difficulty.

Elements of Project Formulation

Project formulation is by itself an analytical management aid. It enables the entrepreneur to arrive at the most effective project decision. Project formulation exercise normally includes such aspects as follows.

1. Feasibility Analysis;
2. Techno-Economic Analysis;
3. Project Design and Network Analysis;
4. Input Analysis;
5. Financial Analysis;
6. Social Cost Benefit Analysis; and
7. Project Appraisal.

(1) ***Feasibility Analysis:*** This is the very first stage in project formulation. At this stage, the project idea is examined from the project view of whether to go in for detailed investment proposal or not. As project idea is examined in the context of internal and external constraints, three alternatives could be considered. First, the project idea seems to be feasible, second, the project idea is not a feasible, we proceed to the third step, if not feasible, we abandon the idea and if sufficient data are not available, we make more efforts to collect the required data and design development.

(2) ***Techno-Economic Analysis:*** In this step, estimation of project demand potential and choice of optimal technology is made. As the project may produce goods or services, it is imperative to know the market for such goods or services produced. Market analysis is also in-built in this step. The choice of technology itself will be based on the demand potential and aid in project design. Techno-economic analysis gives the project a unique individuality and sets the stage for detailed design development.

(3) ***Project Design and Network Analysis:*** This important step defines individual activities which constitute the project and then is presented. A detailed work plan of the project is prepared with time allocation for each activity and presented in a network drawing. Project design is the heart of the project entity. This paves the way for detailed identification and qualification of the project inputs, an essential step in the development of the financial and cost-benefit profile of the project.

(4) ***Input Analysis:*** The step assesses the input requirements during the construction of the project and also during the operation of the project. In the earlier step, a project was divided into several activities. Now it is better to see to the inputs required for each activity and sum it up to get at the total input requirements on the qualitative and quantitative terms. Input includes materials, human resources etc. Input analysis also considers the recurring as well as non-recurring resource requirements of the project and evaluate the feasibility of the project from the point of view of the availability of these resources. This will aid in assessing the project cost itself, which in turn is necessary for financial analysis or cost-benefit analysis.

(5) *Financial Analysis:* This stage mainly involves estimating the project costs, estimating its operating costs and fund requirements. Financial analysis also helps in comparing various project proposals on a common scale, thereby aiding the decision-maker. Some of the analytical tools used in financial analysis are discounted cash flow, cost-volume- profit relationship and ratio analysis. It is very essential to take caution in preparing financial estimates. The objective of this strategy caution is to develop the project taking into consideration resources and also to identify these characteristics. Investment decisions whether made for the provision of goods or services involve commitment of resources in future. Since investment proposition has a very long time horizon, it is absolutely necessary to exercise due care and foresight in developing project financial forecasts.

(6) *Cost Benefit Analysis:* Cost Benefit Analysis is a process by which you weigh expected costs against expected benefits to determine the best (or most profitable) course of action. Under this analysis, estimates of social cost and social benefit are made and presented for computation of social profitability of the project. While the cost and benefits under the financial analysis are estimated employing market price based on financial objectives, this cost benefit analysis considers them only at certain imputed prices based on social or national objectives. The information gathered would be used mostly for setting the social profitability criteria for public sector project appraisal and evaluation. Social cost benefit analysis is now an internationally recognized system of project appraisal even though no standard methodology is available for it.

(7) *Project Appraisal:* Project appraisal is the overall viability evaluation of a project with a view to finding out its practical utility and soundness before actual execution. The term appraisal means 'assessment'. Appraisal is a critical assessment or evaluations of the whole project in order to find out its real worth or utility. It is in addition to feasibility study and is usually undertaken independently by expert agency. Appraisal is a technique of reviewing the entire project plan for removing deficiencies of all types in the existing project, if any. Such appraisal is actually a type of rechecking and reanalyzing of the entire project with suitable techniques in the light of current developments in the government policies, market situation and technological changes. The basic purpose is to find out the true worth of the project. It also aims at finding out the drawbacks and weaknesses in the existing project and to suggest ways and means of removing them. The purpose is to make rechecking of the whole project and to introduce certain modifications, if required and to make the project perfect in all respects. This avoids the possibility of failure of the project at the lowest level.

Industrial projects frequently need to be appraised by expert individuals or agencies. Such appraisal stage comes often and again in the life of every business project. Initial appraisal of a project is usually undertaken at the planning stage of the project. In addition, it is necessary during the course of the execution and also after the completion of the entire project. Appraisal of a project before actual execution is important as it enables the promoters or sponsors to reject them, if found defective or unsound. Such appraisal is particularly needed in the case of big projects where crores of rupees are to be invested. The purpose of appraisal is to make an impartial evaluation of the project by an independent expert agency and also to rectify defects or deficiencies in it before execution. In the process of appraisal, special attention is given to various aspects like the cost of the project, technology used for production, sources of financing, market for the product, competence of the management and financial results (profit, turnover, sales revenue, etc.) of the project.

Break–even Analysis

An organisation is said to be at break-even point when its level of sales (or revenue) is such that it neither results in a profit nor a loss. That is, the total sales (or revenue) at that level is equal to the total costs. This point, at which the total sales (or revenue) are equal to the total costs, is called the break-even point (BEP).

The total cost of an organisation can be roughly divided into two categories, *viz.*, the variable (or direct) costs and fixed (or indirect) costs. The variable costs are those which are directly connected with the product and vary in direct proportion to the production. For example, in the case of a manufacturer, the raw materials used, the labour cost, fuel, water and electricity consumed for production, etc. So, by definition the variable costs will be NIL when there is no production. On the other hand, fixed costs are incurred whether there is any production or not. For example, rent for premises, salaries for establishment, insurance charges, etc.

In other words, the variable costs vary in total according to the level of production but remain constant per unit of production, whereas the fixed costs remain constant in total whatever is the level of production but vary per unit depending on the level of production. If the level of production is high, then the fixed cost per unit will be comparatively lower than when the level of production is low. When both the variable costs and the fixed costs are reduced from the sales, what remains is the profit. Thus, we can express it as: $S - (V+F) = P$ where S = sales, V = variable costs, F= fixed costs and P = profit. Or we can also say: $S - V = F+P$

When only the variable cost is reduced from the sales, what remains is called the contribution. It is so-called because it represents the amount contributed by sales, after meeting the variable cost, towards the fixed expenses and the profit. Therefore:

$S–V=C=F+P$ where C represents contribution.

As stated earlier, when the level of sales is at the BEP, the organisation neither earns a profit nor incurs a loss, i.e., P=0. We can therefore say that at the BEP

$S–V=C=F$ since P=0

Hence, the contribution from sales is equal to the fixed expenses at the BEP and thus there is neither profit nor loss. It follows that when the level of sales is less than the level of sales at the BEP, the organisation will incur loss; i.e., P will be a negative figure.

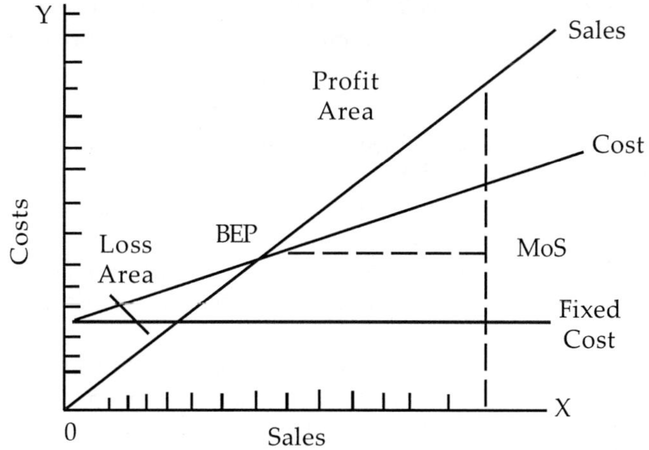

We can also express the BEP graphically and this is called a break-even chart. There are various types of break-even charts and the simplest among these is as above:

From the alongside graph it will be noted that the point at which the total sales curve intersects the total cost curve is the BEP. The area between the total cost curve and the total cost curve to the right of the BEP represents the profit. Such an area to the left of the BEP represents loss. The most important aspect revealed by a break-even chart is the Margin of Safety (MoS). This is the distance, to the right of the BEP, between the BEP and the expected sales.

The financial institutions, banks, etc., lay great stress on a wide MoS. If the MoS is comparatively narrow it means that,

(a) Fixed costs are high, and
(b) Even a minor reduction in the actual sales achieved as compared to the expected sales will bring the organisation dangerously near its BEP and therefore, the risk of the organisation going into a loss is higher.

If the MoS is comparatively wider then,

(a) The fixed costs constitute a lower percentage of the total costs,
(b) Unless the drop in the actual sales achieved is significant as compared to the expected sales, the organisation will continue to make profits.

Hence, the risk factor is very low when the MoS is wide and the risk factor will be high when the MoS is narrow.

Break-even analysis is also used within the organisation to choose between the various products the unit is capable of manufacturing and arrive at an optimum mix of products for manufacture which will maximize the profits of the organisation. This is done by the comparison of the contributors (i.e., sales less variable costs) of the different products, with the fixed costs related to the product as well as the fixed costs of the organisation as a whole.

The main limitations of break-even analysis are the difficulty faced in classifying the costs into variable and fixed costs. Further, there are many items of costs which tend to remain constant within a certain range of production and vary when the level of production increases or decreases beyond this range. These are called semi-variable or semi-fixed costs.

What is a Project?

The Project Management Institute (PMI) defines project as "a temporary endeavour undertaken to create a unique product or service". It can be defined as a finite task to be completed. ***Webster****, new 20th Century Dictionary, defines a project as a scheme, design, a proposal of something intended or devised.*

Some of the attributes that characterize projects are as below:

(a) ***Purpose:*** The project has a well-defined end goal. The goal itself might be made up of several sub-goals. A project can be subdivided into several subtasks, which must be completed in order to achieve the project goals. A project with several subtasks will need careful planning to co-ordinate costs, timing and precedence of other subtasks.

(b) ***Life Cycle:*** Projects have well-defined life cycles. From small beginnings, they build up in size and finally must be terminated. Sometimes, the projects get phased into the normal operations of the firm.

(c) ***Uniqueness:*** Each project is going to be different from the other projects. No two projects will be alike, even though there are a lot of projects with many common elements. That means that a project cannot be reduced to a routine activity and each project needs a customized approach.

What is Project Report?

The Project Report or business plan is a written statement of what an entrepreneur proposes to take up. It is a kind of guide frost or course of action what the entrepreneur hopes to achieve in his business and how is he going to achieve it. In other words, project report serves like a kind of big road map to reach the destination determined by the entrepreneur. Thus, a project report can best be defined as a well evolved course of action devised to achieve the specified objective within a specified period of time. So to say, it is an operating document.

Contents of a Project Report

The following are contents of a project report:

(1) Objective and scope of the report;
(2) Product characteristics (specifications, product uses and application, standards and quality);
(3) Market position and trends (installed capacity, production and anticipated demand, export prospects and information on import and export, price structure and trends);
(4) Raw materials (requirement of raw materials, prices, sources and properties of raw materials);
(5) Manufacture (processes of manufacture, selection of process, production schedule and production technique);
(6) Plant and machinery (equipment and machinery, instruments, laboratory equipment, electric load and water supply and the essential infrastructure);
(7) Land and building (requirement of land area, building, construction schedule);
(8) Financial implications (fixed and working capital investment, project cost and profitability);
(9) Marketing channels (trading practices and marketing strategy);
(10) Personnel (requirements of staff, labour and expenses on wage payment).

The project report is prepared for submission to the financial institutions for the grant of land and other financial concessions. An entrepreneur can himself prepare the report, otherwise assistance from experts can be sought. There are several organizations which help entrepreneurs in the preparation of reports. The Small Industries Service Institutes (SISI) helps the entrepreneur in this regard. State government also helps the entrepreneur in matters of financial assistance towards this end.

Significance of Project Report

An objective without a plan is a dream. The preparation of a project report is of great significance for an entrepreneur. The project report serves two essential functions:

First and most important, the project report is like a road map. It describes the direction the enterprise is going in, what its goals are, where it wants to be, and how it is going to get there. It also enables the entrepreneur to know that he is proceeding in the right direction. Some hold the view that without well spelt out goals and operational methods/tactics, most businesses flounder on the rocks of hard times.

The **second** function of the project report is to attract lenders and investors. Although, it is not mandatory for the small enterprises to prepare project reports, yet it is useful and beneficial for them to prepare the project reports for various reasons. The preparation of project report is beneficial for those small enterprises which apply for financial assistance from the financial institutions and the commercial banks. It is on the basis of project report that the financial institutions make appraisal if the enterprise requires financial assistance or not. If yes, how much? Similarly, other organizations which provide various assistance such as work shed, raw materials, seed/margin money, etc., are equally interested in knowing the economic soundness of the proposal. In most cases, the quality of the firm's project report weighs heavily in the decision to lend or invest funds.

Importance of a Project Report

Project report is of great importance. It highlights the practicability of a project in terms of different factors like economy, finance, technology and social desirability. It is needed by the entrepreneur for carrying out expansion or starting a new production line. These may be carried on by individuals like engineers and scientists, bankers or institutions, consultancy services and development banks.

An important aspect of the report lies in determining the profitability of the project and minimizing risks in the execution of the project.

Summing Up

Introduction

Project Management is used extensively by various organizations to accomplish their pre-determined goal and objectives. Various models, formulae, and charts have been developed to help upcoming entrepreneur to manage their projects effectively. The Project Management Institute, defines Project management as 'the application of knowledge, skills, tools, and techniques to project activities to meet project requirements.'

Concept of Project Formulation

Project formulation is the systematic development of a project idea for the eventual objective of arriving at an investment decision. It has the built-in mechanism of ringing the danger bell at the earliest possible stage of resource utilization. Project formulation involves a step by step investigation and development of project idea.

Project formulation is a process involving the joint efforts of a team expert. Each member of the team should be familiar with the board strategy, objectives and other ingredients of the project.

Project team should consist of experts in major substantive fields of the project. Depending on the situations any large project should comprise the following team members.

(a) One industrial economist;

(b) One market analyst;

(c) One or more technologist/engineer specializing in the appropriate industry;

(d) One mechanical and/or industrial expert;

(e) One civil engineer, if needed;

(f) One management accounting expert.

Need for Project Formulation

The entrepreneur in the developing country has to encounter a number of problems while establishing a new project. These problem cause greater concern to many enthusiastic entrepreneur. However, they could be saved to a greater extend by undertaking a project formulation exercise at the appropriate time.

Selection of Appropriate Technology; Influence of External Economics; Dearth of Technically Qualified Personnel; Resources Mobilization; and Knowledge about Government Regulations.

Significance of Project Formulation

A well-formulated project is the best passport for obtaining the required assistance from financial institutions. When there is a situation of resource constraint and the available resources are allocated to various projects based on their importance and viability, a well formulated project formulation is the best way of selling a project idea to a financing agency.

Elements of Project Formulation

Project formulation is by itself an analytical management aid. It enables the entrepreneur to arrive at the most effective project decision. Project formulation exercise normally includes such aspects as follows:

Feasibility Analysis; Techno-economic Analysis; Project Design and Network Analysis; Input Analysis; Financial Analysis; Social Cost Benefit Analysis; and Project Appraisal.

Break-even Analysis

An organisation is said to be at break-even point when its level of sales (or revenue) is such that it neither results in a profit nor a loss. That is, the total sales (or revenue) at that level is equal to the total costs. This point, at which the total sales (or revenue) are equal to the total costs, is called the break-even point (BEP).

The total cost of an organisation can be roughly divided into two categories, *viz.*, the variable (or direct) costs and fixed (or indirect) costs. The variable costs are those which are directly connected with the product and vary in direct proportion to the production.

We can express it as: S- (V+F)=P where S= sales, V= variable costs, F= fixed costs and P= profit. Or we can also say: S-V=F+P

When only the variable cost is reduced from the sales, what remains is called the contribution. It is so-called because it represents the amount contributed by sales, after meeting the variable cost, towards the fixed expenses and the profit. Therefore:

S-V=C=F+P where C represents contribution.

As stated earlier, when the level of sales is at the BEP, the organisation neither earns a profit nor incurs a loss, i.e., P=0. We can therefore say that at the BEP

S-V=C=F since P=0

Hence, the contribution from sales is equal to the fixed expenses at the BEP and thus there is neither profit nor loss. It follows that when the level of sales is less than the level of sales at the BEP, the organisation will incur loss; i.e., P will be a negative figure.

Break-even analysis is also used within the organisation to choose between the various products the unit is capable of manufacturing and arrive at an optimum mix of products for manufacture which will maximize the profits of the organisation. This is done by the comparison of the contributors (i.e., sales less variable costs) of the different products, with the fixed costs related to the product as well as the fixed costs of the organisation as a whole.

What is a Project?

The Project Management Institute (PMI), defines project as "a temporary endeavour undertaken to create a unique product or service". It can be defined as a finite task to be completed. **Webster**, *new 20th Century Dictionary, defines a project as a scheme, design, a proposal of something intended or devised.*

Some of the attributes that characterize projects are as below: Purpose; Life Cycle; and Uniqueness.

What is Project Report?

The Project report or business plan is a written statement of what an entrepreneur proposes to take up. It is a kind of guide frost or course of action what the entrepreneur hopes to achieve in his business and how is he going to achieve it.

Contents of a Project Report

The following are contents of a project report:

(1) Objective and scope of the report.

(2) Product characteristics (specifications, product uses and application, standards and quality).

(3) Market position and trends (installed capacity, production and anticipated demand, export prospects and information on import and export, price structure and trends).

(4) Raw materials (requirement of raw materials, prices, sources and properties of raw materials).

(5) Manufacture (processes of manufacture, selection of process, production schedule and production technique).

(6) Plant and machinery (equipment and machinery, instruments, laboratory equipment, electric load and water supply and the essential infrastructure).

(7) Land and building (requirement of land area, building, construction schedule).

(8) Financial implications (fixed and working capital investment, project cost and profitability).

(9) Marketing channels (trading practices and marketing strategy).

(10) Personnel (requirements of staff, labour and expenses on wage payment).

The project report is prepared for submission to the financial institutions for the grant of land and other financial concessions. An entrepreneur can himself prepare the report, otherwise assistance from experts can be sought. There are several organizations which help entrepreneurs in the preparation of reports. The Small Industries Service Institutes (SISI) helps the entrepreneur in this regard. State government also helps the entrepreneur in matters of financial assistance towards this end.

Significance of Project Report

An objective without a plan is a dream. The preparation of a project report is of great significance for an entrepreneur. The project report serves two essential functions:

First and most important, the project report is like a road map. It describes the direction the enterprise is going in, what its goals are, where it wants to be, and how it is going to get there.

The **second** function of the project report is to attract lenders and investors.

Importance of a Project Report

It highlights the practicability of a project in terms of different factors like economy, finance, technology and social desirability. These may be carried on by individuals like engineers and scientists, bankers or institutions, consultancy services and development banks.

An important aspect of the report lies in determining the profitability of the project and minimizing risks in the execution of the project.

ANNEXURE I

APPLICATION ID

OFFICIAL USE

Application Form For Financial Assistance Under Prime Minister's Employment Generation Programme (PMEGP)

Preference for sponsoring agency of the project to Bank: (**mark √**)

KVIC KVIB DIC Rural Urban

To

....

....

Details in blocks should be entered in **CAPITAL LETTERS** only

1. Name of the applicant/Institution Name
2. Date of Birth
3. Sex Male Female
4. Father's Name/Spouse's Name/Contact Person's Name (if Institution):
5. Communication Address:

   Taluka/Block:

   District:

   E-mail: Contact No.
6. Address of proposed location of unit: Rural Urban

   Taluka/Block:

   District:
7. Name of the preferred Bank Name and Address in the area for project sanctioned

   Bank Name:

   Address:

   Taluka/Block:

   District:

   Branch code:
8. Qualification

   Academic Technical
9. Whether Entrepreneur Development Programme (EDP at least 2 weeks) undergone: (mark √) Yes No

   Name and Address of Training Institute Period of training Certificate Issue Date

   From to
10. Whether the applicant belongs to (mark √)

    SC ST OBC PHC Ex-serviceman Minority Hill Boarder Area General
11. Whether the project for Manufacturing unit/Business/Service unit (Mark √)

12. Name of the project/business activity proposed:
13. Amount of loan required (in ₹)
    Building type (own/leased/rented) Capital Expenditure Loan Working capital/cash credit limit Total
14. Details of earlier or current Loan/Grant and Subsidy availed from Central/State Govt., Scheme/ or any other similar scheme.

Activity of the Project with Address Amount (in ₹) Year of Sanction

I certify that all information furnished by me is true; and that I and any of my dependant have not borrowed any money under Subsidy Linked Scheme from any Central/State Government or Bank for establishing any such project.

Date **Signature of the applicant**

Note:

- Own contribution must be invested 5% for SC/ST/OBC/PHC/Women/Ex-servicemen/North East Region/Hill Border Area and 10% for General.
- Total Project Cost should not exceed ₹ 25 lakh for Manufacturing unit ₹ 10 lakh for Business/ Service unit.
- Applicant will not be entitled for additional Margin Money (Subsidy) in case of Own Contribution over and above the prescribed limit.
- VIIIth pass for Manufacturing Unit above ₹ 10 lakh project cost and under Service Sector above ₹ 5 lakh.
- Application should be submitted complete in all respect along with attested copies of the following documents:
    1. Certificate of qualification-academic and technical (if project cost above ₹ 5 lakh under business/ service industry or above ₹ 10 lakh under Manufacturing industry.)
    2. Relevant Certificate for SC/ST/OBC/Minority/Ex-servicemen/PHC
    3. If Entrepreneur Development Programme (EDP) training undergone (at least for two weeks) then submit photocopy of the certificate.

For Official Use only (Rejected/To be placed before District Task Force Committee)
Reasons (if rejected):

Place: **Signature, Name and Designation of Officer**

Date: **KVIC/KVIB/DIC**

9 LEGAL ISSUES FOR THE ENTREPRENEUR

Introduction, What is Intellectual Property? Legal Issues in Setting up the Organisation, Patents, Categories of Patents, The Patent Application, Patent Infringement, Trademark, Trademark Registration, Categories of Trademarks, Copyright, Infringement of Copyright, Trade Secrets, Licensing, Summing Up.

Introduction

In the year 1947, the **General Agreement of Tariff and Trade (GATT)** came into existence. International trade got regulated in accordance with terms of this agreement. It was felt over the year that the agreement needed to be upgraded. There was trade negotiation and discussions among the nations for evolving a universally acceptable and applicable agreement.

During the 1980s **Multinational Corporation and International Agencies** began showing interest for including intellectual property as an area of discussions at the GATT. The developed nations wanted statutory protection for their intellectual property, i.e., patents, trademarks and designs that were being infringed on a large-scale in the developing countries. The developing countries exploited the commercial benefits of such intellectual property without being made liable in any manner for the damages caused to the interest of the developed nations who invested considerable funds in research and development. Of such intellectual property, was their argument, for example, the formula of drugs available in India is often borrowed from the results of research and trial undertaken in other developed nations. Developed nations were helpless in protecting their inventions and innovations. In the absence of universal legal provinces, each country followed its domestic legislation on intellectual property law, which were often or even in some cases absent. The developed nations therefore, actively started campaigning for a universally applicable and enforceable system on Intellectual Property Law. In 1986 the Uruguay Round of negotiation began under the GATT which concluded in Marrakesh on 15 April with signing of "Final Act". This final act contains 28 agreements, TRIPS being one of them. One of the discussions taken in Marrakesh was formation of the world trade organization. WTO agreement is a package deal. The member countries have to accept all of the agreement *in toto* and cannot opt out of any one of the provisions without quitting WTO itself.

What is Intellectual Property?

Intellectual property includes patents, trademarks, copyrights, and trade secrets which represents important assets to the entrepreneur and should be understood even before engaging the services of an attorney. Too often entrepreneurs, because of their lack of understanding of intellectual property, ignore important steps that they should have taken to protect these assets.

Legal Issues in Setting up the Organisation

There are many options that an entrepreneur can choose in setting up an organization, it will be necessary to understand all the advantages and disadvantages of each, regarding such issues as liability, taxes, continuity, transferability of interest, cost of setting up, and attractiveness for raising capital. Legal advice for these agreements is necessary to ensure that the most appropriate decisions have been made.

Patents

Patents refers to a grant of some privileges, property or the authority made by the Government or the Sovereign of the country to one or more individuals. The instruments by which such grant is made is known as 'Patents'.

The patents give the entrepreneurs a right to prevent anyone else from making, using or selling the defined invention. Moreover, if an inventor has been granted a patent, in the process of producing or marketing the invention he or she may find that it infringes on the patent rights of others.

Categories of Patents

(1) ***Utility Patents:*** Utility patents basically grants the owner protection from anyone else making, using, and /or selling the identified invention and generally reflects protection of new, useful, and unobvious processes such as film developing, machines such as photocopier, compositions of matter such as chemical compounds or mixture of ingredients, and articles of manufacture such as the toothpaste pump. A utility patents has term of 20 years, beginning of the date of filing patents and trademark office (PTO).

(2) ***Design Patents:*** Covering new, original, ornamental, and unobvious designs for articles of manufacture, a design patent reflects the appearances of an object. These patents are granted for 14 years terms and like the utility patent, provide the inventor with a negative right excluding the others from making, using, or selling an article having the ornamental appearances given in the drawings included in the patent.

(3) ***Plant Patents:*** These are issued under the same provisions as utility patents and are for new varieties of plants.

The Patent Application

The patent application must contain a complete history and description of the inventions as well as claims for it usefulness. In general, patent application will contain the contents of provision and complete specification to be filled with the application describing the invention, method of performing, claim of invention and the provision for technical informations, along with the provision for international application for invention, respectively

Patent Infringement

A patent confers the exclusive right on the patentee to make, distribute or sell the invention in India. An infringement would be when any of these rights is violated. A patentee may assign a license all or some of these rights. The exercise of the right so transferred in favor of the assignee or the licensee by the assignor or the licensor would not amount to infringement of the patent.

In case of the product patent, the rights of the patentee are increased by anyone who makes or supplies that substance commercially. In case of process patent, the use of such a method or process in India by anyone or other than the patentee amounts to infringement.

Whether the act of person other than the patentee amounts to infringement or not would depend upon:

(a) the extent of the monopoly right conferred by the patent which is interpreted from the specifications and claims contained in the application of the patentee. Any action which falls outside the scope of the claims would not amount to infringement.

(b) whether he is infringing any of the monopoly right of the patentee to make, distribute or sell the invention.

Trademark

The Trade and Merchandise Marks Act was passed in the year 1958. Since then it had been amended several times. Moreover, in view of developments in trading and commercial practices, increasing globalization of trade and industry, the need to encourage investment flows and transfer of technology and the need to simplify and harmonize trademark management systems, it was considered necessary to bring out comprehensive legislation on the subject. Accordingly the Trademarks Bills, 1999, was introduced in the parliament.

Trademarks Act, 1999, define a mark as:

'Mark' includes a device, brand, heading, label, ticket, name, signature, word, letter, shape of goods, packaging or combination of colours numeral shape of goods, packaging or combination of colours or any combination thereof.

Trademark Registration

Filing of the trademark registration must meet four requirements:

(1) Completion of the writing form;

(2) A drawing of the mark;

(3) Five Specimens showing actual use of the mark;

(4) Each trademark must be applied separately.

Upon receipt of this information, the PTO assigns a serial number to the application and sends a filing receipt to the applicant.

Accepted trademark is published in the Trademark Official Gazette to allow any party 30 days to oppose or request an extension to oppose. If no opposition is filed, the registration is issued. The trademark is given an initial 20 years registration with 20 years renewable terms. In the fifth to sixth year, the registrant is required to file an affidavit with the PTO indicating that the mark is currently in commercial use. If no affidavit is filed, the registration is cancelled.

Categories of Trademarks

There are four categories of trademarks:

(1) ***Coined Marks:*** Coined marks denote no relationships between the mark and goods or services and afford the possibility of expansion to a wide range of products. For instance; Mercedes, Kodak.

(2) ***Arbitrary Marks:*** An arbitrary mark is one that has another meaning in other languages and is applied to a product or service. For instance, apple.

(3) ***Suggestive Marks:*** Suggestive mark is used to suggest certain features, qualities, ingredients, or characteristics of a product or service. It differs from an arbitrary mark in that it tends to suggest some describable attributes of the products or services. For instance, Halo Shampoo.

(4) ***Descriptive Marks:*** Descriptive marks must have become distinctive over a significant period of time and gained consumer recognition before it can be registered. The mark then is considered to have secondary meaning, that is, it is descriptive of particular product or service. For instance; Rubberoid as applied to roofing materials that contain rubber.

Copyright

Copyright is a unique kind of intellectual property. *The right which person acquires in a work, which is a result of his intellectual labour, is called his copyright.* The primary function of copyright law is to protect the fruits of man's work, labour, skill or test from being taken away by other people.

The copyright law has become especially relevant because of the tremendous growth of the use of the Internet, especially to download music, literary work, pictures, and videos, to name a few. Although software was added to copyright law in 1980, the issues surrounding access to material on the Internet has led to major legal battles for the entertainment industry.

The statutory definition of copyright means the exclusive right to do or authorize other(s) to do certain acts in relation to –

(1) Literary, dramatic or musical works;
(2) Artistic work;
(3) Cinematograph film; and
(4) Sound recording.

Registration of Copyright

Copyrights are registered with the Library of Congress and will not usually require an attorney. All that is necessary is that the form, two copies of the work and the appropriate fee be sent to the Register of Copyrights. The term of copyright is the life of the author plus 50 years. If the author is an institution, the term of copyright is 75 years from publication.

Infringement of Copyright

A copyright grants protection to the creator of original work and prevents such work from being copied or reproduced without consent. The creator of a work can prohibit anyone from:

(1) Reproducing the work in any form, such as print, sound, video, etc.;
(2) Recording the work in compact disks, cassettes, etc.;
(3) Broadcasting it in any form;
(4) Translating it into other languages; and
(5) Using the work for a public performance, such as a stage drama or musical performance.

A Copyright is infringed when someone, without the permission of the copyright holder, does any of the above, which only the copyright holder has the exclusive right to do. The Copyright Act provides for both civil and criminal remedies for infringement of copyrights. The Registrar of Copyrights has the power to prevent the import of infringing copies.

Trade Secrets

An entrepreneur may prefer to maintain an idea or process as confidential and to sell or license it as a trade secret. Trade secret is recognized under a governing body of common law in each state. Employees involved in working with an idea or process may be asked to first sign a confidential information agreement that will be protect against their giving out the trade secret either while an employee or after leaving the organization. The holder of the trade secret has the right to sue any signee who breaches such an agreement.

Licensing

Licensing is an important marketing strategy for entrepreneurs who wish to start a new venture but need permission to copy or incorporate the patent, trademark, or copyright with their ideas. Licensing may be defined as an agreement between two parties, where one party has proprietary rights over some information, process, or technology protected by a patent, trademark, or copyright. This arrangement, specified in a contract, requires the licensee to pay a royalty or some other specified sum to the holder of the proprietary rights in return for permission to copy the patent, trademark, or copyright.

Summing Up

Introduction

The developing countries exploited the commercial benefits of such intellectual property without being made liable in any manner for the damages caused to the interest of the developed nations who invested considerable funds in research and development. Developed nations were helpless in protecting their inventions and innovations. In their absence of universal legal provinces, each country followed its domestic legislation on intellectual property law, which were often lacks or even in some cases absent. The developed nations therefore, actively started campaigning for a universally applicable and enforceable system on Intellectual Property Law.

What is intellectual property?

Intellectual property includes patents, trademarks, copyrights, and trade secrets represent important assets to the entrepreneur and should be understood even before engaging the services of an attorney. Too often entrepreneurs, because of their lack of understanding of intellectual property, ignore important steps that they should have taken to protect these assets.

Patents

Patents refers to a grant of some privileges, property or the authority made by the Government or the Sovereign of the country to one or more individuals.

Categories of Patents

Utility patents; Design patents; and Plant patents: These are issued under the same provisions as utility patents and are for new varieties of plants.

The Patent Application

The patent application must contain a complete history and description of the inventions as well as claims for its usefulness. In general, patent application will contain the contents of provision and complete specification to be filled with the application describing the invention, method of performing, claim of invention and the provision for technical information's, along with the provision for international application for invention, respectively

Patent Infringement

An infringement would be when any of these rights is violated. Whether the act of person other than the patentee amounts to infringement or not would depend upon:

(a) the extent of the monopoly right conferred by the patent which is interpreted from the specifications and claims contained in the application of the patentee. Any action which falls outside the scope of the claims would not amount to infringement.

(b) whether he is infringing any of the monopoly right of the patentee to make, distribute or sell the invention.

Trademarks Act, 1999 define a mark as: 'Mark' includes a device, brand, heading, label, ticket, name, signature, word, letter, shape of goods, packaging or combination of colours numeral shape of goods, packaging or combination of colours or any combination thereof.

Trademark Registration

Filing of the trademark registration must meet four requirements:

(1) Completion of the writing form;
(2) A drawing of the mark;
(3) Five Specimens showing actual use of the mark;
(4) Each trademark must be applied separately.

Upon receipt of this information, the PTO assigns a serial number to the application and sends a filing receipt to the applicant.

Accepted trademark is published in the Trademark Official Gazette to allow any party 30 days to oppose or request an extension to oppose. If no opposition is filed, the registration is issued. The trademark is given an initial 20 years registration with 20 years renewable terms. In the fifth to sixth year, the registrant is required to file an affidavit with the PTO indicating that the mark is currently in commercial use. If no affidavit is filed, the registration is cancelled.

Categories of Trademarks

There are four categories of trademarks:Coined marks; Arbitrary marks; Suggestive marks; and Descriptive marks

Copyright

The statutory definition of copyright means the exclusive right to do or authorize other(s) to do certain acts in relation to –

(1) Literary, dramatic or musical works;
(2) Artistic work;
(3) Cinematograph film; and
(4) Sound recording.

Registration of Copyright

Copyrights are registered with the Library of Congress and will not usually require an attorney. All that is necessary is that the form, two copies of the work and the appropriate fee be sent to the Register of Copyrights. The term of copyright is the life of the author plus 50 years. If the author is an institution, the term of copyright is 75 years from publication.

Infringement of Copyright

A copyright grants protection to the creator of original work and prevents such work from being copied or reproduced without consent. The creator of a work can prohibit anyone from:

(1) Reproducing the work in any form, such as print, sound, video, etc.;
(2) Recording the work in compact disks, cassettes, etc.;
(3) Broadcasting it in any form;
(4) Translating it into other languages; and
(5) Using the work for a public performance, such as a stage drama or musical performance.

A Copyright is infringed when someone, without the permission of the copyright holder, does any of the above, which only the copyright holder has the exclusive right to do. The Copyright Act provides for both civil and criminal remedies for infringement of copyrights. The Registrar of Copyrights has the power to prevent the import of infringing copies.

Trade Secrets

An entrepreneur may prefer to maintain an idea or process as confidential and to sell or license it as a trade secret. Trade secret is recognized under a governing body of common law in each state.

10 RELEVANT ACTS

Introduction, Factories Act, 1948, The Trade Union Act, 1926, Workmen's Compensation Act 1923, Employees State Insurance Act, 1948, The Shops and Establishments, Act, 1948 Summing Up.

Introduction

The Constitution of India maintains that the Union of India is a sovereign and a socialist republic. With this objective in mind, the Parliament of India has enacted various laws for the welfare and prevention of exploitation of the working class. The need was specially felt as the workers who were usually poor and powerless had no defence against the power of the industrialists. Also it was very easy to sack workers and find quick replacements due to the acute problem of unemployment that was existing, as even now it may be noted that some of the basic protection to the working class were enacted and made applicable to India before India got independence.

The modern industrial scenario has changed drastically. The workers are better organized into unions and there are increasing instances of employer-employee conflicts. This leads to loss of production as also a loss to the national economy. Labour legislation has been enacted to serve as a framework for the resolution of such conflicts as also the provision of basic amenities for the worker. The legislation is subjected to periodic review but the basic essence of the legislation remains the same. The legislation that are taken up are as under:

(1) Factories Act, 1948

(2) The Trade Union Act, 1926

(3) Workmen's Compensation Act, 1923

(4) Employees State Insurance Act, 1948

(5) Shops and Establishments Act, 1948

Factories Act, 1948

The Factories Act, 1948, was passed with the main objective of protecting the interest of the workers who were exploited a lot. The Act seeks to regulate the working conditions in factories, regulate health, safety and welfare measures, provide for annual paid leave and has a special provision for young people, women and children who may be working in factories.

The provisions of the Factories Act, 1948, are:

A. Safety Measures

(1) ***Fencing of machinery:*** Every moving part of the machinery and every dangerous part of the machinery has to be fenced to prevent contact with the workers, as it could result in accidents.

(2) ***Working with machinery in motion:*** The machinery that has to be examined or maintained in motion has to be operated by a trained person wearing tight clothes so that they do not get caught in the moving parts which could result in serious accidents.

(3) ***Employment of young people on dangerous machines:*** No young person can work on any machine unless he has been trained and has been made aware of dangers arising out of it.

(4) ***Striking gear and devices for cutting of powers:*** Suitable striking gear or some other mechanical appliances should be used and maintained for cutting off power; also driving belts should not be allowed to be in motion when not in use.

(5) ***Self-acting machines:*** Self-acting machines should be installed according to possibility and in dangerous condition so that the danger to workers is minimized.

(6) ***Prohibition of employment of women and children near cotton openers:*** No woman or children should be employed for pressing cotton where as cotton opener is at work.

(7) ***Pits, sumps, openings in floors etc:*** Any opening in the ground is dangerous to workers; all such openings should be covered or securely fenced.

(8) ***Excessive weights:*** No person should be asked to lift carry or shift a heavy load that is likely to cause an injury to him.

(9) ***Protection to eyes:*** Suitable screens or goggles should be provided for the protection of the eyes of the persons wherever there is danger of the eyes getting harmed.

(10) ***Precautions against dangerous fumes:*** No person shall be allowed to enter any enclosed space that is likely to contain dangerous fumes.

(11) ***Precautions in case of fire:*** Easy escape routes should be provided to the workers in case of fire. Care should be taken to remove all sorts of likely causes of blockades like door locks, fasteners, etc. Escape exits and fire escape routes should be clearly painted in a language that the workers can read and understand.

(12) ***Safety of building and machinery:*** The factory, inspectors should serve a notice to employer if they find a building or machinery risky to the workers. He can give his opinion in regard to the measures to be taken to reduce the risk.

(13) ***Maintenance of the buildings:*** The buildings should be properly maintained in such a manner so as to avoid any danger to the worker.

B. Working Hours

The Factories Act, 1948, specifies the following about the number of working hours:

I. For Adults

(1) No adult worker should be allowed to work in a factory for more than 48 hours per week.

(2) The workers should get one day off per week as a weekly holiday.

(3) The worker should get a compensatory holiday if he works on a holiday.

(4) The worker should not be allowed to work for more than 9 hours a day in the factory.

(5) The worker should be given half an hour of rest after every five hours that he works.

(6) In case of the spread over duty, no worker should be made to work for more than ten and half hours including the period of rest.

(7) The worker should be paid over-time, if he has to work for more than 9 hours in a day.

(8) Generally, no women shall work in the factory between 7 p.m. and 6 a.m. and in no case between 10 p.m. and 5 a.m.

II. For Children

(1) No child below 14 years can be employed in the factory.

(2) Those children who work in the factory should not be made to work for more than four and five hours per day and between 7 p.m. and 6 a.m.

C. Health Measures

The health measure pertaining to the health of the workers mentioned in the Factories Act, 1948, are:

(1) All measures should be taken to ensure that the factory is clean and free from the effluents.

(2) Proper arrangement should be made to disperse the wastes and effluents.

(3) All work places should be adequately ventilated and proper temperature maintained.

(4) No room in the factory should be overcrowded so as to risk a life of the worker.

(5) All the parts of the factory wherein the workers work or pass should be well lit, be it natural light or artificial.

(6) Arrangement for safe drinking water should be made in the factory at convenient points.

(7) There should adequate toilet facilities, well ventilated and well lit with separate facilities for men and women.

(8) Spittoons should be provided within the easy reach, so that workers do not spit and dirty the place.

D. Welfare Measures

The Factories Act, 1948, specifies that the factories should compulsorily provide certain minimum welfare measures to the workers and the measures are:

(1) Washing facilities should be provided at easily accessible points separately for men and women.

(2) There should be provision for storing and drying clothes.

(3) There should be facilities for sitting as far as possible as a worker gets tired faster when standing.

(4) All first aid facilities should be provided to be used by the worker in case of injury.

(5) There should be a canteen maintained by the employer when there are more than 250 workers employed in the factory.

(6) Shelters and rest-rooms should be provided by the employer wherein more than 150 workers are employed in the factory.

(7) Crèches for children upto age 6 years should be provided in the factories employing more than 30 women.

(8) Welfare officers should be appointed in the factories employing more than 500 workers.

Penalties for Violation of the Factories Act, 1948

(1) ***Penalty for offences:*** The penalty for the violation of the provisions of the Factories Act, 1948, are

(a) Imprisonment for the period of upto 3 months or

(b) A fine of upto ₹ 2,000/- or

(c) Both fine and imprisonment as mentioned above.

(2) ***Penalty for the repetition of offence:*** An employer convicted for repeating the offence of violation of the Factories Act, 1948, for the second time can be sentenced to 6 months imprisonment and fine of upto ₹ 5,000/-.

(3) ***Penalty for obstruction of Inspectors:*** Any employer who conceals or fails to present the documents asked for by the inspectors or prevents any worker from testifying before the inspectors can be imprisoned for a period of upto 3 months or a fine of upto ₹ 500 or both depending on the severity of the case.

(4) ***Penalty for offence by workers:*** Any worker violating the provisions of the Factories Act, 1948, can be fined an amount of upto ₹ 20/-.

The Trade Union Act, 1926

In India, there is an acute problem of unemployment. Hence, lot of workers can be easily available. This gives an upper hand to the industrialists who tend to exploit the workers. Also, if the worker has any problem the industrialist (employer) would either not meet the worker or does not care about its solution. So with a view to protect the interests of the workers and safeguard workers unity. Unions have been formed with an objective of collective bargaining from the employer.

The trade union can be defined as any combination temporary or permanent that is formed with the intention of regulating the relations between

(a) Workmen and employers; or
(b) Workmen and workmen; or
(c) Employers and employers.

The aims and objectives of the trade union are:

(1) To secure fair and favourable treatment to employees.
(2) To safeguard common labour interests.
(3) To solve labour problems by negotiating with the employers on behalf of the workers based on the principle of collective bargaining.
(4) To ensure the safety of workers.
(5) To enhance the opportunities for promotion and professional training.
(6) To secure educational, cultural and recreational facilities.
(7) To secure a platform to express ideas in the decision making process on matters concerning the workers.

The main principle of the trade union is the collective bargaining capacity. The trade union can force the employer to come to terms with its demands by the use of strikes, slow production tactics etc., if negotiations fail. The total production process can be brought to a standstill if there is only one union for the company and it has a strong following.

The Trade Union Act, was enacted and made applicable to India with a view to legitimize and regulate the trade unions i.e., the voice of the workers. The main provisions of this Act are :

(1) ***Registration:*** Registration of the Trade Union is not compulsory but it is desirable as only, then can the officers and members claim immunity against civil and criminal proceedings in certain cases. The formalities for registration are :

At least seven members who wish to form a trade union should apply to the Registrar of Trade Unions of the state where the trade union is to be located. The trade union would be only registered if the Executive Committee is constituted and certain other provisions of the Act are met.

(2) ***Cancellation of Registration:*** Registration of a Trade Union can be cancelled if:

(a) The Trade Union applies to do so.
(b) The Registration is obtained by fraud.
(c) The Trade Union has ceased to exist.
(d) The Trade Union has contravened any provisions of the Act.

The Registrar of Trade Unions has to act in cases 'b', 'c' and 'd' but after issuing a two months written notice to the Trade Union citing the reason.

(3) ***Dissolution of the Union:*** The Union can be dissolved after issuing a notice to the Registrar of Trade Unions signed by the secretary and seven members of the union within 14 days of the dissolution.

(4) ***Membership:*** The right to be a member of the Trade Union is available to the person who is above 15 years of age. However, an executive member should be atleast 18 years of age, should not be convicted and sentenced to imprisonment by any court for any offence involving moral turpitude unless 5 years have passed since his release.

(5) ***Legal Protection to the Trade Union against Civil and Criminal Actions:*** The Trade Union is legally protected against

   (a) Being charged as a criminal conspiracy.

   (b) Certain types of suits pertaining to the Trade Union in the civil courts.

(6) ***Funds:*** The Trade Unions may have a fund from the contribution of its members which can be used to further the political and general interests of its members.

(7) ***Auditing:*** It is obligatory on the part of registered Trade Union to send the Registrar of Trade Unions an audited statement of its income and expenses, assets and liabilities, every year.

Workmen's Compensation Act, 1923

Workmen's Compensation Act, 1923, can be considered to be a Welfare Act. It is the main protective Act of the labour class of India and has been amended to include fresh provisions that are needed in modern times due to the changes in circumstances. However, the basic essence of the Act remains the same. So it is essential to have a good idea of the Act. This Act is applicable to the whole of India except Jammu and Kashmir and in cases of negligence of the worker. Its aim is to prevent accident and in case of accident to provide compensation to the workers depending on the injuries sustained while on duty. It imposes legal obligations on the employers to compensate the workers. This makes the employees to take suitable measures either by using new technology or proper safety training to avoid accidents.

Criteria for compensation by the employer

The criteria for the liability of the employer to pay compensation in case of death or injury of the worker due to an accident while on duty depend on the following conditions:

(a) It should be proved that the injury to the worker is caused while on duty in case of instantaneous injury or death.

(b) It should be proved that the injury was caused during the course of the workers employment in case of injury which was caused over a period of time.

(c) It should be proved that the injury was caused due to the work assigned to the workers.

(d) It should be proved that the injury was caused and enhanced due to the work and the resulting strain from the work.

Wages

Wages are well defined in "the Act as the compensation given". It is calculated on the basis of its wages as per the Act as under:

(a) One twelfth of the total wages of the worker if he was employed for the previous 12 months.

(b) An average monthly wages of a worker doing identical work under the same employer or in the same locality if there was no worker employed by the same employer. This is to be considered when the worker has worked for the period of less than one month.

(c) 30 times the daily wages of a worker in all other cases.

Amount payable as compensation

The amount payable to the worker as compensation for an injury would depend upon which category his injury falls in. there are four categories of injuries:

(a) Injury leading to death;
(b) Injury leading to permanent total disablement;
(c) Injury leading to permanent partial disablement;
(d) Injury leading to temporary disablement.

(a) ***Compensation payable in case of injury leading to death:*** In case of an injury sustained by a worker in the course of his work resulting in his death, then the compensation is to be paid by the employer to his dependant. The amount would depend on the wages of the worker as specified in the Act. The Act specifies 20 slabs for the compensation depending on the wages. The compensation should be paid in one lump sum.

(b) ***Compensation in case of injury leading to permanent total disablement:*** When the injury to a worker does not result in death, but complete and permanent disablement, then the amount of compensation would be decided again on the basis of the wages earned by the worker. The Act specifies the slabs for the compensation. The permanent total disablement would mean a disablement that has completely destroyed the earning capability of the worker as a result of the injury.

(c) ***Compensation payable in case of the injury leading to permanent partial disablement:*** Permanent partial disablement would mean a disablement that has partly affected the earning capability of the worker as a result of the injury. In other words, the worker can work but not as a normal person. The amount payable in the case would depend on the extent of percentage of the permanent partial disablement. In this case, the worker is entitled to receive periodic payment to make good his earning capacity.

(d) ***Compensation to be payable in case of the injury leading to temporary disablement:*** Temporary disablement would mean a disablement of the worker that has affected his earning capability for the short period of time as a result of the injury. This disablement should continue for minimum 3 days or more after the day of the accident, i.e., in the case of the injury.

In this case too, the worker is eligible for compensation based on his wages for as long a period as he suffers from the disablement the compensation can be given periodically.

Occupational diseases

Occupational diseases are those that a worker gets due to the type of the job he does over a period of time. For instance, cement factory workers are bound to suffer from dust allergies. The Act has identified many occupations which result in occupational diseases and has indicated the type of disablement and compensation payable under each of them.

Officials responsible for the implementations of the Act

The medical examination of the injured worker should be done by a qualified doctor without any charge. The worker may forfeit his right to compensation in cases where he has to be present in the person for medical examination and he has not done so.

Normally, all cases of death and permanent total disablement are referred to the Commissioner of the workmen's compensation who decides on the case and the mode of payment in case of death of the worker. The Commissioner has to initiate action within 10 days of receipt on the information. The employer has to deposit the amount due to the worker (i.e., dependants) with the Commissioner.

If the parties are dissatisfied by the decision of the Commissioner, then they can approach the High Court. Also, the Commissioner can refer a question of law to the High Court for a decision and act according to the decision.

Employees State Insurance Act, 1948

The Employees State Insurance Act, can be termed as an act to serve as social security to the worker. It aims at striving for the social and economic justice to the labour class.

There is a certain maximum salary limit set to be eligible for the ESI scheme. This limit is changed from time to time by the government. Under this Act, medical care is provided and in case of the death of the worker due to the injury, pension is provided to the dependants of the workers. The benefits under the E.S.I. Act, can be classified into the following categories. They are:

(1) Sickness Benefits;
(2) Maternity Benefits;
(3) Disablement Benefits;
(4) Dependents Benefits;
(5) Medical Benefits; and
(6) Funeral Benefits.

(1) *Sickness Benefits:* An employee insured by the E.S.I. Act is given periodical payment when the sickness is certified by the duly appointed medical practitioner.

Sickness benefit is given to the person under the following conditions:

(1) The sickness of the person who is insured occurs during the benefit period and the contribution for the corresponding period payable with regard to the insured person for not less than thirteen weeks has been made.
(2) The benefit is payable for a maximum number of 91 days in any continuous period of 365 days.
(3) No benefit is payable for an initial period of 2 days in between two successive claims for sickness benefits, if he falls sick again within a time span of 15 days.
(4) The daily rate of the sickness benefit is an amount equivalent to one half the assumed average daily wages.
(5) Claims for extended sickness benefits may also be entertained if the E.S.I. considers the circumstances of the case based on the medical certificate issued to the person by an Insurance Medical Officer.

(2) *Maternity Benefits:* The Act provides for periodical payments in case of confinement or miscarriage or the sickness arising out of pregnancy, confinement, premature birth or miscarriage, to an insured woman worker certified for such payment.

The daily rate of the maternity benefits is twice the standard rate of benefit corresponding to the full average daily wages of the woman concerned during the corresponding contribution period.

This benefit is payable for a maximum of 12 weeks.

(3) *Disablement Benefits:* Disablement benefits are payable for employment-related injuries which include occupational diseases, at the following rates, in case of:

(a) Temporary disablement, the cash payment is to be made at the full rate during the period of disability provided it lasts for more than 7 days. The full rate means 62.5 percent of the average daily wages of the concerned person during the preceding 58 weeks.
(b) Permanent partial disablement, the cash payment is to be made at certain percentage of the full rate depending on the loss of earning capacity.
(c) Permanent total disablement, the cash benefit is to be paid at the full rate for the full life span of the concerned person.

(4) *Dependants Benefits:* Dependants benefits are given to the dependants of insured person whose death has occurred as a result of the employment related injury. The rates applicable are as follows:

(a) An amount of 3/5th of the full rate would be paid to the widow during her life or till remarriage.

(b) An amount of 2/5th of the full rate would be paid to each legitimate or adopted son until the age of 18 years.

(c) An amount of 2/5th of the full rate to each legitimate unmarried daughter until the age of 15 years of marriage whichever is earlier.

(d) The dependants benefits may be paid to the parents of the deceased person if he does not have any of the above.

(e) The total sum to be distributed among the dependants, however, should not exceed a sum equal to full rate.

5. *Medical Benefits:* All the previous benefits only give the benefits in the form of cash. The medical benefits are given in kind. The benefits under this category are :

(a) Free medical treatment in case of the sickness, employment injury and maternity.

(b) The treatment may be either at an E.S.I. dispensary or at the hospital visited by insurance doctors.

(c) The medical benefits are also extended to the family of the insured person.

(d) Expenses are given or arrangement done to provide artificial limbs, artificial teeth and spectacles free of cost.

(e) Ambulance and other forms of transport are also made available free of cost.

6. *Funeral Benefits:* In case of death of an insured employee, the funeral benefit is to be paid to the eldest surviving member of the family or to the person who would spend money on the funeral of the deceased. This claim must be made within three months of the death of the insured person.

Shops and Establishments Act, 1948

Shops and Establishments Act, to provide for the regulation of conditions of work and employment in shops, commercial establishments, restaurants, theatres and other establishments and for matters connected therewith.

Registration of Establishments and renewal of registration certificates:

(1) Within the period specified, the employer of every establishment shall send to the Inspector concerned, a statement in the prescribed form together with such fees as may be prescribed, containing:

- (a) The name of the employer and the manager, if any;
- (b) The postal address of the establishment;
- (c) The name, if any, of the establishment;
- (d) Category of the establishment; and
- (e) Such other particulars as may be prescribed.

(2) On receipt of the statement and the fees, the Inspector shall, on being satisfied about the correctness of the statement, register the establishment in the Register of Establishments in such manner as may be prescribed and shall issue in the prescribed form a registration certificate to the employer who shall display it at a prominent place in the establishment.

(3) The period in respect of establishments mentioned in (i) below for filing the statement and depositing the fees as required shall be as specified against it in column (2) above.

Establishments Period

(i) Establishments existing on the date on which this Act comes into force. Ninety days from the date on which the Act comes into force.

(ii) New Establishments, ninety days from the date on which the establishment commences its work.

(4) The Inspector may, on receipt of an application made by the employer together with the fees prescribed therefore, renew the registration certificate for a period not exceeding five years commencing from the date of its expiry.

(5) Every application for the renewal of the registration certificate shall be made in such form and in such manner as may be prescribed so as to reach the Inspector not later than thirty days before the date of its expiry, Provided that an application for the renewal of a registration certificate received not later than thirty days after its expiry may be entertained by the Inspector on the applicant paying such penalty, not exceeding twenty-five rupees, as may be prescribed.

(6) An applicant for the renewal of a registration certificate shall, until communication of orders on his application, be entitled to act as if the registration certificate had been renewed.

(7) In the event of any doubt or difference of opinion between an employer and the Inspector as to the category to which an establishment would belong, the Inspector shall refer the matter to the prescribed authority which shall after such inquiry as it thinks proper decide the category of such establishment and its decision shall be final for the purposes of this Act.

Maintenance of registers, records etc

(1) Subject to the control of the Government, an employer shall maintain such registers and records and display such notices, as may be prescribed. All such registers and records shall be kept, and all such notices shall be displayed on the premises of the establishment to which they relate.

(2) Every employer shall on demand produce or cause to be produced for inspection by an Inspector all registers, records and notices required to be kept by or under this Act.

(3) Every employer shall submit such returns relating to his business, in such manner and within such period, and to such authority as may be prescribed.

(4) Every employer shall give an order of appointment to his employee in the establishment before such employee joins the service, provided that in the case of an employee in the service at the commencement of this Act, the employer shall give such order of appointment within a period of three months from the date of such commencement.

Summing Up

Introduction

The Constitution of India maintains that the Union of India is a sovereign and a socialist republic. With this objective in mind, the Parliament of India has enacted various laws for the welfare and prevention of exploitation of the working class. The modern industrial scenario has changed drastically. The workers are better organized into unions and there are increasing instances of employer-employee conflicts. This leads to loss of production as also a loss to the national economy. Labour legislation has been enacted to serve as a framework for the resolution of such conflicts as also the provision of basic amenities for the worker. The legislation is subjected to periodic review but the basic essence of the legislation remains the same. The legislation *viz.,* Factories Act, 1948; Workmen's Compensation Act, 1923; E.S.I. Act and The Trade Union Act, 1926, are undertaken.

Factories Act, 1948

The Factories Act, 1948, was passed with the main objectives of protecting the interest of the workers who were an exploited lot. The Act seeks to regulate the working conditions in factories, regulate health, safety and welfare measures, provides for annual paid leave and has a special provision for young people, women and children who may be working in factories.

The provisions of the Factories Act, 1948, are: Safety measures; working hours; health measures; and welfare measures

Penalties for violation of the Factories Act, 1948

Penalty for offences; Penalty for the repetition of offence; Penalty for obstruction of Inspectors; and Penalty for offence by workers

The Trade Union Act, 1926

In India, there is an acute problem of unemployment. Hence, lot of workers can be easily available. This gives an upper hand to the industrialists who tend to exploit the workers. Also, if the worker has any problem the industrialist (employer) would either not meets the worker or does not care about its solution. So with a view to protect the interests of the workers and safeguard workers unity, unions have been formed with an objective of collective bargaining from the employer.

The trade union can be defined as any combination temporary or permanent that is formed with the intention of regulating the relations between

(a) Workmen and employers or
(b) Workmen and workmen or
(c) Employers and employers.

The Trade Union Act, was enacted and made applicable to India with a view to legitimize and regulate the trade unions, i.e., the voice of the workers. The main provisions of this Act are:

Registration; Cancellation of registration; Dissolution of the Union; Membership; Legal Protection to the Trade Union against Civil and Criminal Actions; Funds; and Auditing

Workmen's Compensation Act, 1923

Workmen's Compensation Act, 1923, can be considered to be a Welfare Act. It is the main protective Act of the labour class of India and has been amended to include fresh provisions that are needed in modern times due to the changes in circumstances. However, the basic essence of the Act remains the same. So it is essential to have a good idea of the Act. This Act is applicable to the whole of India except Jammu and Kashmir and in cases of negligence of the worker. Its aim is to prevent accident and in case of accident to provide compensation to the workers depending on the injuries sustained while on duty. It imposes legal obligations on the employers to compensate the workers. This makes the employees to take suitable measures either by using new technology or proper safety training to avoid accidents.

Criteria for compensation by the employer

The criteria for the liability of the employer to pay compensation in case of death or injury of the worker due to an accident while on duty depend on the following conditions:

(a) It should be proved that the injury to the worker is caused while on duty in case of instantaneous injury or death.

(b) It should be proved that the injury was caused during the course of the workers, employment in case of injury which was caused over a period of time.

(c) It should be proved that the injury was caused due to the work assigned to the workers.

(d) It should be proved that the injury was caused and enhanced due to the work and the resulting strain from the work.

Wages

Wages are well defined in "the Act as the compensation given".

Amount payable as compensation

The amount payable to the worker as compensation for an injury would depend upon which category his injury falls in. there are four categories of injuries:

(a) Injury leading to death.

(b) Injury leading to permanent total disablement.

(c) Injury leading to permanent partial disablement.

(d) Injury leading to temporary disablement.

Compensation payable in case of injury leading to death; Compensation in case of injury leading to permanent total disablement; Compensation payable in case of the injury leading to permanent partial disablement; and Compensation to be payable in case of the injury leading to temporary disablement

Occupational Diseases

Occupational diseases are those that a worker gets due to the type of the job he does over a period of time. For instance, cement factory workers are bound to suffer from dust allergies. The Act has identified many occupations which result in occupational diseases and has indicated the type of disablement and compensation payable under each of them.

Officials responsible for the implementations of the Act

The medical examination of the injured worker should be done by a qualified doctor without any charge. The worker may forfeit his right to compensation in cases where he has to be present in the person for medical examination and he has not done so.

Normally, all cases of death and permanent total disablement are referred to the Commissioner of the workmen's compensation who decides on the case and the mode of payment in case of death of the worker. The Commissioner has to initiate action within 10 days of receipt of the information. The employer has to deposit the amount due to the worker (i.e., dependants) with the Commissioner.

If the parties are dissatisfied by the decision of the Commissioner, then they can approach the High Court. Also, the Commissioner can refer a question of law to the High Court for a decision and act according to the decision.

Employees State Insurance Act, 1948

The Employees State Insurance Act, can be termed as an act to serve as social security to the workers. It aims at striving for the social and economic justice to the labour class.

There is a certain maximum salary limit set to be eligible for the ESI scheme. This limit is changed from time to time by the government. Under this Act, medical care is provided and in case of the death of the worker due to the injury, pension is provided to the dependents of the workers. The benefits under the E.S.I. Act can be classified into the following categories. They are: Sickness Benefits; Maternity Benefits; Disablement Benefits; Dependants Benefits; Medical Benefits; and Funeral Benefits.

Shops and Establishments Act,1948

Shops and Establishments Act, to provide for the regulation of conditions of work and employment in shops, commercial establishments, restaurants, theatres and other establishments and for matters connected therewith.

11 SETTING UP A NEW VENTURE

Introduction, Role of small Scale Industries in Industrialization of India, Importance of Small-Scale Industries, Micro, Small & Medium Enterprises, Procedure for Registration of Micro, Small and Medium Enterprises in Goa, Registration of Small-Scale Industries Units, Benefits of Registering, Objectives of the Registration Scheme, Features of the Registration Scheme, Benefits of Provisional Registration, Procedure to get the Provisional Registration, Benefits of Permanent Registration, Procedure to get the Permanent Registration, Features of the Present Procedure for Registration, De-registration, Carrying on Business Clearance, Steps to Start a New Venture, Forms of Business Organizations, Factors Influencing a Suitable Form of Organisation, What is Value Added Tax ? Summing Up, Annexures.

Introduction

Over the years, the developing countries have adopted positive measures to defeat the forces of stagnation. To perform this gigantic task, well-considered and most suited policy of economic development has been framed. The growth process of these countries aims at accelerating the economic development to enhance the social welfare. Infact, the economic change is a part of a wider social change and the economic development is a long-term process of intrinsic growth. Therefore, the task of government policy making has a vital role to play. The policymakers face challenge in selecting the desired objectives and suitable alternatives for stimulating the economic growth. They also require doing a careful examination of the existing institutional framework, social values, economic requirements and their implications, keeping in view the need for rapid social and economic development of the economy.

Nowadays, most of the developing countries are following the thesis that industrialization is a process of growth and as such is organically linked both to the social and economic past and to the parallel processes of social and economic development. The thesis reaffirms the importance of industrialization as an effective means for solving the problems of economic and social progress in developing countries of the world.

Role of Small-scale Industries in Industrialization of India

India is often described as an underdeveloped country. The term 'underdeveloped' implies that the natural resources, manpower and material of the country have not been properly harnessed with the result that the people have to live in poverty. They are underfed and physically weak and their working capacity is low. 'Underdevelopment' implies that the level of real income and capital per head of population is low as judged by the standards in developed countries of North America and Western Europe. In underdeveloped countries, there is no large-scale application of the fruits of scientific and technological advances to agriculture and industry. Subsistence production is generally important for the people, the markets are comparatively narrow and manufacturing industry is usually unimportant.

In many developing countries, manpower is relatively abundant. It is, therefore, imperative that their full and effective utilization should become a focal point of socio-economic policies. Emphasis has to be laid on small-scale industries to absorb the surplus manpower in these countries.

The Small-scale Industry (SSI) has been recognized as one of the most appropriate means of developing the industrial economy of backward countries. Small-scale industries facilitate the tapping of resources which otherwise would remain unused. These resources included entrepreneurship, capital, labour and raw materials. SSIs can mobilize rural savings which may otherwise remain idle or may be spent on luxuries or channeled into non productive ventures. They are fairly labour intensive. Small-scale Industries create employment opportunities at a relatively low capital cost. In India, there is a basic problem of absorbing the surplus manpower in non-agricultural jobs and providing additional employment opportunities for the growing population.

Small-scale Industries contribute significantly to the strengthening of the industrial structure. Small-scale Industries serve as seed-beds of entrepreneurship. They serve the developing economy not only by their output of goods but also by functioning as a nursery of entrepreneurial and managerial talent. This role of Small-scale Industries is of decisive importance in any economy. Such industries lead to the creation of employment opportunities not only in large cities and towns but also in smaller towns and far-flung regions. The establishment of Small-scale Industries have made possible to reverse the current trend of the migration of the people from rural to urban areas.

Soon after independence our national leaders recognized the role of Small-scale Sector in the development of the economy of India and laid a solid foundation for its accelerated development through active policy support and creation of an institutional frame work. The Industrial Policy Resolutions of the Government of India, from 1948 to 1991, visualized integrated growth of both the large and small-scale sectors and recognized the social and economic contribution of Small-scale Sector. These Industrial Policy Resolutions states that the Government of India would stress the role of cottage and village and Small-scale Industries in the Development of the national economy. The policy further envisaged that the decentralized sector should acquire sufficient vitality to be self supporting and its development be integrated with that of the Large-scale Industry.

The concept, small-scale industry covers a wide range of activities and its definition changed from time to time. *The latest definition (July, 1990) of small-scale industries is quite broad-based. All industries with a capital investment of ₹ 20 lacs in plant and machinery are classified as small- scale industries. The smaller units with a capital investment of ₹ 2 lacs in plant and machinery are classified as tiny units. Units with a capital investment in plant and machinery varying between ₹ 20 lacs and ₹ 25 lacs are classified as ancillary industries.*

The development of small scale sector has been important in India because of the following reasons: **First,** the small-scale unit requires less capital outlay and at the same time, it provides more employment than the large-scale sector. **Second,** a small-scale unit does not require highly sophisticated technology. It can, therefore, be useful in backward areas where the people have yet to be trained to meet the challenge of sophisticated technology.

Importance of Small-scale Industries

Apart from their inherent usefulness in terms of numerical superiority, small-scale industries play a vital role in the economic growth of developing countries as discussed below:

(i) ***Utilization of Resources:*** Small-scale Industries facilitate the tapping of resources which otherwise would remain unused. These resources include entrepreneurship, capital labour and raw materials. They can mobilize rural savings which may otherwise remain idle or may be spent on luxuries or channeled into non-productive ventures.

(ii) ***Employment Generation:*** Since they are fairly labour-intensive small-scale industries create employment opportunities at a relatively low–capital cost. In India, there is basic problem of absorbing the surplus manpower in non-agricultural jobs and providing additional employment opportunities for the growing population.

(iii) ***Generation of Foreign Exchange:*** Small-scale Industries facilitate substantial foreign exchange savings and earnings. A wide range of consumer and simple produced goods, now being imported, can be economically produced domestically on a small scale basis.

(iv) ***Diversification of Industrial Structures:*** Small-scale Industries contribute significantly to the strengthening of the industrial structure. Many more articles can be produced economically by the small-scale industries than that of large-scale industries.

(v) ***Entrepreneurial Development:*** Small-scale Industries serve as seedbeds of entrepreneurship. They serve the developing economy not only by their output of goods but also by functioning as a nursery of entrepreneurial and managerial talent. This role of Small-scale Industries is of decisive importance in any economy where the industrial structure consists of a few large-scale and medium sized ones, on the one hand, and of large numbers of traditional industries such as artisan units, handicrafts and cottage industries on the other.

(vi) ***Reverses the Trend of Migration from Rural to Urban Areas:*** The concentration of industrial and other activities has given birth to the phenomenon of the so called pockets of development where economic and social change is achieved at much faster rate than in the outlying rural districts.This trend, although predominant, can be checked and corrected through the establishment of small-scale industries. For one thing, such industries lead to the creation of employment opportunities on a dispersed basis not only in large cities and towns but also in smaller towns and far flung regions. The establishment of small-scale industries would, therefore, make it possible to reverse the current trend of migration of the people from rural to urban areas.

Micro, Small and Medium Enterprises

The **'Micro, Small and Medium Enterprises Development (MSMED) Act – 2006,'** has been implemented by the Government of India with effect from **2nd October, 2006.** Under the Act, Enterprises (Industries) have been classified into four categories namely -

- Micro Enterprises;
- Small Enterprises;
- Medium Enterprises; and
- Large Enterprises.

The definition classifying Micro, Small, Medium and Large Enterprises is as given below:-

(a) Enterprises engaged in the manufacture or production of goods pertaining to any industry,

  (i) a micro enterprise, where the investment in plant and machinery does not exceed twenty-five lakh rupees;

  (ii) a small enterprise, where the investment in plant and machinery is more than twenty-five lakh rupees but does not exceed five crore rupees;

  (iii) a medium enterprise, where the investment in plant and machinery is more than five crore rupees but does not exceed ten crore rupees;

  (iv) a large enterprise, where the investment in plant and machinery is more than ten crore rupees

(b) Enterprises engaged in providing or rendering of services,

(i) a micro enterprise, where the investment in equipment does not exceed ten lakh rupees;

(ii) a small enterprise, where the investment in equipment is more than ten lakh rupees but does not exceed two crore rupees; or

(iii) a medium enterprise, where the investment in equipment is more than two crore rupees but does not exceed five crore rupees.

Procedure for Registration of Micro, Small and Medium Enterprises in Goa

The registration of Micro, Small and Medium Enterprises are done in two stages as follows:

Stage I- Provisional

The prospective entrepreneurs who intends to establish a micro or small enterprise or a medium enterprise engaged in manufacturing or production of goods or in providing or rendering or services, at his discretion has to file the Entrepreneurship Memorandum of Micro, Small or as the case may be, of Medium Enterprises, with District Industries Centre, Directorate of Industries, Trade and Commerce, Government of Goa.

The District Industries Centre on receipt of the Entrepreneurship Memorandum (EM) will fill all the codes in the EM and will issue an acknowledgment allotting Entrepreneurs Memorandum number, date of issued and Category of the unit within Five days of the receipt of the EM. This registration will be valid for two years.

The provisional registration formalities are simple and no elaborate details are required to be provided. However, any supporting documents while filling up the application should be provided, if the same are mentioned in it. It will be also be helpful to provide a brief note on the proposed project highlighting salient features.

Stage II- Permanent/Final

Once the Entrepreneur start the production or starts providing or rendering services they have to file of the Entrepreneurs Memorandum to District Industries Centre.

In case of non-filing of document of the EM within two years, Memorandum filed by the Entrepreneur will become invalid.

In case of change in the investment in plant and machinery or in equipment; or change of products and that of services or addition in products or service, the entrepreneur/enterprise which have already filed Entrepreneurs Memorandum has to inform the District Industries Centre of the same in writing within three months of the change.

Documents required for final/permanent registration

(1) N.O.C. from Directorate of Health Services/Primary Health Centre/Urban Health Centre/valid consent order to operate from Goa State Pollution Control Board as the case may be except in case of items specifically exempted by the Government under specific order/Notification from time to time.

(2) The unit listed under green category shall be exempted from obtaining NOC from Directorate of Health Services/Primary Health Centre/Urban Health Centre/valid consent order from Goa State Pollution Control Board and in that case only Departmental NOC for establishment of the unit is required to be produced. Until Government notifies the list of Green, Orange and Red Category, the present practice shall be followed.

(3) NOC/Trade License from Municipality/Village Panchayats /Corporation for the units established outside the Industrial Estate.

(4) NOC from the owner of the premises in the prescribed format.

(5) House tax payment receipt or any other documentary evidence like electricity bill, water charges bill, a letter from Municipality or Panchayats, etc.

(6) Partnership Deed in respect of Partnership firm duly registered with Registrar of Firms. Memorandum of Association and Articles of Association in respect of Private Limited/Limited Company, duly registered before Registrar of Companies.

(7) Excise license from Commissioner of Excise for liquor units, (alcohol-based products)

(8) Fruit product order for soft drinks and any fruit-based product.

(9) License from Directorate of Food and Drugs Administration for food, drugs, and pharmaceutical products.

(10) License from Inspectorate of Factories and Boilers for the unit having 10 or more workers working with power connection and for unit having 20 or more workers working without power connection. In such cases the acknowledgment of the application by the Inspectorate of Factories and Boilers would serve the purpose.

Registration of Small-scale Industries Units

Small-scale and ancillary units (i.e., undertaking with investment in plant and machinery of less than ₹ 6.00 million and ₹ 7.5 million respectively) should seek registration with the Director of Industries of the concerned State Government.

Registering SSI unit

The main purpose of registration is to maintain statistics and maintain a roll of such units for the purpose of providing incentives and support services.

States have generally adopted the uniform registration procedures as per the guidelines. However, there may be some modifications done by States. It must be noted that small industries is basically a State subject.

Benefits of Registering

The registration scheme has no statutory basis. Units would normally get registered to avail some benefits, incentives or support given either by the Central or state Govt. the regime of incentives offered by the Centre generally contains the following:

- Credit prescription (Priority sector lending), differential rates of interest etc.
- Excise Exemption Scheme.
- Exemption under Direct Tax Laws.
- Statutory support such as reservation and the Interest on Delayed Payments Act. (it is to be noted that the Banking Laws, Excise Law and the Direct Taxes Law have incorporated the word SSI in their exemption notifications. Though in many cases they may define it differently. However, generally the registration certificate issued by the registering authority is seen as proof of being SSI).

State/UTs have their own package of facilities and incentives for small-scale industries. They relate to development of industrial estates, tax subsidies, power tariff subsidies, capital investment subsidies and other support. Both the Centre and the State, whether under law or otherwise, target their incentives and support packages generally to units registered with them.

Objectives of the Registration Scheme

They are summarized as follows:

- To enumerate and maintain a role of small industries to which the package of incentives and support are targeted.
- To provide a certificate enabling the units to avail statutory benefits mainly in terms of protection.
- To serve the purpose of collection of statistics.
- To create nodal centers at the Centre, State and District levels to promote SSI.

Features of the Scheme

Features of the scheme are as follows:

(1) DIC is the primary registering centre.

(2) Registration is voluntary and not compulsory.

(3) Two types of registration are done in all States. First a provisional registration certificate (PRC) is given. And after commencement of production, a permanent registration certificate is given.

(4) PRC is normally valid for 5 years and permanent registration is given in perpetuity.

Benefits of Provisional Registration

(1) This is given for the pre-operative period and enables the units to obtain the term loans and working capital form financial institutions/Banks under priority sector lending.

(2) Obtain facilities for accommodation, land other approvals etc.

(3) Obtain various necessary NOCs and clearances from regulatory bodies such as Pollution Control Board, Labour Regulations etc.

Procedure to get the Provisional Registration

(a) Fill in Application Form in duplicate.

(b) A declaration that the proposed unit is not owned/controlled by or subsidiary to any other Industrial Undertaking.

(c) A detailed scheme of the proposed unit (if project cost exceeds ₹ 40.00 lacs and/or if it comes under Special category under Pollution Control).

(d) Pollution Control Certificate for Consent to establish usually issued by DIC except special Red where activities relates to within the purview of SSI.

  i. A site clearance certificate from Local Body/Local Self-govt.

  ii. A requisite fee has to be deposited based on the project cost and category in the branch of UBI, earmarked for, in favour of Pollution Control Board.

(e) However, the Provisional certificate will be issued subject to production of specific clearance of the concerned Department for specialized items, if any.

Benefits of Permanent Registration

Enables the unit to get the following incentives/concessions:

(1) Excise exemptions.

(2) Income Tax exemption and Sales Tax exemption as per State Govt., Policy.

(3) Incentives and concessions in power tariff etc.

(4) Price and purchase preference for goods produced.

(5) Availability of raw materials depending on existing policy.

Procedure to get Permanent Registration

(a) Fill in Application Form in duplicate.

(b) Documents regarding constitution of SSI unit:

   i. In case of limited company–the certificate of incorporation and article of memorandum of the association.

   ii. In case of registered society—copy of registration certificate.

   iii. In case of industrial co-operative—copy of cooperative registration certificate.

   iv. In case of partnership firm—copy of regd. partnership agreement.

(c) Purchase Documents /Cash Memos/ Sale Agreement, with payment receipt showing the original value of Plant and Machinery. An affidavit in case document in respect of purchase of Plant and Machinery/Tools/Implements, not available.

(d) An Affidavit in the prescribed format is to be submitted to the effect that the formation/activity is well within the purview, procedures and norms laid down by the authority.

(e) Pollution Control Certificate for Consent to Operate (COO) from the appropriate authority depending on the category of industry.

(f) However, the Permanent certificate will be issued subject to production of specific clearance of the concerned Department for specialized items, if any.

Features of the Present Procedure for Registration

Features of the present procedures are as follows:

(1) A unit can apply for PRC for any item that does not require industrial license. Units employing less than 50/100 workers with/without power can apply for registration.

(2) Unit applies for PRC is prescribed application form. No field enquiry is done and PRC is issued.

(3) PRC is valid for five years. If the entrepreneur is unable to set up the unit in this period, he can apply afresh at the end of five years period.

(4) Once the unit commences production, it has to apply for permanent registration on the prescribed form.

The following form the basis of evaluation:

(1) The unit has obtained all necessary clearances whether statutory or administrative, e.g., drug license under drug control order, NOC from pollution Control Board, if required etc.

(2) Unit does not violate any location restrictions in force, at the time of evaluation.

(3) Value of plant and machinery is within prescribed limits.

(4) Unit is not owned, controlled or subsidiary of any other industrial undertaking as per notification.

De-Registration

A Small-scale Unit can violate the regulations in the following ways which will make it liable for de-registration:

(1) It crosses the investment limits.

(2) It starts manufacturing any new item or items that require an industrial license or other kind of statutory license.

(3) It does not satisfy the condition of being owned, controlled or being a subsidiary of any other industrial undertaking.

(4) Also, If the unit/enterprise remained closed continuously for a period exceeding one year.

(5) If the units/enterprise failed/refused or avoided to give full and truthful information as called upon by the registering authority from time to time and in particular for half yearly report.

Before de-registering the unit, a Show Cause Notice to the party should be sent by registered post at the address given in the application form and 30 days time will be given for reply. Action to de-register unit/enterprise will be taken only after the expiry of 30 days time. Any unit/enterprise aggrieved by the order of de-registration can appeal to the authority notified by the State Government within 30 days of receipt of intimation of the same.

Carrying on Business (CoB) Clearance

The same information for Carrying on Business (CoB) clearance required. Industrial undertakings which cross the limit of investment as prescribed in the definition of SSI by process of natural growth will need a "Carrying on Business" license before crossing the ceiling limit from DGTD.

Steps to start a New Venture

While setting up a new unit, there is a lot of excitement as well as pressure on the entrepreneur. In this excitement there is likelihood that entrepreneurs may choose the wrong path.

Therefore, it is necessary once the entrepreneur decides to set up a unit, **first step** which one has to take is to identify the right product, type of raw material required to manufacture the product and whether it is locally available or not; type of machinery/equipment required; market survey etc. and lastly the location to set up the unit.

The **second step**, which the entrepreneur requires to decide is; what type of organizational form of business he would like to choose, depending on finance, i.e., whether proprietary concern; partnership or private limited company.

In the **next step**, the entrepreneur has to choose scale of operation, i.e., whether he/she would like to set up unit in micro, small or medium. The category/definition of a micro, small, medium or large is given in terms of the investment in plant and machinery alone by the unit.

Lastly, the entrepreneur has to decide how he/she is going to arrange finance, as no enterprise/unit can take off without monetary support. No doubt financial assistance for Micro/Small Enterprise/Unit is available from various financial institutions like Goa Economic Development Corporation; National Small Industries Corporation Limited; Small Industries Development Bank of India; Commercial/Co-operative Banks; Khadi and Village Industry Board/Commission, etc.

(a) ***Selection of Product:*** An entrepreneur should select the product which has widespread market and good profitability, hence, it becomes necessary to opt genuine and proper product.

The product should be accepted everywhere, it should earn a reputation for entrepreneur, and it should also get profit and market leadership. Therefore, he has to select the product very carefully.

If the entrepreneur knows technical process and experience for manufacturing the product, while selecting, then it will be more beneficial to him. If he or his colleagues does not know anything about product, it is not advisable to accept that product.

The product with good profitability should be opted. It enjoys many concessions and other benefits to manufacture a product for which the Government has given preference.

Current and future prospects for the products for local and foreign market should be inspected. Some specific gains can be obtained if some products are being manufactured at prescribed industrial zones, i.e., special economic zone, agro export zone etc.

Besides this, the location of SSIs are preferred where raw materials, machinery, skilled workers are easily available.

Process for selection of product can be described as given:

(1) A man thinks to start business, for this some positive and negative factors are responsible.
(2) Information is gathered from various sources about which product is to be manufactured.
(3) Information gathered about various products are arranged in sequence.
(4) Useless and unnecessary details are eradicated.
(5) Rest of the information is analyzed and arranged scientifically.
(6) Every opportunity is being scrutinized keeping various standards in mind.
(7) Micro inspection is being done for every information and reviewed thereafter.
(8) Information gathered is arranged in sequence according to profitability and benefit.
(9) The best product is selected.

(b) ***Preliminary Preparation of the Project Report:*** In the preliminary preparation stage, certain basic information and details are collected for the purpose of analysis. The preparation of a project report requires investigation of various aspect of the project. It is the initial broad testing of the project selected for detailed investigation. It relates to certain broad economic aspects like market demand, investment required and margin of profit likely to be available. The practical utility of the project from the point of view of actual execution is investigated at this stage. Preliminary scrutiny of the proposed project is desirable to find out the possible success of the project. This should be done before proceeding with extensive investigation and detailed planning of the project. The preliminary investigation may suggest that the market for the proposed product is extremely limited or that the product will not have regular demand or that the margin of profit may be very limited. Financial institution need project report because the lending institution certainly desires to study the soundness of the proposed project in detail before granting a loan. The financial institutions now appoint expert staff for the scrutiny of project reports.

(c) ***Selection of Form of Ownership:*** The most commonly chosen forms of ownership for SSI are

(a) Sole proprietorship;
(b) Family ownership;
(c) Partnership; and
(d) Private Limited Company.

The first two forms are mostly preferred for having unified control over the unit. The next two forms, highly facilitate the pooling of financial resources, managerial and technical skills, and business experience. However, to an appropriate extent especially where the family ties and resources are strong, partnerships are in no way distinguishable from family concerns.

(d) ***Selection of Site:*** The third important step is choosing of a suitable plot for factory or shed. In this regard, an entrepreneur has five options open to him. He can choose a land from an industrial area developed by the State Development Corporation, Directorate of Industries, where necessary industrial infrastructure has been provided. The second option is factory sheds in industrial estate constructed by the State Industrial Development Agency and provided with adequate infrastructural facilities. Or he may choose from plots/sheds developed by private developers (i.e., Private Industrial Estates). Information about this type may be obtained from newspaper advertisements or real estate agents. He may buy private land and develop the same for industrial use. However, in this case he/she is to obtain permission from District Collector and/or his subordinate officers.

While selecting a site, an entrepreneur has to take into consideration the following factors:

(a) The site is situated in one's native place;
(b) The site enjoys most or all incentives provided by the Government;
(c) The site is near a market;

(d) The site is near the source of labour supply and raw materials; and
(e) The site has modern infrastructural facilities.

Before locating his plant in a particular area he should ascertain whether the area is a declared industrial area or not. Detailed information about areas classification is available at the District Industries Centre. With the information obtained the entrepreneur can decide whether the proposed industry can be started or not.

(e) *Designing Capital Structure:* The initial capital of a new venture comes from the following sources:
(a) Own Capital;
(b) Long-term loans from friends and relatives; and
(c) Term loans from banks and financial institutions.

In recent years, the institutional lending has increased rapidly, but it has not yet become the dominant source of funds for small industry. Banks play an important role in providing working capital finance. However, an analysis of capital structure of small-scale units reveals that the support from financial institutions is not adequate and that they should gear up their administrative machinery and produce better performance in order to fulfill the objectives and targets adequately.

(f) *Invite Quotations for Equipment/Machinery:* Various accessories are required in the business unit for storing, handling, measuring, weighing the materials, producing, etc. Such accessories should be selected carefully involving low investment and the operating expenses, providing greater safety and maximum utilization of space. Bins, racks flat, pallets, box pallets and skid platforms are used for storing the materials and other purposes. The material handling equipment can be classified as manual and mechanical which includes hand trolley, mobile jib cranes, and roller conveyors, etc. The size and number of these equipment should be selected keeping in view the needs of the form of ownership and the nature and the quantity of materials to be handled. Sometimes, suppliers are selected out of the list of suppliers registered with the unit for the supply of goods or sometimes quotations or price bids or tenders are invited from the prospective suppliers. On studying the terms of supply and the quality and quantity of goods, suppliers are selected out of the bidders or tenderers.

(g) *Acquisition of Manufacturing Know-how:* Many institutions like government research laboratories, research and development divisions of industries and also individual consultants provide the manufacturing know-how. In the case of ancillary units, it is provided by the main unit itself, if the promoter of the ancillary unit needs it. Sometimes, it is provided by the plant and machinery suppliers, both domestic as well as foreign. Apart from this, foreign technical collaboration for know-how is possible subject to the approval of the Government. The scale of operation is linked closely with technology, financial resources available and market demand envisaged. National laboratories, CSIR and RDC provide information on the feasible scale of operation relevant to the manufacturing know-how that is sought for by the applicant.

(h) *Preparation of Project Report:* It is necessary to prepare a project report according to the format of the loan application of the concerned term lending institution. An entrepreneur may get these reports done by a consultant or technical consultancy organisation. The report normally covers important items like sources of finance-long term and short-term, Availability of machinery and technical know-how, sources of labour and raw materials, market potential and overall profitability. All these are systematically estimated and presented balancing the opportunities and constraints. It has not always been possible for consultants to submit reports which could be straight away relied upon by financial or licensing agencies. It is felt that the development agencies themselves should play a more positive role in the preparation of feasibility reports. The project report being compiled by the entrepreneur should accomplish the purpose of providing a **"birds-eye view"** of the entire spectrum of activity. The following matter should be given due consideration while preparing the project report:

(i) ***Technical feasibility:*** Technical feasibility would encompass factors such as description of the product specification to be adopted, raw materials available as per requirements, outline of manufacturing process inclusive of a "flow chart process", quality control measures, power supply, availability of water, transport facilities, and communication network.

(ii) ***Economic viability:*** It essentially involves compilation of demands for domestic and export markets, most appropriate installed capacity requirements, capturing a substantial share of market sale, revenue expected, and suitable price structure and so on.

(iii) ***Financial implications:*** Project costs covering "Non-recurring expenses" such as land and buildings,plant and machinery, equipment, pre-operative expenses, and so on and "Recurring Expenses" such as working capital needs, raw material needs, and wages for personnel and so on will have to be worked out in detail. The probable cost of production over a period of 5 years to be assigned and expenses such as fixed and variable expenses and break-even analysis should be presented. Besides, profit per month, percentage of profit on total investment and percentage of profit on expected sale should also be computed and furnished.

(iv) ***Managerial Competency:*** The new entrepreneur manager entering the small-scale sector should devote his full attention to the new venture and should consider the product line chosen as a "Major Economic Activity".

(i) ***Registration Process:*** Every industry doesn't require registration but to gain from various government. schemes it is necessary, otherwise they are lapse. In this reference, small-scale industries must prefer to get registration for the benefit of government schemes like fiscal, financial, administrative, structured, etc. It is also preferable to get shed in industrial zone subsidy, loan and financial aid according to government. schemes to trade in import-export market, to bid for government. tenders and to participate in other marketing schemes. The main purpose of Registration is to maintain statistics and maintain a roll of such units for the purpose of providing incentives and support services. States have generally adopted the uniform registration procedures as per the guidelines. However, there may be some modifications done by States. It must be noted that small industries is basically a state subject.

Small-scale and ancillary units (i.e., undertaking with investment in plant and machinery of less than ₹6.00 million and ₹7.5 million respectively) should seek registration with the Director of Industries of the concerned State Government.

There is a district industrial centre in every district. These centres undertake registration process. Registration application needs to be submitted to general manager of the Centre duly filled with required details and with necessary documents. If the entrepreneur has decided upon a suitable product and is actively considering the establishment of an industrial unit, he would be initially issued a provisional (temporary) SSI Registration Certificate. It is usually provided for a period of one year, and subsequently renewed for two periods of 6 months each. If the entrepreneur is not in a position to commence production on account of circumstances beyond his own control, extension of the provisional registration period would be considered.

(j) ***Municipal license:*** If an industry is to be started within the area limit of Municipal Corporation, it needs to take required permissions from such bodies. Construction map/blueprints for factory has to be passed through municipal town planning department. He has to consent on proper use of machinery and to take permission for machinery installation. These permissions are required according to various laws. Industries need to pay fees and submit some documents to **State Panchayat Ordinance or Municipal Corporation Acts** to get such permissions, as the case may be.

(k) ***Power Connection:*** There are two categories of power, *viz.*,

(1) The Low Tension (LT), and

(2) The High Tension (HT).

A consumer can avail LT only if the connected load is 75 HP and below. In respect of the cases where the connected load is between 75 HP and 130 HP, the consumer has the option to avail either LT supply or HT supply. If the connected load exceeds 130 HP, the unit is classified as HT consumer. Most of the small-scale units fall under the LT category. To get power connection, the New Entrepreneur has to make an application to the **Assistant Divisional Engineer, Electricity Department of the concerned State Government;** the load applicable for the new unit would be decided. Permission for electric connection and electric load capacity has to be taken from **State Electricity Board.** It needs to consult **Chief Electrical Inspector Commissioner** of electricity dept. for inspection and approval of electrical connection. The new entrepreneur may have to pay security deposit amounting to three month's power connection. To avoid delay in getting power connection, formal application may be given when step is taken.

(l) ***Other Statutory Obligations:*** Besides these, the entrepreneur also has to fulfill the following obligations before proceedings with his business endeavor:

- It is compulsory to register under **State Shops and Establishment Act, 1948.**
- An NOC is to be obtained for pollution control from **State Pollution Control Board** and a letter certifying it free from risk or hazard.
- ISI certification is taken for quality assurance from **Bureau of Indian Standards.**
- An Agmark certificate can be obtained from **Directorate of Marketing and Inspection, Central Rural Development Ministry. Government of India** for agro-products/though this is not compulsory but it is necessary.
- GST number is to be taken from **State Sales Tax Dept.**
- A registration under **P.F. Act (Adulteration Control Act)** is required.
- Permission to be taken from **Steam Boiler and Smock Nuisance Department** under boiler inspection and verification and smock nuisance.
- I.T. and PAN number to be taken from **Central I.T. Dept.**
- An inspection and permission need to be taken for heavy vehicles/refer van mobile precooling unit from **R.T.O.**
- A process for excise number, inspection and collection are to be done from **Central Excise Department.**
- If the unit comes within the purview of the **Factories Act,** e.g., employs 10 persons with power or 20 without power, registration with the Inspector will be required.

(m) ***Arrangement of Finance:*** The funding requirements of a project are of:

(i) Long-term requirements for acquiring fixed assets like land and building plant and machinery and for security deposits.

(ii) Short-term loans for working capital in the form of key loan/cash credit/bill discounting, etc.

Term loans for fixed assets are provided by the State Financial Corporation and Commercial Banks. State Financial Corporation extends financial assistance by availing the refinance facilities available with the Small Industries Development Bank of India in most of the cases. Rate of interest varies depending on the amount of term loan sanctioned and is generally based on the Reserve Bank of India Guidelines.

(n) ***Place Order for Machinery:*** While purchasing the machinery, entrepreneur should check on the ability of available suppliers/dealers to supply the specified quality. He should consider the financial viability and dependability of various suppliers and should check their delivery records and consult other entrepreneurs if necessary. It is always a live issue whether to utilize one source or several sources for any one item. By utilizing a simple source, the suppliers may offer special concession and cooperation but the buyer may suffer at the same time from a reduction in competitive pressure. A common practice which is felt to provide the best answer is to give a contract for large portion through competitive bidding. This permits full cooperation from the larger suppliers and to obtain special consideration from them especially when it is required. Once the entrepreneur finalized the suppliers, the immediate step is to place the orders with the same as decided in the prescribed form. This acts as a contract between the entrepreneur and the suppliers to supply the equipment and other accessories in the desired quality and quantity at the agreed price within a time period.

(o) *Procurement and Installation of Machinery:* Acquisition of machinery is not a child's game. Machinery capable of accomplishing the expected assembly must be well thought-out. Machinery preferred must know how to cope up with the order projected or comply with the standard of the turnover forecasted. Incidentally, the backing of professional personality must be taken into thought. Sometime, layout plays significant function while choosing the correct form of equipments and accessories.

Procurement of requisite type of machine facilitates smooth and well-organized implementation of production process. Setting up of machinery is influenced by certain factors associated with the production process, viz., volume of work to be handled, and the product to be manufactured including their components etc. Installation has to be completed by entrepreneur under the assistance of technically-educated-experienced personnel.

(p) *Recruitment and Training of staff:* Entrepreneur required skilled/unskilled/semi-skilled workers executive officers and so on, to meet his various business endeavors. He has to use different tools and techniques to recruit the most efficient and reliable staff.

Entrepreneur must be practical in nature. Casual approach may put the business at risk. High-quality staff may become an asset to his organization. Organization advancement not only depends on the boss but also depends on the excellence and dexterity of staff for the reason that designation of power is trouble-free but satisfying the assignment via self-responsibility, self-discipline, truthfulness, and dedication is rest in the hands of the staff.

Decision on the best staff minimizes further training. Training is the need of the organization because every organization has their own ways and means of achieving needs. Even experience persons have to undergo training at the beginning of his new placement. Training should be provided for staff that will be using the program to ensure that there is a reduction in the risk of errors.

(q) *Procurement of Input:* Through procurement function, entrepreneur operates as a customer. Accordingly, it is susceptible to the marketing strategies of the vendors from whom it obtains the materials that are required for its operation. Depending upon the extent to which the business unit requires outside suppliers and it is not self-sufficient, the importance of the buying function increases. Here, purchased inventory may be divided into two major groups:

(a) Materials required for production; and
(b) Materials required for maintenance of plant and equipment.

Here, entrepreneur can either purchase manufactured and assembled items or can dcal primarily with basic raw materials and commodity markets.

(r) *Trials Run and Commencement of Commercial Production:* The thorough testing of programs before they become operational is needed. This should also involve the use of 'benchmarks' to determine the optimum time taken for a program. Such benchmarks may be of use to an entrepreneur in checking whether programs have subsequently been tampered with, for example, a new program had just been devised by an enterprise and was put online immediately with no major trials. Within two months, it was apparent that the program contained major flaws and it took 12 months for the program and the problems it caused to be put right.

Entrepreneurs can go ahead with his production activities. To facilitate effective, efficient and uninterrupted production of goods and services, entrepreneurs should well in advance plan the procedure of placing the orders with the dealers/suppliers, acquisition, installation and utilizations of the machinery and equipment.

Forms of Business Organizations

Business may be defined as "an activity" in which different persons exchange something a value, whether goods or services for mutual gain or profit. Organization of business would, therefore, refer to a scheme of assigning duties upon some definite basis to persons engaged in a particular undertaking.

In order to accomplish a definite target need an organization in one form or the other. Every business enterprise with the motive of profit making therefore, requires an organization which will facilitate carrying on the functions involved in the business operation. What form of business organization you choose depends upon whole host of factors such as whether one can raise the finance alone or not, whether one is comfortable running business alone or not, whether the orders you have got is only as a project basis or otherwise.

The growth of industrial and commercial activities has given rise to many kinds of organizations. From the point of view of ownership, the following are some of the main forms of business organizations:

(a) Sole Trading Concern or Sole Proprietorship;
(b) Partnership;
(c) Joint Hindu Family Business;
(d) Joint Stock Company; and
(e) Co-operative Societies.

(a) Sole Trading Concern or Sole Proprietorship: Sole trading concern is the oldest, simplest and most common form of business concern. A Proprietorship concern is a concern owned by a single individual who will be responsible for all the activities involved in business operation. No registration is required and the unit can commence operations immediately. His liability being unlimited, he is personally responsible to all the creditors of the business. He alone bears the complete risk of success or failure of the business.

According to **Encyclopedia of Business and Commerce** *"A sole trading concern is a form of business organization in which an individual invests only his capital, uses his own skill and intelligence in the management of its affairs and is entitled to earn all the profits as also is solely responsible for all risks of ownership".*

Characteristics of Sole Proprietorship

(1) ***Individual initiative:*** This business is started by the initiative of a single person. He prepares the blue prints of the venture and arranges various factors of production. He may employ other persons for assistance but ultimate authority and responsibility lies with him. All the profits and losses are taken by the single individual.

(2) ***Unlimited liability:*** In sole trade business liability is unlimited. The proprietor is responsible for all losses arising from the business but his private property is also liable for business obligation.

(3) ***Management and control:*** The proprietor manages the whole business himself. He prepares various plans and executes them under his own supervision. There may be some persons to help him but ultimate control lies with the owner.

(4) ***Motivation:*** One person is the sole owner of the business. He takes all profits and bears losses, if any. There is a direct relationship between efforts and reward. If he works more, he will earn more. He is motivated to expand his business activities. He will not like to enter speculative business because the risk involved is more.

(5) ***Secrecy:*** All important decisions are taken by the owner himself. He keeps all the business secrets only to himself. Business secrets are very important for small business. By retaining business secrets he avoids competitions entering the same business.

(6) ***Proprietor and proprietorship are one:*** Legally the sole trader and his business are separate entities; loss in his business is his loss. Liabilities of the business are his liabilities.

(7) ***Owners and business exist together:*** In sole trade business there is no separate existence of the business with the owner. The business and owner exist together. The business is dissolved, if the owner dies, becomes insolvent or is removed from the scene.

(8) ***Limited area of operations:*** A sole trade business has generally a limited area of operations, the reason being the limited resources and managerial abilities of the sole trader. He can arrange limited funds only and will be able to supervise a small business. Since all decisions are to be taken by the proprietors so the area of business will be limited with his managerial abilities.

Advantages

The advantages of Sole proprietorship would include the following:

- Ease in formation;
- The Owner's complete control over the business;
- A direct motivation to work hard and succeed;
- Maintenance of absolute business secrecy;
- Possibility of quick and timely decisions;
- Personal contacts with employees, customers and others;
- Flexibility in operations;
- Minimal government regulation and interference; and
- Economic and efficient management.

Disadvantages

The following may be listed as the disadvantages that an individual proprietorship would suffer from:

- Limited capital resources;
- Limited managerial ability or technical expertise;
- Limited avenues for diversification and growth;
- Limited personal liability for business losses; and
- Uncertain life and lack of continuity.

(b) Partnership Firm: *A partnership has been defined by the* ***Indian Contract Act*** *as "the relationship which subsists between persons, who have agreed to combine their property, labour or skill in some business and to share the profits thereof between them."*

The Indian Partnership Act, 1932, *has defined partnership as follows: "Partnership is the relation between persons who have agreed to share the profits of a business carried on by all or any of them acting for all."*

For a partnership organization, a partnership deed has to be prepared among the partners. The partnership can be registered or unregistered. A registered partnership has the right to sue the outsiders or partners, but an unregistered partnership can be sued, but has no powers to sue outsiders.

Characteristics of Partnership

Thus, persons who enter into a partnership are individually called the partners, collectively referred to as the partnership firms, and they conduct their business under a firm name.

Essential characteristics of a partnership may be briefly outlines as follows:

- There should be two or more persons;
- An agreement must have been entered into;
- There must be a lawful business in existence;
- Sharing of profits or losses is to be done;
- Every partner is an agent of every other partner;
- The management is to be collective;
- There is a non-transferability of interests;
- The liability of partners is unlimited; and
- All activities are to be carried out in almost good faith.

Advantages

The partnership mode of business organization enjoys the following advantages:

- Ease in formation;
- Larger financial resources;
- Managerial ability;
- Flexibility;
- Division of risk; and
- Credit-worthiness.

Disadvantages

The partnership form of organization suffers from the following major disadvantages:

- Possibility of conflict;
- Risks of implied authority;
- Unlimited liability; and
- Instability.

Procedure for Registration

The registration of a firm may be effected at anytime by sending by post or delivery to the Registrar of the area in which any place of the business or the firm is situated or proposed to situate, a statement in the prescribed form accompanied by the pre-prescribed fee stating:

(a) The firm name

(b) The place or principle place of business of the firm

(c) The names of any other places whether the firm carries on business.

(d) The date when each partner joined the firm

(e) The names in full and permanent address of the partners, and

(f) Statement of the firm. The statement has to be signed by all partners, or by their agents specially authorized in the behalf.

When the Registrar of Firm is satisfied that all the provisions have been duly complied with, then he records an entry of the statement in the register of firms and files the statement and issues a certificate of registration.

(c) *Joint Hindu Family Business:* The Joint Hindu Family form of business is one in which the undivided family possesses some property and **'Karta'**, the head of the family, operates it.

The Joint Family Business arises out of the provisions of the Hindu law, and so is not governed by the Indian Partnership Act 1932.

Advantages

(1) ***Continuity:*** It need not be dissolved on the insolvency or death of any member.

(2) ***Centralized management:*** the management being centralized in the hands of the **'Karta'** leads to discipline and efficiency in the firm's operations.

(3) ***Unlimited membership:*** This form is not limited in membership by law. Hence, a large family would automatically mean more coparceners.

(4) ***Limited liability:*** The liability of all the coparceners being limited, with the exception of the **'Karta'**, is a prime advantage of this form.

Disadvantages

The chief disadvantages marking this form of business may be listed as the following:

(1) ***Lack of congruence between effort and reward:*** Though the 'Karta' looks after the business, the rewards are shared by all the coparceners

(2) ***Limited financial resources:*** This form has relatively limited financial resources, nor can it raise funds as the joint stock company can.

(3) ***Limited managerial ability:*** Since the management invested with the family head under law, it does not endure any criterion for the decision making powers to be centered in him other than age. This may handicap the business owing to the **'Karta's** lack of relevant knowledge, qualification, vision or innovativeness.

(4) ***Relative instability:*** This form of business is dependent on the continuance of the joint family system itself, which is gradually disintegrating in the face of rapid modernization and the consequent social mobility.

(d) ***Joint Stock Company:*** A Joint Stock Company is an artificial person created by law with a perpetual succession and a common seal. **The Companies Act, 1956,** *defines a Joint Stock Company under section 566 as under: "A Joint Stock Company means a company having a permanent paid-up or nominal share capital of fixed amount divided into shares, also of fixed amount, held and transferable as stock, and formed on the principle of having for its members only the holders of those shares or stock and no other persons."*

Characteristics of a Joint Stock Company may be briefly outlines as follows:

(i) ***Association of persons:*** A company is an association of persons joining hands with a common motive. A private limited company must have at least two persons and a public limited company must have at least seven members to get it registered. Furthermore, the number of shareholders should not exceed fifty in private companies but there is no maximum limit of the members in a public limited company.

(ii) ***Independent legal entity:*** The Company is created under law. It has a separate legal entity apart from its members. The Company is not bound by the acts of its members, and members do not act as agents of the company. A person can own its share and can be its creditors too. The life of the company is independent of the lives of its members. The company can sue and be sued in its own name.

(iii) ***Limited liability:*** The liability of its shareholders is limited to the share of his value in case the company incurs huge liability the shareholders can only be called upon to pay the unpaid balance of their shares.

(iv) ***Common seal:*** A company cannot put its signatures. The law requires every company to have seal and get its name engraved on it.

(v) ***Transferability of shares:*** The shares of a company can be transferred by its members, whenever, the members want to dispose off the shares, they can do by following the procedure devised for this purpose.

(vi) ***Separation of ownership and management:*** The ownership and management are in two separate hands. The companies are managed by Boards of Directors. The shareholders do not get any right to participate in company management. The right to manage company affairs is vested in the directors who are elected representatives of the shareholders.

(vii) ***Perpetual existence:*** The continuity of the company not affected by death, lunacy or insolvency of its shareholders. The company can be wound up only by the operation of law.

(viii) ***Corporate finance:*** A joint stock company generally, raises large amounts of funds. Since there is no limit on number of maximum members in public companies. Large amounts of sources can be raised from persons in different walks of life.

(ix) ***Centralized and delegated management:*** A joint stock company is an autonomous and self governed body. The shareholders elect Board of Directors in general body meeting for managing the company. All important decisions are taken in democratic way.

(x) ***Publication of accounts:*** A joint stock company to file annual statements with the registrar of companies at the end of a financial year.

Advantages

(i) ***Accumulation of large resources:*** A company can collect large sums of money from large number of shareholders. There is no limit on the number of shareholders in a public company.

(ii) ***Limited liability:*** The liability of members in a company form of organization is limited to the nominal value of the shares they have acquired. If the shares are partly paid then he can be required to pay only the unpaid value of the share.

(iii) ***Continuity of existence:*** It is an entity with perpetual succession. The members of a company may go on changing from time to time, but that does not affect the continuity of a company.

(iv) ***Efficient management:*** In company form of organization, ownership is separate from management. It enables the company to appoint experts and qualified persons for managing various business functions. The efficient management will help the company to expand and diversify its activities.

(v) ***Economies of large-scale production:*** The increase in scale and size of the business will result in economies in production, purchase, marketing and management etc. These economies will enable the company to produce goods at a lower cost thus resulting in more results.

(vi) ***Transferability of shares:*** The shares of a company are freely transferrable. The shareholders can dispose of the shares, at any time by following the procedure devised for this purpose. The facility of transferring shares encourages many persons to invest.

(vii) ***Social benefits:*** The company form of organization mobilizes scattered savings of the community. These savings can be better used for productive purposes. The society is supplied with enough quantity of goods.

Disadvantages

The company form of organization suffers from the following drawbacks:

(i) ***Difficulty in formation:*** Promotion of a company is not an easy task. Number stages are involved in company promotion. A lot of legal formalities are required to be performed at the time of registration.

(ii) ***Separation of ownership and management:*** The ownership and management of public company is in different hands. The management may indulge in speculative business activities. There is no direct relationship between efforts and rewards. The management does not take personal interest in the working of the company.

(iii) ***Lack of secrecy:*** The management of companies remains in the hands of many persons. Everything is discussed in the meetings of Boards of Directors. The trade secrets cannot be maintained.

(iv) ***Delay in decision making:*** All important decisions are taken either by the Board of Directors or are referred to general house and not by single individual. If some business opportunity arises and a quick decision is needed, it will not be possible to arrange meetings all of a sudden.

(v) ***Excessive state regulation:*** A large number of rules and regulations are framed for the working of the companies. The companies will have to follow rules even for their internal working. The government tries to regulate the working of the companies because large public money is involved.

(vi) ***Concentration of economic power:*** The company form of organization has helped concentration of economic power in a few hands. Some persons become directors in a number of companies and try to formulate policies, which promote their own-interests. Interlocking of directorship and establishment of subsidiary companies has facilitated concentration of economic power in the hands of a few business houses.

(vii) ***Fraudulent management:*** The promoters and directors may indulge in fraudulent practices. The management is in the hands of those persons who have not invested much in the company.

(viii) ***Evils of factory system:*** The company form of organization leads to large scale production. The evils of factory system like insanitation, air pollution, congestion of cities are attributed to joint stock companies.

(e) ***Cooperative Societies:*** The cooperative movement has been the outcome of the economic and social imbalances caused by the Industrial Revolution. Cooperative societies have acquired significance in both capitalist countries like US and Japan as well as socialist countries.

According to **International Labour Organization** *"A cooperative is an association of persons (usually of limited means) who have voluntarily joined together to achieve a common economic end, through the formulation of a democratically controlled business organization, making equitable contributions to the capital required and accepting a fair share of risks and benefits of the undertaking,"*

Characteristics of Cooperative Societies

(1) A cooperative society is a voluntary association of persons.

(2) Membership is not restricted on the basis of caste, sex, creed, colour or religion, but may be limited to the employees of a particular company.

(3) A cooperative undertaking must seek registration under the Cooperative Societies Act, 1912, or under the relevant Cooperative Societies Act of the state government.

(4) A cooperative society, like a Joint Stock Company, has a separate legal existence, distinct from its members.

(5) The capital of a cooperative is raised from among its members in the form of share capital.

(6) The primary aim of a cooperative is service to its members, though it may also in the process happen to earn reasonable profits for itself.

(7) The cooperative is managed by a managing committee, elected by its members.

(8) Any trading surplus earned by a cooperative may be distributed among its members as dividend, though not exceeding 10 per cent of it.

(9) Each member has only one vote, irrespective of the number of shares held by him or her.

(10) The Cooperative has to submit annual reports and accounts to the Registrar of Societies.

Factors Influencing a Suitable Form of Organisation

When an entrepreneur proposes to undertake a business, he has to choose a suitable form of organization. While selecting a appropriate form of organization, he has to keep in mind the merits and demerits of every form. The choice has to made both at the time of setting up a new enterprise and at the time of expansion and growth of an existing concern.

The selection of a suitable form of business organization is an important management decision. This decision affects the success of a business firm. It is a long-term commitment which cannot be changed easily. As such, selection of the form of business organization is a matter of careful deliberation and judgment. Broadly speaking, the entrepreneur has the choice of three principal kinds of business – sole proprietorship, partnership and company.

For choosing a suitable form of organization an entrepreneur has to take into consideration several factors. They are:

(1) ***Types of Business:*** This is an important factor having a direct bearing on the choice of a form of organization. In small trading, businesses, professions and personal service traders, sole proprietorship is predominant. The partnership is suitable, in all these cases where sole proprietorship is suitable provided the business is to be carried on a slightly bigger scale. Business activities requiring pooling of skills and funds e.g., wholesale trade, stockbrokers etc., are better organized as partnership. Manufacturing organizations are large size are more commonly set up as private and public companies. Similarly, large chain stores, multiple shops, super bazaars, engineering companies are in the form of companies.

(2) ***Scope of Operations:*** In case of large-scale operations, the company form is suitable because large sized enterprises require large financial and managerial resources which are beyond the capacity of a single person or a few persons. If the scale of operations of business activities is small, sole proprietorship is suitable. If the scale of operations is modest – neither too small nor too large, partnership is preferable. The scale of business operations depends upon the size of demand for goods and services.

(3) ***Degree of Direct Control and Management:*** If the entrepreneur desires direct control over its operations, he will prefer sole proprietorship. But if he is not interested in or bothered about the direct control and management, he may choose partnership or company form of organization.

(4) ***Amount of Capital Funds Required:*** If the business requires huge amount of capital company is best form of organization. If the capital is to be required is small, a sole proprietorship or partnership form of organization would be suitable. Requirements of growth and expansion should also be considered in making the choice. There is maximum scope for expansion in case of a company. Where the funds required initially are small and scope for expansion is not desired, proprietorship or partnership is a better choice.

(5) ***Size of the Risk:*** The volume of risk and the willingness of owners to bear, it is an important consideration. If an individual is ready to bear all risks and liabilities of the business, he may opt for sole proprietorship. A business with wider risks and more liabilities is generally started in the form of partnership or company. Due to limited liability and a large number of shareholders, there is maximum diffusion of risks in a company.

(6) ***Continuity of the Concern:*** Sole proprietorship has a limited life because they are not fundamentally perpetual. An illness of owner or his death can end the business partnerships are also unstable. A company is the most stable and permanent form of organization. The life of the company is not dependent upon the life of the owners.

(7) ***Adaptability of Administration:*** In case of sole proprietorship, the responsibility for policy and operations lies with one individual. This may be both good and bad depending upon the ability of the individual. Motivation is very high in sole proprietorships. In a partnership, the division of responsibility may lead to disagreements. Thus, a partnership lacks centralized administration. In a company administration is centralized in the hands of few executives and professionals.

(8) ***Comparative Tax Advantage:*** Corporate profits are subjected to uniform rate of taxation and if the expected profits from business are going to be huge, it is better to start such a business on company basis. Profits earned by sole proprietor or a partner are subjected to progressive rate of taxation, i.e., the rate of tax goes on increasing with increase in volume of profits. Thus, proprietorships and partnerships face a lower tax burden at moderate levels of income.

(9) ***Cost, Procedure and Government Regulation:*** Proprietorships and partnerships are subjected to little regulation and control by the Government while companies and cooperatives are subject to severe restrictions and formalities. Sole proprietorship and partnerships are easiest, cheapest and most convenient forms of organization.

It must be noted that these factors are interrelated and interdependent. For instance, the amount of capital required and degree of risk involved depends upon the nature and volume of business operations. The degree of control and the division of profits are both related to risk and liability. Therefore, an entrepreneur should not consider these factors in isolation. The interrelationship between these factors should be duly considered.

The basic consideration in the choice of a form of ownership is the nature and size of business. All other factors are dependent on this basic consideration. The scope and plan of organization will also vary with the size and nature of business. In a grocery store, for example, the organization will be simple as few employees will be needed.

What is Value Added Tax?

Value Added Tax is the tax on value addition made by a seller on his purchases. In short it is called a VAT. Value addition is the difference between selling price and the purchase price. Whatever tax a seller pays at time of purchase on raw materials or other inputs is called Input Tax. The tax a person is liable to pay at the time of sales is called Output Tax. Value addition or VAT is the tax which is calculated as a difference between output tax and input tax.

Every registered dealer other than a composition dealer as a pay net tax payable which is to be worked out as under:

Less

Output tax ——————→ Tax paid on admissible purchases

(Charged on sale of goods)

= Net tax payable, i.e, VAT to be deposited during the period.

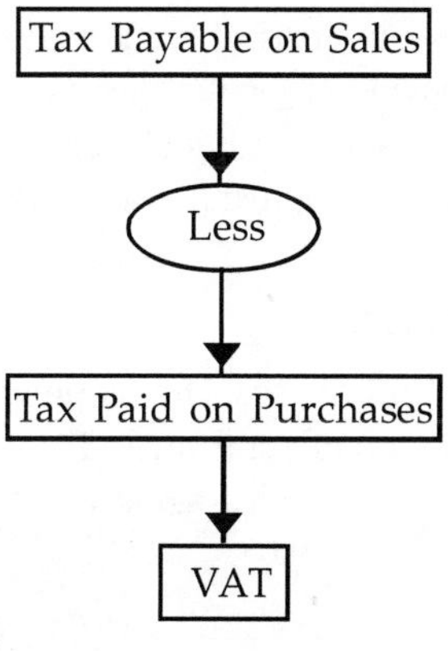

Summing Up

Introduction

Over the years, the developing countries have adopted positive measures to defeat the forces of stagnation. To perform this gigantic task, well-considered and most suited policy of economic development has been framed. The growth process of these countries aims at accelerating the economic development to enhance the social welfare. Therefore, the task of government policymaking has a vital role to play. The policymakers face challenge in selecting the desired objectives and suitable alternatives for stimulating the economic growth.

Nowadays, most of the developing countries are following the thesis that industrialization is a process of growth and as such is organically linked both to the social and economic past and to the parallel processes of social and economic development. The thesis reaffirms the importance of industrialization as an effective means for solving the problems of economic and social progress in developing countries of the world.

Role of Small–scale Industries in Industrialization of India

India is often described as an underdeveloped country. The term 'underdeveloped' implies that the natural resources, manpower and material of the country have not been properly harnessed with the result that the people have to live in poverty. They are underfed and physically weak and their working capacity is low. 'Underdevelopment' implies that the level of real income and capital per head of population is low as judged by the standards in developed countries of North America and Western Europe. In under developed countries, there is no large-scale application of the fruits of scientific and technological advances to agriculture and industry. Subsistence production is generally important for the people, the markets are comparatively narrow and manufacturing industry is usually unimportant.

In many developing countries, manpower is relatively abundant. It is, therefore, imperative that their full and effective utilization should become a focal point of socio-economic policies. Emphasis has to be laid on small scale industries to absorb the surplus manpower in these countries.

The concept, small scale industry covers a wide range of activities and its definition changed from time to time. The latest definition (July, 1990) of small scale industries is quite broad based. All industries with a capital investment of ₹ 20 lacs in plant and machinery are classified as small-scale industries. The smaller units with a capital investment of ₹ 2 lacs in plant and machinery are classified as tiny units. Units with a capital investment in plant and machinery varying between ₹ 20 lacs and ₹ 25 lacs are classified as ancillary industries.

Importance of Small-scale Industries

Apart from their inherent usefulness in terms of numerical superiority, small-scale industries play a vital role in the economic growth of developing countries as discussed below:

Utilization of Resources; Employment Generation; Generation of Foreign Exchange; Diversification of Industrial Structures; Entrepreneurial Development; and Reverses the trend of migration from rural to urban areas.

Micro, Small and Medium Enterprises

The 'Micro, Small and Medium Enterprises Development (MSMED) Act – 2006' has been implemented by the Government of India with effect from 2nd October, 2006. Under the Act, Enterprises (Industries) have been classified into four categories namely -

- Micro Enterprises;
- Small Enterprises;

- Medium Enterprises; and
- Large Enterprises.

Procedure for Registration of Micro, Small and Medium Enterprises in Goa

The registration of Micro, Small and Medium Enterprises are done in two stages as follows:

Stage I- Provisional

The prospective entrepreneurs who intends to establish a micro or small enterprise or a medium enterprise engaged in manufacturing or production of goods or in providing or rendering or services, at his discretion has to file the Entrepreneurship Memorandum of Micro, Small or as the case may be, of Medium Enterprises, with District Industries Centre, Directorate of Industries, Trade and Commerce, Government of Goa.

The District Industries Centre on receipt of the Entrepreneurship Memorandum will fill all the codes in the EM and will issue an acknowledgment allotting Entrepreneurs Memorandum number, date of issue and Category of the unit within Five days of the receipt of the EM. This registration will be valid for two years.

The provisional registration formalities are simple and no elaborate details are required to be provided. However, any supporting documents while filling up the application should be provided, if the same are mentioned in it. It will be also be helpful to provide a brief note on the proposed project highlighting salient features.

Stage II- Permanent/Final

Once the Entrepreneur starts the production or starts providing or rendering services they have to file the Entrepreneurs Memorandum to District Industries Centre.

In case of non-filing of document of the EM within two years, Memorandum filed by the Entrepreneur will become invalid.

In case of change in the investment in plant and machinery or in equipment; or change of products and that of services or addition in products or service, the entrepreneur/enterprise which have already filed Entrepreneurs Memorandum has to inform the District Industries Centre of the same in writing within three months of the change.

Documents required for final/permanent registration

(1) NOC. from Directorate of Health Services/Primary Health Centre/Urban Health Centre/valid consent order to operate from Goa State Pollution Control Board as the case may be except in case of items specifically exempted by the Government under specific order/Notification from time to time.

(2) The unit listed under green category shall be exempted from obtaining NOC from Directorate of Health Services/Primary Health Centre/Urban Health Centre/valid consent order from Goa State Pollution Control Board and in that case only Departmental NOC for establishment of the unit is required to be produced. Until Government notifies the list of Green, Orange and Red Category, the present practice shall be followed.

(3) NOC/Trade License from Municipality/Village Panchayats /Corporation for the units established outside the Industrial Estate.

(4) NOC from the owner of the premises in the prescribed format.

(5) House tax payment receipt or any other documentary evidence like electricity bill, water charges bill, a letter from Municipality or Panchayats, etc.

(6) Partnership Deed in respect of Partnership firm duly registered with Registrar of Firms. Memorandum of Association and Articles of Association in respect of Private Limited/Limited Company, duly registered before Registrar of companies.

(7) Excise license from Commissioner of Excise for liquor units, (alcohol-based products)

(8) Fruit product order for soft drinks and any fruit-based product.

(9) License from Directorate of Food and Drugs Administration for food, drugs, and pharmaceutical products.

(10) License from Inspectorate of Factories and Boilers for the unit having 10 or more workers working with power connection and for unit having 20 or more workers working without power connection. In such cases the acknowledgment of the application by the Inspectorate of Factories and Boilers would serve the purpose.

Registration of Small-scale Industries Units

Small-scale and ancillary units (i.e., undertaking with investment in plant and machinery of less than ₹ 6.00 million and ₹ 7.5 million respectively) should seek registration with the Director of Industries of the concerned State Government.

Registering SSI unit

The main purpose of registration is to maintain statistics and maintain a roll of such units for the purpose of providing incentives and support services.

States have generally adopted the uniform registration procedures as per the guidelines. However, there may be some modifications done by States. It must be noted that small industries is basically a State subject.

Benefits of Registering

The registration scheme has no statutory basis. Units would normally get registered to avail some benefits, incentives or support given either by the Central or State Govt., the regime of incentives offered by the Centre generally contains the following:

- Credit prescription (Priority sector lending), differential rates of interest etc.
- Excise Exemption Scheme.
- Exemption under Direct Tax Laws.
- Statutory support such as reservation and the Interest on Delayed Payments Act.

State/UTs have their own package of facilities and incentives for small-scale. They relate to development of industrial estates, tax subsidies, power tariff subsidies, capital investment subsidies and other support. Both the Centre and the State, whether under law or otherwise, target their incentives and support packages generally to units registered with them.

Objectives of the Registration Scheme

They are summarized as follows:

- To enumerate and maintain a role of small industries to which the package of incentives and support are targeted.
- To provide a certificate enabling the units to avail statutory benefits mainly in terms of protection.
- To serve the purpose of collection of statistics.
- To create nodal centers at the centre, State and District levels to promote SSI.

Features of the Registration Scheme

Features of the scheme are as follows:

(1) DIC is the primary registering centre.

(2) Registration is voluntary and not compulsory.

(3) Two types of registration are done in all States. First a provisional registration certificate (PRC) is given. And after commencement of production, a permanent registration certificate is given.

(4) PRC is normally valid for 5 years and permanent registration is given in perpetuity.

Benefits of Provisional Registration

(1) This is given for the pre-operative period and enables the units to obtain the term loans and working capital form financial institutions/Banks under priority sector lending.

(2) Obtain facilities for accommodation, land other approvals etc.

(3) Obtain various necessary NOCs and clearances from regulatory bodies such as Pollution Control Board, Labour Regulations etc.

Procedure to get the Provisional Registration

(a) Fill in Application Form in duplicate.

(b) A declaration that the proposed unit is not owned/controlled by or subsidiary to any other Industrial Undertaking.

(c) A detailed Scheme of the proposed Unit (if project cost exceeds ₹ 40.00 lacs and/or if comes under Special category under Pollution Control).

(d) Pollution Control Certificate for Consent to establish usually issued by DIC except special Red where activities relates to within the purview of SSI.

  i. A site clearance certificate from Local Body/Local Self Govt.

  ii. A requisite fee has to be deposited based on the project cost and category in the branch of UBI, earmarked for, in favour of Pollution Control Board.

(e) However, the Provisional certificate will be issued subject to production of specific clearance of the concerned Department for specialized items, if any.

Benefits of Permenant Registration

Enables the unit to get the following incentives/concessions:

(1) Excise exemptions.

(2) Income Tax exemption and Sales Tax exemption as per State Govt. Policy.

(3) Incentives and concessions in power tariff etc.

(4) Price and purchase preference for goods produced.

(5) Availability of raw material depending on existing policy.

Procedure to get Permanent Registration

(a) Fill in Application Forms in duplicate.

(b) Documents regarding constitution of SSI unit:

  i. In case of limited company- the certificate of incorporation and article of memorandum of the association.

  ii. In case of registered society – copy of registration certificate.

  iii. In case of industrial co-operative - copy of cooperative registration certificate.

  iv. In case of partnership firm- copy of Regd. Partnership agreement.

(c) Purchase Documents /Cash Memos/ Sale Agreement with payment Receipt showing the original value of Plant and Machinery. An affidavit in case document in respect of purchase of Plant and Machinery/Tool/Implements, not available.

(d) An Affidavit in the prescribed format is to be submitted to the effect that the formation/ activity is well within the purview laid down procedures and norms laid down by the authority.

(e) Pollution Control Certificate for Consent to Operate (COO) from the appropriate authority depending on the category of industry.

(f) However, the permanent certificate will be issued subject to production of specific clearance of the concerned department for specialized items, if any.

Features of the Present Procedure for Registration

Features of the present procedures are as follows:

(1) A unit can apply for PRC for any item that does not require industrial license. Units employing less than 50/100 workers with/without power can apply for registration.

(2) Unit applies for PRC is prescribed application form. No field enquiry is done and PRC is issued.

(3) PRC is valid for five years. If the entrepreneur is unable to set up the unit in this period, he can apply afresh at the end of five years period.

(4) Once the unit commences production, it has to apply for permanent registration on the prescribed form.

The following form basis of evaluation:

(1) The unit has obtained all necessary clearances whether statutory or administrative. e.g. drug license under drug control order, NOC from pollution Control Board, if required etc.

(2) Unit does not violate any location restrictions in force, at the time of evaluation.

(3) Value of plant and machinery is within prescribed limits.

(4) Unit is not owned, controlled or subsidiary of any other industrial undertaking as per notification.

De-registration

A Small-scale Unit can violate the regulations in the following ways which will make it liable for de-registration:

(1) It crosses the investment limits.

(2) It starts manufacturing any new item or items that require an industrial license or other kind of statutory license.

(3) It does not satisfy the condition of being owned, controlled or being a subsidiary of any other industrial undertaking.

(4) Also, If the unit/enterprise remained closed continuously for a period exceeding one year.

(5) If the units/enterprise failed/refused or avoided to give full and truthful information as called upon by the registering authority from time to time and in particular for half yearly report.

Before de-registering the unit a Show Cause Notice to the party should be sent by registered post at the address given in the application form and 30 days time will be given for reply. Action to de-register unit/enterprise will be taken only after the expiry of 30 days time. Any unit/enterprise aggrieved by the order of de-registration can appeal to the authority notified by the State Government within 30 days of receipt of intimation of the same.

Carrying on Business (CoB) Clearance

The same information for Carrying on Business (CoB) clearance required. Industrial undertakings which cross the limit of investment as prescribed in the definition of SSI by process of natural growth will need a "Carrying on Business" license before crossing the ceiling limit from DGTD.

Steps to Start a New Venture

Steps to be followed by an entrepreneur to start with his unit:

Selection of Product; Preliminary Preparation of the Project Report; Selection of Form of Ownership; Selection of Site; Designing Capital Structure; Invite Quotations for equipment/Machinery; Acquisition of Manufacturing Know-how; Preparation of Project Report; Registration Process; Municipal License; Power Connection; Other Statutory Obligations; Arrangement of Finance; Place Order for Machinery; Procurement and Installation of Machinery; Recruitment and Training of staff; Procurement of Input; and Trial Run and Commencement of Commercial Production

Forms of Business Organizations

In order to accomplish a definite target need an organization in one form or the other. Every business enterprise with the motive of profit making therefore, requires an organization which will facilitate carrying on the functions involved in the business operation. What form of business organization you choose depends upon whole host of factors such as whether one can raise the finance alone or not, whether one is comfortable running business alone or not, whether the orders you have got is only as a project basis or otherwise. Some of the main forms of organizations are Sole Trading Concerns; Partnership; Joint Hindu Family Business; Joint Stock Company; and Co-operative Societies.

Factors Influencing a Suitable Form of Organisation

When an entrepreneur proposes to undertake a business, he has to choose a suitable form of organization. While selecting a appropriate form of organization, he has to keep in mind the merits and demerits of every form. The choice has to made both at the time of setting up a new enterprise and at the time of expansion and growth of an existing concern.

For choosing a suitable form of organization an entrepreneur has to take into consideration several factors. They are:

Types of Business; Scope of Operations; Degree of direct control and management; Amount of capital funds required; Size of the Risk; Continuity of the concern; Adaptability of Administration; Comparative Tax Advantage and Cost, Procedure and Government Regulation.

What is Value Added Tax?

Value Added Tax is the tax on Value addition made by a seller on his purchases. It in short is called a VAT. Value addition is the difference between selling price and the purchase price. Whatever tax a seller pays at time of purchase on raw materials or other inputs is called Input Tax. The tax a person is liable to pay at the time of sales is called Output Tax. Value addition or VAT is the tax which is calculated as a difference between output tax and input tax.

ANNEXURE II

GOVERNMENT OF DELHI
OFFICE OF THE COMMISSIONER OF INDUSTRIES
CPO BUILDING, KASHMERE GATE, DELHI – 110 006

APPLICATION FORM FOR PROVISIONAL REGISTRATION AS SMALL–SCALE INDUSTRIES (TO BE FILLED IN DUPLICATE)

INSTRUCTIONS

1. Write/type in block (capital) letters.
2. Fill up whichever is applicable
3. Use English alphabets/Arabic numbers while filling up blocks (to help computerization). Leave one blank after each word.
4. While filling the form, use the following procedure :
   (i) Name of unit e.g. KAMAL ENTERPRISES/G.K. ENTERPRISES

K	A	M	A	L	E	N	T	E	R	P	R	I	S	E	S	

G	K	E	N	T	E	R	P	R	I	S	E	S

   (ii) Pin Code: e.g. 110041

1	1	0	0	4	1

   (iii) Date: e.g. 23rd June 1959

1	9	5	9

   (iv) Quantity(kg) e.g. 90 kg

0	0	0	0	9	0

   (v) Amount (₹ In thousands) e.g. ₹ 5000/- 0

0	0	0	5

   (vi) Fill up appropriate codes in the block wherever applicable.

Example 1: Yes – 1, No. – 2, NA-3.
If NA fill up-3

Example 2: Category: SSI-1, Anc-2, Tiny-3, SSSBE-4, EOU-5, If Tiny fill up-3

5. Block/boxes marked (*) are to be filled by office [3]
6. Applicant should sign all copies

ANNEXURE III

GOVERNMENT OF DELHI
OFFICE OF THE COMMISSIONER OF INDUSTRIES
CPO BUILDING, KASHMERE GATE, DELHI – 110 006
PROVISIONAL REGISTRATION

The application is accepted for Provisional Registration as a SSI/SSSBE unit for the manufacture of items/activities as stated in the application form.

Provisional Registration No.: | | | | | | | | | | |

Date of Issue:

| | | | | | | |

Category of unit (S.No.3)

Signature

Name and designation of Registering Authority

1. The endorsed application form is a part of the certificate of registration.
2. The provisional registration is valid for a period of five years from the date of issue.
3. The provisional registration will automatically lapse at the end of the validity period or the date of commencement of production, whichever is earlier.
4. If an applicant/unit unable to set up the unit within the validity period, the applicant/unit has the option to apply afresh for provisional registration using standard procedure.
5. The provisional registration is given to enable the unit to obtain all facilities/clearance etc. required in the pre-production stage.
6. The provisional registration is subjected to any or all conditions that may be imposed by the Registering Authority.

ANNEXURE IV

GOVERNMENT
DIRECTORATE OF INDUSTRIES
APPLICATION FOR PERMANENT REGISTRATION AS SMALL–SCALE INDUSTRIES
(TO BE FILLED IN TRIPLICATE)

INSTRUCTIONS

1. Write/type in block (capital) letters.
2. Fill up whichever is applicable.
3. Use English alphabets/Arabic numbers while filling up blocks (to help computerization).
4. Leave one blank after each word.
5. While filling the form, use the following procedure. I) Name of the unit e.g. KAMAL ENTERPRISES/G.K ENTERPRISES

K	A	M	A	L	E	N	T	E	R	P	R	I	S	E	S

G	K	E	N	T	E	R	P	R	I	S	E	S

(ii) Pin Code: e.g. 110041

1	1	0	0	4	1

(iii) Date: e.g. 23rd June 1959

2	3	0	6	5	9

(iv) Quantity (kg) e.g. 90kg

0	0	0	0	9	0

(v) Amount (₹ in thousands) e.g. ₹ 5000/-

0	0	0	0	5

(vi) Fill up appropriate codes in the blocks wherever applicable

Example 1: Yes-1, No-2, NA-3 | 3 |
If NA fill up-3

Example 2: Category: SSI-1, Anc-2,
Tiny-3, SSSBE-4, Eou-5 | 3 |

If Tiny fill up-3 5, Block/boxes marked (*) are to be filled by office. 6. Applicant should sign all copies. Abbreviations used:
SSI: Small Scale Industries, ANC: Ancillary Industrial Undertaking, SSSBE: Small Scale Service and business enterprise, TINY: Tiny Enterprise, EOU: Export Oriented Unit, NA: Not applicable.

ANNEXURE V

GOVERNMENT OF DELHI
OFFICE OF THE COMMISSIONER OF INDUSTRIES
CPO BUILDING, KASHMERE GATE, DELHI
FORM

1. Name of Unit/Applicant
2. Address of communication

   Tel.: Pin Code :

3. Category of Unit
   SS1-1, ANC-2, SSSBE-3, TINY-4, EOU-5
4. Location:
   Place/Town
   Tehsil/Taluk
   District
   State
5. Type of organization:
   Proprietory-1, Partnership-2, Pvt. Company-3, Cooperative-4, Others-5
6. Nature of activity :
   Manufacturing/Assembly (01)
   Processing (02)
   Job work (04)
   Repairing/Servicing (08)
7. Main items of manufacture/activities.
   (i) Name
   Code:*
   (ii) Name
   Code:*
   (iii) Name
   Code:*
   (iv) Name
   Code:*

(v) Name

Code:*

8. Investment in Fixed assets (₹ in '000)

(i) Land

(ii) Building

(iii) Plant and Machinery

(iv) Other fixed assets Name

TOTAL Name

9. Investment in Plant and Machinery (Original value ₹ in '000)

Note: Should exclude items whose value is not taken into account while computing the investment, please enclose project profile in case value of investment in Plant and Machinery exceeds ₹ 40 lacs.

10. Power Load

H.P

(1 H.P. = 0.795 K.W.)

11. Employment

(i) Management and Office Staff

(ii) Supervisory and Workers

12. Date of commencement of production (estimated)

Signature of Applicant (Authorized Person)

Date:

Name of proprietor/partner/managing director

FOR OFFICE USE ONLY

Application No

NIC Code

Block Code

District Code

State Code

Location of Unit

(Conforming -1, Non-conforming-2)

Whether the items of manufacture/activity require an industrial license

Yes-1, No.-2

12 ENTREPRENEURIAL SUPPORT

Introduction, Entrepreneurship Development Institute of India, National Institute for Entrepreneurship and Small Business Development, Small Industries Development Organization, National Alliance of Young Entrepreneurs, State Bank of India, District Industry Centre, Small Industries Service Institutes, Small Industries Development Bank of India, State Financial Corporations, National Small Industries Corporation Limited, National Bank for Agriculture and Rural Development, Rajiv Gandhi Udyami Mitra Yojana, District Rural Development Agency, Khadi and Village Industries Commission, Goa Handicraft, Rural and Small-scale Industries Development Corporation, Goa Industrial Development Corporation, Economic Development Corporation, Summing Up.

Introduction

Small-scale Industries Board is an apex advisory body constituted by the Government of India to render advice on all the issues pertaining to the SSI sector. The Department of SSI and Agro and Rural Industries was created under the Ministry of Industry, Government of India, to formulate policy framework and initiate appropriate programmes and schemes for the promotion of SSIs in the country. The range of functions of the development include the setting up of a network of institutions to render services of a varied nature like, techno-economic and managerial aspects, training, testing facilities, marketing assistance, etc. These activities are supported by a host of other Central/State Departments, Agencies, and Autonomous Institutions all over the country.

Industry Associations provide support to the SSI sector and offer a common platform to raise industry-related issues. Government policies, in recent years, have stressed the increasing role of Industry Associations in the setting up of common facilities and other ventures in the area of technology, marketing and other support services.

Entrepreneurship Development Institute of India (EDI)

This is a key organization to play a vital role to develop entrepreneurship. It is not working for profit. It has been established by the inspiration and joint efforts of IDBI, IFCI, ICICI, and SBI. The Govt. of Gujarat has allotted 23 – acre land to build grand a campus of this organization. This is an autonomous and independent body.

This organization has successfully managed various training programme for entrepreneurship development and proved that people of any class can own a business and respectfully earn their livelihood. It has proved that the belief that entrepreneurs are born, not made, is untrue. This organisation has proved with it's activity and performance that entrepreneurship can be developed with properly planned efforts. To make it happen EDI has helped to set up 12 state level entrepreneurship development centers and institutes.

Main activity of EDI is to identify entrepreneur by the programmes of self employment and small industries development, later on it trains and inspires them to set up and develop small as well as village industries. From 1986 to 1990, EDI, with the help of Ford Foundation had applied three years programme in three states to develop entrepreneurship. 150 non-government volunteer organizations work to carry out programmes of this organization.

EDI has executed Micro Enterprise Development Programmes (MEDPs) as well as other programmes in the period of more than 13 years with the help of NGOs. It has groomed many entrepreneurs from rural and town area. This organization had carried out GIO MEDPs programmes and trained 15243 rural youth in a decade.

Besides above EDI also works to strengthen capability of NGOs. It has trained 325 workers of more of more than 200 NGOs. More than 150 NGOs, had managed MEDPS. They did it either independently or with EDI. Chief Managers of more than 250 NGOs had participated in various training schools. They were encouraged by realistic information about small scale industries about development of finance transactions and had developed their activity. It was undertaken by micro credit programmes. NGO and banks hold dialogues for easy finance to entrepreneurs. 40 bank managers are given detailed idea about financial requirements of entrepreneurs start their business immediately after completion of training.

More than 100 chief executive officers and senior workers who are associated with NGOs have been given high level managerial training. These officers were from U.P., H.P., Rajasthan and Haryana.

The Government in centre and state has approved the successful performance and activities of EDI. The international institutes, which work for development of entrepreneurship, have helped EDI. Thus EDI has been helped by world famous organizations like World Bank, Common Wealth secretariat, UNIDO, ILO, British Council, Ford Foundation etc. It has been appreciated by declaring it *"Centre of Excellence"* for its global achievements by United Nations Economic and Social Commission for Asia and Pacific (ESCAP) Bangkok, Thailand and India.

EDI is a national resources organization. It is committed training, research and education of entrepreneurship. It explores novel techniques for such training. Training and educational material is also provided to trainees by learned experts. Experience and experiments are also shared with them.

EDI has a nationwide network. The organizations fully working to develop entrepreneurship are connected with it. It is also associated with Inter regional centre for entrepreneurship and investment training sponsored by Government of India and United Nations, Industrial development organization. It is also concerned with national science and technology entrepreneurship development board.

In education field it works for entrepreneurship development of present entrepreneurs, micro enterprise, micro finance development, development of entrepreneurship, promoting organizations, environment for entrepreneurship, research and development in entrepreneurship etc..

EDI felt that to reach the people and to prepare skilful entrepreneurs, industrial education and training is the best medium, hence, it emphasizes on them. Entrepreneurship education is main activity of EDI. EDI plans faculty development programmes for engineering colleges and schools. It arranges summer camp for children and young people to inspire them to be capable entrepreneur. More over EDI plans seminars, workshops to apply entrepreneurship, education for future prospects and for educationists, policy decision makers, administrators etc.

EDI holds skill-based development programme for the rising demand of training in the fields like rural market capacity. Unit- wise finance distribution, in house financial management in NGOs etc. EDI arranges training and development programmes keeping the necessities of rural entrepreneurship programmes NGOs and voluntary organizations training and expansion programmes, self-employment for rural youth etc., in mind. EDI plans programmes for the NGOs to manage their finance system, accounts, and individual administration properly as well as to groom youth to be the best entrepreneurs. It under taker specific activities to develop rural markets and microcredit based rural business.

EDI encourages entrepreneurs who are running and managing their business to develop and expand their activity. It also works for small entrepreneurs to improve their activity. For this objective EDI holds programmes for performance improvement programmes, development programmes, inter entrepreneurship programmes for exports, small industries management help programme etc. To develop entrepreneurship EDI arranges specific programmes for skillful work-based management as well as to develop technology and unit in enterprise. EDI continuously strives to improve its depth and strongest to develop entrepreneurship development programmes and their organizations. For the same it arranges basic training programmes, skill development programmes and open entrepreneurship information programmes for trainees. These programmes considerably help to improve the performance at existing and potential entrepreneurs. Officers and managers of development organizations, financial organizations, also help this organization. EDI holds research programme for entrepreneurship environment.

A new entrepreneurship research centre which is founded by national science and technology entrepreneurship development board also associated with EDI. EDI is going to set up laboratories and testing centers in industrial area through this (above) institute. The entrepreneurs who develop technology are inspired by this because it provides information about developed technology. Besides these EDI has a separate centre named Centre for Research and Entrepreneurship Education and Development (CREED) for developing research for training and education about entrepreneurship. EDI bridges practical and theoretical concepts of entrepreneurship.

EDI's activity for the development of entrepreneurship, grooming of new entrepreneurs identification of business opportunities, project evaluation etc. are worldwide appreciated. Due to excellent performance of EDI, the Government of India and UNIDO has sponsored Inter-regional centre for entrepreneurship and investment training.

National Institute for Entrepreneurship and Small Business Development (NIESBUD)

This is a paramount to co-ordinate activities of those organizations who arrange training classes for entrepreneurship development. It was established in 1960, under society act and has commenced its activity since 1983. It works as Secretariat of National Entrepreneurship Development Board which enact policies for entrepreneurship.

It provides standardized syllabus and training to various groups and concerned. The govt., provides full fund for the programmes of this organization. It holds programmes having high demand or not held by other institutes with such programmes, it inspires, encourages, develops and expands entrepreneurship.

The organization (NIESBUD) works for those institutes working directly or indirectly in the field of entrepreneurship and tries to make them stronger.

Its main objective is to develop and expand entrepreneurship and the institutes working in this field. It helps to make the activity of such institutes more efficient and result oriented.

Its second object is to identify potential entrepreneurs and to train them, to help them, to provide detailed information, to exchange of the people working in this field. It also works for improvement in policy and programmes to be helpful in the formation of concerned policies.

A governing council has been formed to provide direction to this organization. Union minister of industry holds its office of chairman and minister for state of industry ministry holds the office of vice chairman of NIESBUD. It arranges programmes keeping various people in mind who are involved in various activities. In this context NIESBUD holds various programmes for entrepreneur their supporting agencies, professionals, gov.'s agencies. NGOs and for the people working for the development of entrepreneurship, it arranges special programme trainers, training promoters, entrepreneurs of small industries etc. It also arranges programmes for small aid, continuous education programme, Entrepreneurship–based programmes are held for senior administrators. In the same way for the teachers, research analyst of IIT, professors of engineering colleges, senior officers of merchant banks, SIDO, Shramik Vidhyapith's officers, arrange special training classes.

NIESBUD continuously evaluates its programmes and makes necessary amendments according to current requirements. Thus necessary amendments are made according to requirements of entrepreneurship and small industry development. NIESBUD also works to create warm atmosphere according to changing condition of society for entrepreneurs, as well as to get support and co-operation from society.

Thus, NIESBUD plays a significant role to develop entrepreneurship and small industries, nationwide specialty of its activity is that it doesn't work in the fields which are less important, less necessary and the fields in which other organizations are working. It works in the field having rising demand and in which others are not working. It also helps other agencies, institutes concerned with the same field.

It tries to improve efficiency of the top most officers of finance and industrial field by training and educating them and for the development of their organizations.

It provides direction to the government to enact policies and programmes for entrepreneurship. Industry ministry and specific important ministers are associated with this organization, which denotes its worth and importance.

NIESBUD's activity defers from EDI. Both are having same goal but carry out different task. EDI works is connected with rural entrepreneurship and self-employment whereas NIESBUD does not involve itself in them, hence, money and efforts are not wasted.

Its structure and activities are flexible. It is continuously changes itself according to changing condition, demand, economic and industrial condition. It continuously evaluates its performance, programmes, policies, structure, etc., it arranges its programmes according to demand and requirement of industries and entrepreneurs.

However, it has more power than EDI, also having a widespread field and work area, though it has not reached to all existing and potential entrepreneurs. The impression is such that it works only in cities. It has not reached wider class of rural entrepreneurs like EDI has, though it helps a lot to enact and to apply policies and programmes in the field of entrepreneurship.

Small Industries Development Organization (SIDO)

SIDO was established in New Delhi for development of small industries and organizational structure development. It has nationwide network. It provides economic and mechanical services. It is associated with office of small industries, dept. of agriculture and rural industry ministry as well as the Government of India.

SIDO is a nodal agency of central government. It is a paramount organization to enact policies and programmes and to apply coordinate to control and to manage these programmes. It provides many important services to small industries. It provides services of adviser of economic management matters. It helps small entrepreneurs by providing training, some general facilities, testing instrument facility, market aid, etc. All these activities are being carried out by its regional agencies and other specially formed organizations. Among these organizations, small industries service institutes, regional testing centers, field testing centers, field testing stations, tools room, tool design, institutes field process-cum-product development centers etc., are included, moreover 28 small industries service institutes and branches, small industries service institutes have 30 branches to work for this objective. They are situated in state capitals and at other location.

These institutes run programmes to encourage entrepreneurship and provide advice to entrepreneurship. It holds surveys at state and district level to explore potentiality of industrial development. 4 regional and 10 zonal testing centers provide testing facility and advice. It also arranges training centers, tools rooms and tool design institute provide training and advice to entrepreneurs for production, product design, their arrangement, and management etc., with coordination of tools manufacturers.

It also sets product-cum process development centre to work as research and development institute where industries are developed in clusterous form. It also helps for product designing, product improvement, development of packaging technology, man power development, training etc.

Besides its zonal agencies there are some specific organizations, like National Small Industries Corporation, New Delhi, which provide machinery to small industries on hire-purchase basis. It also provides market aid, technological help, instrument on hire basis etc., for the purpose of training and development of entrepreneurship. National Institute of Small Industry Extension Training, Hyderabad and National Institute for Entrepreneurship and Small Business Development, New Delhi, carry out related programmes, SIDBI programmes finance small industries. A small industry board has been formed to co-ordinate with central and state governments. It is the highest advisory body. It advises the government about every facet of small industries.

There are many organizations working at state and central level which provide various means and services. They include *"District Industry Centres"*, *"Small Industries Development Corporations"*, *"Industry Commissioners and Supervisors"* etc.

National Alliance of Young Entrepreneurs (NAYE)

It is a national level body for young entrepreneurs. It specially strives for preparing women entrepreneurs. 1975, was the year, observed for maintaining women's status and respect, hence, in the same year NAYE added a women's wing in its structure. It nurtures entrepreneurship in women. It grooms women entrepreneurs in a big scale. It has put in lots of efforts to have a proper place and respect for women in our industrial structure and economy.

NAYE a national institute for young entrepreneurs had hosted a conference in 1975, in New Delhi. In which through discussion about needs of women entrepreneurs, their problems, steps towards development etc. It was also discussed for the women to be independent, self-reliant, and secure their deserved place in the society.

Later in three international conferences, the points of discussion were, maximum productive use of capital development structure and market problems besides these, eight national conferences were held in various parts of the country. Women's wing of NAYE helps women entrepreneurship in all respects. Efforts are being put into increase their production capacity so they can manage their business easily. NAYE helps to identify investment opportunity. It sends a delegation to conferences, trade fairs etc. NAYE represents various authorities to sort out individually the problems of woman entrepreneurs.

Women entrepreneurs are given required information through workshops, conferences, seminars, training progammes etc., and it is seen that they get required facilities. Lobbying is being done by women's wing of NAYE to press, parliament, state assemblies and in other forums for women entrepreneurs. Thus, proper efforts are done for women to secure their deserved place.

In May 1985, "The Association of Women Industrialists/Entrepreneurs of Maharashtra" was established. 400 of its members work to develop women entrepreneurship in the state. NAYE had a vital role in foundation of this association. It has its H.O. at Pune. It has its branches at Mumbai, Nasik, and Aurangabad and at other places. It associates NAYE to market its member's product and hold training progammes.

Thus, NAYE strives hard for upliftment of young entrepreneurs especially women. It has played a considerable role to make women entrepreneurs independent and to live respectfully. It holds workshop, conferences, training classes etc., to create awareness in entrepreneurs.

It has succeeded in uplifting women entrepreneurs and it was appreciated worldwide. This way association for women entrepreneurs covering entire state in Maharashtra was formed. Such association should be formed in every state having branches in all districts to establish women's importance and place in the society and economy. In the same way Self-employed Women's Association (SEWA) has performed better in Gujarat to make women independent.

State Bank of India (SBI)

Activities of India's biggest, widespread, versatile bank, SBI include development of entrepreneurship. It also carries out development-based banking activities along with traditional merchant banking. It is a leading bank at this facet. It was pioneer to form various programmes and schemes for the development of entrepreneurship. It especially manages its programmes to develop industries in backward areas. Since 1978, SBI carries out various programmes to develop entrepreneurship.

In the leading associations working for entrepreneurship, EDI was founded in 1983. NIESBUD was also founded in 1983. SBI also started its activity in 1978 for entrepreneurship. Hence SBI is a leading bank among the organizations working for entrepreneurship. SBI has formed a unique model for the development of entrepreneurship in which a rigorous training of one month is given to entrepreneurs. It covers behaviors training etc. SBI bears all expense of training like stay, food etc.

SBI has three phases of its entrepreneurship development programme.

(1) **The first phase**, includes searching for the person having potentiality for the development of entrepreneurship.

(2) **In second phase**, various programmes are held for the development of such person like management skills, training programmes, inspiration etc.

(3) **In the last phase**, the person is given all necessary aids to develop his business and inspiration as well as encouragement is provided to such entrepreneurs.

SBI has understood the importance of small industries in national development of economy hence, it has financed on large-scale to small industries, small entrepreneurs are also encouraged by SBI. It has made a separate arrangement for finance to small industries. SBI applies development programmes packages keeping specific requirements of small industries in mind. This package has various programmes and schemes. It also includes liberal loan, in which SBI finances up to 75% of project cost, hence, an entrepreneur has to arrange only for balance 25% amount. A technically qualified entrepreneur gets loan to cover the entire project cost. The entrepreneur qualifying in the technical qualification set by bank gets 100% loan besides this under equity fund scheme up to ₹1 lakh is financed as interest free loan to fulfill equity deficit.

Thus, SBI has an important stake in the development process of entrepreneurship in the country. It identifies and trains the entrepreneurs. It finances them to commence their business. Qualified entrepreneurs get loan up to to 100% of cost. Interest free loan is also given to fill equity deficit.

District Industry Centre (DIC)

Morarji Desai Govt. of Janta Morcha party had thought of DIC for decentralized and balanced industrial development as well as for the development of rural and small industries. This programme was commenced on 1st May, 1978, during 7th Five Year Plan. Central and State Government shares 50:50 of the cost of this programme.

DIC operates in every district of the country, 422 approved district industry centers covered 431 districts. Its objectives are to develop tiny, small and rural industries, as well as, to increase employment in villages and backward ares. It works as a single window agency for entrepreneurs, where they carry out most of the tasks of entrepreneurs. It helps to provide all kinds of help to small industries under one roof at district level. Small industries get registration in their district. It performs an important task of helping entrepreneur pre and post finance aids. Especially, it looks to establish more and more industries in rural backward area.

"Prime Minister Rojgar Yojna" is also provided by District Industry Centre to help unemployed youth to be self-employed. This scheme was announced in August'93 and applied on 2nd October 1993. This programme was started with a view to employ 10 lacs unemployed youth through 7 lacs small enterprises. It was anticipated to select beneficiaries by NGO's as well as training and project profile preparation for entrepreneurs. This center provides information about business opportunities to entrepreneurs. It helps entrepreneurs in various phases from preparation of project report to application of project. It helps to avail infrastructure like land, electricity etc., to entrepreneurs. First of all, an entrepreneur has to select a district and secondly, he has to get registration in that centre.

Thus, these centers look after various activities for the development of industries and entrepreneurship in the district. All information can be gathered from one place. All the Govt. Schemes for tiny and small industries are provided by DICs. It provides direction and information from commencement to complete management of business.

This is a scheme in which central and all state governments are equal financial partner. DIC carry out conspicuous activities for industrial development in rural and backward area.

Role of DIC for the promotion of Small-scale and Cottage Industries

(1) Technical support of preparation of Project Report.

(2) Information on sources of machinery and equipment.

(3) Priority in Power Supply/Telephone connection.

(4) Promotion of new Industrial Estates/Growth Centers.

(5) Land/Shed in Industrial Estate.

(6) Approval of Project Reports of special types.

(7) Promotion of Electronic Industries.

(8) Govt. Margin Money Loan under Additional Employment Programme.

(9) Training through Entrepreneurship Development Programme.

(10) Assistance under State Incentives Scheme.

(11) Allotment of Raw Materials.

(12) Financial Assistance under Self-employment Schemes.

(13) Financial assistance through Bank/WBFC/WBSIC/NSIC.

(14) Assistance under Equipment Leasing Scheme through NSIC.

(15) Marketing linkage with Central Govt./ State Govt. Organizations/Undertakings.
(16) Marketing assistance through WBSIC/NSIC/CEO.
(17) Ancillary Industry tie-up with Govt. undertakings.
(18) Marketing information.
(19) Marketing assistance through participation in Exhibitions/Trade Fairs/Buyers-Sellers Meet etc.
(20) Marketing assistance to Handicraft Artisans through participation in Handicrafts Expo and Exhibition inside/outside of the state.
(21) Linkage with organization like WBHDC/WB State Handicrafts Co-operative Society Ltd., Development Commissioners (Handicrafts).
(22) Attending problems related to SSI Registration/Bank loan/ Marketing of Production etc.
(23) Linkage with Research Institutes like CMERI/CGCRI/NML/CFTRI etc., for technology up-gradation and innovation.
(24) Financial Assistance for modernization of Unit.
(25) Skill development training through own workshop/organization like SISI, PDTC/Coir Board/ETDC.
(26) Managerial capability improvement through training, workshop, seminars.
(27) Export assistance.
(28) In plant study of their SSI Units.
(29) Standardization of products.
(30) Sick Unit Revitalization.
(31) National level awards for innovative products/outstanding growth/exports etc.
(32) Promotion of products under Non-conventional Energy Sources.
(33) Assistance under Coir Development Schemes.
(34) Registration of Industrial Cooperative and financial assistance to them.
(35) Pollution control.
(36) Assistance under scheme promoted by W.B Minority Dev. Finance Corporation/KVI Commission/ Board and such other organizations.
(37) Single window assistance through SIDA and District Industries Centrers.
(38) BSAI Loan for Cottage Industries.
(39) Design and Product Development for Handicrafts.
(40) Awards to Handicrafts Artisans.
(41) Development of Lac Industries.
(42) Setting up of Bio-gas plants.

Small Industries Service Institutes (SISIs)

The SISIs are setup to provide consultancy and training to small entrepreneurs-both existing and prospective. The activities of SISIs are co-ordinated by the Industrial Management Training Division of the DCSSIs office there are 28 SISIs and 30 Branch SISIs set up in State Capital and other places all over the country.

The main functions of SISIs include:

(1) To serve as interface between Central and State Governments.
(2) To render technical support services.
(3) To conduct Entrepreneurship Development Programmes.
(4) To initiate promotional programmes.

Credit is the prime input for sustained growth of small sector and its availability continues to be a matter of concern. Credit provided for creation of fixed assets like land, building, and plant machinery is called long-term credit. Credit provided for running the industry for its day to day requirement for purchasing raw materials and other inputs like electricity and water etc., and for payment of wages and salaries is called short-term credit or working capital.

Institutional Arrangement

Small-scale Industrial Sector is provided working capital by commercial banks and in some cases by cooperative banks and regional rural banks. Term loans are provided by State Financial Corporations (SFCs), Small Industries Development Corporations (SIDCs), National Small Industries Corporation (from NSIC) and National Bank for Agriculture and Rural Development (NABARD), Financial assistance from NSIC and to some extent SIDCs is available in the form of supply of machinery on hire purchase basis/deferred payment basis. Small sized SSI and tiny units also get some term loans from commercial banks along with working capital in the form of composite loans.

Refinance to these institutions is provided by the Small Industries Development Bank of India (SIDBI). Such refinance comprises assistance provided to State Financial Corporation Bills, Finance Scheme, Special Capital/Seed Capital Scheme, and to National Small Industries Corporation. Long-term loan are provided to the smalls scale industrial units by SFCs mainly through Single Window Scheme and National Equity Fund as also direct assistance provided to State Financial Corporations in the form of refinance. Some part of working capital for pre-operative expenses is also provided by State Financial Corporations to Small Scale Industrial units under the Single Window Scheme.

Credit to SSI Sector from Public Sector Banks

The Table given below gives the positions with regard to flow of credit to SSI Sector:-

	At the end of March 1995	At the end of March 1996	At the end of March 1997	At the end of March 1998	At the end of March 1998
Net Bank Credit	₹ 16,90,138.00	₹ 8,43,181.00	₹ 8,96,284.00	₹ 1,82,219.00	₹ 46,203.00
Credit to SSI	₹ 25,843.00	₹ 29,845.00	₹ 31,542.00	₹ 38,109.00	₹ 42,674.00
No. of SSI Accounts (in lacs)	32.25	33.77	N.A.	29.64	N.A.
SSI Credit as percentage of Net Bank Credit	15.29	15.99	16.6	17.50	17.33

There is a marginal decline in share of credit to SSI sector as a percentage of net bank credit.

Credit to Tiny Sector

The table below gives the status of credit flow to tiny sector since 1995:-

	At the end of March 1995	At the end of March 1996	At the end of March 1997	At the end of March 1998
Net Credit to Tiny Sector	₹ 7,734.00	₹ 8,183.00	₹ 9,515.00	₹ 10,273.13
Tiny Credit as percentage on net SSI Credit	29.93	27.76	30.20	27.00

The advances outstanding against Tiny sector increased from ₹ 9,515 crores at the end of March, 1997 to ₹ 10,273 crores at the end of March 1998. The share of tiny sector in the advances to SSI sector has, however, decreased from 30.2% at the end of March 1997 to 27% at the end of March, 1998. As per RBI guidelines, 40% priority sector going to SSI has to go to tiny units with in plant and machinery between ₹ 5 lacs and ₹ 25 lacs. Thus, against the target of 60% of SSI credit for tiny units, actual flow at 27% is very low.

Nayak Commitee

Nayak Committee was set up by the Reserve Bank of India in December, Nayak Committee and RBI issued a number of circulars advising the banks to grant working capital to the extent of 20% of the projected annual turnover, timely disposal and setting up of specialized bank branches for SSI loaning in areas of higher SSI concentration.

As a follow up of Nayak Committee recommendations, Finance Minister in the Budget speech of 1995-96, announced a Seven Point Action Plan for improving the flow of credit to small-scale sector consisting of the following:

(i) Time bound action for setting up specialized SSI branches in 85 identified districts; at least 100 such dedicated branches to be opened before the end of 1995-96.

(ii) Adequate delegation of powers at the branch and regional levels.

(iii) Banks to conduct sample surveys of their performing SI accounts to find out whether they are getting adequate credit.

(iv) Steps to be taken to see as far as possible that composite loans (covering both term loans and working capital) are sanctioned to SSI entrepreneurs.

(v) Regular meetings by banks at zonal and regional levels with SSI Entrepreneurs.

(vi) Need to sensitize bank managers and reorient them regarding working of the SSI sector.

(vii) Simplification of procedural formalities by banks for SSI entrepreneurs.

Steps taken by Reserve Bank of India to improve credit flow to SSI sector

(a) The Government had raised the investment limit of SSIs from ₹ 60 lacs to ₹ 300 lacs and for tiny units from ₹ 5 lacs to ₹ 25 Lacs. In order to ensure that credit is available to all segments of tiny sector. RBI has issued instructions that out of funds normally available to SSI sector, 40% be given to units with investment in plant and machinery up to ₹ 5 lacs; 20% for units with investment between ₹ 5 lacs to ₹ 25 lacs and remaining 40 % for other units.

(b) Public sector banks have been advised to operationalise more specialized SSI branches at centers where there is a potential for financing many SSI borrowers. As on March 1998, 370 specialized SSI branches are working in the country.

(c) To extend 'Single Window Scheme' of SIDBI to all districts to meet the financial requirements (both term loan and working capital) of SSIs.

(d) With a view to moderating the cost of credit to SSI units, banks are advised to accord SSI units with a good track record the benefits of lower spread over the Prime Lending Rate.

(e) In order to take expeditious decision on credit proposals of SSI units, banks have been advised to delegate enhanced powers to the branch managers of the specialized SSI branch so that most of the credit proposals are decided at the branch level.

Fresh initiatives announced in the Budget of 1999-2000

In this budget speech the Finance Minister has announced the following measures for improving credit supply to SSI sector:

(a) ***A New Credit Insurance Scheme Launched:*** Inability to provide adequate security to banks and low recovery are often cited as major constraint in flow of investment credit of SSI units. The problem is more acute for export oriented and tiny sector enterprises. To alleviate this problem, the Finance Minister announced that a new credit insurance scheme will be launched.

(b) ***Composite Loan Scheme Limit Enhanced to ₹ 5 lacs:*** The composite loan scheme of SIDBI and commercial banks is designed to case operational difficulties of the small borrowers by presiding term loan and working capital through a single window. The limit for composite loans currently at ₹ 2 lacs has been enhanced to ₹ 5 lacs.

(c) ***Working Capital Limit Enhanced to ₹ 5 Crores:*** For SSI units the working capital is determined by the banks on the basis of simple calculation of 20% of their annual turnover. The turnover limit for this purpose has been enhanced from ₹ 4 crore to ₹ 5 crore.

(d) ***Credit Delivery to Tiny Sector:*** To increase the outreach of banks to the tiny sector, lending by banks of Non-Banking Financial Companies (NBFCs) or other financial intermediaries for purposes of on-lending to the tiny sector is being included within the definition of priority sector for bank lending.

High Level Committee for Credit (Kapur Committee)

In December, 1997, Reserve Bank of India has appointed a One-man Committee under the Chairmanship of **Shri S.L. Kapur**, former Secretary (SSI), Government of India, to suggest measures for improving the delivery system. The Committee has submitted its report to RBI on 30th June, 1998. Some of the major recommendations of the Committee are:-

(i) Special treatment to smaller among small industries;

(ii) Enhancement in the quantum of composite loans;

(iii) Removal of procedural difficulties in the path of SSI advances;

(iv) Sorting out issued relating to land including removal of stamp duty and permitting equitable mortgages;

(v) Allowing access to low-cost funds to Small Industries Development Bank of India (SIDBI) for refinancing SSI loans.

(vi) Non-obtaining of collaterals for loans up to ₹ 2 Lacs;

(vii) Setting up of collateral reserve fund to provide support to first party guarantees;

(viii) Setting up of a Small Industries Infrastructure Development Fund for developing industrial areas in/around metropolitan and urban areas;

(ix) Change in the definition of sick SSI units;

(x) Giving statutory powers to State Level Inter-Institutional (SLIIC);

(xi) Setting up a separate guarantee organization and opening of 1,000 additional specialized branches;

(xii) Enhancement of SIDBIs role and status to match with that of National Bank for Agriculture and Rural Development (NABARD).

Kapur Committee has made 126 recommendations out of which RBI has already accepted 40 recommendations for implementations.

Amendment of interest on delayed payment act

To tackle the problem of settlement of dues of SSI units by large companies interest on Delayed Payment Act has been amended. The following amendments have been made in the Act:

(a) The payment has to be made within 120 days to the SSI supplier from the date of acceptance of the goods by the buyer;

(b) Interest on delayed payment has been revised from 5% above the floor rate to one and half time the prime lending rate charged by SBI;

(c) Mechanism has been prescribed for settling disputes by Industry Facilitation Councils to be set up by State Governments through notification.

Small Industries Development Bank of India (SIDBI)

SIDBI was set up by an Act of Parliament, as an apex institution for promotion, financing and development of industries in small scale sector and for coordinating the functions of other institutions engaged in similar activities. It commenced operations on April 2, 1990. SIDBI extends direct/indirect financial assistance to SSIs, assisting the entire spectrum of small and tiny sector industries on All India basis.

The range of assistance comprising financing, extension support and promotional, is made available through appropriate schemes of direct and indirect assistance for the following purposes:-

- Setting up new projects;
- Expansion, diversification, modernization, technology upgradation, quality improvement, rehabilitation of existing units;
- Strengthening of marketing capabilities of SSI units;
- Development of infrastructure for SSIs; and
- Export promotion.

Direct Assistance Schemes

Directly assists SSIs under Project Finance Scheme, Equipment Finance Scheme, Marketing Scheme, Vendor Development Scheme, Infrastructural Development Scheme, ISO-9000, Technology Development and Modernization Fund, Venture Capital Scheme, assistance for leasing to NBFCs, SFCs, SIDCs and resource support to institutions involved in the development and financing of small-scale sector.

These Schemes are mainly targeted at addressing some of the major problems of SSIs in areas such as high tech project, marketing, infrastructural development, delayed realistic of bills, obsolescence of technology, quality improvement, export financing and venture capital assistance.

Indirect Assistance Schemes

Under its indirect schemes, SIDBI extends refinance of loans to small scale sector by Primary Lending Institutions (PLIs) *viz.*, SFCs, SIDCs and Banks. At present, such refinance assistance is extended to 892 PLIs and these PLIs extend credit through a network of more than 65,000 branches all over the country.

All the schemes of SIDBI both direct and indirect assistance are in operation in all the States of the country through 39 regional/branch offices of SIDBI.

Promotional and Development Activities

SIDBI is actively involved in promoting tiny and small-scale industries by means for its promotional and developmental activities through suitable professional agencies for organizing Entrepreneurship Development Programmes, Technology Upgradation & assistance under Mahila Vikas Nidhi to bring about economic empowerment of women specially the rural poor by providing them avenues for training and employment opportunities.

A	Refinance against term loans in respect of projects/activities eligible for assistance under the Scheme	Interest on term loans for fixed assets and working capital advances (excluding interest tax) (% p.a)	Interest on Refinance (% p.a)
	(i) Upto and inclusive of ₹ 25,000/-	12.00	9.00
	(ii) Over ₹ 25,000/- and upto ₹ 2 Lakh	Not exceeding 13.5	10.5

B	Refinance against term loans in respect of projects/activities eligible for assistance under TDMF and ISO 9000 Schemes (Applicable to all eligible institutions) (except RRBs)	Interest on term loans (excluding interest tax) (% p.a)	Interest on Refinance (% p.a)
	(i) Upto and inclusive of ₹ 25,000/-	12.00	9.00
	(ii) Over ₹ 25,000/- and upto ₹ 2 Lakh	Not exceeding 13.5	10.50
	(iii) Over ₹ 2 lakh	Not exceeding 14.00	12.00

Performance

SIDBIs efforts have resulted in increased flow of credit to SSI sector since inception as indicated below

Year	Sanction	Disbursement
1990-91	2410	1839
1991-92	2847	2028
1992-93	2909	2146
1993-94	3357	2672
1994-95	4706	3390
1995-96	6066	4801
1996-97	6485	4585
1997-98	7484	5241

SIDBI's Assistance to

(i) Tiny units About 89.2 per cent of the number of projects assisted under Refinance Scheme during 1996-97, were tiny, receiving assistance upto ₹ 5 lakh per project. The sanctions for such projects accounted for 39.6% of the total amount of sanctions in 1996-97, as against 36.0% during the previous year.

(ii) Women entrepreneurs—Under various schemes assistance amounting to ₹ 19.7 crores was given to 1067 women entrepreneurs during 1996-97.

(iii) Backward Areas—During 1996-97, projects emanating from backward areas received assistance to the tune of ₹ 775 crores of sanction which accounted for 37% of total assistance under Refinance Scheme of SIDBI.

Measures to Simplify Rules/Regulations

- To fill the gaps in the existing structure of credit delivery mechanism to the small scale sector, Small Industries Development Bank of India (SIDBI) keeps on effecting simplification of procedures, liberalization of new schemes and introduction of new schemes.
- Endeavour of SIDBI is to ensure that no worthwhile proposal is denied credit for want of funds.
- Norms lay down by Reserve Bank of India and Government of India are followed by SIDBI for granting assistance to SSI units.

Liberalization effected

- Enhancement in the ceiling on loan amount of the Composite Loan Scheme to ₹ 2 lakh from the earlier ceiling of ₹ 50,000/- to ensure timely availability of term loan and working capital to the small units. The scheme was also liberalized to include units in all areas other than metropolitan areas.
- Scope of Technology Development and Modernization Fund Scheme and Refinance Scheme for Technology Development and Modernization has been expanded to cover non-exporting SSIs/Ancillary units graduating out of SSI sector for assistance under the Scheme.

- Scope of Single Window Scheme has been enlarged to cover modernization, technology up-gradation in addition to new SSI units. Project outlay under the scheme has been gradually raised from ₹ 30 lacs to ₹ 100 lacs. Simultaneously, the sub-limits for working capital and term loan components have been done away with.

Main Schemes of SIDBI

National Equity Fund Scheme which provides equity support to small entrepreneurs setting up projects in Tiny Sector.

Technology Development and Modernization Fund for providing finances to existing SSI units for technology up gradation/modernization.

Single Window Scheme to provide both term loan for fixed assets and loan for working capital through the same agency.

Composite Loan Scheme for equipment and/or working capital and also for work sheds to artisans, village and cottage industries in Tiny Sector.

Mahila Udyam Nidhi (MUN) Scheme provides equity support to women entrepreneurs for setting up projects in Tiny sector.

Scheme for financing activities relating to marketing of SSI products provides assistance for undertaking various marketing related activities such as marketing research, R&D, product up gradation, participation in trade fairs and exhibitions, advertising branding, establishing distribution networks including showroom, retail outlet, ware housing facility, etc.

Equipment Finance Scheme for acquisition of machinery/equipment including Diesel Generator Sets which are not related to any specific project.

Venturecapital Scheme to encourage SSI ventures/sub-contracting units to acquire capital equipment, as also requisite technology for building up of export capabilities / import substitution including cost to total quality management and acquisition of ISO-9000 certification and for expansion of capacity.

ISO 9000 Scheme to meet the expenses on consultancy, documentation, audit, certification fee, equipment and calibrating instruments required for obtaining ISO 9000 certification.

Micro Credit Scheme to meet the requirement of well managed Voluntary Agencies that are in existence for at least 5 years; have a good track record and have established network and experience in small savings-cum-credit programmes with Self–help Groups (SHGs).

New Schemes

(i) To enhance the export capabilities of SSI units;

(ii) Scheme for Marketing Assistance;

(iii) Infrastructure Development Scheme;

(iv) Scheme for acquisition of ISO 9000 certification;

(v) Factoring Service;

(vi) Bills Re-discounting Scheme against inland supply bills of SSIs; and

(vii) Major Schemes.

Technology Development and Modernization Fund

SIDBI has set up Technology Development and Modernization Fund (TDMF) Scheme for direct assistance of Small-scale industries to encourage existing industrial units in the sector, to modernize their production facilities and adopt improved and updated technology so as to strengthen their export capabilities. Assistance under the scheme is available for meeting the expenditure on purchase of capital equipment acquisition of technical know-how, upgradation of process technology and products with thrust on quality improvement, improvement in packaging and cost of TQM and acquisition of ISO-9000 series certification.

SIDBI in July 1996 had permitted SFCs and promotional banks to grant loans for modernization projects costing up to ₹ 50 Lacs. The coverage of the TDMF scheme has been enlarged, *w.e.f.*, 1.9.1997. Non-exporting units and units who are graduating out of SSI sector are now eligible to avail assistance under this scheme.

National Equity Fund

National Equity Fund (NEF) under Small Industries Development Bank of India (SIDBI) provides equity type assistance to SSI units, tiny units at one per cent service charges. The scope of this scheme was widened in 1995-96 to cover all areas excepting Metropolitan areas, raising the limit of loan from ₹ 1.5 lacs to ₹ 2.5 lacs and covering both existing as well as new units:

(a) The following are eligible for assistance under the scheme:-
   (i) New projects in tiny small-scale sectors for manufacture preservation or processing of goods irrespective of the location (except for the units in Metropolitan areas).
   (ii) Existing tiny and small-scale industrial units and service enterprises as mentioned above (including those which have availed of NEF assistance earlier), undertaking expansion, modernization technology upgradation and diversification irrespective of location (except in Metropolitan areas).
   (iii) Sick units in the tiny and small-scale sectors including service enterprise as mentioned above, which are considered potentially viable, irrespective of the location of the units (except for the units in Metropolitan areas).
   (iv) All industrial activities and service activities (except Road Transport Operators).
(b) Project cost (including margin money for working capital) should not exceed ₹ 10 lacs in the case of new projects in the case of existing units and service enterprises, the outlay on expansion/modernization/technology upgradation or diversification or rehabilitation should not exceed ₹ 10 lakh per project.
(c) There is no change in the existing level of promoters' contribution at 10% of the project cost. However, the ceiling on soft loan assistance under the Scheme has been enhanced from the present level of 15% lakh per project to 25% of the project cost subject to a maximum of ₹ 2.5 lakh per project.

State Financial Corporations (SFCs)

In pursuance of the SFCs Act, 1951, SFCs were set up mainly to finance small and medium-scale units. Their area of operation is generally restricted to the concerned States. SFCs also assist small-scale units for their modernization and technology up gradation programmes by providing soft loans, restructuring the sick small-scale units through rehabilitation schemes and through equity type assistance under SIDBIs seed capital scheme.

At present, there are 18 SFCs (including TIIC which was set up as company) in existence for more than 40 years and operate as Regional Development Banks. The SFCs have played an important role in the evolution and growth of small and medium-scale industries in their respective states. They provide financial assistance to industrial units by way of term loans, direct subscription to equity, guarantees, etc. Over the years SFCs have expanded their activities and coverage of assistance.

One-man Committee set up by RBI under the Chairmanship of former Secretary, SSI and ARI, to look into various problems regarding credit flow to SSI sector and support appropriate measures for their redressal has given the following recommendations in its report submitted to RBI which are being processed by them:-

- Restructuring of weaker SFCs by the Government.
- Funds for lending under Single Window Scheme by SFCs should be placed by SIDBI with the SFCs in adequate measures.
- Each SFC should get into an MoU with one or two Public Sector banks and participate in joint lending in which both term loan and working capital is provided jointly. For example, 80 per cent of the term loan could be given by SFC and 20 per cent by bank. In case of working capital which may be sanctioned at the same time as term loan, the proportion could be reversed, i.e., 80 per cent by bank and 20 per cent by SFC. However, the working capital account is managed and supervised by the bank through its specialized SSI branches.
- SIDBI should sign MoU with the State Governments to provide some assistance to SFC prior to the approval of assistance packages by the Government of India/SIDBI.
- The staff of SFCs has to be adequately trained and SIDBI may be asked to make arrangements for this purpose.

National Small Industries Corporation Limited (NSIC)

National Small Industries Corporation Ltd. (NSIC), an ISO 9001, certified company, since its establishment in 1955, has been working to fulfill its mission of promoting, aiding and fostering the growth of small scale industries and industry related small scale services/business enterprises in the country. Over a period of five decades of transition, growth and development, NSIC has proved its strength within the country and abroad by promoting modernization, up gradation of technology, quality consciousness, strengthening linkages with large and medium enterprises and enhancing exports projects and products from small industries.

NSIC carries forward its mission to assist small enterprises with a set of specially tailored schemes designed to put them in a competitive and advantageous position. The schemes comprise of facilitating marketing support, credit support, technology support and other support services.

Marketing

Marketing, a strategic tool for business development, is critical to the growth and survival of small enterprises in today's intensely competitive market. NSIC acts as a facilitator to promote small industries products and has devised a number of schemes to support small enterprises in their marketing efforts, both in and outside the country. These schemes are briefly described as under:

(1) *Consortia and Tender Marketing:* Small Enterprises in their individual capacity face problems to procure and execute large orders, which inhabit and restrict their growth. NSIC accordingly adopts Consortia approach and forms consortia of units manufacturing the same products, thereby easing out marketing problems of SSIs. The Corporation explores the market and secures orders for bulk quantities. These orders are then distributed to small units in tune with their production capacity. Testing facilities are also provided to enable units to improve and maintain the quality of their products conforming to the standard specifications.

(2) *Single Point Registration for Government Purchase:* NSIC operates a Single Point Registration Scheme under the Government Purchase Programme, wherein the registered SSI units get purchase preference in Government Purchase Programme exemption from payment of Earnest Money Deposit etc. The units registered are issued tender sets free of cost.

(3) *Performance and Credit Rating Scheme for Small Industries:* To enable small enterprises to ascertain the strengths and weaknesses of their existing operations and take corrective measures to enhance their organizational strength. NSIC is operating a Performance and Credit Rating Scheme through empanelled agencies like ICRA, ONICRA, Duns and Bradstreet (D&B), CRISIL, FITCH, CARE and SMERA. Small enterprise has the liberty to choose among any of the rating agencies empanelled with NSIC. Rating agencies will charge the credit rating fee according to their policies. The benefits to small enterprises are as follows:

- An independent, trusted third party opinion on capabilities and credit worthiness of SSI units.
- Good rating to enhance the acceptability of the SSI units with Banks. FIs, SSIs' customers and buyers.
- Facilitate prompt credit decisions from Banks on proposals of SSI units.
- 75% of the credit rating fee subject to a maximum of ₹ 25,000/- will be reimbursed to the small enterprise having a turnover up to ₹ 50 lakh by way of grants.
- 75% of the credit rating fee subject to a maximum of ₹ 30,000/- will be reimbursed to the small enterprise having a turnover above ₹ 50 lakh to ₹ 200 lakh by way of grants.

(4) *Technology Support:* Technology is the key to enhancing a company's competitive advantage in today's dynamic information age small enterprises need to develop and implement a technology strategy in addition to financial, marketing and operational strategies and adopt the one that helps integrate their operations with their environment, customers and suppliers.

NSIC offers small units the following support services through its technical services centers and extension centers

- Advising on application of new techniques.
- Material testing facilities through accredited laboratories.
- Product design including CAD.
- Common facility support in machining, EDM, CNC, etc.
- Energy and environment services at selected centers.
- Classroom and practical training for skill upgradation.

NSIC Technical Services Centers are located at the following places:

Name of the Centre		Focus area
Chennai	...	Leather & Footwear
Howrah	...	General Engineering
Hyderabad	...	Electronics & Computer Application
New Delhi	...	Machine Tools and related activities
Rajkot	...	Energy Audit and Energy Conservation activities
Rajpura (Pb)	...	Domestic Electrical Appliances
Aligarh (UP)	...	Lock Cluster, Die and Tool Making

On a case to case basis, SIDBI has also started Working Capital Finance and Non-fund facilities like Bank Guarantees and opening of inland and foreign LCs.

SIDBI also operates subsidy schemes for Food Processing Industry and Textiles Industry.

National Bank for Agriculture and Rural Development (NABARD)

NABARD is set up as an apex Development Bank with a mandate for facilitating credit flow for promotion and development of agriculture, small-scale industries, cottage and village industries, handicrafts and other rural crafts. It also has the mandate to support all other allied economic activities in rural areas, promote integrated and sustainable rural development and secure prosperity of rural areas. In discharging its role as a facilitator for rural prosperity NABARD is entrusted with:

(1) Providing refinance to lending institutions in rural areas;

(2) Bringing about or promoting institutional development; and

(3) Evaluating, monitoring and inspecting the client banks.

Besides this pivotal role, NABARD also:

- Acts as a coordinator in the operations of rural credit institutions.
- Extends assistance to the government, the Reserve Bank of India and other organizations working in the field of rural development.
- Offers training and research facilities for banks, cooperatives and organizations working in the field of rural development.
- Helps the state governments in reaching their targets of providing assistance to eligible institutions in agriculture and rural development.
- Acts as regulator for cooperative banks and RRBs.

Credit Functions

Refinance against Investment Credit: This is a long-term refinance facility. It is intended to create income generating assets in the following:

- Agriculture and allied activities.
- Artisans, small-scale industries, tiny sector, village and cottage industries, handicrafts, handlooms, power looms, etc.
- Activities of voluntary agencies and self-help groups working among the rural poor.

The credit is normally provided for a period of 3 to 15 years. Investment credit leads to capital formation through asset creation. It induces technological up gradation resulting in increased production, productivity and incremental income to farmers and entrepreneurs.

Criteria

The technical feasibility of the project, financial viability and generation of incremental income to ultimate borrowers thereby enabling them to have a reasonable surplus after repayment of the loan installments are the necessary conditions for sanctioning investment credit. The period of loan ranges between 3 and 15 years depending on the purpose for which it is provided.

The beneficiaries of the programme are individuals/group of individuals, SHGs, proprietary/ partnership concerns, companies, state-owned corporate or cooperative societies.

The refinance is usually 90% to 100% of the loan amount. The balance, wherever applicable, will be met by the banks or the concerned state governments or the Government of India in the case of SCARDBs. With a view to ensure credit flow to certain thrust areas, such as special category beneficiaries like SC/ST members, self-help groups, etc., the quantum of refinance is enhanced to 100%.

Refinance Schemes

Enterprise Loan Scheme (ELS): The refinance schemes which are in force, *viz.*, Integrated Loan Scheme (ILS) and Composite Loan Scheme (CLS) have been merged and modified into a new scheme, i.e., Enterprise Loan Scheme (ELS).

Salient features: Institutions eligible for drawal of refinance, Commercial Banks, Regional Rural Banks, State Cooperative Banks, State Cooperative Agriculture and Rural Development Banks and Scheduled Primary Urban Cooperative Banks.

Borrowers: Individuals, artisans, small entrepreneurs, groups of individuals, associations (formal and informal), proprietary/partnership firms, Co-operatives societies, registered institutions/trusts, NGOs/ voluntary agencies, private and public limited companies, financed institutions etc.

Purpose: To set up new units as well as for modernization/renovation/expansion/diversification of existing units and also for replacement of old and obsolete machinery even if the units were not initially financed by the banks and refinanced by NABARD. To change over to new process of manufacturing/ introduction of new technology/computerization etc., for expansion/ diversification, any unit which is in existence for at least two years will be eligible.

For acquisition of new machinery and equipments resulting in additional production capacity and/ or improving productivity or introducing new product/product line, etc. (The total cost of investment in Plant and Machinery including that of modernization/renovation/expansion/diversification of the existing units to be financed should not exceed the SSI limit prescribed by the Govt. of India).

Eligible activities: All manufacturing, processing, marketing and approved service activities in the SSI sector with emphasis on Cottage, Village, Tiny Industries, Rural Artisans and Rural Crafts. All activities in rural areas or benefitting rural areas that are income generating and /or employment generating, including all service sector activities, are eligible activities under NFS for refinance assistance.

Project Components: For block and/or working capital requirements of tiny/SSI/Service sector units. In respect of cottage and village industries, artisans, etc., a component for consumption credit could be built in the Working Capital component keeping in view the value of the family labour engaged in the productive activity. If a unit avails Working Capital alone, the ceiling for refinance limit per unit shall be limited to ₹ 10 lakh. Block capital will include the following:

Cost of land (to the extent of borrowers down payment), workshed, plant and machinery, equipment and tools, computers, technology upgradation, project formulation and consultancy charges, preliminary and pre-operative expenses, etc., and working capital for one operating cycle.

While sanctioning loans, banks may carefully work out the credit requirements of the borrowers both for term loans and working capital. The quantum of working capital component may be assessed taking into account the incremental requirement also for a reasonable period within which the unit is expected to stabilize. Also, wherever the loan includes both term loan and working capital components, while drawing up the repayment schedule, it may please be ensured that, as far as possible, the working capital component of the loan is recovered after the block capital component is repaid, so that the unit will have adequate funds for meeting the working capital requirements.

Repayment period of loan: The repayment period should be fixed between 2 years and 10 years with a need based moratorium of up to 18 months for individual cases, based on the debt servicing capacity of the borrower and taking into account the nature of activity to be financed, operating cycle, cash flow and the borrower's sustenance needs.

Soft Loan Assistance Scheme for Margin Money

Objective: The objective of the scheme is to provide financial assistance to the prospective entrepreneurs who have the requisite talents and traits of entrepreneurship, but lack necessary monetary resources of their own for setting up units/implementing projects under NABARD refinance schemes for non-farm sector, SEMFEX II borrowers and innovative, high tech projects, export oriented units, agro-processing schemes, and agriculture graduates for setting up a agriclinics and agribusiness centers covered under the farm sector.

Eligibility: The loan assistance towards margin money will be available to the entrepreneurs/ promoters comprising individuals, proprietary/partnership concerns, and groups of individuals, industrial co-operative societies, government/quasi-government agencies, promotional agencies, development corporations, registered and charitable institutions and voluntary organizations. Soft Loan Assistance for Margin Money will not be available for SRWTO schemes and Rural Housing.

Mode of Assistance

Margin Money assistance will be by way of soft loans to the entrepreneur/promoter.

Schemes under pre–sanction procedure

Term Loan to SSI units (through CBs and Scheduled Primary Urban Cooperative Banks)

Borrowers

Individuals, Proprietary/Partnership concerns, Private/Public Limited Companies, Promotional/ Developments Organizations, State Level Federations/Corporations, Joint Sector Undertakings.

Purpose

Setting up of new units and modernization/ renovation/ expansion/ diversification of existing units (other than agro-industries).

Eligible items for investment

- Land and Site Development (including cost of land up to margin money required to be brought in by the borrower).
- Construction of work shed (including civil structure, go downs for storage, market outlets and other essential amenities).
- Plant and Machinery (including machinery/equipment required for packaging and preservation)
- Equipment and tools.
- Delivery van.
- Project formulation and consultancy charges.
- Preliminary and pre-operative expenses.
- Margin for working capital.

Repayment period

3 to 10 years with moratorium of 12 months

Debt Equity Ratio (DER) 3:1

Rajiv Gandhi Udyami Mitra Yojana

Introduction: World over, micro and small enterprises (MSEs) are recognized as an important constituent of the national economies, contributing significantly to employment expansion and poverty alleviation. Recognizing the importance of micro and small enterprises, which constitute an important segment of Indian economy in terms of their contribution to country's industrial production, exports, employment and creation of entrepreneurial base, the Central and State Governments have been implementing several schemes and programmes for promotion and development of these enterprises.

The small-scale industries in India, including the tiny or micro industries and service/business entities, collectively refereed as micro and small enterprises (MSEs) have a long history of promoting inclusive, spatially widespread and employment-oriented economic growth. In terms of employment generation, this segment is next only to agriculture.

Objective: The objective of Rajiv Gandhi Udyami Mitra Yojana(RGUMY) is to provide handholding support and assistance to the potential first generation entrepreneurs, in completion of various formalities and in dealing with various procedural and legal hurdles and in completion of various formalities required for setting up an enterprise.

Target Group: The scheme is targeted to assist potential first generation entrepreneurs, which have already successfully completed entrepreneurship/skill development training of at least two weeks duration, or have undergone vocational training from ITIs.

Implementation Agencies

The scheme would be implemented through various lead agencies, i.e., Udyami Mitras, *viz.*,

(1) Existing national level Entrepreneurship Development Institutions (EDIs).

(2) Micro, Small and Medium Enterprises Development Institutes (MSMEDIs)/Branch MSMEDIs.

(3) Central/State Government public sector enterprises (PSEs) involved in promotion and development of MSEs, e.g., National Small Industries Corporation (NSIC) and State Industrial Development Corporations etc.

(4) Selected State level EDIs and Entrepreneurship Development Centers (EDCs) NGOs, Industry Associations and other organizations engaged in entrepreneurship development and promotion of micro and small enterprises.

Activities of Under Mitra

The selected lead agencies, i.e., Udyami Mitras would be expected to render following services:

(1) Networking, coordinating and follow up with various Government departments/agencies/organizations and regulatory agencies on the one hand and with support agencies like Banks/Financial Institutions, District Industries Centers (DICs), technology providers, infrastructure providers on the other hand, to help the first generation entrepreneurs in setting up their enterprise. Udyami Mitras are expected to help the first generation entrepreneurs in:

(a) Identification of suitable project/product/enterprise and preparation of bankable project report for the same.

(b) Creation of the proprietorship firm/partnership firm/company/society/Self-help Group (SHG) etc.

(c) Filing of Memorandum (as prescribed under MSMED Act, 2006).

(d) Accessing bank loans, admissible capital subsidy/assistance under various schemes of the Central/State Government and other agencies/organizations/financial institutions/banks etc., by networking with respective agencies.

(e) Assistance and support in establishment of work shed/office.

(f) Sanction of power load/electricity connection.

(g) Selection of appropriate technology and installation of plant and machinery/office equipment etc.

(h) Obtaining various registration/licenses/clearances/objection certificates (NOCs) etc., from the concerned regulatory agencies/Government departments/local bodies/Municipal authorities etc.

(i) Allotment of Income Tax Permanent Account Number (PAN) and Service Tax/Sales Tax/ VAT registration etc.

(j) Sanction of working capital loans from the banks.

(k) Arranging tie up with raw material suppliers.

(l) Preparation and implementation of marketing strategy for the product/service and market development.

(m) Establishment linkage with a mentor for providing guidance in future.

(n) Creation of web page and email address.

2. Once the enterprise has been successfully set up, the Udyami Mitras will also monitor and follow up on the functioning of the enterprise for a further period of minimum 6 months and provide help in overcoming various managerial, financial and operational problems.

Financial Assistance To Udyami Mitras

Rates of financial assistance: For setting up of service enterprises, Udayami Mitras would be provided handholding charges at the rate of ₹ 4000/-(Rupees four thousand only) per trainee that would include a Central Grant of ₹ 3000/-(Rupees three thousand only) under RGUMY and contribution of ₹ 1000/-(Rupees one thousand only) to be contributed by the beneficiary.

For setting up of micro manufacturing enterprises, having investment(in plant and machinery) up to ₹ 25,00,000/- the handholding charges would be ₹ 6000/- (Rupees six thousand only) including a Central grant of ₹ 5000/- (Rupees five thousand only) under RGUMY and ₹ 1000/- (Rupees one thousand only) to be contributed by the beneficiary.

For the beneficiaries from special category, i.e., SC/ST/ physically handicapped/women/beneficiaries from North-eastern Region, the beneficiaries contribution of ₹ 1000/- shall also be provided as a grant under RGUMY.

District Rural Development Agency (DRDA)

Introduction: Poverty alleviation through self-employment and wage-employment programme is the theme of rural development. It is District Rural Development Agency (DRDA) at the District level which oversees the implementation of different anti-poverty programme. DRDA came into existence with effect from 1/4/1980. Previously it was known as Marginal Farmer and Agricultural Land Development Agency (MFALDA). Later on it became Small Farmer Development Agency (SFDA). These agencies were only to cater the development of marginal farmers and agricultural labourers in rural area. Now DRDA has embraced manifold activities for upliftment of rural poor.

DRDA has become an autonomous agency having its own governing body registered under Society Registered Act. 1960. After 73rd, Amendment Act pased in the year 1993, President of Zilla-Parishad is the Chairperson of the governing body and the District Collector is its Chief Executive Officer.

Activities

I. Self-employment Programme
II. Wage-employment Programme

Role

I. Principal facilitators for drawing of plan and programmes.
II. Allocates funds, maintains accounts and collects Utilization Certificates.
III. Coordinates executive agencies, financial institutions, NGOs, Government and Panchayati Raj Institutions at different levels.
IV. Supervises and monitors various programmes implemented in the field.
V. Ensures successful implementation of the programmes.
VI. Keeps Zilla Parishad and Government informed through reports and returns.
VII. Creates awareness and transparency amongst the common people.
VIII. Safeguards the interest of SC/ST., Women and Physically Handicapped Persons.

The main **objectives** of the agency are:-

1. To identify the families living below the poverty line through survey conducted by the Govt., servants working at field level.
2. To give financial assistance to these BPL families through banks and govt., sponsored schemes.

3. To draw up model plans through technical departments, for executing the labour generating schemes such as Employment Assurance Scheme.

The main schemes implemented by DRDA are as follows:

✪ Swarnayanti Gram Swarozgar Yojna (SGSY)

SGSY aims at establishing a large number of micro enterprises in the rural areas. The main objective is to bring assisted BPL families above poverty line in three years (Below an annual income of ₹ 20,000/-, a family is considered below poverty line). To remove poverty SGSY is conceived as programme covering all the aspects of self-employment, *viz.,* organization of the rural poor into self-help groups and the capacity building, planning of activity clusters, infrastructures build up, credit and marketing. It lays emphasis on skill development through well-designed training courses. The swarojgaries are financed through the banks on the basis of their projects. The subsidy is at 30% of the project cost, subject to a maximum of ₹ 7,500/- for general classes and 50% or ₹ 10,000/- respectively for SC/ST. For group of swarojgaries the subsidy will be 50% of the project cost subject to maximum of ₹ 1.25 lakh. There is no limit on subsidy for irrigation projects. The funds under this scheme are shared by the Centre and State govt., in ratio of 75:25 respectively.

✪ Jawahar Gram Samridhi Yojna (JGSY)

Primary objective of JGSY is to develop village infrastructure by creating durable assets and its secondary objective is generation of supplementary employment for the unemployment poor the rural areas. The programme is implemented as a centrally sponsored scheme on the basis of 75% funds from the Centre and 25% funds from the State govt.

For the weaker sections of the society special safe guards are provided, such as 22.5% of the annual allocation is earmarked for SCs/STs. individual beneficiary schemes living below poverty and 30% of the employment opportunities are served for women. The programme is implemented through village panchayats.

All works that result in the creation of durable assets can be taken up as per the felt need of the community. However priority is given to

(i) Infrastructure for SC/ST habitations.

(ii) Community infrastructure for education, link roads and street roads.

The Panchayats will execute the work with the approval of Gram Sabah. No other administrative or technical approval is required to execute the works/schemes up to ₹ 50 thousand.

✪ Employment Assurance Scheme (EAS)

The primary objective of the EAS is the creation of additional wage employment opportunities through manual work for the rural poor living below the poverty line while the secondary objective is the creation of durable assets for the benefit of the community. The programme is implemented as a centrally sponsored scheme on cost sharing basis between the centre and the state in the ratio of 75:25 respectively.

The programme is open to all the rural poor who are in need of wage employment. However, the preference is given to SCs/STs. the programme is implemented through Zilla Panchayat. 70% of the received funds is allocated to Block Panchayats in the ratio of their population and the remaining 30% is allocated to Zilla Panchayat, but the Zilla Panchayat is responsible for the approval of annual action plan including the funds of Block Panchayat. However Zilla Panchayat may take into consideration the proposal of Block Panchayat. Zilla Panchayat is also responsible for entrusting works to implementing agencies, supervision and co-ordination of works and furnishing of necessary reports through DRDA.

The programme is implemented departmentally only. Contractors are not permitted to be engaged for the execution of any work. Works taken up are labour intensive. At least 60% of the labour component is maintained against the allocated funds.

✪ Indira Awas Yojana (IAY)

Introduction: Housing is one of the basic requirements for human survival. For a normal citizen owning a house provides sufficient economic security and status in society. For a shelterless person a house brings about a profound social change in his existence endowing with an identity, thus integrating him with his immediate social milieu. IAY was a sub-scheme of JRY. Since 1st January, 1996, it has been delinked from JRY and has been made an independent scheme.

Objective: The objectives of IAY is primarily to help construction of fireproof dwelling units for members of SC/ST, Freed Bonded Labourers and also non SC/ST rural poors living below the poverty line by providing them 100% free of cost.

Target Group—(Beneficiary)

The following are the criteria for selection of Indira Awas Yojana (IAY) beneficiary:

(i) He must belong to BPL family living in rural area.

(ii) Person belonging to SC/ST category will be given preference.

(iii) Freed bonded labourers.

(iv) Non-SC/ST rural poor enlisted in BPL.

(v) Widow or next to kin of defense personnel or Paramilitary forces killed in action, subject to condition that:

a. They reside in rural area.

b. They are not covered any other shelter rehabilitation scheme.

c. They are homeless.

(vi) Reservation of 3% of fund under IAY for disabled person below poverty line.

✪ Watershed Development

Introduction: Watershed development originally managed by national wasteland development board under Ministry of Environment and Forest. It is now placed under Ministry of Rural Development and Department of Land Resources. The main objective of this programme for development of waste lands in non-forest areas, checking of land degradation, putting such waste land into sustainable use and increasing bio mass, availability of fuel wood, fodder and restoration ecology, etc., thus, concept of watershed development is integrated and nurtured with multidisciplinary activities in the area. At present Ministry of Rural Development and Department of Land Resources, Government of India funding watershed development programmes under DPAP, DDP, and Integrated Wasteland Development Plan (IWDP) etc. This programme is intended to be taken up in rainfed and drought-prone areas especially predominated by SC/ST population and preponderance of wasteland.

Objectives

(1) The basic objective of this scheme is to take up integrated wastelands development based on village/micro watershed plans. These plans are prepared after taking into consideration of the land capability, site condition and local need of the people.

(2) The scheme also helps in generation of employment in rural areas besides enhancing people participation in wasteland development programme at all stages. This leads equitable sharing of benefits and sustainable developments. Thus, it aims at the capacity building and empowerment of village community and involvement of PRIs and NGOs in implementation transfer of funds as well as decision making process at grass roots level.

(3) It covers management of natural resources like land, water, vegetative cover and raising land productive and mobilization of human resources are the chief factors and watershed development programme.

Targeted person

(i) Local residents inside the watershed area.

(ii) Poor families specially SC/ST persons in rainfed areas where economic condition of the people is relatively less due to problems of less production, scanty rain and degradation of land.

(iii) Members of SHGs and UGs.

(iv) Usufruct right given to landless persons out of common resource management.

Implementing Agency

Watershed development programme is generally sponsored by the Central Government and funds are released to ZP/DRDA for implementation of the programme. District level water shed development advisory committee in ZP/DRDA selects the Project Implementing Agencies (PIAs). It could be an autonomous organization, Public Sector Undertaking, Voluntary Organisation and Block development officer or any Government Organisation specially dealing with land, water and agriculture etc., the PIA remains in-charge of implementation of watershed projects.

Activities: The following major activities are taken up under the scheme:

(i) Soil and moisture conservation measures like terracing, bounding, trenching vegetative barriers, etc.

(ii) Planting and sowing of multipurpose trees, shrubs, grasses leguas and pasture land development.

(iii) Encouraging natural regeneration.

(iv) Promotion of agro-forestry and horticulture.

(v) Wood substitution and fuel wood conservation measures.

(vi) Measures needed to disseminate technology.

(vii) Training extension and creation of greater degree of awareness among the participants.

(viii) Encouraging people's participation and community contribution.

(ix) Community mobilization through self-help groups (SHGs) and Users Group.

(x) Afforestation

(xi) Repair, restoration and upgradation of existing common property, assets and structures in watershed areas to obtain optimum and sustainable benefits from previous investments.

(xii) Development of small water harvesting structures such as low cost farm ponds, nallahs, bunds checks dams and percolation tanks, etc.

(xiii) Development of Animal Husbandry, i.e., dairy, duckery, piggery and fisheries etc.

All these activities are to be covered up in the watershed areas within four years of project period. Structure of watershed development organization in the District.

✪ Below Poverty Line Family

Introduction: Identification of families lying below poverty line is the essential factor for successful implementation of all anti-poverty programmes, i.e., SGSY, JGSY and IAY etc. It is a method of survey adopted for selection of rural poor families who are living below poverty line. Previously during 8th five year plan a house having income below ₹ 11,000/- was recognized as BPL family. The following provisions were made for identification of BPL families as per survey made in the year 1997.

(i) Families are divided into different categories on consideration of income, family condition, numbers of earning members and household goods used by the families. In addition to income, expenditure of family members also comes to the zone of consideration.

(ii) Each surveyor engaged by District Administration will go around door to door and fill up the index "A" form. If a particular household answers any one of the parameter of form "A" from Sr. No. 2 to 6 then, Index "B" form is not required to be filled up. If household indicates negative of all the above questionnaire then Index "B" form should be filled up.

Procedure for selection of BPL family

(i) Families under below poverty line are identified by means of household survey done by door to door in every five year.
(ii) No families should be repeated or left out.
(iii) Index "A" form is filled up by the surveyor for every household.
(iv) If a particular household refers positive to any one of the questionaire Sr.No. 2 to 6 of survey index "A" form, then index "B" form should not be filled in.
(v) If all the questions referred negative, Index "B" form should be filled up.
(vi) Abstract of Index "A" and "B" form are placed before the Gram Sabah for approval after discussion. Gram Sabah has right to decide ineligible household for deletion.
(vii) Provisional approved copy will be published in the noticeboard of GP and PS for inviting objection.
(viii) Objection application will be enquired into by the competent authority engaged by District administration.
(ix) Identification of BPL families by correct, concrete and transparent manner is the sole objective of the BPL survey.

What are the parameters for selection of BPL family?

The household which comes under all or any one of the following criteria would not be considered for inclusion in BPL family.

(1) Whether a household has more than 2 hectares or of crop land (one hec., in case of irrigated land).
(2) Does he possess pucca house?
(3) Whether income of family above ₹ 1700=00 per month froms self-employment?
(4) Whether family has following consumable household articles. (articles completely unused would be deleted)
   (a) T.V.
   (b) Fridge
   (c) Ceiling Fan
   (d) Motorcycle/scooter/moped
   (e) Three wheeler vehicle. (Not Rickshaw)
(5) Does the family have following agricultural implements?
   (a) Tractor
   (b) Power Tiller
   (c) Paddy Thresher
(6) Data entry of BPL families.

After completion of all work, provisional BPL list is sent to Computer Cell of DRDA for Computerization of all records, the information of BPL list is intimated to Government for final approval. The approved BPL list is kept in GP, PS and DRDA level for reference.

✪ Rajiv Gandhi Swavlamban Rozgar Yojna (RGSRY)

The Rajiv Gandhi Swavlamban Rozgar Yogna has been designed, developed and promoted by the Delhi Khadi & Village Industries Board, with the help of Government of NCT of Delhi, to provide employment opportunities to the unemployed youth, artisans, trained professionals, skilled technocrats and entrepreneurs by promotion/expansion of permissible industries, professions, tertiary and service sector in the UT of Delhi.

The salient features of RGSRY Scheme are as under:-

1. Eligibility

(i) All commercial professionals;

(ii) Passed out candidates from any Technical /Professional Institution recognized by Government and its autonomous/undertaking bodies without any training; and

(iii) Small-scale Industrial units shall become eligible for financial aid of loan within the limits of budget under the purview of Delhi Khadi & Village Industries Board Rajiv Gandhi Swavlamban Rozgar Yogna. Small-scale industrial undertaking should have total investment of plant, machinery and equipment not exceeding the ceiling prescribed for small-scale units by the Central Government from time to time and must be located within the National Capital Territory of Delhi. Anyone of the following can avail loan under the scheme:-

   (a) School/College dropouts above the age of 18 years.

   (b) Individual entrepreneur.

   (c) Trade professionals.

   (d) Artisan

   (e) Small-Scale Industrial units which have total investment of plant, machinery and equipment not exceeding the ceiling prescribed for small-scale units by the Central Government from time to time and must be located within the National Capital Territory of Delhi, shall also become eligible for financial aid or loan.

   (f) P assed out candidates from any technical/professional institute recognized by the Government or its authorized undertakings, without further training.

2. Jurisdiction, Purpose and Quantum of Assistance

(1) Financial aid as loan under these rules may be granted to the eligible projects pertains to any of the following groups/sectors:-

(i) Secondary Sector (Tiny/Cottage Industries)

(ii) Tertiary Sector (Trade, Transportation, Hostels, Restaurants without liquor and meat etc.)

(iii) Service Sector.

However, detailed list of above categories be decided by the Delhi Khadi & Village Industries Board subject to terms & conditions, provisions of local bodies and Delhi Master Plan.

(2) *Quantum of loan:-*

(i) The quantum of loan granted under this scheme, to proposed and functioning units shall not exceed ₹ 3 lacs provided that concerned entrepreneur shall make at least 10% contribution of amount demanded as loan from the DKVIB and promoter. In case of weaker sections, i.e., SC/ST/OBC/Physically Handicapped/Women Entrepreneur/Ex-servicemen only 5% contribution is required.

(ii) Loans shall not be sanctioned to such parties who have already been advanced loan for the same or similar purpose by the Government or any Government controlled financial institutions and has not been repaid in full with interest or has been misutilised and /or misapplied.

(iii) Govt. of Delhi would provide subsidy @ 15% of the project cost subject to the ceiling of ₹ 7,500/- per e ntrepreneur. In case of more than one entrepreneur joining together and setting up a project under partnership, subsidy would be calculated for each partner separately, @ 15% of this share in the project cost, limited to ₹ 7,500/- each partner. Subsidy component would be adjusted to the borrower's loan account after a period of two years from the date of disbursement of loan. Subsidy component would be recovered from the borrower along with interest in cases where the loan amount has been found not utilized for the purpose for which it was released. No subsidy, In case where the loan amount has been found not utilized for the purpose of which, it was released, 18% interest along with principal amount may be recovered.

(3) *Submission of Application:* The borrower shall submit the application to the DKVI Board on the prescribed form as per direction of the DKVI Board.

(4) *Tenure of Loans and Repayment:* Every loan with interest thereon shall be repaid in full within 5 years in equal quarterly installments. The recovery of loan may be started after a gap of 12 months from the date of release of loan amount. However, interest on released amount will be recoverable from the first quarter, from the date of release of loan amount. To ensure timely recovery, borrower shall provide equal numbers, of post dated cheques for quarterly installments of principlal amount including interest due as on date of installment fixed by the DKVI Board.

The borrower shall ensure for timely encashment of each and every cheque. Incase of any default, DKVI Board will be entitled to take action against him/her and/or sureties as prescribed under the law.

The borrower shall be bound to confirm the loan balance within one month after expiry of each financial year.

(5) *Rate of Interest:* The loan granted under this scheme shall bear interest as prescribed by the Govt. of NCT of Delhi from time to time. The interest on loan will accrue from the date of its disbursement and where the loan is in installments, interest shall run on each installment from the date of disbursement of such installment. No interest subsidy.

(6) *Rate of Interest:* The DKVI Board shall charge 18% interest for late payment of overdue installments as prescribed by the Government of Delhi.

(7) *Security of Loans:* Procedure to be followed as per commercial banks.

(8) *Training:* Since the scheme envisages conversion of energy of school dropouts or those who have not gone beyond school education as well as of college dropouts, emphasis would be on skill formation/enhancement of the selected candidates selected by the DKVIB. The primary purpose of imparting skills to the candidates is for enabling them to take up self-employment. DKVIB shall prepare training modules of about three months duration in respect of identified areas in consultation with the NGOs, Training institutions under the Government. The focus, therefore, will be on skill formation and entrepreneur development, basic component of which would be:-

(i) Skill formation.
(ii) Elements of bookkeeping.
(iii) Simple knowledge of marketing.
(iv) Acquaintance with product costing.
(v) Familiarization with project financing by banks and other financial institutions.

The expenditure likely to be incurred on the training shall be paid by DKVIB. Once the training is successfully completed, the training institution will give a certificate to each of the trainees. Industries department will do secretarial work and release of funds for the DKVIB.

(9) *Marketing Support:* Under this scheme the following arrangements are proposed for extending marketing support to the beneficiaries who avail financial assistance under this scheme:

(i) Display of their products in Delhi Emporium as per availability of space.
(ii) DSIIDC/Cooperative Stores can get the products manufactured by the selected entrepreneurs and market the same in their own brand name.
(iii) Allowing such entrepreneur to participate in trade fairs particularly in Delhi Pavilion.
(iv) Allowing such entrepreneurs to participate in the exhibitions organized by Delhi Khadi & Village Industries Board or any other Govt. Organisation.

(v) Forming cooperatives of entrepreneurs manufacturing same or similar type of products under common brands.

(vi) Issue of certificates to the beneficiary unit to get the recognition in the market/society.

(10) *Publicity:* Intensive publicity should be made out by DKVIB through print/electronic/ mass media and also by field motivation of the beneficiaries. The electronic media are now mostly common in use such as TV/Radio. Such mode of communication will help in increasing mass awareness of the scheme.

(11) *Utilization of Loan:* (1) The borrower shall utilize the loan for the specific purpose for which it is advanced within three months. However, Managing Director of the DKVI Board will be competent to grant maximum three months grace for the utilization of amount released by the DKVI Board. After six months, no further concession will be allowed and in case of non-utilization of funds within the maximum permissible period, loan amount will be treated as mix-utilized and DKVI Board will be liable to make recovery of entire amount along with 18% interest, prescribed from time to time by Delhi Govt., if any, incurred, in addition to the amount of loan provided by the DKVI Board.

(2) If the borrower utilizes the financial assistance received from the DKVI Board in violation of the provisions of these loan rules or instructions of the DKVI Board, the amount of loan shall be treated as miss-utilized and shall invite interest @18% along with principal amount may be recovered.

(12) *Charge of the DKVI Board:* The DKVI Board shall have the first charge on all the assets created or to be created by the borrower out of the loan received or any portion thereof. The borrower shall not create any further charges of these assets without the prior approval of the DKVI Board.

(13) *Hypothecation of assets:* Procedure to be adopted as followed by commercial banks.

(14) *Sale and/or Transfer of Assets:* The borrower shall not sell or transfer or let out any machinery, building, implements, sheds or any other immovable's created out of the funds received from the DKVI Board, without the prior permission of the DKVI Board, till the repayment of the entire dues of the DKVI Board.

(15) *Maintenance of the Books and its Inspection:* After giving the utilization papers and inspection shall be done by DKVIB/Industries Department staff to ascertain the utilization of the loan for the purpose it was given to them. There will be not need of audit by auditors of Delhi Govt. and Central Govt. No.T.A/D.A will be charged from the borrower.

(16) *Audit of Accounts:* No need

(17) *Execution of Agreement Deed:* Procedure to be followed as per commercial banks.

Khadi and Village Industries Commission (KVIC)

The KVIC established by an Act of Parliament in 1957, is engaged in planning, promoting and implementing programmes for the development of Khadi and Village Industries in rural areas. Besides producing Khadi, 116 village industries are implementing various projects ranging from poultry, tanning, carpentry, blacksmithing, weaving and designing of musical instruments. While Khadi is produced only by registered co-operative societies and charitable trusts, it is from village industries that entrepreneurs get help. The manufacture, supply of looms and weaving equipment have all been brought under a central supply system by the commission which is also working towards standardization of various components of the charkha from the Bureau of Indian Standards.

The Khadi and Village Industries Commission (KVIC) will be receiving monitory assistance of nearly ₹ 6 billion from the Asian Development Bank. This aid will be given for upgrading the technological aspect of almost 300 Khadi and village industries enterprises. More than 9 lakh workers are associated with Khadi industry. KVIC provides employment to approximately 8.8 lakh people.

Goa Handicraft, Rural and Small-scale Industries Development Corporation (GHRSSIDC)

Goa Handicrafts, Rural and Small-scale Industries Development Corporation Limited (GHRSSIDC), a Govt. of Goa Undertaking, set up in 1980 performs the role of encouraging, promoting and marketing the numerous of Goan Handicrafts by making these items available through its varieties of outlets. A fully Owned Govt. Corporation primarily deals with the promotion of arts and handicrafts in Goa in addition to assisting Rural and Small-scale Industrial units and others. GHRSSIDC is enthusiastically engaged in development of handicrafts with the objective of assisting the artisans in marketing their products through the 10 emporia in Goa. GHRSSIDC create a strong brand for **"APARANT"** Goan handicrafts to help in marketing the handicrafts. The objective of this organization is to ensure that every tourist who visits Goa purcharses real Goan handicrafts from **"APARANT"** emporia.

GHRSSIDC identifies potential and talented persons in Goa who have wholehearted interest in producing handicrafts items based on Goan Art and Culture. Such promising persons are also imparting by organizing training in a batch of 20 each. After imparting training to the artisans, Corporation extends them marketing assistance. The sole objective of developing handicrafts artisans is to make them self employed by producing the handicrafts items for which the Corporation extends marketing outlets

The main functions of the Corporation include:

- Procurement and supply or raw materials and extending marketing assistance to small-scale industries units.
- Promoting and developing handicrafts by opening sales outlets, participating in exhibitions and encouraging artisans to participate in training programmes sponsored by development Commissioner (handicrafts), Govt. of India all over Goa which includes coconut shell craft, sea shells, jute bags, wax craft, etc.
- Conducting design development workshops, seminars, demonstrations etc for artisans, rural youth, members of Self-help Groups, women etc.

The above schemes shall be implemented through the Goa Handicrafts, Rural and Small-scale Industries development corporation ltd:

- Scheme for providing subsidy for clay idol makers.
- Scheme for conducting training programmes in various handicrafts and allied items, design development and technology up gradation workshops for capacity building and to create self-employment opportunity for urban and rural youth/women, and un-employee
- Scheme for marketing support and dovumentation of goan handicrafts scheme for handicrafts artisans for participating in interstate crafts mela, exhibitions and interstate tour for visiting handicrafts establishments in other states within the country.
- Pension for National/State/Merit Certificate Winners.
- Group Insurance Scheme for crafts-persons.
- Insurance Schemes for Hospitalization for crafts persons.
- Workshed and Workshed-cum-housing scheme for Handicraft Artisans.
- Setting up of Craft Development Centre.

The Goa Handicraft, Rural and Small-scale Industries Development Corporation Ltd., is implementing the preferential purchase scheme since 1999, for the benefit of registered small-scale industries located in the State of Goa. The scheme is intended to provide encouragement to the SSI units by giving a preferential treatment to the various items produced by the SSI units. This Corporation has been set up with an intention to promote the traditional arts and crafts fashioned by Goan artists/artisans. Besides this the

Corporation performs various other functions such as procurement and distribution of indigenous and imported raw materials and also assists the SSI Units to procure raw materials and market their products. Through establishment of Emporia units products are exhibited and sold.

The GHRSSIDC has identified the following items:

- Ceiling and pedestal fans
- Disinfectants
- Coir mattresses
- CFL fixtures/switches
- Hose assemblies
- Paver blocks
- Air conditioning equipment and assembly/repairs
- Chalks
- Notebooks

In addition, as and when new items, which are required by Govt. organizations, are identified by the GHRSSIDC, and then the same shall be added to the rate contract.

Terms and Conditions: Terms and conditions for the empanelment of units for supply of stores and other items to various Goa Govt. Departments/Semi Govt. Departments/Public Sector undertakings spread all over Goa for a period of 18 months from the date of acceptance of the rate, or till the finalization of subsequent rate contract whichever is earlier.

Job Specifications: The SSI units shall be required to submit their most competitive rates in respect of individual items as per the schedule of specification of various items attached along with this tender.

The units shall be required to sign a performance bond in a prescribed performa and shall execute the work order/supply orders as and when placed by GHRSSIDC which are to be supplied to various Govt. Departments within the stipulated time limit. The rates to be offered by selected units shall be applicable for free delivery all over Goa even for items in small quantities.

In case, there are more than one SSI units which respond to the tender for supply of various items, then the GHRSSIDC upon the approval of the rate contract committee, will reserve the right to empanel any or all the parties who have participated in the tender, provided they match the lowest rates obtained in the tender process and also provided they fulfill all the terms and conditions of the tender. Further the GHRSSIDC, subject to the approval of rate contract committee also reserves the right to allocate a certain percentage of the quantity of the various items to be supplied under this scheme to the party, which has quoted the lowest in respect of the concerned item. In such a case where the party which has quoted the lowest in respect of certain items, expresses the inability in writing, of his/her unit to supply the items reserved for his unit, then the GHRSSIDC will allocate this quantity among the other empanelled units, subject to the guidelines formulated by the rate contract committee. In case parties fail to supply the items within a reasonable time period not exceeding 30 days, then, the GHRSSIDC will reserve the right to blacklist the party from the scheme.

In case the party which has quoted the lowest in this rate contract, backs out after the tenders are opened or during the process of finalization and acceptance of the lowest quoted rates or after signing of the performance bond, then the same will be viewed very seriously by the GHRSSIDC and the said party will be black listed from participating in future tenders floated by the GHRSSIDC. Moreover, the GHRSSIDC will take up the matter with the Directorate of Industries for cancellation of the permanent registration as SSI unit of the concerned unit.

Once the unit executes a performance bond, then the said unit will have to keep the rates valid for a period of 18 months from the date of signing of the bond or till the signing of the rate contract whichever is earlier.

Job Estimate: The GHRSSIDC does not offer any guarantee as to any definite volume of orders/ minimum size of orders that will be placed on the selected units at any time throughout the period of the contract. Subject to the guidelines finalized by the rate contract committee in this regard, the GHRSSIDC will distribute the orders among the selected units as and when the indents are received from the organizations.

Validity and Acceptance of The Tender: The selected units shall keep their rates for 18 months for the purpose of finalizing the rate contract. The rate shall remain constant during the entire duration of the rate contract which shall be up a maximum period of 18 months or till the finalization of subsequent rate contract, whichever is earlier. In case the unit fails to honor this clause and refuse to accept orders then the GHRSSIDC shall reserve the right to take action against the unit, which may even, be black listed and barred from participating in the rate contract in future. This rate contract scheme will not have any price escalation clause and it shall be the responsibility of the quoting unit to anticipate fluctuation in prices of inputs at the time of submitting their lowest and most competitive rates.

Scope of Contract: The contract covers the supply, testing and handing over in satisfactory working condition, the "goods" as per the detailed specifications instructions contained in the contract document.

All specifications, drawings, data provided to the units by the GHRSSIDC in connection with this Tender/Rate Contract are hereby incorporated herein and a part hereof.

The units promised that their pricing to indenting departments is consistent and units shall maintain a strict and consistent pricing policy.

Units further certify that the pricing under the contract is not higher than the pricing to any other customer. Units guarantees GHRSSIDC the goods covered in the Purchase Order;

- It has goods title to any and all goods supplied hereunder and said goods will be free and clear of any and all liens and encumbrances;
- Any and all goods supplied, hereunder, will be of merchantable quantity;
- Any and all goods supplied hereunder shall be fit for the particular use intended, free from defects, whether patent or latent, in material and workmanship, and shall confirm to all contract specifications and requirements;
- The units shall in the performance of its obligations, hereunder, comply with all and shall not violate any applicable International/Sovereign Government laws, rules and regulations.
- The foregoing guarantees shall survive acceptance of goods by the Purchaser and shall be in addition to any warranties of additional scope given in this contract.
- The prices agreed under the contract are firm, fixed, and non-revisable and form as indivisible sum payable as consideration for the total scope of work under this contract.
- Should the GHRSSIDC require additional quantity of the contracted goods, the GHRSSIDC shall have the option to increase the quantity (either full or part covered under the contract) on the same terms and conditions of this contract, and the shipment of any such extra quantity shall be made by the units within such delivery schedule as agreed to between the GHRSSIDC and the units.

Extension of Delivery Period: If the completion of systems/components is delayed for reasons of *force majeure* such as acts of God, acts of public enemy, acts of Government, fires, floods, epidemics, quarantine restrictions, illegal strikes and freight embargoes, the units shall within 21 days from the date of such occurrence, give notice to the GHRSSIDC in writing of his claim for extension of delivery period. The GHRSSIDC on receipt of such notice may agree to extend the contract delivery date as may be reasonable but without prejudice to other terms and conditions of the contract.

Delay in Completion/Liquidated Damages: If the units shall fail to deliver the systems/components/items within the time specified in the contract, the GHRSSIDC shall recover from the units as liquidated damages as may be decided by the rate contract committee. Systems/components/items will be deemed to have been delivered only when all essential component parts are also delivered. If any essential components are not delivered in time, the entire system/components/items will be considered as delayed until such time the missing parts are delivered.

Default Liability: Should either party fail to execute its obligations under this contract as per the time schedule specified in the contract or should there be any default or breach of any of the provisions of this contract by either party, and such breach is not corrected within thirty (30) days after notice in writing specifying the nature of breach, either party may terminate further performance of this contract forthwith.

No termination shall affect any right or obligation of either party accrued prior to such termination.

In the event the GHRSSIDC terminates the contract in whole or in part The GHRSSIDC reserves the right to purchase upon such terms and in such a manner as it seems appropriate, stores similar to that terminated and the units shall be liable to the GHRSSIDC for any additional costs for such similar stores and/or liquidated damages for delay until such reasonable time as may be required for the final supply of stores.

Packing: The units shall pack and create all systems/components for air/sea/rail/road shipment in a manner suitable to withstand a tropical humid climate and tropical rainforest conditions, in accordance with internationally accepted practice and in such a manner so as to afford protection from damage and deterioration in transit by road, rail, air/sea/waterways. The units shall ensure that each box/unit of shipment is legibly and properly marked for correct identification.

Guarantee/Warranty: The systems/components/items supplied under this contract shall be guaranteed by the units for a period of 12 months from the date of final acceptance at purchaser's site, against defective material, design or manufacture.

During the period of guarantee, the units shall remedy all defects in design, materials and workmanship that may develop under normal and proper use of the systems/components in accordance with the units's recommendations contained in the operating manuals upon written notice from the GHRSSIDC who shall indicate in what respect the systems/components are faulty.

If within the warranty period some defects are noticed, rectification will have to be carried out by unit at their own expense.

Language and Measures: All documents pertaining to the contract including specifications, schedules, notices, correspondence, operating and maintenance instructions, drawings or any other writings shall be written in English language.

The metric system and generally accepted international standard of measurement shall be used exclusively.

Indemnity: The units shall warrant and be deemed to have warranted that all goods and supplied against this contract are free and clean of infringement of any patent, copyright or trademark, and shall at all times indemnify the GHRSSIDC against all claims which may be made in respect of the systems/components/items for infringement of any right protected by patent, registration of design or trademark.

Assignment: This contract shall ensure to the benefit of and be binding upon the successors and assigns of the parties hereto. It will not be assigned in whole or in part by either party without the prior written consent of the other.

If the units dissolves or goes into bankruptcy or causes to be wound up except for reconstruction purposes or carries on its business under a receiver, the representatives in law of the Estate of the seller or any such receiver, liquidator or any person in whom the contract may be vested shall forthwith give notice thereof in writing to the GHRSSIDC and shall remain liable for the successful performance of the contract and nothing aforesaid shall be deemed to relieve the units or its successors of its obligations under this agreement under any circumstances.

Settlement of Disputes and Conflicts: In the event of any dispute, conflicts, controversy or difference which may arise between the parties hereto, out of or in relation to or in connection with this contract or for the breach thereof, the parties hereto shall in the first instance do their utmost to settle such dispute, conflicts, controversy or difference amicably. Where the parties hereto fail to settle such dispute, conflicts, controversy or difference within sixty (60) days (or such longer period as may be mutually agreed upon) of the written notice given by either party to the other of its existence, then such dispute, controversy or difference shall be finally settled by arbitration in accordance with the rules of Indian Arbitration and Conciliation Act, 1996 (Act 1996) or any other Laws and regulations in force, by a Sole Arbitrator to be appointed by the Chairman of Rate Contract Committee. The fact that the Arbitrator is a Government Servant, that he had to deal with the matters to which the contract relates or that in the course of his duties as a Government Servant, has expressed views on all or any of the matters in dispute or difference shall not be an objection. In the event of the arbitrator being unable to act for any reason or resigning or his mandate having been terminated for any reason or his award being set-aside by the Honourable Court for any reason, it shall be lawful for the sitting Chairman of Rate Contract Committee to appoint another Arbitrator in place of the out-going Arbitrator in the manner aforesaid. No person other than the person appointed by the Chairman of Rate Contract Committee as aforesaid shall act as Arbitrator.

If the value of the claim in reference does not exceed ₹ 1,00,000/- (Rupees INR One Lakh Only) the Arbitrator shall not be required to state the reasons upon which Award is based. The arbitrators' award shall be final and shall not be subject to appeal to any court, and may be entered in the court of competent jurisdiction for execution forthwith. The venue of the Arbitration shall be at Panaji, Goa. Both parties to the contract shall bear the Arbitration expenses equally. Notwithstanding to any pending reference to arbitration, both parties will proceed with the execution of their commitments under the present contract until the arbitration award is known.

Applicable Law and Jurisdiction: The law governing the formation, application, performance, interpretation of this rate contract and the legal enforcement of the purchase order is Indian Law with venue in Panaji Goa, India.

Quality Control

- The goods manufactured and supplied shall be of good quality and shall conform to the specifications laid down in the schedule. The indenting departments may take the assistance of SISI Margao, QTC Corlim, Engineering College, Farmagudi or ETDC as far as quality is concerned, if felt necessary and the cost if any on account of quality checking shall be recovered by GHRSSIDC from the concerned unit.
- The items to be manufactured and supplied should conform to ISI specifications.
- Registered SSI Units must compulsorily have manufacturing facility in Goa. Stock transfer from other units located outside Goa will not be permissible under this rate contract. If it is observed

that the material is imported from outside the state and is not actually manufactured by the unit, then the GHRSSIDC shall reserve the right to stop placing of orders on the concerned unit.

- In case of steel furniture manufacturers, the CR sheets shall have to be compulsorily procured from the rate contract and the sheets either of SAIL/ESSAR make. This price will be informed to the concerned units upon request in order to enable them to calculate the price of steel furniture.
- Alternatively the steel furniture manufacturers can quote the prices of steel furniture by considering the input cost of CR sheet from the open market. The indenting department will be given a choice of steel furniture.

Pre-inspection of Stores by The Units: The unit should satisfy themselves that the stores/materials are in accordance with the specifications and fully conform to the required specification by carrying out a thorough pre-inspection of each lot of the stores before actually tendering the same for inspection to the indenting department. Such precaution on the part of the units minimizes the chances of rejection and consequences thereof.

Earnest Money Deposit: Each Tender (only non SSI Units) shall be accompanied with a sum of ₹ 20,000/- as Earnest Money Deposit by D.D/Pay order payable on any nationalized bank favoring GHRSSIDC, Panaji and in case of units registered with Directorate of Industries, Govt of Goa, a sum of ₹ 500/- will be payable as EMD in the manner stated above. SSI units registered with DTC in Goa, benefits will be available as per Govt. Notification No.3/40/2003-IND (iii).

Security Deposit: Security deposit in the form of Performance Bond based on the terms and conditions of this tender document will have to be executed by the short listed units at a later date upon finalization of the rate contract.

Payment: Though the GHRSSIDC will make all possible efforts to obtain the payment from the indenting departments within a period of 30 days, however, it does not offer any assurance on the exact time period since as a matter of current policy, the payment are made as soon as corresponding payment is received from the Govt. departments against submission of the following documents.

(i) Commercial certified and signed invoice in duplicate describing the goods shipped, quantity, unit rate and their total CIF destination value excluding on site testing, installation and commissioning charges, for which separate invoice to be raised.

(ii) Declaration by the units that the contents in each package are not less than those entered in the invoices.

Delivery Schedule: The delivery of the goods will have to be made free of cost to the consignee destination within the stipulated delivery period not exceeding 30 days.

Service Charges: The GHRSSIDC shall be liable to collect commission two percent (2%) of the net value of the orders from the empanelled/short listed registered SSI units, under the scheme. This commission shall be deducted at the time of releasing the payment to SSI units once the corresponding payment from the indenting departments.

Rejected Goods: If the consignee rejects in part or full due to lack of quality, non conformation to specifications, etc., then, the items, will have to be replaced by the shortlisted Unit within the stipulated period at their own cost and expense.

Risk Purchase: If the selected Unit fails to complete the supply within 30 days of delivery schedule period and if the consignee makes risk purchases on account of the default made by the empanelled unit, then full cost of risk purchase shall be borne by the concerned unit.

Penalty: In the event of failure to supply the goods or in case of other default in specification and quality of goods, the penalty imposed by the consignee as liquidated damages for late delivery etc., will have to be borne by the Units.

Important Instructions to The Unit Participation in The Rate of Contract: The rates quoted should be competitive and must be applicable for a maximum period of 18 months and minimum period of 12 months. The taxes/excise duties or any other charges if applicable should be mentioned separately in the tender. In case the party fails to do so, then further addition of taxes will not be allowed once the rates are finalized. The units should read the above terms and conditions very carefully and submit their quotation accordingly. If the tender is misleading or if the unit backs out from the tender process after the tender is opened, then the same will be viewed very seriously and the said unit will run the risk of being blacklisted and de-registered.

Goa Industrial Development Corporation (GIDC)

Before the liberalization, Goa's economy was mainly based on agriculture and to a large extent on the mining industry. Industrial activity in Goa was basically an offshoot of mining industry. Iron ore mining in Goa was solely export-oriented catering to the post world war industrial activities in countries like Japan and Western Europe. Development in mining industry in Goa gave rise in a small way to industrial activity in supporting areas of infrastructure, servicing and job works of mining equipments, vehicles etc. However, after Goa's liberalization due to various steps taken by the Government, the industrial scenario has undergone a vast change.

One of the important activities of this agency has been to identify land for setting up industrial estates keeping in mind the concept of balanced industrial development in various parts of the State without disturbing the fragile ecology of Goa. The areas have to be within the industrial zones as per the regional plan prepared by the Town and Country Planning Department. The other aspects that are kept in mind while selecting the land are availability of transport, water, power supply, urban infrastructure, communication facilities and reasonable cost. After identifying the land, the site plan indicating the survey no.s, plot no.s, etc., is prepared. At the time of preparation of the layout, care is taken to see that ecological features and tourism development plans in the State are not disturbed. Goa has a tremendous tourism potential. Care is also taken to keep adequate land for open space and green area. Further some area is reserved for common industrial facilities as well. The total units established in the estates are over 1600 generating an employment to around 30,000 people. The units ranging from tiny to large-scale manufacture a diverse range of products from food processing to modern sophisticated computer peripherals, defense and telecommunication equipment.

Objectives: The Goa, Daman and Diu Industrial Development Corporation (GDDIDC) was established by the Government of Goa, Daman and Diu in February, 1966, under the provisions of Goa, Daman and Diu Industrial Development Act, 1965, with the aims and objectives of securing and assisting in the rapid and orderly establishment of industries in Industrial Areas and Industrial Estates in Goa. One of the important activities of the Corporation is to identify land of sizeable area for setting up of Industrial Estates.

In pursuance of the above objectives, the GDDIDC (now renamed Goa IDC) has so far established twenty-two Industrial Estates in Goa, Daman and Diu, *viz.*, Corlim, Margao, Sancoale, Daman, Mapusa, Tivim, Bicholim, Kakoda, Honda, Bethora, Canacona, Kundaim, Diu, Tuem, Verna, Cuncolim, Pilerne, Marcaim, Pissurlem, Colvale, Shiroda and Sanguem. 22 Industrial Estates set up by the Corporation shall be provided with the state of art infrastructure facilities in stipulated time frame. Uninterrupted electric power, necessary water supply, network of good roads; easy and fast transportation is available in most areas and will be made available wherever they do not exist. The Government will revamp the functioning of the Goa Industrial Development Corporation, and make efforts to energize the Corporation to provide proper infrastructure and facilities, for setting up of Industries and attracting investment in Goa.

At present, GOA-IDC has a programme of expansion of Industrial Estates as well as establishment of new Industrial Estates to meet the demand of the industry to set up their projects in Goa. In order to cope up with the pace of industrialization in Goa, a Special Land Acquisition Cell has been set up to gear up the land acquisition proceedings.

Economic Development Corporation (EDC)

EDC is primarily a financial institution established by the Government of Goa to promote industrial investment within the State (earlier Union Territory). EDC has been assisting units located in the Union Territory of Daman, Dadra and Nagar Haveli also.

EDC Ltd, earlier known as Economic Development Corporation of Goa, Daman & Diu Limited was incorporated on 12th March, 1975, as limited company to act as the State Industrial Development Corporation. It has also been accorded the twin status of SFC by IDBI and SIDBI.

During the first decade after inception EDC took upon entrepreneurial role to pursue development and growth of specific industrial sectors like pharmaceuticals, light engineering, electronics, telecommunications etc. Subsequent to economic liberalization in the nineties, the corporation continues its financial lending operations as a main activity.

The EDC Limited, originally known as the Economic Development Corporation of Goa, Daman & Diu Limited (EDC) incorporated on 12th March, 1975, as a public limited company under the Companies Act, 1956, has been the State financial institution set up by the Govt. of Goa with the prime objective to promote industrial development. The area of operation of EDC in addition to Goa is in the Union Territory of Daman, Diu, Dadra and Nagar Haveli.

It has been acting as a State Industrial and Investment Corporation. Besides, it has also been accorded the twin status of State Financial Corporation (SFC) by IDBI/SIDBI.

The equity capital of the company is not only subscribed by the Govt. of Goa but also Daman & Diu Administration and IDBI. The present shareholding of the Corporation as on 31/03/2008 is as follows:

	Percentage	Amount (₹ In lacs)
Government of Goa	81.81%	₹ 6,620.26
IDBI	14.25%	₹ 1,153.22
Administration of Daman & Diu	3.94%	₹ 319.00
	100%	₹ 8,092.00

STATUS OF EDC FUNDING (AS ON 31/03/2008)

Cumulative sanctions	₹ 85,530.91 lacs
Cumulative disbursements	₹ 56,611.85 lacs
Cumulative recovery	₹ 81,109.47 lacs
Units assisted	5,744 nos.

The present staff strength of EDC is 94, comprising mainly of professionals from various disciplines.

Objectives of EDC

EDC has been a professionally managed organization and acts as on excellent delivery channel for conversion of the Government policies and delivering them to the citizens.

The main objectives of the company are:

(1) To carry on the business of an investment company by providing financial assistance to Entrepreneurs for starting, expanding, modernizing their activities in the following:

(a) Small and Medium Entrepreneurs in the industrial sector;

(b) Tourism sector;

(c) Medial Infrastructure;

(d) Service sector;

(e) Construction sector;

(f) Infrastructure Development.

(2) To extend financial assistance by means of various financial products, either fund–based or non fund-based.

(3) To participate in other development works, projects, schemes as mandated by the Government.

(4) To encourage and promote participation of capital in various forms like equity, preference or debentures in industrial enterprises and other economic activities.

(5) To identify and motivate entrepreneurs to set up industries and assist them in the spadework by providing required training and guidance.

(6) To offer and act as an agent for the disbursement of various schemes, incentives concessions and benefit on behalf of the State and Central Government to units and enterprises assisted by EDC.

Other activities: The Corporation has developed Patto Plaza admeasuring about 1,77,000 sq.mts. at Panaji, Goa. The land was reclaimed and leveled after it was acquired. Infrastructural facilities like road, footpaths, drains, electrification and parking spaces were constructed.

The plots in the complex have been leased out to various parties, which include SBI, Bharat Petroleum, LIC, Bank of India, ESIC, Registrar of Companies, Regional Provident Fund, Income Tax Dept., Passport Dept., Dempos, Sesa Goa Ltd., Govt of Goa, DLF Ltd., Parsvnath Developers Ltd. Many buildings and important offices have come up in the complex.

The FAR for the land is 2.50:1, the location is about 2kms., from assembly complex in the State of Goa. EDC Ltd., has plans to develop more land on lines of Patto Plaza in the State of Goa.

Brief Details of Loan Scheme

Name of Scheme	Eligibility	Purpose Features	Salient Contribution	Promoters Equity Ratio	Debt	Repayment the Period
General Term Loan	Proprietary, Partnership or limited concerns new or existing	To set up a new industrial unit or expand, diversify the existing unit.	Industrial units engaged in manufacture, preservation or processing of of goods, repairs and maintenance or servicing etc.	25%	3:1 for SSI below ₹ 10.00 lacs other wise 2:1	8-10 years including 6 months to 2 year moratorium
Equipment Finance Scheme	Existing concerns having good track record and sound financial position for at least 4 years	To acquire identifiable item of equipment and machinery	75% of the cost of the	25%	3:1 for the equipment cost	2.5 years including moratorium of 6-12 months.
Acquisition of DG Set	Existing unit	To acquire a DG set for captive use and the shed/room for housing.	75% of the cost	25%	3:1 for the equipment cost	Normal 5 to 8 years
Pollution Control Equipment	Existing unit intending to control/prevent Pollution	To acquire pollution control equipment by new units, or existing units	75% of the cost	25%	3:1	Normal 5 to 8 years
Acquisition of computers	New or existing units	To acquire computer	75% of the cost	25%	3:1	Normal 3-5 years
Quality Control Facilities	New or existing unit and quality evaluation for inputs as well as out puts	To provide facilities of testing SSI units not to ₹ 7.5 lacs Moratorium could be upto 3 years.	75% of the cost. Loan limit for	25%	3:1 3 years	8 years include.

Scheme for indigenization or import stitution	Units promoted or by Technician Entrepreneurs/ Professionals existing for at least 3 years/ profit for 2 years	To develop new products aimed at indigenization/ import substitution	Maximum ₹ 5 lacs per product. Repayment not to exceed 5 years		The total envisage expenditure to be financed	5 years including 1 year moratorium
Scheme for mfg. and installation renewable energy/energy saving systems	Units engaged in mfg of related items	To acquire or to mfg. equipment falling under of renewable energy systems like solar heaters, windmill and energy systems based on big mass. Energy saving devices likes high efficiency wood burning stoves, economizers.	75% of the cost	25%	3:1	8 years with moratorium of 1 1/2 years
Scheme for hotels/ restaurant projects	The hotel must have minimum 10 rooms of which 25% should have attached bath with one for every 4 of the remaining rooms	To establish new hotel/restaurant or for expansion	The facilities should be as prescribed as per the starred category. Maximum term loan of 75% of the cost of the assets	Minimum 30%	1:1	10 years including 2 years moratorium
Tourism Related Activities	Facilities should be recommended and approved by Tourism Dept.	To set up tourism related facilities like amusement part, cultural centres, restaurants, tourist service agencies	Facilities should be located in the tourist's areas. Maximum term loan of 75% of cost of assets	25%	3:1 below ₹ 10 lacs otherwise 2:1	10 years including 2 years moratorium

Hospitals/Nursing Homes	Allopathic Doctor promoters with post graduation qualifications are eligible for new/expansion/ modernization of hospitals nursing homes	To set up small hospitals, nursing homes, polycli-inics, special clinics, etc	Minimum 10 beds Maximum 50 beds should provide conce-ssional medical facilities to low income group maximum cost of project upto ₹ 10 crores	25%	3:1 below ₹ 10 lacs otherwise 2.1	10 years includ-ing 2 years moratorium
Acquisition electro-medical and other equipment	Qualified medical practitioner can apply.	To acquire electro-medical and diagnostic equip-ment. Generator can be included	Maximum upto ₹ 60 lacs	25%	3:1 below ₹ 10 lacs otherwise 2:1	5-8 years of including 1 year moratorium
Scheme for qualified professionals	Qualified profe-ssionals in the field of manag-ement, account ancy, medicine, architecture & engg.	To establish pro-fessional practice/ consultancy	Cost of land and building shall not exceed 50% of total cost. Maximum cost upto ₹ 20 lacs	25%	3:1 below ₹ 10 lacs otherwise 2:1	5 years with 1 year moratorium
Scheme of loan assis-tance for construction of residential/reside-ntial cum commercial complexes	Proprietary/Par-tnership Limited companies	For construction of residential/ residential cum complexes	Maximum assis-tance limited company ₹ 500 lacs Partnership -₹ 250 lacs Prop-rietary –₹ 120 lacs Debt Equity Ratio 1.5:1	30% commercial	1.5:1	5 years with a moratorium of 18 months
Loan assist ance for units sold under auction	Proprietary/ partnership/ limited company	For purchase of fixed assets sold under auction and creation of new fixed assets	Security margins for fixed assets purchased under auction -40% for new assets 30%	25%	3:1below ₹ 10 lacs 2:1 otherwise	5years with a moratorium of 18 months

National equity fund scheme (NEF)	The assistance is available to new projects in tiny and SSI sector or expan sion/moderni zation/ diversifi cation-ion and potentially viable sick units.	To support the entrepreneur for his contribution by way of soft loan	Project cost shall not include working capital margin and shall not exceed ₹ 50 lacs. The soft loan shall have 5% service charge. No security is to be insisted upon.	10% of project cost.	2:1	7 yrs. Incl.3 yrs moratorium
Mahila Udyam Nidhi Scheme (MUN)	Protect set up women entrepreneurs. service activities	To establish new industrial projects as also 15% of the project cost by way of soft loan. No security including collateral is needed.	Equity assistance to women entrepreneur maximum	Maximum 10%	3:1	10yrs. Incl; 5yrs moratorium
Single Window Scheme (SWS)	New projects with project cost and working capital requirements upto ₹ 100 lacs.	To extend working capital also along with the term loan.	Requirement of working capital as per the prevailing norms.	25% minimum on on fixed and current assets	3.1 upto ₹ 10 lacs otherwise 2.1	L8yrs,Incl. 11/2yrs. Morato rium......W.C, Moratorium 8yrs. Incl.3yrs, Moratorium
Scheme for marketing organisation	Individuals partnerships, limited companies, experienced in marketing village and small industry products	To set up new sales outlets or undertake renovation/ expansion of existing outlets for marketing VSI products	Cost of project not to exceed ₹ 25 lacs.	25%	2:1	5-8yrs

- Depending on the merit of the case and economic development, the above stipulations are amended by the corporation while granting the assistance.
- Promoter's contribution does not include unsecured loans.
- For loans above ₹ 10.00 lacs, Debt. Equity ratio is 2:1.

Summing Up

Introduction

Small-scale Industries Board is an apex advisory body constituted by the Government of India to render advice on all the issues pertaining to the SSI sector. The Department of SSI and Agro and Rural Industries was created under the Ministry of Industry, Government of India, to formulate policy framework and initiate appropriate programmes and schemes for the promotion of SSIs in the country. The range of functions of the development include the setting up of a network of institutions to render services of a varied nature like, techno-economic and managerial aspects, training, testing facilities, marketing assistance, etc. These activities are supported by a host of other Central/State Departments, Agencies, and Autonomous Institutions all over the country.

Industry Associations provide support to the SSI sector and offer with a common platform to raise industry-related issues. Government policies, in recent years, have stressed the increasing role of Industry Associations in the setting up of common facilities and other ventures in the area of technology, marketing and other support services.

Entrepreneurship Development Institute of India (EDI)

This is a key organization to play a vital role to develop entrepreneurship. It is not working for profit. It has been established by the inspiration and joint efforts of IDBI, IFCI, ICICI, and SBI. The Govt. of Gujarat has allotted 23 – acre land to build a grand campus of this organization. This is an autonomous and independent body.

This organization has successfully managed various training programme for entrepreneurship development and proved that people of any class can own a business and respectfully earn their livelihood. It has proved that the belief of entrepreneurs are born, not made, is untrue. This organisation has proved with it's activity and performance that entrepreneurship can be developed with properly planned efforts. To make it happen EDI has helped to set up 12 state level entrepreneurship development centers and institutes.

Main activity of EDI is to identify entrepreneur by the programmes of self employment and small industries development, later on it trains and inspires them to set up and develop small as well as village industries.

EDI has been helped by world famous organizations like World Bank, Commonwealth Secretariat, UNIDO, ILO, British Council, Ford Foundation etc. It has been appreciated by declaring it "centre of excellence" for its global achievements by United Nations Economic and Social Commission for Asia and Pacific (ESCAP) Bangkok, Thailand and India.

National Institute for Entrepreneurship and Small Business Development (NIESBUD)

This is a paramount to co-ordinate activities of those organizations who arrange training classes for entrepreneurship development. It was established in 1960, under society act and has commenced its activity since 1983. It works as Secretariat of National Entrepreneurship Development Board which enact policies for entrepreneurship.

It provides standardized syllabus and training to various groups and concerned. The govt. provides full fund for the programmes of this organization. It holds programmes having high demand or not held by other institutes with such programmes it inspires, encourages, develops and expands entrepreneurship.

The organization (NIESBUD) works for those institutes working directly or indirectly in the field of entrepreneurship and tries to make stronger.

Its main objective is to develop and expand entrepreneurship and the institutes working in this field. It helps to make the activity of such institutes more efficient and result-oriented.

Its second object is to identify potential entrepreneurs and to train them, to help them, to provide detailed information, to exchange of the people working in this field. It also works for improvement in policy and programmes to be helpful in the formation of concerned policies.

Small Industries Development Organization (SIDO)

SIDO was established in New Delhi for development of small industries and organizational structure development. It has nationwide network. It provides economic and mechanical services. It is associated with office of small industries dept.of agriculture and rural industry ministry as well as the Government of India.

SIDO is a nodal agency of central government. It is a paramount organization to enact policies and programmes and to apply co-ordinate to control and to manage these programmes. It provides many important services to small industries. It provides services of adviser of economic management matters. It helps small entrepreneurs by providing training, some general facilities, testing instrument facility, market aid, etc.

National Alliance of Young Entrepreneurs (NAYE)

It's a national level body for young entrepreneurs. It specially strives for preparing women entrepreneurs. 1975, was the year, observed for maintaining women's status and respect, hence in the same year NAYE added as women's wing in its structure. It nurtures entrepreneurship in women. It grooms women entrepreneurs in big scale. It has put in lots of efforts have a proper place and respect for women in our industrial structure and economy.

Women entrepreneurs are given required information through workshops, conferences, seminars, training progammes etc. and it is seen that they get required facilities. Lobbying is being done by women's wing of NAYE to press parliament, state assemblies and in other forums for women entrepreneurs. Thus, proper efforts are done for women to secure their deserved place.

In May 1985, "The Association of Women Industrialists/ Entrepreneurs of Maharashtra" was established. 400 of its members work to develop women entrepreneurship in the state. NAYE had a vital role in foundation of this association. It has its H.O. at Pune. It has its branches at Mumbai, Nashik, and Aurangabad and at other places. It associates NAYE to market its member's product and hold training progammes.

Thus NAYE strives hard for upliftment of young entrepreneurs especially women. It has played a considerable role to make women entrepreneurs independent and to Olive respectfully. It holds workshop, conferences, training classes etc., to create awareness in entrepreneurs.

State Bank of India (SBI)

Activities of India's biggest, widespread, versatile bank SBI include development of entrepreneurship. It also carries out development based banking activities along with traditional merchant banking. It is a leading bank at this facet. It was pioneer to form various programmes and schemes for the development of entrepreneurship. It especially manages its programmes to develop industries in backward area. Since 1978, SBI carry out various programmes to develop entrepreneurship.

District Industry Centre (DIC)

Morarji Desai, Govt. of Janta Morcha party had thought of DIC for decentralized and balanced industrial development as well as for the development of rural and small industries. This programme was commenced on 1st May, 1978, during 7th Five Year Plan. Central and State Government shares 50:50 of the cost of this programme.

DIC operates in every district of the country, 422 approved district industry centers were covered 431 districts. Its objectives are to develop tiny, small and rural industries, as well as, to increase employment in villages and backward area. It works as a single window agency for entrepreneurs, where they carry out most of the tasks of entrepreneurs. It helps to provide all kinds of help to small industries under one roof at district level. Small industries get registration in their district. It performs an important task of helping entrepreneur pre and post finance aids. Especially it looks after to establish more and more industries in rural backward area.

"Prime Minister Rojgar Yojna" is also applied by District Industry centre to help unemployed youth to be self-employed. This scheme was announced in August'93 and applied on 2nd October 1993. This programme was started with a view to employ 10 lacs unemployed youth through 7 lacs small enterprises. It was anticipated to select beneficiaries by NGOs as well as training and project profile preparation for entrepreneurs. This center provides information about business opportunities to entrepreneurs. It helps entrepreneurs in various phases from preparation of project report to application of project. It helps to avail infrastructural like land, electricity etc., to entrepreneurs. First of all an entrepreneur has to select district and secondly he has to get registration in the centre.

Thus these centers look after various activities for the development of industries and entrepreneurship in the district. All information can be gathered from one place. All the Govt. Schemes for tiny and small industries are applied by DICs. It provides direction and information from commencement to complete management of business.

This is a scheme in which central and all state governments are equal financial partner. DIC carry out conspicuous activities for industrial development in rural and backward area.

Small Industries Service Institutes (SISIs)

The SISIs are setup to provide consultancy and training to small entrepreneurs-both existing and prospective. The activities of SISIs are coordinated by the Industrial Management Training Division of the DCSSIs office there are 28 SISIs and 30 Branch SISIs set up in State Capital and other places all over the country.

The main functions of SISIs include:

(1) To serve as interface between Central and State Governments.
(2) To render technical support services.
(3) To conduct Entrepreneurship Development Programmes.
(4) To initiate promotional programmes.

Small Industries Development Bank of India (SIDBI)

SIDBI was set up by an Act of Parliament, as an apex institution for promotion, financing and development of industries in small scale sector and for coordinating the functions of other institutions engaged in similar activities. It commenced operations on April 2, 1990. SIDBI extends direct/indirect financial assistance to SSIs, assisting the entire spectrum of small and tiny sector industries on All India basis.

State Financial Corporations (SFCs)

In pursuance of the SFCs Act, 1951, SFCs were set up mainly to finance small and medium scale units. Their area of operation is generally restricted to the concerned States. SFCs also assist small scale units for their modernization and technology up gradation programmes by providing soft loans, restructuring the sick small-scale units through rehabilitation schemes and through equity type assistance under SIDBIs seed capital scheme.

National Small Industries Corporation Limited (NSIC)

National Small Industries Corporation Ltd. (NSIC), an ISO 9001, certified company, since its establishment in 1955, has been working to fulfill its mission of promoting, aiding and fostering the growth of small scale industries and industry related small scale services/business enterprises in the country. Over a period of five decades of transition, growth and development, NSIC has proved its strength within the country and abroad by promoting modernization, upgradation of technology, quality consciousness, strengthening linkages with large and medium enterprises and enhancing exports projects and products from small industries.

National Bank for Agriculture and Rural Development (NABARD)

NABARD is set up as an apex Development Bank with a mandate for facilitating credit flow for promotion and development of agriculture, small-scale industries, cottage and village industries, handicrafts and other rural crafts. It also has the mandate to support all other allied economic activities in rural areas, promote integrated and sustainable rural development and secure prosperity of rural areas. In discharging its role as a facilitator for rural prosperity NABARD is entrusted with,

(1) Providing refinance to lending institutions in rural areas.
(2) Bringing about or promoting institutional development and
(3) Evaluating, monitoring and inspecting the client banks.

Besides this pivotal role, NABARD also

- Acts as a coordinator in the operations of rural credit institutions.
- Extends assistance to the government, the Reserve Bank of India and other organizations working in the field of rural development.
- Offers training and research facilities for banks, cooperatives and organizations working in the field of rural development.
- Helps the state governments in reaching their targets of providing assistance to eligible institutions in agriculture and rural development.
- Acts as regulator for cooperative banks and RRBs

Rajiv Gandhi Udyami Mitra Yojana

World over, micro and small enterprises (MSEs) are recognized as an important constituent of the national economies, contributing significantly to employment expansion and poverty alleviation. Recognizing the importance of micro and small enterprises, which constitute an important segment of Indian economy in terms of their contribution to country's industrial production, exports, employment and creation of entrepreneurial base, the Central and State Governments have been implementing several schemes and programmes for promotion and development of these enterprises.

The small scale industries in India, including the tiny or micro industries and service/business entities, collectively refereed as micro and small enterprises (MSEs) have a long history of promoting inclusive, spatially widespread and employment-oriented economic growth. In terms of employment generation, this segment is next only to agriculture.

District Rural Development Agency (DRDA)

Poverty alleviation through self-employment and Wage-employment programme is the theme of rural development. It is District Rural Development Agency (DRDA) at the District level which oversees the implementation of different anti-poverty programme. DRDA came into existence with effect from 1/4/1980. Previously it was known as Marginal Farmer and Agricultural Land Development Agency (MFALDA). Later on it became Small Farmer Development Agency (SFDA). These agencies were only to cater the development of marginal farmers and Agricultural Labourers in rural area. Now DRDA has embraced manifold activities for upliftment of rural poor.

DRDA has become an autonomous agency having its own Governing Body registered under Society Registered Act. 1960. After 73rd amendment act past in the year 1993 President of Zillah - Parished is the Chairperson of the Governing Body and the District Collector is its Chief Executive Officer. The main schemes implemented by DRDA are as follows:

✪ Swarnayanti Gram Swarozgar Yojna (SGSY)

SGSY aims at establishing a large number of micro enterprises in the rural areas. The main objective is to bring assisted BPL families above poverty line in three years (Below an annual income of ₹ 20,000/- a family is considered below poverty line). To remove poverty SGSY is conceived as programme covering all the aspects of self employment *viz.* organization of the rural poor into self help groups and the capacity building, planning of activity clusters, infrastructures build up, credit and marketing. It lays emphasis on skill development through well designed training courses. The swarojgaries are financed through the banks on the basis of their projects. The subsidy is at 30% of the project cost, subject to a maximum of ₹ 7,500/- for general classes and 50% or ₹ 10,000/- respectively for SC/ST. For group of swarojgaries the subsidy will be 50% of the project cost subject to maximum of ₹ 1.25 lakh. There is no limit on subsidy for irrigation projects. The funds under this scheme are shared by the centre and state govt. in ratio of 75:25 respectively.

✪ Jawahar Gram Samridhi Yojna (JGSY)

Primary objective of JGSY is to develop village infrastructure by creating durable assets and its secondary objective is generation of supplementary employment for the unemployment poor the rural areas. The programme is implemented as a centrally sponsored scheme on the basis of 75% funds from the centre and 25% funds from the State govt.

✪ Employment Assurance Scheme (EAS)

The primary objective of the EAS is the creation of additional wage employment opportunities through manual work for the rural poor living below the poverty line while the secondary objective is the creation of durable assets for the benefit of the community. The programme is implemented as a centrally sponsored scheme on cost sharing basis between the centre and the state in the ratio of 75:25 respectively.

✪ Indira Awas Yojana (IAY)

Housing is one of the basic requirements for human survival. For a normal citizen owning a house provides sufficient economic security and status in society. For a shelter less person a house brings about a profound social change in his existence endowing with an identity, thus integrating him with his immediate social milieu. IAY was a sub-scheme of JRY. Since 1st January 1996, it has been delinked from JRY and has been made an independent scheme.

✪ Watershed Development

Watershed development originally managed by national wasteland development board under Ministry of Environment and forest. It is now placed under Ministry of Rural Development and Department of Land Resources. The main objective of this programme for development of waste lands in non-forest areas, checking of land degradation, putting such waste land into sustainable use and increasing bio mass, availability of fuel wood, fodder and restoration ecology etc. thus concept of watershed development is a integrated nurture with multi disciplinary activities in the area. At present Ministry of Rural Development and Department of Land Resources, Government of India funding watershed development programmes under DPAP, DDP, and Integrated Wasteland Development Plan (IWDP) etc. This programme is intended to be taken up in rainfed and drought - prone areas especially predominated by SC/ST population and preponderance of wasteland.

✪ Below Poverty Line Family

Identification of families lying below poverty line is the essential factor for successful implementation of all anti-poverty programmes, i.e., SGSY, JGSY and IAY etc. It is a method of survey adopted for selection of rural poor families who are living below poverty line. Previously during 8th Five Year Plan a house having income below ₹ 11,000/- was recognized as BPL family.

✪ Rajiv Gandhi Swavlamban Rozgar Yojna (RGSRY)

The Rajiv Gandhi Swavlamban Rozgar Yogna has been designed, developed and promoted by the Delhi Khadi & Village Industries Board, with the help of Government of NCT of Delhi, to provide the employment opportunities to the unemployed youth, artisans, trained professionals, skilled technocrats and entrepreneurs by promotion/expansion of permissible industries, professions, tertiary and service sector in the UT of Delhi.

Khadi and Village Industries Commission (KVIC)

The KVIC established by an Act of Parliament in 1957, is engaged in planning, promoting and implementing programmes for the development of Khadi and Village Industries in rural areas. Besides producing Khadi, 116 village industries are implementing various projects ranging from poultry, tanning, carpentry, and blacksmithing, weaving and designing of musical instruments. While Khadi is produced only by registered co-operative societies and charitable trusts, it is from village industries that entrepreneurs get help.

Goa Handicraft, Rural and Small-scale Industries Development Corporation (GHRSSIDC)

The Goa Handicraft, Rural and Small-scale Industries Development Corporation Ltd., is implementing the preferential purchase scheme since 1999, for the benefit of registered small-scale industries located in the State of Goa. The scheme is intended to provide encouragement to the SSI units by giving a preferential treatment to the various items produced by the SSI units.

Goa Industrial Development Corporation (GIDC)

GOA-IDC has a programme of expansion of Industrial Estates as well as establishment of new Industrial Estates to meet the demand of the industry to set up their projects in Goa. In order to cope up with the pace of industrialization in Goa, a Special Land Acquisition Cell has been set up to gear up the land acquisition proceedings.

Objective

One of the important activities of the Corporation is to identify land of sizeable area for setting up of Industrial Estates. The Government will revamp the functioning of the Goa Industrial Development Corporation, and make efforts to energize the Corporation to provide proper infrastructure and facilities, for setting up of Industries and attracting investment in Goa.

Economic Development Corporation (EDC)

EDC is primarily a financial institution established by the Government of Goa to promote industrial investment within the State (earlier Union Territory). EDC has been assisting units located in the Union Territory of Daman, Dadra and Nagar Haveli also.

EDC Ltd., earlier known as Economic Development Corporation of Goa, Daman & Diu Limited was incorporated on 12th March 1975, as limited company to act as the State Industrial Development Corporation. The area of operation of EDC in addition to Goa is in the Union Territory of Daman, Diu, Dadra and Nagar Haveli.

It has been acting as a state Industrial and investment Corporation. Besides, it has also been accorded the twin status of State Financial Corporation (SFC) by IDBI/SIDBI.

Objectives of EDC: EDC has been a professionally managed organization and acts as on excellent Delivery Channel for conversion of the Government policies and delivering them to the citizens.

Other activities: The Corporation has developed Patto Plaza admeasuring about 1,77,000 sq.mts. at Panaji, Goa. The land was reclaimed and leveled after it was acquired. Infrastructural facilities like road, footpaths, drains, electrification and parking spaces were constructed.

13 INCENTIVES AND SUBSIDIES

Introduction, Subsidy, Incentive, Need for Incentives, Central Level Subsidies and Incentives, Subsidies and Incentives in Goa, Self-employment Schemes: (a) Chief Minister's Rozgar Yojana; (b) Prime Ministers Rozgar Yojana, Seed Capital Assistance, Summing Up.

Introduction

Entrepreneurs in India are offered a number of incentives with their incredible contributions to economic development. Entrepreneurs play a significant role in industrialization. **Firstly**, they encourage effective resource mobilization of capital and skill which might otherwise remain unutilized and idle. **Secondly**, they induce backward and forward linkages which stimulate the process of economic development in the country. **Thirdly**, as a catalyst or agent of change their role is confined to economic, social, cultural and attitudinal changes required for the successful economic development.

Mrs. Joan Robinson has given a "Golden Age" idea in her economic development concept. She said that the society enters in Golden period when total production, total capital and product value are continuously increasing – simultaneously manpower and per capital production are also increasing. It occurs only when industrial production is ever increasing. Industrial development depends on entrepreneurship.

Subsidy

'Subsidy' denotes a single lump sum which is given by a Government to an entrepreneur to cover the cost. The term 'bounty' denotes a bonus or financial aid given to an industry to help it to compete with other units in the country or in a foreign market.

Incentive

The term 'incentive' means encouraging productivity. It is a motivational force which makes an entrepreneur take a right decision and act upon it. Broadly, incentives include concessions, subsidies and bounties stated above. Economic incentives - both financial and non-financial - push an entrepreneur towards decisive decision and action. The objective of incentives is to motivate an entrepreneur to set up a new venture in the larger interest of the nation and the society.

Need for Incentives

The need for incentives and subsidies arises for the following reasons:

(1) ***To Correct Regional Imbalances in Development:*** The usual package of incentives and concessions has been, however, the experience of industrial administration, department of industries, district level officers, development corporations, etc., that what is lacking in the backward districts is the overall existing environmental growth. One of the ways is to identify pockets of savings of different activity groups like traders, businessmen, agriculturists, professionals, etc., and provide them with relevant information as well as suitable incentives to offset the disadvantages prevailing in such places. Industrial policy uses incentives both to correct the market imperfections and to accelerate the process of industrialization so as to drive forces of supply and demand to reach the equilibrium level. Such a policy then aims at inducing some entrepreneurs or sections of the community to locate their industrial limits in areas selected by government rather than that of their own choice. Regional balances can also lead to effective utilization of regional resources, removal of disparities in income and levels of living and contribute to a more integrated society.

(2) ***To Promote Entrepreneurship by Removing Economic Constraints:*** As for the economic constraints, the new entrants in the field face many impediments on account of inadequate infrastructures. The new entrepreneur suffers because of distances separating central administrative organs from entrepreneurs and their projects, deficiency of various supporting services such as market intelligence, entrepreneurial guidance and training, technical consultancy and merchant banking facilities, lack of an institutional mechanism to provide full-time management personnel complementary to that of the new entrepreneurs, and finally, from in–sufficient orientation of the promotional institutions, barring a few exceptions, at the state level to the needs of new entrepreneurs.

(3) ***To Provide Competitive Strength, Survival and Growth:*** Some of the incentives are concerned with the establishment of industries while others are concerned with the survival and growth of industries. Several incentives are confined to the first few years of the establishment of the unit while a few of them are made available over a long period. Instances may be cited of the reservation policy for SSIs due to which a small firm can hope to compete in the market to which entry for large units are barred. If these units are already established and are brought under the reservation policy later; it will be a case of incentives to support its competitive strength. For a newcomer, the reservation is an incentive to enter the industry itself. A price preference improves its competitive strength.

Central Level Subsidies and Incentives

(1) ***Central Investment Subsidy Scheme:*** This was introduced in 1971, and has been modified from time to time. The scheme is for encouraging setting up of industries in centrally notified backward areas. For setting up industries in Category "A" backward areas, subsidy is allowed at the rate of 25% subject to a maximum of ₹ 25 lakh (enhanced to ₹ 50 lakh for setting up electronics industry in hilly districts). It is 15% and 10% subject to a maximum of ₹ 15 lakh and ₹ 10 lakh for category 'B' and 'C' districts respectively. MRTP/FERA companies are not eligible for subsidy in Category 'C' areas. Entrepreneurs who set up nucleus plants in Category 'B' and 'C' districts/areas are legible for 20% and 15% subsidy, subject to a maximum of ₹ 20 lakh and ₹ 15 lakh respectively. Since the inception of the scheme and upto December, 1989, a total sum of ₹ 855.46 crore reimbursed to States/Union Territories excluding Delhi and Chandigarh.

(2) ***Transport Subsidy Scheme:*** The Scheme was introduced in 1971 and is applicable to remote and inaccessible areas. It covers the entire North Eastern Region including Sikkim, Jammu and Kashmir, and Himachal Pradesh, hill districts of Uttar Pradesh, Lakshadweep and Andaman and Nicobar Islands and Darjeeling District of West Bengal. Identified promotional institutions which transact business on behalf of small, village and cottage industries are also eligible for transport subsidy. Transport subsidy is paid on the transport costs of industrial raw materials which are brought into and finished goods which are taken out of these areas to identified rail heads/ports. In the North Eastern region subsidy is available at the rate of

90% and for Himachal Pradesh, hill districts of Uttar Pradesh and Darjeeling District of West Bengal, it is 75%. It is also available at the rate of 90% for movement of raw materials within the N.E. region and at the rate of 50% for movement of finished goods in this region from one state to another state. For airlifting of electronic components/products from Calcutta airport to the airport nearest to the locations of the industrial units in this region subsidy is allowed at the rate of 75% and vice versa.

(3) ***Central Assistance for Infrastructural Development in No-Industry Districts under the Old Scheme:*** To assist State Governments in taking up infrastructural development in one or two identified growth centers in each no-industry district, the Centre gives financial assistance which is limited to one-third of the total cost of infrastructural development, subject to a maximum of ₹ 2 crore per district. Two types of patterns have been laid down for the purpose:

Pattern I

₹ 2 crore as subsidy from the Central Government.
₹ 2 crore as share of the State Government.
₹ 2 crore as loan from IDBI on concessional terms.

Pattern II

₹ 2 crore as subsidy from the Central Government.
₹ 4 crore as share of the State Government.
₹ 5 crore as loan from IDBI on concessional terms after the shares of State and Centre are spent.

For States in the N.E. region, the scheme has been further liberalized. In a total project of ₹ 4 crore, the Centre's shares would be 50%, i.e., ₹ 2 crore per district and the State Governments have the option to fund the balance of ₹ 2 crore either from their own funds or by raising a loan from IDBI. Construction of sheds, subject to a ceiling of 25% of the total cost, has been allowed in the case of this region only.

So far 51 growth centers in 44 districts of the States of Rajasthan, Orissa, and Karnataka, UP, Bihar, Maharashtra, West Bengal, Tripura, Nagaland, AP and Mizoram have been approved by the Government for development of infrastructural facilities. A sum of ₹ 15.42 crore has been released for creating infrastructural facilities in the States of Rajasthan, Orissa, UP, Karnataka, MP, Maharashtra, Mizoram, Bihar and West Bengal till December 1988.

New Scheme for Growth Centers: The Government has announced on June 3, 1988, the decision to set up 100 growth centers throughout the country over the next five years or so. These growth centers would be endowed with infrastructural facilities on par with the best available in the country, particularly in respect of power, water, and telecommunication and banking. Each growth centre would be provided with funds of the order of 25-30 crore in order to create infrastructural facilities of a high order.

The States/Union Territories have been asked to identify double the number of growth centers allocated to them but the final selection of these will be done by the Centre. The State Governments are also free to include any of the growth centers already approved under the erstwhile scheme for developing such centres in the 'No-industry districts'.

The growth centre's shall not be located within 50 kms of the boundary of 7 cities with a population of above 25 lakhs, 30 kms from the boundary of 2 cities with a population of above 15 lakhs but below 25 lakhs and 15 kms from the boundary of 12 cities with a population of 7.5 lakh but below 15 lakhs.

The growth centers shall be located close to district sub-divisional/block/taluka/headquarters or developing urban centers. The broad financing pattern for development of infrastructure in the selected growth centers will be as follows:

1.	Central Government (Equity)	₹ 10 crore
2.	State Government (Equity)	₹ 5 crore
3.	All India Financial Institutions (including ₹ 2 crores as Equity)	₹ 4 crore
4.	Nationalized Banks	₹ 1 crore
		₹ 20 crore
5.	Market borrowings	₹ 10 crore
	Total	₹ 30 crore

The growth centers selected under this scheme will be included in Category 'B' (unless it is already in Category 'A') of the list of backward areas and will be entitled to all incentives available from time to time for Category 'B' areas. The State Governments have been requested to make suitable provisions in their States/Union Territories Plan for the development of these growth centers.

(4) *Duty Drawback to the Exporters:* For a product exported from India, the manufacturer would have paid duties as under:

(i) Import duties on raw materials and components imported; and

(ii) Excise duty on the items manufactured in India.

The Customs and Central Excise Duty Drawback Rules, 1971, provide for refund of such duties to the exporter on the export being completed.

Duty drawback is allowed only in respect of all items wherein such raw materials and components have been used on which duty either of customs or excise has been paid. There are two types of rates of drawback: (i) all-industry rate and (ii) brand rate. All-industry rate is applied to all exporters alike. The brand rate is applicable only to particular manufacturers. The brand rate is fixed on application and furnishing of information to the authorities by the exporter. Brand rate can be so fixed where the all-industry rate does not exist, or where the existing rate of drawback is less than 80% of the duty paid.

For claiming the drawback, the exporter should file with the customs the triplicate copy of the shipping bill within 60 days after the customs officer at the port has given 'Let Export Order'. On a fortnightly basis, the drawback entitled to the exporter will be remitted to his account with his bank. If the rate of drawback is yet to be fixed, the exporter can make a provisional claim. The final disbursement will be made on fixation of the rates.

To help the exporter tide over the financial difficulty faced due to the delay in disbursement of the duty drawback, the Government has formulated the Duty Drawback Scheme, 1976. Under this scheme, the exporter can get interest-free finance from his bank and export eligible goods and producing a provisional certificate as to his entitlement of drawback.

(5) *Duty Exemption Scheme to the Exporters:* The scheme enables the exporter to import materials without payment of customs duty. The licence issued under this scheme is known as 'Advance Licence'. The items allowed to be imported under these licences are such as are to be used in the manufacture of goods to be exported from India.

The advance licences are issued to manufacturers-exporters subject to actual user condition. Generally, the scheme is applicable only to those export products in which there is a minimum value addition of 33%. The licence will bear a suitable export obligation.

The licensing authority issuing a license under this scheme will also simultaneously issue a connected Duty Exemption Entitlement Certificate. Exempt materials imported against a licence under this scheme should be utilized for the manufacture of the resultant products specified in the Duty Exemption Entitlement Certificate. The license holder should execute a bond with bank guarantee and lodge it with the licensing authority.

After exports, the Duty Exemption Entitlement Certificate duly completed by the customs will have to be surrendered to the licensing authority in fulfillment of the export obligation imposed. No duty drawback will be allowed on the products exported/supplied under this scheme.

(6) *Excise Rebate to the Exporters:* Finished goods which are subject to excise duty for home consumption are exempt from the duty when they are exported. The scheme is also applicable where exported goods contain excisable goods in their manufacture.

The exporter can avail of this facility in either of the following methods, where finished goods are excisable:

(i) ***Export under bond:*** Under this method, the exporter has to execute a bond in favour of Central Excise Authorities. The amount of the bond will be equal to the duty on the estimated maximum outstanding of goods leaving the factory without paying the duty and pending acceptance of their proof of export by excise authorities. No excise need be paid by the exporter.

(ii) ***Refund of duty:*** If the duty is already paid, after export is made, the exporter should make a claim with the Centre Excise authorities. After verification of the claim, the excise authorities will arrange for the refund of the central excise.

Where the excisable materials have been used in the manufacture, similar to the above arrangement, the exporter can avail of the facility of manufacturing under bond or he can claim refund after the duty is paid.

(7) *Marketing Development Assistance to the Exporters:* The Government of India has instituted a Marketing Development Fund for providing grants-in-aid for the development of markets for Indian products abroad, for compensatory support for export commodities and for other export promotion efforts. The fund gets its resources from the allocation of General Budget.

The fund is administered by a committee consisting of the Secretaries of the Departments of Economic Affairs and Expenditure and Commerce. Various schemes (i.e., export promotion activities) falling under the grants-in-aid are processed by different sub-committees.

Assistance under MDF is available to organizations like Export Promotion Councils, Commodity Boards, India Trade Promotion Organisation, etc., and individual exporters approved by such organizations.

The extent of assistance differs depending upon the scheme. Generally it ranges between 50% and 60%. Some of the schemes eligible for assistance under the fund are :

(a) Commodity survey/study within the country for determining export potential;
(b) Market survey abroad;
(c) Publications for issue within the country or abroad;
(d) Participation in exhibitions abroad;
(e) Setting up showrooms, warehouses, after sales service establishments;
(f) Research and development;
(g) Consultancy services;
(h) Setting up foreign offices.

The application for assistance should be sent to the Marketing Department Assistance Committee at the Ministry of Commerce through the approved organization like Export Promotion Council and Commodity Board.

(8) *Supply of Raw Materials:* Units engaged in exports are given priority in the allotment of scarce raw materials such as steel. In certain cases, the raw materials are arranged to be supplied at international prices, much below the internal prices.

IPRS: The International Price Reimbursement Scheme for steel and pig iron provides for reimbursement to the exporter of the difference in international and domestic price of specified categories of iron and steel used in export of engineering goods. The reimbursement is made through the Engineering Exports Promotion Council.

(9) ***Export Oriented Units/Export Processing Zone:*** Units undertaking to export their entire production of goods may be set up under the Export Oriented Units Scheme. Such units may be engaged in manufacture, production of software, horticulture, agriculture, acquaculture, animal husbandry or similar activity. Units engaged in service activities may also be considered on merits.

Free Trade Zone or Export Processing Zone is an industrial estate, cordoned off from domestic tariff area, where trade barriers applicable to the rest of the economy do not apply and where export-oriented units can operate free of import duties or quantitative restrictions and are given other advantages including tax exemptions. Seven free trade zones have been set up in India at Santa Cruz (Mumbai), Kandla, Chennai, Kochi, Noida, Falta (Kolkata), and Visakhapatnam.

Units in the free trade zone and export oriented units (outside the zone) are similarly placed with regard to conditions and benefits bestowed on them.

Facilities for Units in the Export Processing Zone

- Developed plots/ready-buildings to suit project requirements.
- Single-point clearance of new projects within 40-65 days.
- Automatic approvals of proposals by the Development Commissioner on certain conditions.
- No licence required for import of capital goods, raw materials, consumables, spares etc.
- Duty free import of capital goods and equipment from preferred sources.
- Second-hand capital goods allowed to be imported.
- Sourcing of capital goods from domestic manufacturing/leasing companies allowed.
- Exemption from Central Excise Duty and other levies on products manufactured within the zone.
- Complete exemption from Income Tax on profits for a period of five years.
- Foreign equity participation up to 100% permissible.
- Remittance of profits and dividends by foreign investors/NRIs allowed fully after payment of taxes.
- Up to 25% production and 5% rejects can be sold in domestic market on payment of appropriate duties.
- Re-export of unused imported goods allowed, subject to certain conditions.
- Imported machinery becoming obsolete allowed to be disposed of, subject to payment of custom duty on depreciated value.
- Sub-contracting part of job work to units in the domestic market may be allowed.
- Concessional finance available for investment and working capital.
- Assured power supply, preferential power connection.
- Supplies from domestic market to the units in the zone treated as deemed export.
- Export finance banks or special concessional rate of interest.
- Green card to units for getting facilities like telephone, telex, cement, steel, etc. on priority basis.
- Containers loaded by units in SEPZ not to be inspected or other points, so long the seals are intact.
- Private bonded warehouses permissible for stack and sale of duty-free materials, components, etc., to SEEPZ units.
- And many more....

Other Facilities/Provision being made available in SEEPZ

- Security as per norms laid down by the customs for SEEPZ.
- Paved internal roads, street lights, water supply, etc.
- Container space on rental basis.

- Customs clearance centre within the Diamond Industrial Park.
- Railway station within 1 km. Surat Airport, Magdalla Sea Port and highway within 15 km.
- Office premises available in the International Trade Centre of the park.
- Health centre, school, recreation club, theatre coming soon.
- Hotel by an international chain of hotel soon to come up.
- Excellent green and clean environment.
- Administrative support by the promoters to users in preparing their application for units in the zone.

(10) *Export Houses, Trading Houses and Star Trading Houses:* A registered exporter is a person holding valid registration certificate issued by an Export Promotion Council, Commodity Board or other registering authority designated by Government for the purpose of export promotion.

The exporter may be registered as an Export House or a Trading House or a Star Trading House if the average FOB value of physical exports during the preceding three licensing years is not less than ₹ 10 crores, ₹ 50 crores and ₹ 250 crores respectively. The registration may also be granted if the FOB value of exports during the preceding licensing year was not less than ₹ 15 crores (export house), ₹ 75 crores (trading house) and ₹ 300 crores (star trading house).

These houses are entitled for special import licences for import of such items included in the Negative List of Imports, under a scheme notified on this behalf. They are also eligible for opening of foreign currency accounts in India and abroad, Marketing Development Assistance and to execute legal undertaking in lieu of bank guarantee to cover the export obligation.

(11) *Export Promotion Capital Goods Scheme:* The scope of the EPCG scheme has been enlarged, following amendments to the EXIM Policy in 1996. The major provisions of the scheme are as follows:

(a) Capital goods may be imported with a license under the EPCG Scheme. Capital goods (including spares up to 20 per cent of the Cost-Insurance-Freight, value of the capital goods) may be imported at a concessional rate of customs duty according to the conditions given in the table below, subject to an export obligation to be fulfilled over a period of time. The period for fulfillment of export obligation is reckoned from the date of issue of the import license.

Duty	Export Obligation	Period
15% CIF Value	Four times CIF Value	5 years
Zero Duty (in case CIF value is ₹ 200 million or more)	Six Times CIF value	8 years

(b) Export obligation shall be in Free on Board basis. However, in the case of zero-duty imports, the licence holder may apply for the fulfillment of the export obligation by exporting four times the CIF value of the capital goods on net foreign exchange basis within a period of eight years.

(c) Under the scheme, manufacturer exporters, merchant exporters and service providers are eligible to import capital goods.

(d) EPCG licence holders may fulfill their export obligation through supply of intermediate products, but without claiming benefits provided for deemed exports.

(12) Foreign Currency Accounts for Exporters: Exporters with a net foreign earnings of ₹ 4 crore and over during the preceding year may be permitted by Reserve Bank to maintain foreign currency accounts in US dollar or sterling pound, with SBI, public sector banks and foreign banks operating in India.

Only one account shall be maintained which will have no cheque facility. No overdraft can be granted in the account. The exporter availing this facility should route all export documents through the designated branch of the bank. Credit to the foreign currency account will be approved method of liquidation of post shipment advances. RBI will fix ceiling on balance to be maintained in the account. Excess over that shall be converted into rupees promptly.

If exports arrange foreign currency overdraft/revolving lines of credit from banks abroad for financing their imports RBI may consider their keeping foreign currency accounts abroad. Mirror account shall be maintained by a bank in India. They cannot avail pre shipment/post shipment finance except to the extent of rupee expenditure.

(13) *Other Benefits:* Some of the other benefits available to exporters can now be listed.

(a) Exemption from sales tax.

(b) Exemption from income tax.

(c) Training facilities in India and abroad.

(d) Availability of concessional finance from banks and Exim Bank.

(e) Credit insurance cover from ECGC.

(f) Pre shipment inspection facilities.

(g) Foreign exchange for business visits abroad and for participation in trade fairs and exhibitions abroad.

(h) Special import licences for items in negative list.

Thus, it may be seen that no efforts have been spared in providing all possible facilities and incentives to exports.

Subsidies and Incentives in Goa

(1) Capital Contribution Scheme, 2008.

Introduction: The Scheme is designed to support local entrepreneurs, promote industrial units which venture out and develop special products based on locally developed technology.

Objectives: The objectives of the Scheme are as follows:

(1) To give financial support to local entrepreneurs.

(2) To support existing functional units to venture out and expand.

(3) To support locally developed technology.

Quantum of Subsidy

(1) The quantum of contribution under this Scheme shall be subject to budgetary provisions and in case of sick units under revival plan. The applications which are not considered during the fiscal year shall lapse and fresh applications are required to be filed during the next financial year.

(2) Maximum capital contribution up to ₹1.00 crore per unit will be available under this Scheme subject to the condition that contributions of promoters should be equal or more than the capital contribution by the Government. However, this restriction/condition shall not be applicable to sick units.

(3) The capital contribution will be for a period of 5 years as may be indicated in the sanctioned order with guaranteed return of 6% or actual profit.

(4) The beneficiary shall submit post dated cheques for repayment as a security towards the amount sanctioned. In case of failure of realization of the cheques so produced, the beneficiary shall be liable to be prosecuted as per the relevant provisions of the Act.

(5) The units shall submit collateral security equal to the quantum of contribution sought or equal to the tune the unit is eligible. In case of failure to repay, the security so produced shall be forfeited.

(6) Preference:

   (1) Preference will be given to the units in the small scale sector, units involved in research and development, technical oriented, units and the units run by women entrepreneurs/clusters.

(2) In case of the Goa Sick Industrial Unit Revival and Rehabilitation Scheme, 2008, the capital contribution will be in proportion as indicated in the Goa Sick Industrial Unit Revival and Rehabilitation Scheme, 2008 and subject to:
(a) The unit generating net revenue in VAT/ST or any other tax of the Government of Goa.
(b) The actual generation of net tax revenue during the preceding year (in proportion) as indicated in the Goa Sick Industrial Unit Revival and Rehabilitation Scheme, 2008.

(2) Preferential Purchase Incentives for Micro and Small Enterprises Scheme, 2008

Introduction: To give effect to the provisions of said policy, the Government of Goa has decided to formulate a Preferential Purchase Incentives Scheme for Micro and Small Enterprises.

Objectives: This Scheme is intended to encourage and give boost to Micro and Small-scale Enterprise Sector and needs to be complied with utmost care. Non-compliance of provisions of this Scheme shall be viewed seriously and the Officer concerned shall be personally held liable.

Benefits: Under this Scheme Micro and Small Enterprises permanently registered with the Directorate of Industry, Trade and Commerce, Goa shall be given special treatment in any tender floated by Government Department/Autonomous Bodies/Corporations/Semi-government Departments or any purchases made by them, as under :

(1) Micro and Small Enterprises shall be allowed to match to lowest tender price floated by non Small-scale Units provided its quoted price is within 15% of lowest quoted price floated by Non Micro and Small Enterprises;
(2) In case of contractual tenders for installation, commissioning of machinery/items, etc., the preference of quoted price, the pro-rata percentage over and above the lowest quotation shall be granted to the concerned Micro or Small Enterprises for being qualified to match the lowest one.
(3) For the purpose of availing benefit under this Scheme, the Micro and Small Enterprises shall be required to match standard of quality as required by the State Government Department.
(4) The Scheme shall be applicable even for purchase of computer hardware and other electronic items except in cases of purchases of Education Department, under this Scheme.
(5) The tender documents shall be supplied to Micro and Small Enterprises at the rate of maximum upto ₹ 200/-.
(6) Earnest money shall be required to be deposited and the same shall be to the maximum of ₹ 500/-.
(7) No other security deposit is required.
(8) Priority in payment shall be ensured to Micro and Small Enterprises and the payment shall be affected by the concerned Department within 60 days from the delivery of goods or completion of tendered work, failing which the Department shall be liable to pay an interest at the rate of 0.75 % per month.

(3) Goa State Financial Incentives to the Industries for Certification and Patenting Scheme, 2008

Introduction: Units which obtain Indian Standard Institute and International Standard Organisation Certification or any other International Certification and/or patent right on products and/or processes, need to be specially encouraged. Such units provide a benchmark of excellence and serve as a model for others to emulate. Therefore, this Scheme is introduced for industrial units to provide financial incentives for achieving the benchmark of excellence.

Objectives: The main objectives of this Scheme are as follows:

(a) To encourage the industrial units to obtain National and International Certification and patent rights in order to maintain requisite standards of quality of products/processes.

(b) To give boost to the industrial units to achieve the benchmark of excellence and service as a model for others to emulate.

(c) To promote healthy qualitative industrial growth in the State of Goa.

Quantum of Assistance

(1) Under this Scheme, financial assistance/subsidy to the extent of ₹ 2 lacs or the actual expenses incurred whichever is less will be granted per unit. The actual expenses will not include charges of Lodging/boarding, refreshment, travel etc., but will include only the actual charges incurred to obtain the certificate.

(2) Under the Scheme financial incentive can be availed once in a lifetime of the unit, irrespective of change in ownership/constitution or product provided that after such a change in ownership/constitution/product; if the applicant becomes ineligible to use such certification under which the benefit is availed than the unit will once again be eligible to avail the benefit under this Scheme provided that the loss of certification due to inadequacies in the unit shall not be reason enough to avail this benefit for the second time.

(4) Incentives to Encourage Consumption of Local Raw Material Scheme, 2008

Objectives: The main objective of this Scheme is to encourage consumption of local raw material; thereby encouraging units manufacturing such raw materials and also to encourage economics of villages supplying/producing such raw materials including those in Horticulture business/Food Processing/Cluster.

Eligibility

(1) Only those units under green and specified orange category shall be eligible under this Scheme.

(2) Only those units which are permanently registered with the Directorate of Industries, Trade and Commerce or cleared by High Powered Co-ordination Committee (HPCC) or any Committee or authority formed to grant such clearance for investment in the State shall be eligible under this Scheme. This Scheme will be applicable only to Micro, Small and Medium-scale Enterprises as defined under MSMED Act.

(3) The unit consuming minimum 50% of its raw materials (in value) from local sources shall be eligible for the benefit on pro-rate terms with those consuming 60% and above, which will be considered for 100% benefit under this Scheme.

Nature of Incentive

Once a unit becomes eligible under this Scheme, following incentives shall be granted in proportion to the quantum of local raw materials consumed by such unit for a period of five years from the date of first approval:

(1) The unit consuming local raw materials below 50% of total raw materials consumed by such unit shall not be considered for any benefit. The unit consuming local raw materials from 50% to 60% of total raw material consumed, by such unit; shall be given benefit proportionately considering 50% consumption at zero level and 60% consumption at 100% level (units consuming more than 50% local raw materials of its total raw materials shall get benefit of 100%). For the purpose of calculating the percentage level; the raw materials to finished goods ratio shall be considered as 0.4 (minimum) and 0.6 (maximum).

(2) Following benefit shall be granted to the eligible units:-

   (a) The eligible unit shall be considered for reimbursement to the extent of maximum 90% Sales Tax paid by such unit and subject to quantum based on (1) above.

   (b) The eligible unit shall be considered for incentives in the form of subsidy on power and water bills annually. 25% subsidy will be given to the eligible units on total expenditure incurred by the unit on power and water tariff subject to maximum 2 lacs per annum and as per proportion indicated in (1) above.

(5) Goa State Export Market Development Scheme, 2008

Introduction: To give effect to the provisions of the said policy, the Government of Goa is pleased to introduce this Scheme for the industrial units engaged in export and set up in Goa, by providing assistance in the form of interest free loan.

Objectives: The main objectives of the Scheme are as follows :

(a) To encourage the Goan Industries to improve export markets.

(b) To support the Goan Industries to establish their goods firmly in export market, thereby, generating growth and employment.

Quantum of Loan: Maximum interest free loan up to ₹ 5.00 lacs will be provided under this Scheme.

Purpose for Assistance

(a) Interest free loan under this Scheme up to ₹ 5.00 lacs will be provided for participating in Shows/Exhibitions outside India.

(b) Interest free loan up to ₹ 5.00 lacs will also be provided for market study tour out of India.

(c) One unit can avail this facility only once under this Scheme in lifetime.

(d) If the original unit have already taken benefits under this Scheme, then the sold/transferred unit shall not be eligible to derive any benefits under this Scheme.

(e) If there is any dispute in interpreting (a) to (d) above, then the decision of the Director, Directorate of industries, Trade and Commerce, shall be final and binding.

(6) Interest Subsidy Scheme, 2008

Introduction: In an effort to boost economic growth in the State, it is proposed by the Government of Goa to provide subsidy to the Micro and Small Enterprises on interest payable by them. This will be a very attractive incentive to the investors who could then invest more and seek better returns for themselves and for the State.

Objectives: The main objectives of this Scheme are as follows :

(a) To give boost to the Micro and Small Enterprises in the State.

(b) To provide incentives to small investors for making their enterprises viable financially.

(c) To promote industrial growth in the State and create an optimistic environment for the small investor and local entrepreneurs to invest.

Quantum of Subsidy

(a) Incentives shall be given to eligible units to the extent of 1½% of the total net turnover or 30% of the interest paid by the units, whichever is less, subject to a ceiling of ₹ 5.00 lacs per annum.

(b) For the purpose to this Scheme, net turnover means turnover not including taxes, such as, sales tax and excise as also net of any discount.

(c) Any additional benefit granted to Women Entrepreneurs by Government of India/Government of Goa under any Scheme of any Department.

(7) Incentives to Women Entrepreneurs Scheme, 2008

Introduction: The Government of Goa is pleased to frame this Scheme for the benefit of those units which are set up by women entrepreneurs, to give them additional incentives.

Objectives:The objective of this Scheme is to encourage women entrepreneurship and encourage women to start industry for self-employment.

Incentives

(1) 5% additional benefit under Local Employment Subsidy Scheme. This is over and above what is eligible under the original Scheme.

(2) Preference in Capital Contribution and under Special Capital Contribution Schemes.

(3) In case of Interest Subsidy Scheme prescribed limit of 1½% of turnover will be increased to 2% and 30% of interest paid will be increased to 35%, however, subject to overall ceiling of ₹ 8.00 lacs.

(8) Goa State Employment Subsidy Scheme for the Industries, 2008

Introduction: For effective implementation of new Industrial Policy, the Government of Goa is pleased to introduce the Goa State Employment Subsidy Scheme for the Industries, 2008, for industrial units to be set up and the units already set up in the State of Goa. The Scheme will be in operation as per the period indicated herein. However, the Government may decide to extend or curtail the period of the same without effecting the benefits already availed.

Objectives: The main objectives of this Scheme are:

(a) To promote industrial growth in the State of Goa.

(b) To create a healthy environment for setting up new industrial units in the State of Goa.

(c) To revive sick industrial units in the State of Goa.

(d) To give boost to provide employment to local youths.

(e) To create manpower suitable to the needs of the Industry.

Quantum of Subsidy

For determining the quantum of subsidy, the State is divided into developed and less developed talukas, Pernem, Satari, Bicholim, Sanguem, Quepem and Canacona are less developed talukas. The rest shall be treated as developed talukas.

- For new units in developed talukas, the subsidy shall be 25%.
- For new units in less developed talukas additional 10% incentives will be given in the subsidy.
- For existing micro and small industrial units in developed talukas, the subsidy shall be 10%.
- For existing micro and small industrial units in less developed talukas additional 5% benefit will be given in the subsidy.
- For sick units, under revival plan, it shall be defined by the appropriate authority, subject to maximum 25% and shall be uniform across the State.

Under any circumstances, the total quantum of subsidy shall not exceed 40% including all the additional benefits under this and various other Schemes.

(9) Grant-in-Aid Scheme to provide Financial Assistance to the Mahila Mandals

Background: The women in Indian Society play significant role in shaping the family and its members; socially, educationally, culturally and economically too. The women are the milestones of the society, should be aware and educated in different arts 7 skills; which are required in their day to day activities or for providing good services/facilities to their family members.

The women in Indian Society are not united, they are segmented. For the development of the society/families the women should be united and it is required to inculcate in the minds of women the concept of togetherness.

Today, the concept of Self-help Groups and Mahila Mandals has highlighted the concept of togetherness and implemented several programme for the well-being of the women. Mahila Mandals have actively involved in several socio-cultural activities of educating, training and socializing the women.

To encourage the activities of Mahila Mandals and to strengthen them, the Scheme of Grant-in-Aid to Mahila Mandal has been formulated, by which financial assistance shall be sanctioned to undertake socio-educational activities.

Objective of the Scheme: The objective of the Scheme is to provide financial assistance to Mahila Mandals for training/orientation for members of the Mahila Mandals for generating their own activity for self-employment.

Target Group: The Scheme is applicable to all the Mahila Mandals duly registered before the competent authority within the State of Goa and are operating successfully.

Financial Assistance

1. Under the Scheme an amount of ₹ 5000/- (Rupees Five Thousand only) shall be sanctioned as annual grants to the registered Mahila Mandal for successful functioning in the Goa State.
2. Financial assistance of ₹ 2000/- (Rupees Two Thousand only) shall be sanctioned to the registered Mahila Mandals having at least 20 members for undertaking any gainful self-employment activity.

Pattern of assistance

Each Mahila Mandal shall be disbursed following grants:

1. ₹ 5000/- as annual Grant-in-Aid for registered Mahila Mandal for successful functioning in the Goa State.
2. ₹ 2000/- shall be sanctioned per course for purchase of raw materials to every Mahila Mandal for conducting any activity for self-employment.
3. Resourceful persons may be provided by the Directorate for each course of activity through CDPO's.

Self-employment Schemes

(a) Chief Minister's Rozgar Yojana (CMRY)

I Eligibility

(i) ***Age:*** for all educated unemployed 18-40 year in general; relaxable by 5 yrs in case of widow, disabled person, scheduled caste, scheduled tribe, other backward class person.(Additional relaxation of 5 years for general as a well as reserved categories could be considered by the Task Force committee, to be approved by the Chairman EDC, depending upon genuineness of the case/project. However, such relaxations during the year shall not exceed 5% of the total sanctioned cases during previous financial year. Regular ex-Government employees including those who have opted for VRS shall not be eligible for such relaxations.

(ii) ***Educational qualifications:*** VIIth passed relaxable in deserving cases. Preference will be given to those who have technical/professional qualifications. These will include candidates trained by TCPC, GHRSSIDC, Agriculture Department, Forest Department or under any other Government Training scheme.

(iii) ***Family income:*** The income of the beneficiary along with spouse and dependants, and children of minor age shall not exceed ₹ 80,000/-p.a.

(iv) ***Residence:*** Proof of residence for at least 15 years. Documents required residential certificate or passing certificate from Goa Board/Goa University or any document to the satisfaction of the sanctioning authority.

(v) ***Defaulter:*** Should not be a defaulter to any nationalized bank/financial institution/co-operative banks. Further, a person already assisted under other subsidy linked scheme would not be eligible under this scheme.

II Activities covered

All economically viable/legal activities except dealing in alcohol and tobacco.

III Loan Assistance

(a) ***Term Loan:*** Maximum ₹ 2.00 lakhs 4.00 lakhs, including 50% share assistance capital under DITC scheme. Maximum ₹ 4.00 lakhs -6.00 lakhs including 50% share capital under DITC scheme for an individual with professional degree/diploma/I.T.I. including those undergoing special training programmes conducted by authorized Govt. Departments/Corporations.

(b) ***Means of Finance (interest free):*** 10% minimum promoters' contribution 50% share capital under DITC Scheme. 40% term loan under CMRY @ 8% p.a. (5% Promoters Contribution & 45% term loan in case of widow, disabled person, SC/ST/OBC beneficiaries) Share Capital to local entrepreneurs and self-employed scheme 2003.

(c) ***Interest Rate:*** 8% p.a.(Penal & Compound interest not to be charged on term loan)

(d) ***Margin for Loan:*** 10% minimum (5% minimum for widow, disabled person SC/ST/OBC person)

(e) ***Moratorium:*** Maximum one year (Moratorium period at the period discretion of the Task Force Committee)

(f) ***Security:*** First charge of mortgage/Hypothecation of Fixed/ current assets

(g) ***Collateral:*** The applicant has to provide personal guarantee from self and one guarantee (Govt servant or a person owning a house worth ₹ 2.00 lacs or a plot of land of 1000 sq.mts. in Goa). Only personal guarantee by the applicant and parents/spouse/relative of the applicant to be taken for loan amount up to ₹ 1.00 lakh and for loans where the assets financed are fixed assets as tangible security.

(h) ***Loans up to:*** The Task Force Committee could consider proposals up to ₹ 25,000/- depending upon genuineness of the applicant and the project, based on an affidavit of self-declaration of having obtained all clearances from competent authorities, as applicable to their proposed venture.

IV Repayment Schedule

10 years (including moratorium of maximum 1 year) in monthly installments. In case of Loans against vehicles, the maximum repayment may be restricted to 5 years.

V Group Activity

More than one person (not exceeding five) joining together to form a partnership will be eligible for the assistance. The assistance will be multiplies by number of persons joining together. (Prior approval for the government will be required for consideration of proposals involving a group of more than 5 persons.)

VI Default in Repayment

If the borrower fails to repay the loan amount including interest thereon as per repayment schedule, the same shall be recovered under provisions of the Goa Public Monies (Recovery of dues) Act, 1986(PMRA) and or section 29, 30, and 31 of SEC's Act.

VII Application Form/Fees

Eligible persons shall apply in prescribed application form priced at ₹ 25/-, giving details of their project along with requisite documents. Duly completed application form shall be submitted to EDC Ltd., with application fee of ₹ 200.00 (Non-refundable).

VIII Insurance Cover Fund

₹ 200/- per lakh of term loan/share capital will be deducted from the 1st disbursement to create a fund to provide insurance cover to the loan amount/share capital in case of unfortunate disability/death of the beneficiary during currency of the loan. Repayment of principal balance of the loan amount will be done through the Fund.

IX Training

The Science envisages compulsory entrepreneurship training of upto 7 days for the beneficiary to be provided by the Government, after the loan is sanctioned but before disbursement of the loan.

Check List For CMRY Loan Assistance

Application from: Fill up the simple prescribed application from in duplicate along with the following documents:

(a) 2 photographs of the applicant.
(b) Birth certificate.
(c) School leaving or qualification certificate.
(d) Certified copy of ration card.
(e) 15 years residential certificate.
(f) Any other relevant certificate.

Project Report: Fill up the prescribed project report application from in duplicate along with the following documents:

(a) All quotations of assets to be acquired and also of raw material or stock, from authorised dealers.
(b) Registration of the unit wherever necessary.
(c) N.O.C. from Panchayat/municipality.
(d) Any other requisite N.O.C. from Government department or authority as applicable.
(e) N.O.C. on stamp paper and in prescribed format from the owner of the premises where the activity is proposed to be started.
(f) Tax receipt/registration of the shop.
(g) Electricity/Water connection proof (Wherever necessary).

Guarantor: The applicant has to provide one guarantor in the form of Government servant having a minimum monthly take home salary of about ₹ 4000/- or a person owning a residential house worth ₹ 2.00lakhs or a plot of land measuring 1000^2m. Such a guarantor will have to fill in the prescribed from provided with the application along with two photographs and relevant proof, i.e, salary certificate, house tax receipt or form I & XIV, as the case may be. Also, if assets proposed to be acquired have tangible security, no Guarantor is required for loans upto ₹ 1.00 lakh.

Affidavit: The applicant has to file an affidavit on ₹ 20/- stamp paper, duly executed before the competent authority, in the format provided with the application form.

(b) Prime Ministers Rozgar Yojana (PMRY)

District Industries Centre/Directorate of Industries, Trade and Commerce, Government of Goa, Udyog Bhavan, Panaji, Goa implements Prime Minister's Rozgar Yojana (PMRY) for providing self-employment to educated to educated unemployed youth has been in operation since October 2,1993. The scheme is revised, with a view to strengthen, by liberalizing the significant parameters of PMRY, as part of promotional package, for Micro and Small Enterprises approved by Government of India with effect from 1st of April, 2007.

Parameters for Eligibility

(1) ***Age of the Applicant:***

(i) 18 to 35 years for all educated unemployed.

(ii) 18 to 40 for all educated unemployed in North-East States, Himachal Pradesh, Uttaranchal and J & K.

(iii) 18 to 45 years for Scheduled Castes/Scheduled Tribes, Ex-servicemen, Physically disabled and Women.

(2) ***Educational Qualification:*** VIII pass. Preference will be given to those who have been trained for any trade in Government recognized/approved institutions for durations of atleast six months.

(3) ***Family Income:*** The income of the beneficiary along with the spouse or the income of parents of the beneficiaries shall not exceed ₹ 1,00,000/-per annum.

(4) ***Residence:*** Permanent resident of the area for atleast 3 years (Relaxed for married men in Meghalaya and for married women in rest of the country).

(5) ***Defaulter:*** Should not be a defaulter to any bank/financial institution/co-operative bank. Further, a person already assisted under other subsidy linked Government schemes would not be eligible under this scheme.

(6) ***Activities Covered:*** All economically viable activities including agriculture and allied activities but excluding direct agricultural operations like raising crops, purchase of manure, etc., an illustrative list of activities is available at DICs.

(7) ***Project cost:*** ₹ 2.00 lakhs for service and business sectors. ₹ 5.00 lakhs for industries sector, loan to be of composite nature. If two or more eligible persons join together in a partnership, project upto ₹ 10.00 lakhs are covered. Assistance shall be limited to individual admissibility.

Self-help Centre can be considered for assistance under the scheme provided:

- All the members of the self-help group individually satisfy the eligibility criteria laid down under the scheme.
- A self-help group may consist of 5-20 educated unemployed youth.
- No upper ceiling on project cost.
- Loan may be provided as per individual eligibility taking into account requirement of the project.
- SHG may undertake common economic activity for which loan is sanctioned without restoring to onwards lending to its members.
- The subsidy ceiling for self-help group is ₹ 15,000/- per beneficiary subject to a maximum of ₹ 1.25 lakh per self-help group.
- Subsidy may provide to the SHG as the eligibility of individual members taking into account relaxation provided in North Eastern states, Uttarakhand, Himachal Pradesh and Jammu & Kashmir.
- Required margin money contribution (i.e., subsidy and margin to be equal to 20 per cent of the project cost) should be brought in by the SHG collectively.
- The exemption limit for obtaining of collateral security will be ₹ 5 lakh per member of SHG in the industry sector and ₹ 2 lakh per member of SHG project under service/business sector. Banks may consider enhancement in the limit of exemption of collateral in deserving cases.
- Implementing agencies may decide necessity of pre-disbursal training for all the members/ majority of the members of the group.

(8) ***Subsidy and Margin Money:*** Subsidy will be limited to 15% of the margin money project cost subject to ceiling of ₹12,500/- per entrepreneur. Banks will be allowed to take margin money from the entrepreneur varying from 5% to 16.25% of the project cost so as to make the total of the subsidy and the margin money equal to 20% of the project cost.

For North Eastern states, Himachal Pradesh, Uttaranchal and J&K, subsidy @ 15% of the project cost subject to a ceiling of ₹ 15,000/- per entrepreneur may vary from 5% to 12.5% of the project cost so as to make the total of the subsidy and the margin money equal to 20% of the project cost.

(9) *Collateral:* No collateral for units in industry sector with cost upto ₹ 5.00 lakhs (the loan ceiling under the PMRY). For partnership projects under Industry Sector, the exemption limit for obtaining of Collateral. Security will be ₹ 5.00 lakhs per borrower account. For units in service and business sector no collateral for project upto ₹ 2.00 lakhs. Exemption from collateral in case of partnership project will also be limited to an amount of ₹ 2.00 lakh per person participating in the project cost.

(10) *Rate of Interest & Payment:* Normal rate of interest shall be charged. Repayment schedule may range between 3 to 7 years after initial moratorium as may be prescribed.

Reservation

Preference is given to weaker sections including women. Assistance to SC/ST beneficiaries is to be targeted in such a manner that they are benefitted in proportion to their population in the respective district/state. However, the number of SC/ST beneficiaries should not be less than 22.5% & 27% for Other Backward Class (OBCs) candidates are not available, States/UTs Govt., will be competent to consider other categories of candidates under PMRY.

(11) *Training (Entrepreneurship Development Programme):* Each entrepreneurship whose loan is provided for training is as per details given below:

(a) For Industry Sector:

- Duration; 15 to 20 working days.
- Stipend for the EDP participant: ₹ 750/-
- Training Expenditure for EDP Institutions: ₹ 875/-per beneficiary

(b) For Service and Business Sector:

- Duration: 7 to 10 working days.
- Stipend for the EDP participant: ₹ 375/-
- Training Expenditure for EDP Institution: ₹ 875/-per beneficiary.

(12) *Motivational Campaigns:* To improve the success rate of applicants, States/UTs will be allowed target cases.

(13) *Publicity:*

(i) Seminars to be conducted in each district for creating awareness of PMRY in the area in the form of pre-selection motivational campaigns. A resolution may be adopted by each Gram Panchayat for giving wide publicity and awareness about PMRY in their respective jurisdictions.

(ii) To reduce the level of sickness/closure of PMRY units, the District Level Selection Committee/ Task Force Committee be made responsible for the proper scrutiny of applications and selection of viable projects.

(14) *Implementing Agency:* The District Industries Centre & the Directorate of Industries are mainly responsible for Implementation of the Scheme along with the banks.

Parameters of PMRY

Sr. No.	Parameters	Revised
1.	Age	For all educated unemployed 18-35 years in general with a 10 years relaxation for SC/STs, ex-servicemen, physically handi-capped and women.

2.	Educational	VIIIth passed. Preference will be given to those who have been trained Qualification for any trade in Government recognized approved institutions for a duration of at least six months.
3.	Family Income	Neither the income of the beneficiary alongwith the spouse nor the income of parents of the beneficiaries shall exceed ₹ 40,000/-p.a.
4.	Residence	Permanent resident of the area for at least 3 years.
5.	Defaulter	Should not be a defaulter to any nationalized bank/financial institution/cooperative bank. Further, a person already assisted under other subsidy linked Government schemes will not be eligible under this Scheme.
6.	Activities Covered	All economically viable activities including agriculture and allied activities but excluding direct agricultural operations like raising crop, purchase of manure etc.
7.	Project Cost	₹ 1.00 lakh for business sector., ₹ 2.00 lakhs for other activities, loan to be of composite nature. If two or more eligible persons joins together in a partnership project upto ₹ 10.00 lakhs are covered. Assistance shall be limited to individual admissibility.
8.	Subsidy & Margin money	Subsidy will be limited to 15% of the project cost subject to ceiling of ₹ 7,500/- per entrepreneur. Banks will be allowed to take margin money from the entrepreneur varying from 5% to 16.25% of the project cost so as to make the total of the subsidy and the margin money equal to 20% of the project cost.
9.	Collateral	No collateral for project upto ₹ 1 lakh. Exemption from collateral in case of partnership project will also be limited to an amount of ₹ 1.00 lakh per person participating in the project.
10.	Rate of Interest & Repayment Schedule	Normal rate of interest shall be charged. Repayment schedule may range between 3 to 7 years after an initial moratorium as may be prescribed.
11.	Training & Other Assistance	The training expenses and operational expenditure to be covered within the ceiling of ₹ 2,000/- per case. The existing system of revising the scale of expenditure in consultation with the finance for various activities and flexibility would be available to the implementing agencies of the State and Central levels subject to condition that overall training and operating expenses remain within the ceiling of ₹ 2,000/- per case sanctioned.
12.	Implementing Agency	The District Industry Centres and the Directorates of Industries shall mainly be responsible for scheme implementation along with banks.
13.	Linkages of Targets Recovery	Basic minimum targets based on the population and the number of with educated unemployed. Additional targets would be linked to the recovery of loans sanctioned, past performance of sanctions or special circumstances prevailing in the State/UT.
14.	Reservation	Preference should be given to weaker sections including women. The scheme envisages 22.5% reservation for SC/ST and 27% for Other Backward Class (OBCs). In case SC/ST/OBC candidates are not available, State/UTs Govt., will be competent to consider other categories of candidates under PMRY.

Seed Capital Assistance: One of the constraints faced by the entrepreneurs, especially first generation or technical entrepreneurs, is the lack of resources to meet the minimum promoter's contribution. To help the entrepreneurs overcome the problem IDBI has come up with a scheme which has gained popularity as the Seed Capital Scheme. If the project is coming up in non-backward areas, then the project would not be eligible for subsidy. Hence, the entire amount of promoter's contribution would be brought by the contributor himself. This would be reduced to the extent of the subsidy, if the project is coming up in backward areas like (category A, B, or C). The maximum amount which can be sanctioned is to the extent of ₹ 5 lacs per project on the fulfillment of certain conditions.

Objectives of the Scheme: The objective of the scheme is to create new generation entrepreneurs who have the requisite traits of entrepreneurship but whose financial resources are limited. It envisages extension of assistance at a nominal service charge for meeting the risk capital requirements of entrepreneurs. The scheme is expected to promote wider dispersal of ownership and control of industrial undertakings.

Summing Up

Introduction: Entrepreneurs in India are offered a number of incentives with their incredible contributions to economic development.

Subsidy: 'Subsidy' denotes a single lump-sum which is given by a Government to an entrepreneur to cover the cost. The term 'bounty' denotes a bonus or financial aid given to an industry to help it to compete with other units in country or in a foreign market.

Incentive: The term 'incentive' means encouraging productivity. Broadly, incentives include concessions, subsidies and bounties stated above. Economic incentives - both financial and non-financial - push an entrepreneur towards decisive decision and action.

Need for incentives: The need for incentives and subsidies arises for the following reasons:

To correct regional imbalances in development; to promote entrepreneurship by removing economic constraints; and to provide competitive strength, survival and growth.

Central level Subsidies and Incentives

(1) ***Central Investment Subsidy Scheme:*** This was introduced in 1971 and has been modified from time to time. The scheme is for encouraging setting up of industries in centrally notified backward areas.

(2) ***Transport Subsidy Scheme:*** The Scheme was introduced in 1971 and is applicable to remote and inaccessible areas. It covers the entire North Eastern Region including Sikkim, Jammu and Kashmir, and Himachal Pradesh, Hill districts of Uttar Pradesh, Lakshadweep, Andaman and Nicobar Islands and Darjeeling District of West Bengal.

(3) ***Central Assistance for Infrastructural Development in No-industry Districts under the Old Scheme:*** To assist State Governments in taking up infrastructural development in one or two identified growth centers in each no-industry district, the centre gives financial assistance which is limited to one-third of the total cost of infrastructural development, subject to a maximum of ₹ 2 crore per district.

(4) ***Duty Drawback to the exporters:*** For a product exported from India, the manufacturer would have paid duties under import duties on raw materials and components imported and excise duty on the items manufactured in India.

(5) ***Duty Exemption Scheme to the exporters:*** The scheme enables the exporter to import materials without payment of customs duty.

(6) ***Excise Rebate to the exporters:*** Finished goods which are subject to excise duty for home consumption are exempt from the duty when they are exported. The scheme is also applicable where exported goods contain excisable goods in their manufacture.

(7) ***Marketing Development Assistance to the exporters:*** The Government of India has instituted a Marketing Development Fund for providing grants-in-aid for the development of markets for Indian products abroad, for compensatory support for export commodities and for other export promotion efforts.

(8) ***Supply of Raw Materials:*** Units engaged in exports are given priority in the allotment of scarce raw materials such as steel. In certain cases, the raw materials are arranged to be supplied at international prices, much below the internal prices.

(9) ***Export Oriented Units/Export Processing Zone:*** Units undertaking to export their entire production of goods may be set up under the Export Oriented Units Scheme. Such units may be engaged in manufacture, production of software, horticulture, agriculture, acquaculture, animal husbandry or similar activity.

(10) ***Export Houses, Trading Houses and Star Trading Houses:*** A registered exporter is a person holding valid registration certificate issued by an Export promotion Council, Commodity Board or other registering authority designated by Government for the purpose of export promotion.

(11) **Export Promotion Capital Goods Scheme:** The scope of the EPCG scheme has been enlarged, following amendments to the EXIM Policy in 1996. The major provisions of the scheme are as follows:

- (a) Capital goods may be imported with a license under the EPCG Scheme.
- (b) Export obligation shall be in Free on Board basis.
- (c) Under the scheme, manufacturer exporters, merchant exporters, and service providers are eligible to import capital goods.
- (d) EPCG license holders may fulfill their export obligation through supply of intermediate products, but without claiming benefits provided for deemed exports.

(12) ***Foreign Currency Accounts for Exporters:*** Exporters with a net foreign earnings of ₹ 4 crore and over during the preceding year may be permitted by Reserve Bank to maintain foreign currency accounts in US dollar or sterling pound, with SBI, public sector banks and foreign banks operating in India.

(13) ***Other Benefits:*** Some of the other benefits available to exporters can now be listed: Exemption from sales tax and income tax; Training facilities in India and abroad; Availability of concessional finance from banks and Exim Bank; Credit insurance cover from ECGC; Pre shipment inspection facilities; Foreign exchange for business visits abroad and for participation in trade fairs and exhibitions abroad; and Special import licenses for items in negative list

Subsidies and Incentives in Goa

(1) ***Capital Contribution Scheme, 2008:*** The Scheme is designed to support local entrepreneurs, promote industrial units which venture out and develop special products based on locally developed technology.

(2) ***Preferential Purchase Incentives for Micro and Small Enterprises Scheme, 2008:*** To give effect to the provisions of said Policy, the Government of Goa has decided to formulate a Preferential Purchase Incentives Scheme for Micro and Small Enterprises.

This Scheme is intended to encourage and give boost to Micro and Small-scale Enterprise Sector and needs to be complied with utmost care. Non-compliance of provisions of this Scheme shall be viewed seriously and the Officer concerned shall be personally held liable.

(3) ***Goa State Financial Incentives to the Industries for Certification and Patenting Scheme, 2008:*** Units which obtain Indian Standard Institute and International Standard Organisation

Certification or any other International Certification and/or patent right on products and/or processes, need to be specially encouraged. Such units provide a benchmark of excellence and serve as a model for others to emulate. Therefore, this Scheme is introduced for industrial units to provide financial incentives for achieving the benchmark of excellence.

(4) ***Incentives to Encourage Consumption of Local Raw Material Scheme, 2008:*** The main objective of this Scheme is to encourage consumption of local raw material; thereby encouraging units manufacturing such raw material and also to encourage economics of villages supplying/ producing such raw materials including those in Horticulture Business/Food Processing/Cluster.

(5) ***Goa State Export Market Development Scheme, 2008:*** To give effect to the provisions of the said policy, the Government of Goa is pleased to introduce this Scheme for the industrial units engaged in export and set up in Goa, by providing assistance in the form of interest free loan.

(6) ***Interest Subsidy Scheme, 2008:*** In an effort to boost economic growth in the State, it is proposed by the Government of Goa to provide subsidy to the Micro and Small Enterprises on interest payable by them. This will be a very attractive incentive to the investors who could then invest more and seek better returns for themselves and for the State.

(7) ***Incentives to Women Entrepreneurs Scheme, 2008:*** The Government of Goa is pleased to frame this Scheme for the benefit of those units which are set up by women entrepreneurs, to give them additional incentives.

The objective of this Scheme is to encourage women entrepreneurship and encourage women to start industry for self-employment.

(8) ***Goa State Employment Subsidy Scheme for the Industries, 2008:*** For effective implementation of new Industrial Policy, the Government of Goa is pleased to introduce the Goa State Employment Subsidy Scheme for the Industries, 2008 for industrial units to be set up and the units already set up in the State of Goa.

(9) ***Grant-in-Aid Scheme to provide Financial Assistance to the Mahila Mandals:*** The objective of the Scheme is to provide financial assistance to Mahila Mandals for training/orientation for members of the Mahila Mandals for generating their own activity for self-employment.

Self-employment Schemes

(a) Chief Minister's Rozgar Yojana (CMRY)

CMRY is designed for all educated unemployed 18-40 year in general; relaxable by 5 yrs in case of widow, disabled person, scheduled caste, scheduled tribe, other backward class person.(Additional relaxation of 5 years for general as a well as reserved categories could be considered by the Task Force committee, to be approved by the Chairman EDC, depending upon genuineness of the case/project. VIIth passed relaxable in deserving cases. Preference will be given to those who have technical/professional qualifications.

(b) Prime Ministers Rozgar Yogana (PMRY)

District Industries Centre/Directorate of Industries, Trade & Commerce, Government of Goa, Udyog Bhavan, Panaji, Goa implements Prime Minister's Rozgar Yogana (PMRY) for providing self-employment to educated unemployed youth has been in operation since October 2,1993. The scheme is revised, with a view to strengthen, by liberalizing the significant parameters of PMRY, as part of promotional package, for Micro and Small Enterprises approved by Government of India with effect from 1st of April, 2007.

Seed Capital Scheme

To help the entrepreneurs overcome the problem IDBI has come up with a scheme which has gained popularity as the Seed Capital Scheme. This would be reduced to the extent of the subsidy, if the project is coming up in backward areas like (category A, B, or C). The maximum amount which can be sanctioned is to the extent of ₹ 5 lacs per project on the fulfillment of certain conditions.

14 TAXATION BENEFITS

Introduction, Taxation support for Small-Scale Sector, The Taxation Benefits to Small-scale Industries, Summing Up

Introduction

India has a well developed tax structure. The power to levy taxes and duties are distributed among the three tiers of Government, in accordance with the provisions of the Indian Constitution. The main taxes/duties that the Union Government is empowered to levy are — Income Tax (except tax on agricultural income, which the State Governments can levy), Customs duties, Central Excise and Sales Tax and Service Tax. The principal taxes levied by the State Governments are — Sales Tax (tax on intra-State sale of goods), Stamp Duty (duty on transfer of property), State Excise (duty on manufacture of alcohol), and Land Revenue (levy on land used for agricultural/non-agricultural purposes), Duty on Entertainment and Tax on Professions and Callings. The Local Bodies are empowered to levy tax on properties (buildings, etc.), Octroi (tax on entry of goods for use/consumption within areas of the local bodies), Tax on Markets and Tax/User Charges for utilities like water supply, drainage, etc.

In the wake of economic reforms, the tax system in India has under gone a radical change, in line with the liberal policy. Some of the changes include:- rationalization of tax structure; progressive reduction in peak rates of customs duty; reduction in corporate tax rate; customs duties to be aligned with ASEAN levels; introduction of value added tax; widening of the tax base; tax laws have been simplified to ensure better compliance. Tax policy in India provides tax holidays in the form of concessions for various types of investments. These include incentives to priority sectors and to industries located in special area/regions. Tax incentives are available also for those engaged in development of infrastructure.

Industrial growth may be motivated by way of a reduction in the normally applicable tax liability in the form of tax rate. In the early stages of the developmental programmes for small-scale industries, the government had provided a number of taxation benefits with adequate incentives. Concessions are granted on the basis of product line, and the concessions refer to excise duties, taxes on specific inputs such as capital equipment, intermediate goods, etc., of all privileges that small-scale which give small enterprise an important cut-throat edge. Taxation concessions not only encourage growth of small-scale industries but also inspire entrepreneurship production and marketing of quality goods. There is increase in employment, industrial production, national income and in return increased revenue to the exchequer, which will offset the loss on account.

In a developing country like India, Small-scale Industries play a significant role in economic development of the country. They are a vital segment of Indian economy in terms of their contribution towards country's industrial production, exports, employment and creation of an entrepreneurial base. These industries by and large represent a stage in economic transition from traditional to modern technology. Small industry plays a very important role in widening the base of entrepreneurship. The development of small industries offers an easy and effective means of achieving broad based ownership of industry, the diffusion of enterprise and initiative in the industrial field.

Given their importance, the Government policy framework right from the First Plan has highlighted the need for the development of SSI sector keeping in view its strategic importance in the overall economic development of India. Accordingly, the policy support from the Government towards Small-scale Industries has tended to be conducive and favourable to the development of small entrepreneurial class. Government accords the highest preference to development of SSI by framing and implementing suitable policies and promotional schemes.

The most important promotional policy of the Government for the SSI's is fiscal incentives in the form of tax concessions and exemptions of direct or indirect taxes leviable on production or profits.

Taxation support for Small-scale Sector

Concession in matters of taxation for industries has three supportive roles. They are:

- Marketing support;
- Investment support; and
- Raw materials support.

Concessions in excise duties and sales tax primarily aim at marketing support; concessions in profits tax/dividend tax etc., offer investment support; whereas concessions in custom duty offer raw-materials support.

Taxation Benefits to Small-scale Industries

The Taxation Benefits available to small-scale industries are enumerated below:

(i) ***Tax Holiday:*** Small-scale industries are exempted from the payment of income-tax on their profits up to 6 per cent per annum of the capital employed. The deduction at the rate of 6 per cent from the total income is allowed in the assessment year in which the unit begins to manufacture, provided that the conditions specified are fulfilled by small-scale industries.

(ii) ***Depreciation:*** A small-scale industry is entitled to a deduction on depreciation account on buildings, furniture, plant and machinery at the prescribed rates. In the case of small-scale industries, the deduction from the actual cost of plant and machinery is allowed up to Rs. 20 lakhs; in the case of any machinery or plant hired by a unit, the actual cost thereof the owner of such machinery or plant. For plant and machinery used in factories working a double or triple shift, an additional allowance called extra shift allowance, is available.

(iii) ***Rehabilitation Allowance:*** A rehabilitation allowance is granted to any small-scale industriesl undertaken in India provided it is used for business purposes within three years, and, whose business is discontinued on account of:

- Flood, typhoon, hurricane, cyclone, earthquake or other natural upheaval;
- Riot or civil disturbance;
- Accidental fire or explosion; and
- Action by an enemy or action taken in combating an enemy.

(iv) ***Investment allowance:*** The investment allowance is allowed at the rate of 25 per cent of the cost of acquisition of new plant or machinery installed, unlike the development rebate, which was allowed at different rates, ranging from 10 per cent to 40 per cent.

(v) ***Expenditure on Scientific Research:*** The following deductions in respect of scientific research are allowed:

- Any expenditure incurred on scientific research related to the business (no capital expenditure);
- Any sum paid to a scientific research association which has as its objects, the undertaking of a scientific research or to a university, college or other institution to be used for scientific research.

(vi) ***Export Markets Development Allowance:*** The expenditure incurred, wholly and exclusively, on the following items is eligible for deduction:

- Advertisement or publicity outside India;
- Obtaining information regarding markets outside India;
- Maintenance of a branch office or agency for the promotion of sales abroad;
- Preparation and submission of tenders samples or technical information;
- Travelling outside India for the promotion of sales;
- Performance of services outside India in connection with, or incidental to the execution of any contract for the supply of such goods, services or facilities outside India; and
- Such other activities as may be necessary for the promotion of sales outside India.

(vii) ***Amortization of Certain Preliminary Expenses:*** A newly-established small-scale industrial unit located in a backward area is allowed a deduction of 20 per cent on its profits and gains. The deduction shall be allowed for ten years, beginning with the commencement of production.

(viii) ***Publication of Books:*** A small-scale industry engaged in the business of publication of books is entitled to claim a deduction of a sum equal to 20 per cent of the profits and gains derived from such business.

(ix) ***Amalgamation of Sick Units:*** The policy of the Government has been to encourage the amalgamation of sick units with profit-making larger units. Income Tax Act has relaxed the provisions relating to carry forward and set off accumulated business loss and the unabsorbed depreciation allowance in certain cases of amalgamation.

(x) ***Profits and Gains:*** With effect from financial year 2005-06, SSIs can claim deductions in respect of profits and gains at the following rates:-

- If SSI unit is owned by a company, the deduction available is 30% for first 10 years.
- If SSI unit is owned by a co-operative society, the deduction available is 25% for first 10 years.
- If any other person owns SSI unit, the deduction to be claimed is 25% for first 10 years.

(xi) ***Excise Concessions:*** The eligibility for excise concessions for SSIs has been based on annual turnover rather than SSI registration. SSI units having turnover less than Rs. 4 crores are only eligible for concessions. Government of India has provided various concessions to SSIs by granting full exemption from payment of central excise duty on a specified output and thereafter slab-wise concessions. Thus concessions in this regard are:-

- SSI units producing goods up to Rs. 100 lakhs are exempted from payment of excise duties.
- SSI units having turnover less than Rs. 60 lakhs per annum need not have a separate storeroom for storing finished products.
- They are not required to maintain any statutory records such as daily stock accounts, etc. Their own records are adequate.
- SSI exemption is available for goods for home consumption as well as goods exported to Nepal and Bhutan.

Summing Up

Introduction

The idea is to stimulate investment in specific directions which in the eyes of the government are particularly helpful from a small-scale industry development standpoint. Taxation benefits relate to Income tax; Excise duty; Sales tax; Electricity duty; Octroi and so on.

Taxation support for Small-scale Sector

Concession in matters of taxation for industries has three supportive roles viz., marketing support, investment support and raw materials support.

The Taxation Benefits available to Small-scale Industries

Tax Holiday; Depreciation; Rehabilitation Allowance; Investment allowance; Expenditure on Scientific Research; Export Markets Development Allowance; Amortization of Certain Preliminary Expenses; Publication of Books; Amalgamation of Sick Units; Profits and Gains; and Excise Concessions.

15 ENVIRONMENT CONCERNS

Introduction, Deforestation and The Global Carbon Cycle, Environment Concerns, Environmental Impact Assessment, Environment Friendly Products, Building Environment Sustainability, Summing Up, Case Study.

Introduction

The environment includes air, water, and land and the inter-relationship that exists among them. The inter-relationship is so delicate that a disturbance to any of these factors would have inevitable repercussion on the other. Man, in his quest for development has unwittingly tampered and transformed the environment. Development activities are a necessary evil as far as the environment is concerned. They cannot be stopped because of the harm they do to the environment, for it will not be pragmatic for man to revert back to a simplistic lifestyle, also the population is exploding and resources are scarce. The provision of minimum needs of food, shelter education and health to our vast masses demand that the basic industries and to consider agriculture specifically, there is growing demand to produce more from the same area of cultivable land, so they resort to improved varieties of seeds, chemical fertilizers and pesticides which create havoc on the environment. But there is no option but to ensure that these developmental activities do not cause much damage to the ecological balance as more the damage, more could further development be hampered. This would mean greater poverty for the poor who depend on the environment for the basic needs.

Protection of the environment is as important as economic developments for the sustenance of a socio-political system aimed at the welfare of the people. The concepts of people's welfare and economic development are totally independent and form the core idea of the concept of sustainable development. Hence, it is imperative that the planners of our country's resources use all their ingenuity and creativity towards charting a development path which is in harmony with nature.

The Ministry of Environment and Forests has been assigned the responsibility of harmonizing the protection of the environment with the development activities. It is the nodal body for the planning, promotion and coordination of various environmental and forestry programmes. It seeks to execute its plans through activities like:

- Survey and conservation of natural resources.
- The assessment of the impact of development projects.
- Incorporation of environment protection measures in the planning process.
- Pollution control.
- Regeneration programmes.

- Enacting legislation.
- Conducting research.
- Education, training and dissemination of environment related information.
- Creating an awareness of the environment.

The State Government, the Central and State Pollution Control Boards, The Indian Council of Forestry, the Wildlife Institute of India, Botanical and Zoological Surveys of India and the other Government agencies play a conducive role in the environment protection activities.

Deforestation and the Global Carbon Cycle

Carbon dioxide (CO_2) is the major gas involved in the greenhouse effect, which causes global warming. All the things that produce CO_2 (like car burning gas) and the things that consume CO_2 (growing plants) are involved in the "global carbon cycle".

Tropical forests hold an immense amount of carbon, which joins with oxygen to form CO_2. The plants and soil of tropical forests hold 460-575 billion metric tons of carbon worldwide. Each acre of tropical forest stores about 180 metric tons of carbon.

Deforestation increases the amount of CO_2 and other trace gases in the atmosphere. When the forest is cut and replaced by cropland and pastures, the carbon that was stored in the tree trunks (wood is about 50 % carbon) joins with oxygen and is released into the atmosphere as CO_2. The loss of forests has a great effect on the global carbon cycle. From 1850 to 1990, deforestation worldwide (including that in the United States) released 122 billion metric tons of carbon in the atmosphere, with the current rate being 1.6 billion metric tons per year. In comparison all the fossils fuels (coal, oil and gas) burned during a year release about 6 billion tons per year.

Releasing CO_2 into the atmosphere increases the greenhouse effect, and may raise global temperature. The role of fossil fuels burned by cars and industry is well known, but tropical deforestation releases about 25% of the amount released by fossil fuel burning. Tropical deforestation, therefore, contributes a significant part of the increasing CO_2 in the atmosphere.

Hydropower Projects and Greenhouse Gas Emission

It is estimated by our esteemed scientists that about one-fifth of India's total global warming is due to large dams. The study titled, "Methane Emission from Indian Large Dams" estimates the total generation of methane from India's reservoirs could be around 45.8 million ton, more than the share of any other country in the world. These gases are produced by the rotting of the vegetation and soils flooded by reservoirs, and of the organic matter (Plants, planktons, algae, etc.). Large dams have been known to be emitters of greenhouse gases like methane, carbon dioxide and nitrous oxide for over a decade now.

Indian hydropower projects are already known for their serious social and environmental impact on the communities and the environment. The fact that these projects also emit global warming gases in such significant proportion should further destroy the myth.

Environment Concerns

The task of an entrepreneur is to ensure that in all of our economic and social processes, we take full account of the environmental costs. Now we are in a situation where land, air and water degradation already constitutes a serious problem in our country. Growing air and water pollution is seriously affecting the quality of our lives. As development proceeds, the use of energy and natural resources will also increase. The challenge ahead is to adopt a pattern and style of development that will not put unsustainable pressure on our resources, particularly, non-renewable ones. The best is the polluter pays.

In case of major industry at least environmental audits must now become a normal routine. Industry must recognize that they have a clear responsibility, not only towards their shareholders, but what is increasingly recognized the world over as stakeholders, particularly towards consumers and the public. That is, in addition to shareholders, industry management has accountability towards consumers, workers, citizens and, of course, to future generations. That is what sustainable development means; a system of growth that does not limit the options of future generations. It is in this context that environmental costs acquire urgency. The pricing system must send right signals, reflecting all environmental costs. Only such means will enable our society to conserve its life support systems. We have to create environment friendly standards without recreating the old license or regulatory system. Industry through self-regulation should provide protection of the environment, energy conservation and conservation of other natural resources. May be there should be countervailing powers utilized by consumers, commuters and environmentalists. It is really a matter of raising environmental consciousness. We need pressures and mechanisms (in the form of regulations) that can goad industry and marketers to constantly use new environment friendly techniques. We should also lay emphasis on renewable substitutes where available, on energy saving and efficiency in all our economic processes. Reckless industrialization, unlimited consumerism leading to very high consumption is responsible for the present ecological damages. The earth has enough for everyone's need but not for everyone's greed. Co-operation with nature can assure harmony and tension free prosperous global life.

Environmental Impact Assessment (EIA)

An Environmental Impact Assessment (EIA) is an assessment of the possible positive or negative impact that a proposed project may have on the environment, together consisting of the environmental, social and economic aspects.

The purpose of the assessment is to ensure that decision makers consider the ensuing environmental impacts when deciding whether to proceed with a project. *The International Association for Impact Assessment (IAIA) defines an environmental impact assessment as "the process of identifying, predicting, evaluating and mitigating the biophysical, social, and other relevant effects of development proposals prior to major decisions being taken and commitments made".* EIAs are unique in that they do not require adherence to a predetermined environmental outcome, but rather they require decision makers to account for environmental values in their decisions and to justify those decisions in light of detailed environmental studies and public comments on the potential environmental impacts of the proposal.

India has a special legislation to provide environmental protection. Under this National Environment Protection Act, environment impact assessment and environment impact statement reports must be made mandatory before launching any new project. EIA must include the cost of impact on the environment produced by a manufacturing project into the sale price of the products. The EIA should be prepared by a panel of experts approved by the regulatory authority. Based upon this, an environment impact statement is prepared. A draft EIS should be circulated to citizens' organizations for comments. Public participation in environmental decision making is essential. Comments of citizens' organizations should be included in the final EIS. Each EIS must consider alternative strategies and actions including no action and their respective environmental impacts. All industries are made to undergo EIA and EIS procedure before granting the green signal for launching any new project. In short, mandatory EIA. must become a public conscience keeper in India as it is in USA, UK, Germany and Japan. The combination of Consumer Protection Act will act as Magna Carta of Eco-consumerism and two together will ensure societal marketing concept in its wider sense. Europe and U.S. are operating in a license free-system. But they have stringent environmental regulations and laws, a strong judiciary and higher public consciousness, a populace which are unforgiving. Our judiciary has fortunately taken active interest in pollution. Government should also evince similar, even greater interest.

Indian public is not yet ready to face the burden of safeguarding their health and environment. India is the only major country which has no mandatory Environmental Impact Assessment (EIA) prior to the initiation of development project.

Environment Friendly Products

Concentrated environmental campaigning has created a strong public opinion for environmental concerns, and as consumer awareness increases, consumer preferences will be expressed through market behaviour and by stakeholders of companies, compelling corporate sector to cater to changing demands created by consumer-citizens. The marketers will realize the seriousness of environmental concerns and issues. They will learn to opt for, and market their products as, 'environmental friendly'. Preference for green consumerism and environment friendly goods will encourage marketers to add a green tint to their marketing strategies reflecting real environmental considerations. Marketers will have to give top priority to environmental protection in India within a few years. In fact, to promote eco-friendly products will become a social responsibility. Preference for environment friendly goods will itself create immense marketing opportunities for manufacturers. Ecomark labels on the products can be an effective promotion/marketing tool.

The new eco-friendly process recently discovered by Indian researchers could prove to be a boon for plastic and pesticide industry where the conventional process yields hazardous by-products and effluent treatment entails heavy costs. The new process has low cost, product purity and high yield. It is also duly patented in 1998. Plastic and pesticide is a very great polluter.

Dapple Dishwasher Powder

Dapple Cleanup Kit

Promotional T-Shirt

Promotional USB Flash Drive

Promotional Lanyards

Bamboo Sport Shirt

Solar Calculator

Biodegradable Cup

Promotional Pens

LED Sign Eco-friendly Corporate Gift

Promotional Pencils

Organic Totel Bags

Eco-friendly Ceramic Mug

Promotional Magnets

Recyclable Aluminum Bike Bottle

Promotional Mug

Promotional Umbrella

Building Environment Sustainability

Remarkable competition is going on among the consumer, industrial and service products. Since society becomes more anxious with the natural environment, businesses have started to adjust their behavior in an attempt to address society's "new" concerns. Judging by the number of large, small and mid-size companies that are setting the trend with green initiatives, Industrialist all over the world are serious about building environmental sustainability into their business practices.

Case-I: New Delhi Transport Corporation (NDTC): This need is greatly influenced by consumer-forums and judiciary. To take an example when Supreme Court ordered the Delhi Government to examine ways and means to reduce pollution in Delhi, it asked the government to introduce clean fuel like Compressed Natural Gas (CNG) in public transport system. This put pressure on petroleum companies for launching clean fuels with low sulphur content and led free petrol. Also the only CNG supply company, Indraprastha Gas Ltd, had to increase its supply. The vehicles had to made appropriate changes. This led to Delhi Transport Corporation becoming the largest CNG powered transport system in the country. Today Indraprastha Gas has 121 CNG distribution station in Delhi with a combined capacity of 16.47 lacs kg gas per day, catering to about 90000 vehicles. This growing concern for the environment led to development in oil and gas exploration, refining and marketing. It also spurred development in the automobile sector which manufactured vehicles that could run on CNG fuel. Also the vehicles have to conform to pollution control norms as laid down by the Govt. like Bharat-III, Ero –II.

Case-II-Suzlon: One Earth Global Headquarters in Pune – India's greenest building, "the world's fourth largest wind-turbine maker is among the greenest and best Indian companies in India. Tulsi Tanti, the visionary behind Suzlon, convinced the world that wind is the energy of the future and built his factory in Pondicherry to run entirely on wind power. Suzlon's corporate building is the most energy-efficient building ever built in India.

Suzlon One Earth Global Headquarters in Pune - India's greenest building

Case-III- Imperial Tobacco Company of India Limited (ITC): Strengthened their commitment to green technologies by introducing 'ozone-treated elemental chlorine free' bleaching technology for the first time in India. The result is an entire new range of top green products and solutions: the environmentally friendly multi-purpose paper that is less polluting than its traditional counterpart.

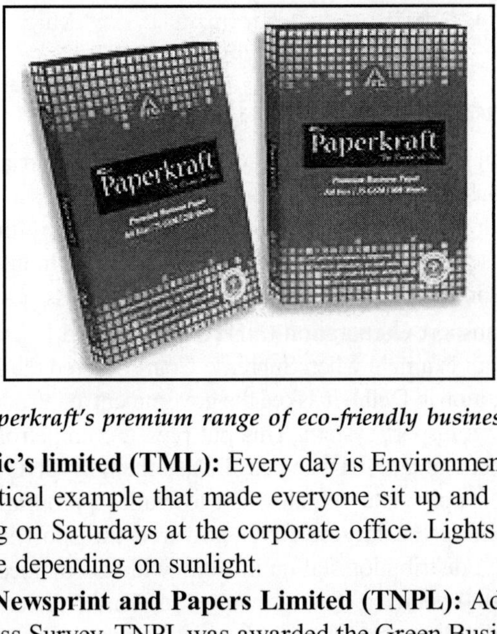

ITC Paperkraft's premium range of eco-friendly business paper

Case-IV: Tata Metallic's limited (TML): Every day is Environment Day at TML, one of the top green firms in India. A practical example that made everyone sit up and take notice is the company's policy to discourage working on Saturdays at the corporate office. Lights are also switched off during the day with the entire office depending on sunlight.

Case-V-Tamil Nadu Newsprint and Papers Limited (TNPL): Adjudged the best performer in the 2009-2010 Green Business Survey, TNPL was awarded the Green Business Leadership Award in the Pulp and Paper Sector. The initiatives undertaken by this top green firm in India includes two Clean Development Mechanism projects and a wind farm project that helped generate 2,30,323 Carbon Emission Reductions earning ₹ 17.40 Crore.

Aerial view of TNPL

Case- VI-Wipro: Wipro is one among the top ten green companies, which climbed to the top five brand league in Green peace's 'Guide to Greener Electronics' ranking. Despite the global financial crisis, Wipro held fast to its commitment towards energy efficiency and was lauded for launching energy star compliant products in the market.

Wipro broadens its green IT initiatives through its participation in "The Green Grid"

Case VII Hindustan Computers limited (HCL): This IT major may be considered as the icon of Indian green initiatives, thanks to the "go green" steps taken in solving the problem of toxics and e-waste in the electronics industry. HCL is committed to phasing out the hazardous vinyl plastic and Brominates Flame Retardants from its products and has called for a Restriction on Hazardous Substances Legislation in India.

The HCL Green Bag campaign that aimed at tackling e-waste

Case-VIII: IndusInd Bank: Green banking has been catching up as among the top Indian green initiatives ever since IndusInd opened the country's first solar-powered ATM and pioneered an eco-savvy change in the Indian banking sector. The bank is planning for more such initiatives in addressing the challenges of climate change.

IndusInd's solar-powered ATM expects to save around 1,980 Kw of energy annually

Case-IX: IDEA Cellular: One of the best Indian companies, IDEA, paints India green with its national 'Use Mobile, Save Paper' campaign. The company had organized Green Pledge campaigns at Indian cities where thousands came forward and pledged to save paper and trees. IDEA has also set up bus shelters with potted plants and tendril climbers to convey the green message.

IDEA's green bus shelter in Mumbai

Case-X: Hero Honda: Hero Honda is one of the largest two-wheeler manufacturers in India and an equally responsible top green firm in India. The company's philosophy of continuous innovation in green products and solutions has played a key role in striking the right balance between business, mankind and nature.

Hero Honda Green Ambassadors: winners of the international inter-school environment quiz competition

Case – XI- National Thermal Power Corporation (NTPC): NTPC Limited has decided to allocate 0.5% of distributable profit annually for its "Research and Development Fund for Sustainable Energy," for undertaking research activities in development of green and pollution free technologies.

Case–XII: Mahindra Group: Mahindra Group has formally announced the launch of project Mahindra Hariyali in which 1 million trees will be planted nation-wide by Mahindra employees and other stakeholders including customers, vendors, dealers, etc. by October 2008, of these, 1,50,000 trees have already been planted by Mahindra employees since September 2007.

Case-XIII: Nokia: Nokia's environmental work is based on life cycle thinking. Nokia's aim to minimize the environmental impact of products throughout the operations, beginning with the extraction of raw materials and ending with recycling, treatment of waste, and recovery of used materials.

Case-XIV-Apple Computer: Potato starch trays made by Dutch Paper Foam protect the new iPhone just launched by Apple Computer which equals 90 percent reduction in the carbon footprint compared to the plastic tray used in the past.

Case-XV-Fuel Tech: Despite its emissions, coal is still widely used in industries all over the world. Since it's an accessible resource for a number of countries, including India and China, very little work has been done to find alternative non-polluting (yet abundant) sources of energy. That's when companies like Fuel Tech step forward. They help coal-powered utilities to reduce the amount of pollution and operate more efficiently. Established in 1987, Fuel Tech has come up with a technology that reduces nitrogen emissions in boilers and furnaces. Its specialty is cleaning up coal and thereby reducing the resulting pollution. Since there are over 550 coal power plants in the US alone, Fuel Tech has come up with a solution to a very pressing problem.

Fuel Tech

Case-XVI-Solar Century: Solar Century is a UK based solar energy company that provides an alternative source of energy to residential and commercial buildings. Their solar energy products provide their customers with electricity and water heating facilities. Solar Century has the potential to generate 4 million kwh of electricity every year and has won various business and design awards for its work. The thing that sets Solar Century apart is that they integrate solar energy systems with standardized building components, making solar part of the fabric of the buildings.

Case-XVII-SweTree: SweTree Technologies is a forest biotech company that improves the productivity of seedlings and trees. They are primarily discovering new ways of increasing the speed of forestation, without using harmful chemicals or fertilizers. SweTree uses its technology to assist reforestation programs to preserve the natural habitat. With so much deforestation going on around us, such technology can help a lot in expediting the replanting process.

SweTree

Case-XVIII- OderSun: Based in Germany, OderSun has been making thin film solar cells since 2002. Instead of using silicon for their solar cells, they use a combination of copper, indium and sulfur and have the advantage of being able to produce energy in a wide variety of sizes and power capacities. The solar cells made by OderSun were used in the Beijing Olympics. They provided their thin film solar modules for the Olympic Park. Their flexibility of form and power makes them the perfect candidate for providing solar cell energy to buildings.

Case-XIX-NanoSolar: While talking about solar tech, we can't ignore NanoSolar role in this field. They manufacture solar electricity panels for cost-efficient energy. The technology used by NanoSolar aims to make solar cells that last as long as silicon solar cells. It has operations in both US and Germany. NanoSolar mass-produces in a global scale, and can thus cater to large projects anywhere in the world. With the rise of sustainable construction in Middle Eastern and European countries, access to their technology is highly valued.

Case-XX-Polyfuel: Designs, develops and manufactures hydrocarbon based fuel cells for increased performance of fuel cells in automotives and electronics. Established back in '99, Polyfuel technology is used in laptops, cell phones and other portable electronic devices manufactured by Consumer Electronic (CE) companies. Because of the abundant availability of the raw material, this is an opportunity for us to move away from traditional fuel sources that are driving the world mad, as it is. This makes Polyfuel a move in the right direction.

Case-XXI-CPower: Delivers energy management services and products enabling its customers to reduce their power usage effectively. In short, they teach companies and organizations how to reduce their electricity consumption through energy management and sustainability technologies. Their clients include businesses, factories and industries with high rates of energy consumption. To encourage companies that are not yet running on renewable energy, clean energy is a good step in the right direction. They give incentives to companies to optimize their energy consumption and earn market payments for those reductions.

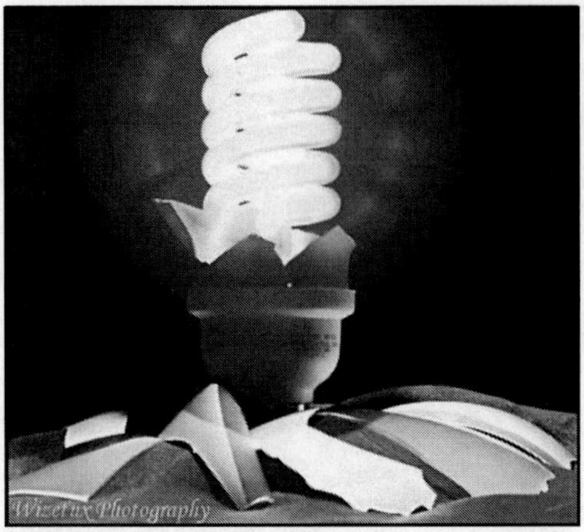

C Power

Case-XXII-Sun Power: Sun Power is another solar product and services company which produces solar cells and panels. It claims to be able to reduce the cost of solar power by 50% bringing them down enough to compete with retail electricity rates by 2012.The solar cells technology produced by Sun Power is used by some high profile companies such as Honda and NASA. With such clients in their portfolio, they're bound to create some more stirs in the industry in the years to come.

Case-XXIII-Solar City: Solar Century also provides solar panels as an alternative source of energy for home owners and businesses. Established in 2006 by brothers Lyndon and Peter Rive, it has become the largest solar power provider in California. The company aims to make solar panels easy to install at reduced rates so that more and more people switch over from conventional electricity to solar power. Their Solar Lease option reduces the installation cost making it an attractive option for customers. Solar City has now extended its business into Oregon and Arizona with plans to extend to 10 more states by the end of 2010.

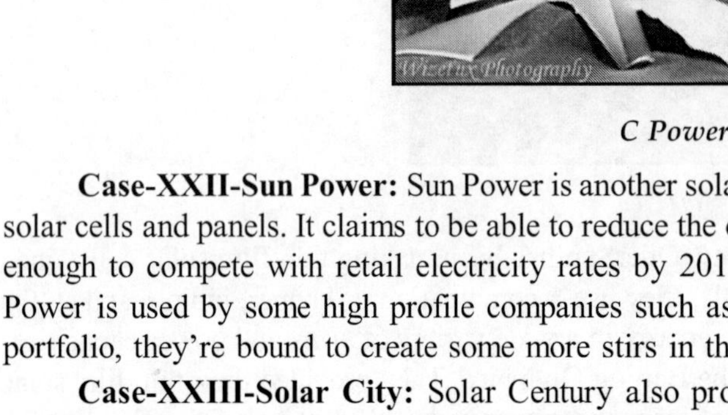

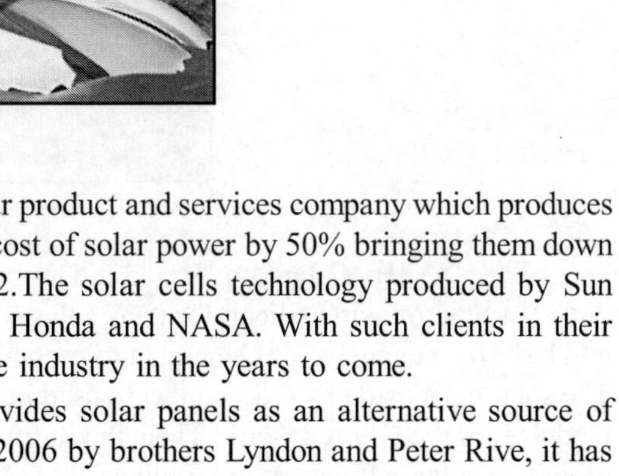

Solar city

Case-XXIV-McDonald: McDonald's bolsters green credentials with recycled biodiesel: McDonald's Corp., the fast-food chain, has bolstered its "green" credentials by announcing that its UK distribution fleet will be powered by biodiesel made of recycled cooking oil from its restaurants. The cooking oil will be collected from about 900 of McDonald's 1,200 restaurants in Britain. "With McDonald's restaurants in the United Kingdom and Ireland selling 143,000 cups of coffee, cappuccino and latter every day, the move is a significant boost to the eco-friendly coffee market. McDonald's fish 110 million pounds per year is also sustainable. Like Wal-Mart, McDonald's sources its seafood to producers that meet standards for sustainability set out by the nonprofit Marine Stewardship Council.

Case-XXV-Parle: Parle products launch "Parle my green planet" campaign. To kick start the initiative Parle will be launching a holistic campaign aimed at reaching out to 5000 schools across 70+ towns and cities in the country with the aim of reducing wastage of plastic, increasing environmental awareness and conserving the ecosystem rather than just complaining about it. Titled the School Giving Program, it is the first in a series of similar environmentally aware campaigns that are planned to be undertaken under the Parle My Green Planet banner.

The School Giving Program – a plantation drive to go green – will focus on collection of wrappers off the streets across the identified 70 plus towns. The program aims at generating awareness amongst children about the need to be responsible towards their environment and how can they contribute towards the same. To encourage this Parle Products has instituted certain awards that will be given out at the end of the exercise. The class to collect maximum wrappers will get the 'Green Class of the School' and the school to collect maximum wrappers will get the title 'Green School of the City'. This initiative also coincides with the Joy of Giving week, India's biggest social Giving programme, initiated by the Give India Foundation.

Case-XXVI-The E2: It is an internet technology and a high speed internet line. In Europe it is called E2 but in US it is called T2. Non-profit internet provider Green Net's new ultra-low power computer can run on a car battery for hours and uses a maximum of nine watts of electricity. Green Net is a not-for-profit, ethical collective internet service provider, geared towards the needs of civil society organizations. Green Net came to existence in the late 80s to support networking efforts within the green movement initially. Green Net's current work focuses on supporting organizations that promote peace, human rights and the environment through the use of Information and Communication Technology (ICTs). Green Net has now joined forces with Aleutia, a producer and distributor of affordable computers worldwide that specializes in distributing affordable computers in the developing world and Africa.

ONGC's green projects contribute to increased environmental awareness among local communities

CaseXXVII-Oil and Natural Gas Company (ONGC): India's largest oil producer, ONGC, is all set to lead the list of top 10 green Indian companies with energy-efficient, green crematoriums that will soon replace the traditional wooden pyre across the country. ONGC's Mokshada Green Cremation initiative will save 60 to 70% of wood and a fourth of the burning time per cremation.

Case-XXVIII-Whirlpool (1994): launched the "Energy Wise" refrigerator, the first CFC free cooler and one that was 30% more efficient than the U. S. Department of Energy's highest standard. For its innovation Whirlpool won the prestigious "Golden Carrot", a $30 million award package. Unfortunately, Energy Wise's sales languished because the CFC-free benefit and energy saving did not offset its $100 to $150 price premium and the refrigerator did not offer additional features or new styles that consumers desired.

Case-XXIX-Coca-Cola: Coca-Cola India has recently formed a separate division for juices to focus on its non-carbonated portfolio as all major food and beverage companies increasingly fortify their health portfolio in a market which is annually growing at 20%. Health products and juices have been at the top of these companies bucket list since they have launched new products and categories to capture a share of the pie. The cola major has been expanding its non-carbonated beverage portfolio with launches like Maaza, Milky Delite, its entry into the dairy segment, the ice tea brand Nestea with its joint venture partner Nestle, besides the fruit-based drinks Minute Maid Pulpy Orange and Minute Maid Fresh.

Summing Up

The task of an entrepreneur is to ensure that in all of our economic and social processes, we take full account of the environmental costs. In case of major industry at least environmental audits must now become a normal routine. Under this National Environment Protection Act, environment impact assessment and environment impact statement reports must be made mandatory before launching any new project. Preference for green consumerism and environment friendly goods will encourage marketers to add a green tint to their marketing strategies reflecting real environmental considerations. Marketers will have to give top priority to environmental protection in India within a few years. In fact, to promote eco-friendly products will become a social responsibility. Preference for environment friendly goods will itself create immense marketing opportunities for manufacturers. Ecomark labels on the products can be an effective promotion/marketing tool.

Case 5- Green Marketing - An Emerging Issue

Introduction

Although environmental issues has prejudiced all actions but very few academic disciplines have inculcated green issues into their writing. Even till date it has not been inculcated, a must be taught subject in almost all management and related higher education level. Smart business houses have accepted green marketing as a part of their approach. While the shift to "green" may appear to be expensive in the undersized period, it will definitely prove to be indispensable and advantageous, cost-wise too, in the long run. The public tends to be incredulous of green claims to begin with and companies can critically damage their brands and their sales if a green claim is discovered to be false or contradicted by a company's other products or practices. Green marketing is a vital constituent of the holistic marketing concept. It is particularly applicable to businesses that are directly dependent on the physical environment; for example, industries like fishing, processed foods, and tourism and adventure sports. Changes in the physical environment may pose a threat to such industries. Many global players in diverse businesses are now successfully implementing green marketing practices.

What is Green Marketing?

According to the American Marketing Association, green marketing is the marketing of products that are presumed to be environmentally safe. Thus, green marketing incorporates a broad range of activities, including product modification, changes to the production process, packaging changes, as well as modifying advertising. Other like terms used are Environmental Marketing or Ecological Marketing.

Green marketing was given prominence in the late 1980s and 1990s, after the proceedings of the first workshop on Ecological Marketing held in Austin, Texas (US), in 1975. According to Mintel, Research Director David Lockwood, about 12% of the U.S. population can be identified as True Greens, consumers who seek out and regularly buy so-called green products. Another 68% can be classified as Light Greens, consumers who buy green sometimes.

According to the Joel Makeover (a writer, speaker and strategist on clean technology and green marketing), green marketing faces a lot of challenges because of lack of standards and public consensus to what constitutes "Green".

According to Peattie (2001), the evolution of green marketing has three phases. First phase, was termed as "Ecological" green marketing, and during this period all marketing activities were concerned to help environment problems and provide remedies for environmental problems. Second phase, was "Environmental" green marketing and the focus shifted on clean technology that involved designing of innovative new products, which takes care of pollution and waste issues. Third phase, was "Sustainable" green marketing. It came into prominence in the late 1990s and early 2000.

Why Green Marketing?

It is really scary to read these pieces of information as reported in the Times recently: "Air pollution damage to people, crops and wildlife in the US totals tens of billions of dollars each year". "More than 12 other studies in the US, Brazil, Europe, Mexico, South Korea and Taiwan have established links between air pollutants and low birth weight premature birth still birth, and infant deaths". As resources are limited and human wants are unlimited, it is important for the marketers to utilize the resources efficiently without waste as well as to achieve the organization's objective.

There is growing interest among the consumers all over the world regarding protection of environment. Worldwide evidence indicates people are concerned about the environment and are changing their behavior. Companies all over the world are striving to reduce the impact of products and services on the climate and other environmental parameters. Marketers are taking the cue and are going green.

Thus, the growing awareness among the consumers all over the world regarding protection of the environment in which they live, people do want to hand down a clean earth to their offsprings. Most of the consumers, both individual and industrial, are becoming more concerned about environment-friendly products. As a result, green marketing has emerged, which aims at marketing sustainable and socially-responsible products and services. Now is the era of recyclable, non-toxic and environment-friendly goods. This has become the new mantra for marketers to satisfy the needs of consumers and earn better profits. Green marketing is the process of developing products and services and promoting them to satisfy the customers who prefer products of good quality, performance and convenience at affordable cost, which at the same time do not have a detrimental impact on the environment. It includes a broad range of activities like product modification, changing the production process, modified advertising, change in packaging, etc., aimed at reducing the detrimental impact of products and their consumption and disposal on the environment.

Marketing Mix of Green Marketing

When companies come up with new innovations like eco friendly products, they can access new markets, enhance their market shares, and increase profits. Just as we have 4Ps product prices, place and promotion in marketing, we have 4ps in green marketing too, but they are a bit different. They are buttressed by three additional Ps, *viz.*, people, planet and profit.

- ***Product:*** The products have to be developed depending on the needs of the customers who prefer environment friendly products. Products can be made from recycled materials or from used goods. Efficient products not only save water, energy and money, but also reduce harmful effects on the environment. Green chemistry forms the growing focus of product development. The marketer's role in product management includes providing product designers with market-driven trends and customer requests for green product attributes such as energy saving, organic, green chemicals, local sourcing, etc. Now companies are offering more eco-friendly alternatives to their customers. Recycled products for example, are one of the most popular alternatives that can benefit the environment. These benefits include sustainable forestry, energy efficiency, water conservation, and a healthy office. One example is the E-commerce business and office supply company Shop let which offers a web tool that allows you to replace similar items in your shopping cart with greener products. Tamar Rosenthal, Co-owner of Dapple introduced Eco friendly baby cleaning products designed specifically for the baby in mind. All of the Dapple products are bleach-free and contain no harmful SLES, parabens, phthalates, dyes or synthetic fragrances (hallelujah!). The line was designed with the help of "green" chemists and input from both parents and pediatricians. It includes a Toy Cleaner, in both spray and wipes, Dish Liquid & Baby Bottle Cleaner, Surface wipes and cleaner and Travel Packs. Coca-Cola India has recently formed a separate division for juices to focus on its non-carbonated portfolio as all major food and beverage companies increasingly fortify their health portfolio in a market which is annually growing at 20%. Health products and juices have been at the top of these companies bucket list since they have launched new products and categories to capture a share of the pie. The cola major has been expanding its non-carbonated beverage portfolio with launches like Maaza Milky Delite, its entry into the dairy segment, the ice tea brand Nestea with its joint venture partner Nestle, besides the fruit-based drinks Minute Maid Pulpy Orange and Minute Maid Fresh.
- ***Price:*** Green pricing takes into consideration the people, planet and profit in a way that takes care of the health of employees and communities and ensures efficient productivity. Value can be added to it by changing its appearance, functionality and through customization, etc. Wal Mart unveiled its first recyclable cloth shopping bag. IKEA started charging consumers when they opted for plastic bags and encouraged people to shop using its "Big Blue Bag".
- ***Place:*** Green place is about managing logistics to cut down on transportation emissions, thereby in effect aiming at reducing the carbon footprint. For example, instead of marketing an imported mango juice in India it can be licensed for local production. This avoids shipping of the product from far away, thus reducing shipping cost and more importantly, the consequent carbon emission by the ships and other modes of transport. Solar City has now extended its business into Oregon and Arizona with plans to extend to 10 more states by the end of 2010.
- ***Promotion:*** Green promotion involves configuring the tools of promotion, such as advertising, marketing materials, signage, white papers, web sites, videos and presentations by keeping people, planet and profits in mind. Indian Tobacco Company has introduced environmental-friendly papers and boards, which are free of elemental chlorine. Toyota is trying to push gas/ electric hybrid technology into much of its product line. It is also making the single largest R&D investment in the every-elusive hydrogen car and promoting itself as the first eco-friendly car company. International business machines Corporation (IBM) has revealed a portfolio of

green retail store technologies and services to help retailers improve energy efficiency in their IT operations. Green marketer can attract customers on the basis of performance, money savings, health and convenience, or just plain environmental friendliness, so as to target a wide range of green consumers. Consumer awareness can be created by spreading the message among consumers about the benefits of environmental-friendly products. Posting of profiles related to green marketing on social networks creates awareness within and across online peer groups. Marketing can also directly target the consumers through advertisements for products such as energy saving compact fluorescent lamps, the battery-powered Reva car, etc. There's an alternative approach to standard promotional products that consumers will truly appreciate as eco-friendly corporate gifts and environmentally-conscious green promotional products of exceptional quality. A division of Corporate Accents Unlimited offers the newest products manufactured from sustainable materials and environmentally safe processes.

Why is Green Marketing chosen by most marketers?

Most of the companies are venturing into green marketing because of the following reasons:

- Opportunity–In India, around 25% of the consumers prefer environmental-friendly products, and around 28% may be considered health conscious. Therefore, green marketers have diverse and fairly sizeable segments to cater to. The Surf Excel detergent which saves water (advertised with the message-"do bucket paani roz bachana") and the energy-saving LG consumers durables are examples of green marketing. We also have green buildings which are efficient in their use of energy, water and construction materials, and which reduce the impact on human health and the environment through better design, construction, operation, maintenance and waste disposal. In India, the green building movement, spearheaded by the Confederation of Indian industry (CII) - Godrej Green business Center, has gained tremendous impetus over the last few years. From 20,000 sq ft in 2003, India's green building footprint is now over 25 million sq ft.
- Social Responsibility–Many companies have started realizing that they must behave in an environment-friendly fashion. They believe both in achieving environmental objectives as well as profit related objectives. The HSBC became the world's first bank to go carbon-neutral last year. Other examples include Coca-Cola, which has invested in various recycling activities. Walt Disney World in Florida, US, has an extensive waste management program and infrastructure in place. Margao Municipal Council has obtained an NOC from the Margao Urban Health Centre for the air-conditioned Sulabh toilet at the Margao Municipal Garden, specifying on the condition of hygiene and maintenance. This was taken due to the complaint lodged by a local school management with the MMC and UHC that sewage from one of the toilets was being discharged into the public drains.
- Governmental Pressure–Various regulations are framed by the government to protect consumers and the society at large. The Indian government too has developed a framework of legislations to reduce the production of harmful goods and by products. These reduce the industry's production and consumers' consumption of harmful goods, including those detrimental to the environment; for instance The Union Ministry of Environment and Forest has extended thc ban on plastic below 40 microns across the country due to the urge of environmental activitists and others who were irked by the clutter of plastic floating around. Government has introduced a minor financial boost to green cars and other green gadgets. The exemption from basic customs duty and concessional rate of central excise duty was extended to cover imported batteries for electric vehicles. Fuel cell-based cars also got a concessional excise duty of 10% in the Budget.
- Competitive Pressure–Many companies take up green marketing to maintain their competitive edge. The green marketing initiatives by niche companies such as Body Shop and Green & Black have prompted many mainline competitors to follow suit. The company aims to make solar panels easy to install at reduced rates so that more and more people switch over from

conventional electricity to solar power. Their Solar lease option reduces the installation cost making it an attractive option for customers. The Chicago Mercantile Exchange, which owns NYMEX, and the Intercontinental Exchange are both consulting the market about a switch in the specification of their near identical gasoil and hearing oil contracts to low-sulphur diesel. Demand for the lighter; low-sulphur product, used as a transport and heating fuel, has grown due to stricter environmental rules in Europe and rising use by Asian motorists.

- Cost Reduction–Reduction of harmful waste may lead to substantial cost savings. Sometimes, many firms develop symbiotic relationship whereby the waste generated by one company is used by another as a cost-effective raw material. For example, the fly ash generated by thermal power plants, which would otherwise contributed to a gigantic quantum of solid waste, is used to manufacture fly ash bricks for construction purposes. CPOWER delivers energy management services and products enabling its customers to reduce their power usage effectively. In short, they teach companies and organizations how to reduce their electricity consumption through energy management and sustainable technologies. Their clients include businesses, factories and industries with high rates of energy consumption. To encourage companies that are not yet running on renewable energy, clean energy is a good step in the right direction. They give incentives to companies to optimize their energy consumption and earn market payments for those reductions.

Conclusion

An intelligent pusher is one who not only convinces the consumer, but also involves the consumer in marketing his product. Green marketing should not be well thought-out as just one more move toward marketing, but has to be pursued with much greater dynamism, as it has an environmental and social aspect to it. With the menace of global warming alarming large, it is extremely important that green marketing becomes the norm rather than an exception or just a fad. Recycling of paper, metals, plastics, etc., in a safe and environmentally harmless manner should become much more systematized and worldwide. It has to become the general norm to use energy-efficient lamps and other electrical goods. Marketers also have the responsibility to make the consumers understand the need for and benefits of green products as compared to non-green ones. In green marketing, consumers are willing to pay more to maintain a cleaner and greener environment. Finally, consumers, industrial buyers and suppliers need to coerce effects on minimize the negative effects on the environment-friendly. Green marketing assumes even more importance and relevance in developing countries like India.

16 MANAGING OPERATION

Production Management: Introduction, Meaning and Definitions, Scope, Optimum Selection of Technology: Introduction, Factors Influencing choice of Technology, Inventory Control: Introduction, Meaning, Objectives and Importance, Materials Management: Introduction, Meaning and Definition, Objectives, Importance of Materials Management, Purchasing: Meaning and Definitions, Objectives, Functions and Procedures, Summing up.

Production Management

Introduction

Production' and 'Marketing' are the two basic operating functions of every industrial enterprise. Production is concerned with the supply side while marketing of goods and services is concerned with the demand side. These two activities are interdependent and one cannot exist without the other. Production of goods and services without marketing is useless and marketing of goods and services without production is not possible. Thus, production decisions constitute one of the most important functions of the top management.

Production is the process by which goods and services are created. In other words, it transforms the inputs (i.e., raw materials, men, machine, management and capital) into output (i.e., goods and services) with the help of certain production processes. Production includes production of goods and production of services. In a manufacturing organization, men, materials and equipment are employed to produce goods and commodities by creating form utility while in service enterprise the production is the discharge of some functions of utility and includes all types of services.

Production function is the basic function of an industrial enterprise around which all other activities of the organization such as purchasing, financing, marketing, storing, personnel, research and development revolve. It is therefore very essential that the production function must be managed effectively and efficiently so as to achieve the organization goals. The main aim of every production system is to produce the goods and services economically to the entire satisfaction of the customers for which they are meant. In order to achieve this aim, it is essential to plan, organize, direct and control the production system. There activities of planning, organizing, directing and controlling comprise the production management.

Meaning and Definitions

Production management is a branch of management which is related to the production function. Production may be referred to as the process concerned with the conversion of inputs (raw materials, machinery, information, manpower, and other factors of production) into output (semi-finished and finished goods and services) with the help of certain processes (planning, scheduling and controlling etc.) while management is the process of exploitation of these factors of production in order to achieve the desired results. Thus production management is the management which by scientific planning and regulation sets into motion the part of an enterprise to which it has been entrusted the task of actual transformation of inputs into output. A few definitions of production management are stated hereunder to understand the meaning of the term clearly:

(1) *"Production management then becomes the process of effectively planning and regulating the operations of that part of an enterprise which is responsible for actual transformation of materials into finished products".*

E.F.L. Brech

The definition seems to be quite incomplete as it ignores the human factors involved in a production process and lays stress only on the materialistic features. **Elwood S. Buffa**, has defined the term in a broader sense as -

(2) *"Production management deals with decision making related to production process so that the resulting goods or services are produced according to specifications in amounts and by the schedule demanded and at a minimum cost".*

Elwood S. Buffa

Thus, production management is concerned with the decision making regarding the production of goods and services at a minimum cost according to the demands of the customers through the management process of planning, organizing and controlling. In order to attain these objectives, effective planning and control of production activities is very essential. Otherwise, the customers shall remain unsatisfied and ultimately certain activities will have to be closed.

Production management, thus, is assigned with the following tasks -

(1) Specifying and accumulating the input resources, i.e., management, men, information materials, machine and capital;
(2) Designing and installing the assembly or conversion process to transform the inputs into output; and
(3) Coordinating and operating the production process so that the desired goods and services may be produced efficiently and at a minimum cost.

Scope

Production management mainly associated with the factory management as the problems of production crept with the development of factory system. Before the evolution of factory system, manufacturing activities are carried on by single person that pose no problem or very insignificant problem of production and therefore question of production management did not arise. But with the inception of factory system, the situation changed and so many problems of production were begun to creep up and necessity arose to tackle with the problems of quality control, layout facilities, meeting the schedules and organization of production activities. Thus, the scope of production management began to develop. In early stage, the stress was on controlling the labour costs because labour cost was the major element of the total cost of production. With the continuing development of factory system, the trend towards mechanization and automation developed and it resulted in the increased costs of indirect labour; more than the direct labour costs. So concerns found it difficult to run the business in these circumstances and evolved so many controlling devices to regulate the cost of production. They had developed device like designing and packing of products, indirect labour cost control, production and inventory control and quality control.

Since the level of production has increased tremendously, so many other production problems have been added to its scope. On the present era of intense competition, the scope of production management is very wide. The production department in an enterprise is not only concerned with the full exploitation of production facilities but also the human factor that indirectly affects the production, utilization of latest techniques of production and the production of quality goods to the satisfaction of customers of the product.

Optimum Selection of Technology

Introduction

When an entrepreneur proposes to undertake a business, he has to choose a suitable technology. The choice he has to make both at the time of setting up a new enterprise and at the time of expansion and growth of an existing concern. The selection of a suitable technology of business organization is an important management decision. This decision affects the success of a business firm. It is a long term commitment cannot be changed easily. As such, selection of the technology is a matter of careful deliberation and judgment.

Choice of technology depends on the nature of the industry, the size of the enterprise, the scale of the output, the requirements of the workers etc. The entrepreneur should bear in mind the product design, plant design, the required tools, the personnel, etc., while planning the technology. Any carelessness, negligence or mistake in this regard can adversely affect the efficiency of the enterprise by raising the costs of production, caused by wastage of labour and materials.

The decision regarding technology cannot be taken once for all at the time of locating the new plant and equipment. It should be flexible enough to accommodate the subsequent changes in the management policies and processes and techniques of production. It will, therefore, be necessary to consider not only the problems and techniques of the initial technology and building design, etc., but also of revision in response to various situational changes. The choice of technology is to be laid out with definite objective, i.e.,

(i) to secure larger production;
(ii) to reduce the costs per unit;
(iii) to maintain the quality;
(iv) to ensure timely delivery of the outputs; and
(v) to minimize the chances of accidents

It should be noted here that the objectives are laudable in themselves; it is often difficult to reconcile all of them in a practical situation. And as such, the highest level of skill and judgment are required to be exercised. For this, close association between the entrepreneurs and experienced engineers is a must.

The Factors Influencing Choice of Technology

The following are some important factors which influence choice of technology and plants and equipments:

(1) ***Nature of the Product:*** The nature of product to be manufactured will significantly affect the choice. The design and the specification of the product to be turned out and its physical and the chemical characteristics including the size, the shape and bulk, would decide the pattern of technology and plant and equipments. If the design of the product is of high quality than the technology may demand complicated mechanical equipment. If the product is a luxury article, it is produced on a limited scale which may minimize specialized equipment. A product categorized as a necessary, would provide the mass market and its technology should consist of a complex of specialized equipment to support longer volume of production.

(2) ***Managerial Policies:*** The choice depends very much on the decisions and policies of the management to be followed in producing a commodity with regard to size of plant, kind and quality of the product; scope for expansion to be provided for, amount of stocks to be carried at any time, etc.

(3) ***Volume of Production:*** Volume of production and the standardization of the product also affect the choice. Standardized commodities will be manufactured on large-scale through the shortened built-in sequence of the plant complex. The turnover of output will be quicker and the lockup of working capital in the form of stock of raw materials and finished goods is reduced thereby.

(4) ***Characteristics of the Building:*** Shape of building, covered and open area, number of storey's, facilities of elevators; starts, parking area, storing place and so on also influence the choice. Although minor modifications may be done to suit the needs of the technology. Special type of construction is needed to accommodate huge or technical or complex or sophisticated machines and equipment.

(5) ***Human Factor and Working Conditions:*** Man is the most important factor of production and therefore special consideration for their safety and comforts should be given while selecting the technology, specific safety items like obstruction - free floor, workers not exposed to hazards, exit etc., should be provided for, sufficient space is also to be provided for free movement of workers. For this, provisions of Factories Act should be followed strictly.

(6) ***Type of Machine and Equipment:*** Machines and equipment may be either general purpose or special purpose. The requirements of each machine and equipment are quite different in terms of their space, speed and material handling process and these factors should be given proper consideration.

(7) ***Climatic Condition:*** Sometimes temperature, illumination and air are the deciding factors in deciding the technology and their installation. For example, in lantern manufacturing industry, the spray painting room is built along the factory wall to ensure the required temperature control and air expulsion and then the process of spray painting may be undertaken.

(8) ***Type of Industry Process:*** This is one of the most important factors influencing the choice of technology. Industries are classified into following main types :

- **(i)** ***Synthetic Processes:*** Synthetic process is one that combines several different ingredients or which involves assembling of numbers of components for manufacturing a final product, e.g., soap, medicines, cement, automobiles, radios, shoes, etc.
- **(ii)** ***Analytical Process:*** Analytical process is one in which final product is obtained by successive processes that separate the final product from the mass of original materials, e.g., oil refining.
- **(iii)** ***Conditioning Industry:*** It is one where finished product is turned out by converting the raw materials, e.g., sugar, textiles, etc.
- **(iv)** ***Continuous Industry:*** This involves a sequence of process solving as a prelude to release of the final product. It is characterized by an uninterrupted flow of operations from raw materials to the completion of the product through integrated facilities, e.g., cement, printing, flour mills, paper, etc.
- **(v)** ***Intermittent Industry:*** Intermittent type of industries is those which manufacture different components on different machines. Such industries may manufacture the parts, store them for some time of necessary and assemble them as and when required according to the market needs, e.g., automobiles, radio sets, ship-building plants, cycle manufacturing plants etc.

These classifications should not be viewed as rigid because many industries are combinations of these processes.

Inventory Control

Introduction

The dictionary meaning of the word inventory is a detailed list of movable goods. But according to management language, inventory is used to designate the aggregate of those items of tangible property which are held for sale in the ordinary course of business and goods which are in process of production for such sale and also goods currently consumed in the production of goods or services. Thus inventory means stock of items kept in reserve for certain period of time. It includes raw materials, work-in-progress or semi-finished goods, finished goods and spares parts for the maintenance of equipment etc. Raw materials are those inputs that are converted into finished products. Work in progress represents semi-finished goods that require some work before they are ready for sale. Finished products are those which are ready for sale.

Every business organization, however big or small, has to maintain inventory and it constitutes an integral part of the working capital. It has been estimated that inventory in Indian industries constitutes more than 60% of current asset. Inventories are significant elements in cost process. Inventories require a significant investment, not only in acquiring them but also in holding them. Investment in inventories is said to be idle but it is unavoidable in any organization–manufacturing or trading so inventory is a necessary evil. For this reason, one requires a careful planning, formulation of policies and procedures appropriate to maintain the stock at some desired level. In other words, this technique of maintaining inventories at appropriate level may be known as inventory control.

Basically there are two approaches to inventory control. One is unit or physical control and the other is value control. Purchase and production department officials use this word in terms of unit control because they are mainly concerned with the control of physical units of inventories while on the other hand financial executives are interested in value so they use the word in terms of value control. These two approaches should be coordinated. The inventories should be maintained at desired level with the minimum investment of capital in acquiring as well as in maintaining them.

Meaning

Inventory means all movable items in store either ready for sale or for consumption in the course of production with a view to convert them into finished stock for sale. Thus, inventory includes stock of raw materials, work in progress, finished goods and accessories. Inventories form an integral part of working capital and require a considerable investment. It is, therefore, necessary to have a control over the inventories.

Inventory Control is a system which ensures the provision of the required quantity of inventories, of required quality, a required time with the minimum amount of capital investment. Thus, the function of inventory control is to obtain the maximum inventory turnover with sufficient stock to meet all requirements.

There are basically two approaches to inventory control *viz.* Unit control and value control. Unit control involves the control over inventories in terms of unit while value control entails the control over inventories in terms of value. These two approaches seem to be conflicting. Unit control of inventories insures stocks for continuity of operations and sales and obviously the greatest insurance against running out of any item at a crucial movement is maintaining huge supplies of everything stored in the plant. It will increase the cost of handling the inventory and investment. If value control is imposed, there is always a risk of running short of materials. Thus, an optimum control is achieved when the required materials can be obtained at a minimum cost through proper planning, formulation of policies and procedure in order to maintain the inventory level at a desired point. The quantum of inventory to be kept is decided after taking into consideration the availability of finance, the quantity-discount allowed, the cost of storage and storage accommodation, order placing and receiving costs, risk of lost due to falling prices, deterioration, evaporation, obsolescence theft etc. economic orders, quantity and time in obtaining delivery. Thus, in the words of **John L. Burbidge**, inventory control is, then, concerned with the control of the quantities and/or monetary values of these items at a predetermined level or within safe limits. Thus, the inventory control management includes the following aspects:

(i) Determining maximum and minimum level establishing time schedules, procedures and lot of sizes for new orders, ascertaining minimum safety levels, coordinating sales production and inventory policies.

(ii) Providing proper storage facilities arranging the receipt disbursements and procurement of materials, developing the form of recording these transactions.

(iii) Assigning responsibilities for carrying out inventory control functions.

(iv) Providing for the reports necessary for supervising the overall activity.

It is, therefore, necessary that proper coordination must be there in the activities and policies of purchase, production and sales department to affect the better inventory control.

Objectives and Importance

Inventory control now-a-days has become unavoidable in any manufacturing process. The basic managerial objectives of inventory control are two-fold:

(i) To avoid over and under investment in inventories; and

(ii) To the right quality of goods of right quantity at proper time and at reasonable price.

The objectives and importance of inventory control are discussed below:

(1) *Availability of Materials:* The first and foremost objective of inventory control management is to make all types of materials available at all times whenever it is required by the production department so that the flow of production may not be interrupted and the production may not be interrupted and the production may not be held up for want of supply of materials. It is, therefore, advisable to maintain a buffer stock of all essential items to move on the production on schedule.

(2) *Minimizing the Wastage:* Inventory control aims at minimizing the wastage of inventory at all levels, i.e., during its storage in go down or at work in the factory. Normal or controllable wastage should strictly be controlled. Wastage of materials by leakage, theft, embezzlement and spoilage due to dust, rust or dirt should be avoided.

(3) *Better services to Customers:* In order to meet the demand of quality goods, it is the responsibility of the concern to produce sufficient stock of finished goods at proper time to execute the orders of customers. It means a flow of production should be kept on.

(4) *Promotion of Manufacturing Efficiency:* Inventory control promotes the manufacturing efficiency of the enterprise by providing right type of materials production because it will improve the morale of workers.

(5) *Control of Production Level:* Proper inventory control helps increasing and maintaining buffer stock of raw materials to meet any eventuality in difficult times. Production variations can also be avoided through proper control of inventories.

(6) *Optimum Level of Inventories:* The management can procure the inventory in time in order to run the plan efficiently, if regular and prompt information about the availability of materials is provided to it. It, thus, helps the management in maintaining the inventory at optimum level keeping in view operational requirements. It also avoids the out of stock danger.

(7) *Economy in Purchasing:* A proper inventory control brings several advantages and economics in purchasing. Management makes every attempt to purchase the inventories in bulk and to take the advantages of favourable market conditions.

(8) *Optimum Investment and Efficient Use of Capital:* From financial point of view, the prime objective of inventory control is to have an optimum level of investment in inventories. There should neither be any deficiency of stock which may obstruct the production flow nor there any excessive inventment in inventories so that it may block the funds of the concern that may otherwise be utilized investment in other activities. So the management must control the quantum of inventories by fixing the minimum and maximum levels and to avoid the deficiency or surplus stock positions.

Materials Management

Introduction

Materials, means the raw materials used in the manufacturing process to be transformed into finished product. In other words, the raw materials of which the finished product is made may be known as materials. The importance of materials in a manufacturing concern needs no explanation because in its absence production is not possible and moreover it affects the efficacy of all men, machines, money and marketing division of an industry. So, the management of materials is the great concern of executives at all levels. There are so many problems attached with the management of materials such as investment in materials, idle funds, storage and obsolescence problems, wastage of materials in handling, etc., which require immediate attention of management so that the cost of production may be reduced to the minimum and the quality of the product may be maintained.

In recent years, the concept of materials management is being widely accepted by industrially advanced countries for more effective coordination and control over materials because materials costs (including investment in materials, handling cost, transportation and storage costs, insurance, wastage and obsolescence costs etc.) constitute a major part of the total cost of the finished product. So, the control over material is essential to arrest the increasing cost of finished product because it is one of the major constituents of cost. Thus, material management is the uniting of activities involved in the acquisition and use of materials employed in the production of finished product.

Meaning and Definition

Materials are of pivotal importance in the manufacturing of a product. No production is possible without materials. Moreover, materials form an important part of the cost of a commodity and therefore proper control over its procurement, issue, movement and use is necessary. So, proper and effective management of materials is the necessity of the hour. Materials management may thus, be referred to an activity having all control over the materials used and the commodities produced by the concern. In the words of **Bethel** and others, *"Materials Management" is a term used to "controlling the kind, amount, location, movement and timing of the various commodities used in and produced by the industrial enterprise".* The materials management involves all activities relating to materials starting right from the time the need of materials arises and ending with its issuance to production. In this way, materials management is also concerned with all the activities of management such as planning, organizing, directing, controlling and coordinating so far as they are related to the materials. According to one of the definition *"Materials management is the planning, directing, controlling and coordinating of all those* *activities concerned with materials and inventory requirements, from the point of their inception to their introduction into the manufacturing processes. It begins with determination of materials quality and quantity, and ends with its issuance to production in time to meet customers' demands on schedule at the lowest cost".*

Thus, materials management covers all aspects of materials and material supply necessary for converting raw materials and ancillary into the desired finished products. It is, thus, concerned with planning and programming of materials and equipment with redesign value-analysis, with marketing research for purchases, with procurement of all materials including capital goods, packing and packing materials, with stores and inventory control, with transportation costs of materials, with materials handling and operation research of materials. Thus, the functions of materials management can be summarized as follows:

(i) Materials Planning and Programming;
(ii) Purchasing of Raw Materials and Capital Goods;
(iii) Inventory Control;
(iv) Receiving, Storekeeping and Warehousing;
(v) Value Engineering and Value Analysis;
(vi) Transportation Internal and External;
(vii) Materials Handling; and
(viii) Disposal of Scrap and Surpluses.

Objectives

The main objectives of materials management are as follows:

(i) To maintain the flow of production by making the raw materials available in time according to the schedule of production.
(ii) Contribution towards higher productivity by arranging the better quality of raw materials at the lowest possible cost through effective purchasing system.
(iii) Reducing the inventory cost by purchasing the economic lots requiring the minimum investment and the maximum utilization value.
(iv) To eliminate extra materials through product design.
(v) To contribute towards competitiveness of the product by conducting the market research and bringing the product according to the demand by the consumers. Special attention should be given to purchasing the materials.
(vi) Increasing the profits of the concern by producing the best quality products using quality materials at the lowest possible cost.
(vii) To buy further best ultimate value, not necessarily the lowest initial price.

Importance

Materials management is a service function and is of a great importance to other sections like manufacturing, marketing, engineering and finance by way of providing assistance to these sections in their operations. Their materials management entails coordination between various departments.

The main objective of materials management is to affect the reduction in the cost of production through efficient purchasing, minimizing wastages in handling, storing and transporting the materials and thus utilizing the materials efficiently. From the national point of view, materials management plays a pivotal role for the success of national plans because efficient materials management can utilize the national resources, efficiently and according to the plans. It also plays an important role in the industrial economy both in public and private sectors. The importance of materials management can be judged from the following advantages:

(i) According to reports materials cost is about 60 to 70 per cent of the total cost of production. Through effective materials management, this cost content may be kept at the lowest level and thus sales price of the commodity can be fixed at reasonable level.

(ii) Indirect cost and the cost of materials movement are well within control.

(iii) Inventory losses are minimized, efficient materials management reduces the risk of loss from fraud and theft and the wastages of materials are reduced.

(iv) Adequate utilization of equipment is ensured because effective utilization of materials is only when the equipment are effectively used.

(v) Loss of time of labour is minimized.

(vi) Cases of late deliveries are most infrequent because delays in production due to non-availability or lack of materials are prevented by arranging the proper supply of materials in required quantities to the production at the right time.

(vii) Length of manufacturing cycle is reduced to the minimum due to effective utilization of men, materials and machine and thus reduces the capital tied up in inventories.

(viii) Congestion of materials in stores and or at different points of manufacturing is avoided.

(ix) Perpetual inventory system and other record facilitaties the preparation of actual material reports to management.

(x) Cost records of materials are made feasible. Cost of materials used in different department or job may be ascertained easily.

Purchasing

Meaning and Definition's

Purchasing is an everyday function of almost everyone and occupies much of the time both of business houses and ultimate consumers. There are three basic types of purchasers:

(i) Industrial buyers who buy raw materials, stores and equipment for manufacturers;

(ii) Merchant buyers who buy goods for resale and include wholesalers, retailers, speculators etc. and

(iii) Ultimate buyers, i.e., only with the first purchasing, i.e., purchasing of raw materials, equipment, stores etc., for the use in the manufacturing process.

Purchasing to a manufacturing concern is of extreme importance because it has its bearing on every vital factor concerning the manufacture, i.e., quantity, quality, cost efficiency, economy, prompt delivery, volume of production etc. It is the scientific purchasing that can save much money, time and efforts of the management.

In manufacturing organization, "purchasing is the procuring of materials, supplies, machines, tools and services required for the equipment maintenance and operation of the business". Purchasing must be of the right quality in proper quantity for delivery at the correct time and at the most favourable price from outside the organization.

In the words of **Walter**, *Industrial purchasing is "the procurement by purchase of the proper materials, machinery, equipment and supplies of stores used in the manufacture of a product adapted to marketing in the proper quantity and quality at the proper time and at the lowest price consistent with the quality desired".*

In simple words, the task of purchasing is related to going to open market, finding the desired materials at the lowest possible price, and selecting the supplier who offers it at that price having the quality of the materials in mind. It is indeed, a specialist activity calling for the commercial rather than the technical training and outlook.

Objectives

The major objectives of scientific purchasing may be stated as follows:

(1) Procurement of required quality and quantity of materials at the best price, not necessary the lowest price.

(2) Procurement of materials which best suits the product and the purposes for which they are intended.

(3) Purchasing for time utility by a schedule, sufficiently in advance of the demands of the production department so that the production work shall not suffer due to lack of materials.

(4) Buying the quantity, which is neither too much, that involves belonging of the capital, nor too little that holds up the regular supply for production.

(5) Improvement of the product with reference to quality and the distribution by means of selection of adequate materials.

(6) Maintaining continuity of supply to ensure production schedule at a minimum of investment.

(7) Avoidance of duplication of materials, leading to waste of materials and equipment.

(8) Maintenance of company, competitive position in the market by having company's quality standards in accordance with the demands of the customers.

(9) Creation of goodwill for the company through dealing with supplies.

(10) Developing fullest cooperation and coordination and maintenance of internal relationship among various departments of the company.

The main task of the purchasing functions is buying for the company by which is meant going into the open market, finding the lowest price at which a standard item is offered, and selecting a supplier who is ready to offer that item at that price. This task is clerical, Scientific or effective purchasing is something more than buying. It is an executive job involving cooperation with other functions, e.g., production, distribution, finance, sales, etc. the purchaser, therefore, does not think solely in terms of buying. Sometimes he thinks himself as producer, sometimes as financier, sometimes as sales manager. In all his varied thinking he works out how he can be most helpful to every phase of business.

Functions of Purchasing Department

The purchasing department in a big industrial concern has to perform the following functions in order to procure right time, in the right quantity and at the right price:

(1) ***Studying the Market and Sources of Supply:*** Having decided to purchase a material, the purchasing agent studies the market and various sources of supply by inviting tenders or inquiries in a prescribed form from the prospective suppliers with full details or by examining catalogues and samples received from time to time or by paying the visits to the prospective supplier's place of work. After detailed study of market and supplier, the agent decides to select the sources of supply. The purchase department should not only have the knowledge of the market or the sources of supply where such items are available but he should also have full details of the manufacturer.

The purchasing department must have full knowledge of the specification of materials requirement of the concern and the resources of supply of these requirements. The purchasing officer or agent must obtain the necessary information from personal knowledge, past records catalogues, buyers' guide and guiding materials about the vendor and he should record all these information, properly classified and suitably indexed in a comparative statement called schedule of quotation.

With the help of these records, the purchasing officer approves the supplies having regard to the reliability of the supplier in supplying the goods in the past, his price movement history, his delivery record and other service required such as technical service attitude towards rejected materials or scrap etc. Before finalizing the deal, he should also consider the current and expected change in government import export and industrial licensing policy and emergence of substitute etc.

(2) *Placing of Order:* Having approved the supplier, the next task is to place an order with the supplier so approved in the prescribed form which forms a contract between the company and the supplier to supply the materials in the desired quantity and quality at the started price within a stipulated period.

(3) *Follow-up of Purchase Order:* The purchase department must contact the supplier from time to time before the date of requirement of the materials as ordered in order to get the assurance for the delivery of goods at the right time as its follow-up measure. It will facilitate the purchase department to arrange for the materials in case the supplier fails to deliver the goods on due date due to any unavoidable circumstances with him so that the production work will not suffer.

(4) *Verifications of Invoices:* On receiving the goods from the supplier, the purchase department will check the invoice presented by the supplier with the order placed by the company:

(a) To ensure that the quality and quantity of materials received is strictly according to the order. At this stage it can obtain the services of experts to ensure the quality of the goods.

(b) To examine the prices and the total amount of the invoice. If there is any change in the price, it should see whether it is approved in advance. If invoice is found correct, it should approve the invoice for payment.

(c) To secure the adjustment on claims for goods received and found not in accordance with the quality and quantity specifications or which are being damaged in transit.

(5) *Other Functions:* Besides above noted activities, the purchase department has to perform the following other functions:

(i) Giving intimation to the department concerned if deliveries are not going to be made on due dates so that necessary steps may be taken to maintain the flow of production.

(ii) Interviewing the supplier's representatives who call on the purchasing agent.

(iii) To organize discussions with the potential and actual suppliers of materials.

(iv) To maintain necessary records for efficient functioning of the department.

(v) To sell absolute materials scrap and rejected articles not approved by the purchasers.

(vi) Supervising, recurring and storekeeping operations.

(vii) Collection of information regarding new goods and services which may be proved better or substitute to the present goods that supply of materials can be restored immediately.

(viii) Preparing annual purchases budget with the help of and in consultation with other departments.

Purchasing Procedure

The main steps in purchasing procedure may be listed as follows:

(1) *Purchase Requisition:* The initiation of purchase begins with the formal request from the various sections or departments to the purchase department to order goods or services. The request is made in purchase requisition slips (a prescribed form) to the purchase department by the departments needing the goods, authorizing the purchase department for procuring the goods as per the specifications given in the slip by the date mentioned on it. Purchases department receives the requisitions from:

(a) Storekeeper for all items in regular use;

(b) Production control department for special materials required for a particular order;

(c) Plant and maintenance engineer for materials required for capital expenditure or special maintenance projects; and

(d) Heads of the departments for special items as filing cabinet, almirah, furniture, etc.

The requisitions are generally prepared in triplicate. The original copy is sent to the purchase department, the second copy is retained by the store or the department initiating the purchase requisition and third one is sent to the costing department.

(2) ***Decision for Purchase:*** On receipt of the purchase requisition, the purchase department then decides what and how much to buy taking into consideration various limitations and constraints in purchasing the goods. As far as possible, the raw materials should be purchased in sufficient quantity, neither less nor more, to continue the flow of production. For purchasing other materials or plant and equipments, the necessary permission should be obtained from the authority concerned and the finance department to release the finance.

(3) ***Study of Market Conditions and Sources of Supply:*** Having taken the decision for the purchase of materials, the purchasing agent should study the market conditions on the basis of market reports as to when and what goods should be purchased. An intensive study should also be made in regard to the source of supply from where the goods can be procured with the help of catalogues, directories, old records, price lists, vendor and purchase records, etc.

(4) ***Selection of Vendor:*** On the basis of the studies of market condition and sources of supply, the purchasing agent selects the vendor keeping in mind the reliability, his price movement history, his delivery records and other services required and his past cooperation. Sometimes, supplier is selected out of the list of supplier registered with the company for the supply of goods or sometimes quotations or price bids or tenders are invited from the prospective supplies. On studying the terms of supply and the quality and quantity of goods, vendor is selected out of the bidders or tenderers.

(5) ***Purchase Order:*** Having selected the vendor or supplier, a purchase order is prepared in the prescribed form by the purchase department and sent to the vendor authorizing him to supply a specified quantity and quality of materials at the stipulated terms at the time and place mentioned therein. It forms a formal contract between the purchaser and the vendor.

(6) ***Receiving of Materials:*** When goods arrive, they are taken delivery of and parcels or packets unpacked and the contents of the packages are checked by the receiving clerk with the order placed by the purchasing department to the vendor. After proper checking, goods are delivered to the store department or to other department that requisitioned them. On checking if any discrepancy is found as regards to quality or quantity, it should immediately be referred to the purchasing department so that the discrepancy may be adjusted or steps may be taken to return the defective or damaged goods in exchange of proper quality material on credit note.

Summing up

Production management

Production is the process by which goods and services are created. In other words, it transforms the inputs (i.e., raw materials, men, machine, management and capital) into output (i.e., goods and services) with the help of certain production processes. Production includes production of goods and production of services.

Production function is the basic function of an industrial enterprise around which all other activities of the organization such as purchasing, financing, marketing, storing, personnel, research and development revolve.

Meaning and Definitions

Production management is a branch of management which is related to the production function. A few definitions of production management are being reproduced, hereunder, to understand the meaning of the term clearly:

"Production management then becomes the process of effectively planning and regulating the operations of that part of an enterprise which is responsible for actual transformation of materials into finished products".

E.F.L. Brech

The definition seems to be quite incomplete as it ignores the human factors involved in a production process and lays stress only on the materialistic features. Elwood S. Buffa, has defined the term in a broader sense as -

"Production management deals with decision making related to production process so that the resulting goods or services are produced according to specifications in amounts and by the schedule demanded and as a minimum cost".

Elwood S. Buffa

Scope

Since the level of production has increased tremendously, so many other production problems have been added to its scope. On the present era of intense competition, the scope of production management is very wide. The production department in an enterprise is not only concerned with the full exploitation of production facilities but also the human factor that indirectly affects the production, utilization of latest techniques of production and the production of quality goods to the satisfaction of customers of the product.

Optimum Selection of Technology

The following are some important factors which influence choice of technology and plants and equipments:

Nature of the Product; Managerial Policies; Volume of Production; Characteristics of the Building; Human Factor and Working Conditions; Type of Machine and Equipment; Climatic Condition; and Type of Industry Process.

These classifications should not be viewed as rigid because many industries are combinations of these processes.

Inventory Control

The dictionary meaning of the word inventory is a detailed list of movable goods. But in according or management language, inventory is used to designate the aggregate of those items of tangible property which are held for sale in the ordinary course of business and goods which are in process of production for such sale and also goods currently consumed in the production of goods or services.

Meaning

Inventory Control is a system which ensures the provision of the required quantity of inventories of required quality a required time with the minimum amount of capital investment. Thus, the function of inventory control is to obtain the maximum inventory turnover with sufficient stock to meet all requirements.

Thus the inventory control management includes the following aspects:

(1) Size of inventory - determining maximum and minimum level establishing time schedules, procedures and lot of sizes for new orders, ascertaining minimum safety levels, coordinating sales production and inventory policies.

(2) Providing proper storage facilities arranging the receipt disbursements and procurement of materials, developing the form of recording these transactions.

(3) Assigning responsibilities for carrying out inventory control functions.

(4) Providing for the reports necessary for supervising the overall activity.

It is, therefore, necessary that proper coordination must be there in the activities and policies of purchase, production and sales department to affect the better inventory control.

Objectives and Importance of Inventory Management

Inventory control nowadays has become unavoidable in any manufacturing process. The basic managerial objectives of inventory control are two-fold:

(i) To avoid over and under investment in inventories; and

(ii) To the right quality of goods of right quantity at proper time and at reasonable price.

The objectives and importance of inventory control may be as follows:

Availability of materials; Minimizing the wastage; Better services to customers; Promotion of manufacturing efficiency; Control of production level; Optimum level of inventories; Economy in purchasing; Optimum investment and efficient use of capital

Materials Management

Materials, as we generally know it, *means the raw materials used in the manufacturing process to be transformed into finished product.* In other words, the raw materials of which the finished product is made may be known as materials. The importance of material in a manufacturing concern needs no explanation because in its absence production is not possible and moreover it affects the efficacy of all men, machines, money and marketing division of an industry. Thus, material management is the uniting of activities involved in the acquisition and use of materials employed in the production of finished product.

Meaning and Definition

Materials are of pivotal importance in the manufacturing of a product. No production is possible without materials. So, proper and effective management of materials is the necessity of the hour. Materials management may thus be referred to an activity having all control over the materials used and the commodities produced by the concern. In the words of **bethel** and others, *"Materials Management" is a term used to "controlling the kind, amount, location, movement and timing of the various commodities used in and produced by the industrial enterprise".* The materials management involves all activities relating to materials starting right from the time the need of materials arises and ending with its issuance to production.

Thus, the functions of materials management can be summarized as follows:

(i) Materials planning and programming;

(ii) Purchasing of raw materials and capital goods;

(iii) Inventory control;

(iv) Receiving, storekeeping and warehousing;

(v) Value engineering and value analysis;

(vi) Transportation internal and external;

(vii) Materials handling; and

(viii) Disposal of scrap and surpluses.

Objectives

The main objectives of materials management are as follows:

- To maintain the flow of production; Contribution towards higher productivity; Reducing the inventory cost;
- To eliminate extra materials;
- To contribute towards competitiveness; Increasing the profits;
- To buy further best ultimate value;
- Contribution towards higher productivity; and
- Reducing the inventory cost.

Importance

The importance of materials management can be judged from the following advantages:

Cost content may be kept at the lowest level; Inventory losses are minimized; Adequate utilization of equipment is ensured; Loss of time of labour is minimized; Cases of late deliveries are most infrequent; Length of manufacturing cycle is reduced to the minimum; Congestion of materials in stores; perpetual inventory system; and Cost records of materials are made feasible.

Purchasing

Meaning and Definitions

Purchasing is an everyday function of almost everyone and occupies much of the time both of business houses and ultimate consumers. There are three basic types of purchasers:

(i) Industrial buyers who buy raw materials, stores and equipment for manufacturers;

(ii) Merchant buyers who buy goods for resale and include wholesalers, retailers, speculators etc. and

(iii) Ultimate buyers, i.e., only with the first purchasing, i.e., purchasing of raw materials, equipment, stores etc., for the use in the manufacturing process.

In the words of ***Walter****, Industrial purchasing is "the procurement by purchase of the proper materials, machinery, equipment and supplies of stores used in the manufacture of a product adapted to marketing in the proper quantity and quality at the proper time and at the lowest price consistent with the quality desired".*

Objectives

The major objectives of scientific purchasing may be stated as follows:

(1) Procurement of required quality and quantity of materials at the best price, not necessary the lowest price.

(2) Procurement of materials which best suits the product and the purposes for which they are intended.

(3) Purchasing for time utility by a schedule, sufficiently in advance of the demands of the production department so that the production work shall not suffer due to lack of materials.

(4) Buying the quantity, which is neither too much, that involves belonging of the capital, nor too little that holds up the regular supply for production.

(5) Improvement of the product with reference to quality and the distribution by means of selection of adequate materials.

(6) Maintaining continuity of supply to ensure production schedule at a minimum of investment.

(7) Avoidance of duplication of materials, leading to waste of materials and equipment.

(8) Maintenance of company, competitive position in the market by having company's quality standards in accordance with the demands of the customers.

(9) Creation of goodwill for the company through dealing with supplies.

(10) Developing fullest cooperation and coordination and maintenance of internal relationship among various departments of the company.

Functions of Purchasing Department

The purchasing department in a big industrial concern has to perform the following functions in order to procure right time, in the right quantity and at the right price:

Studying the Market and Sources of Supply; Placing of Order; Follow-up of Purchase Orders; Verifications of Invoices; and other Functions.

Purchasing Procedure

The main steps in purchasing procedure are: Purchase Requisition; Decision for Purchase; Study of Market Conditions and Sources of Supply; Selection of Vendor; Purchase Order; and Receiving of Materials.

17 HUMAN RESOURCE MANAGEMENT

Human Resource Management: Meaning, Basic Principles of Human Resource Management, Recruitment: Meaning and Definition, Importance of Recruitment Method, Sources of Recruitment, Training and Development, Summing up.

Human Resource Management—Meaning

Human Resource Management (HRM) is a function within an organization that focuses on providing direction for the people who work in the organization. Human resource management is the organization function that deals with issues related to people such as compensation, hiring, performance management, safety, wellness, benefits, employee motivation, communication, administration, and training. HRM enables employees to contribute effectively and productivily to the overall company direction and the accomplishment of the organization's goals and objectives.

Basic Principles of Human Resource Management

Human Resource Management is an approach to the management of people based on four basic principles.

Firstly, human resources are the most important assets an organization has and their effective management is the key to its success.

Secondly, this success is most likely to be achieved if the personnel policies and procedures of the enterprise are closely linked with, and make a major contribution to, the achievement of corporate objectives and strategic plans.

Thirdly, the corporate culture and the values, organizational climate and managerial behavior that emanate from that culture will exert a major influence on the achievement of excellence. This culture must, therefore, be managed, which means that organizational values may need to be changed or reinforced and continuous efforts from the top to the bottom of the organizational hierarchy, will be required to get them accepted and acted upon.

Finally, HRM is concerned with integration, getting all the organizational members involved so as to make them work together with a sense of common purpose.

As **Tom Peters** wrote in, A *Passion for Excellence (William Collins, 1985): "Trust people and treat them like adults, enthuse them by lively and imaginative leadership, develop and demonstrate an obsession for quality, make them feel they own the business, and your workforce will respond with total commitment".*

Thus, HRM involves getting the organization right, providing effective motivation and leadership, obtaining and developing the right people, paying and treating them fairly, and getting them involved in working productively. In the broadest sense, it denotes satisfaction, development, fulfillment and happiness of all the people who work in an organization. The human environment within an organization has to be increasingly viewed as an integral whole. The primary objectives of the people who work in the organization are satisfaction of their own physical, social and psychological needs, the organizational objectives being only of secondary importance to them, though some degree of achievement of which is necessary for the achievement of their own personal or group objectives.

Thus, to summarize, HRM is a strategic approach to the structure, motivation, development and management of an organization's employees, based on four basic principles:

- The effective management of human resources is the key to an organization's success.
- Success is most easily achieved if personal policies are closely linked with the organization's corporate objectives.
- Managerial behavior and the organizational climate exert a major influence on the achievement of excellence.
- The total integration of manpower is essential to success.

In the words of **Lee Lacoca**, the world famous international business tycoon,"... all business operations can be reduced to three words; people, product and profits. People come first. Unless you've got a good team, you can't do much with the other two".

In their pioneering piece of work titled "*In Search of Excellence*", **Peters and Waterman** (1982) emphasized that in order to achieve productivity through people, the management should put into practice the three fundamental values of "treating them as adults, treating them with dignity and treating them with respect."

Recruitment

Meaning and Definitions

Recruitment is the process of searching for prospective employees and stimulating them to apply for jobs in the organization. It is a positive process because it increased the selection ratio by attracting a large number of applications for the advertised jobs.

According to **Dales S. Beach** - *"Recruitment is the development and maintenance of adequate manpower resources. It involves the creation of a pool of available labour upon whom the organization can depend when it needs additional employees."*

According to **Edwin B. Flippo**, *"Recruitment is the process of searching for prospective employees and stimulating them to apply for jobs in the organization."*

Further, **Roger H.Hawk** has written that *"the purposes of a recruitment function are primarily straightforward; to seek out, to evaluate, to obtain commitment from, place and orient the employees to fill positions required for the successful conduct of the work of an organization."*

Recruitment enables the management to select suitable employees for different jobs. It is significant to point out that hiring of employees through selection is a negative process since it involves the taking of suitable candidates for the organization and rejection or elimination of the other applicants.

Importance of Recruitment Method

The method of recruitment that an organization uses directly affects the efficiency of its selection and placement of programme is at least three ways:

(i) It determines the number of qualified applicants applying for a particular position.

(ii) It influences how well the organization meets its obligations to hire minority group members and women. This usually entails advertising in minority newspaper, sending recruitment to minority colleges and high schools and co-operating with such agencies as the urban league that specialize in working with the minority community. It also involves actively searching for qualified women when filling positions not traditionally held by women.

(iii) It can sometimes affect the subsequent turnover rates of employees. Several studies have shown that when recruiters give applicant's realistic expectations about a particular job by pointing out both the positive and negative aspects of it, lower turnover rates result. This is particularly true when the job is fairly complex in terms of the physical and mental demands placed on the incumbents, as in the case of managerial and sales positions.

Other recruiters give applicants unrealistic expectations regarding the company and their future jobs, thereby resulting in frustration, dissatisfaction and early termination. One possible solution to this problem used by several companies is a work sample, which gives the prospective employee a realistic picture of what will be expected of him or her. This involves providing films, video tapes, printed booklets or job visit to realistically depict training and work.

Sources of Recruitment

Sources of manufacture supply can be classified into two broad categories:

(1) Internal, i.e., recruitment from within the enterprise.

(2) External, i.e., recruitment from outside.

(1) ***Internal Sources of Recruitment:*** The very important internal sources of recruitment, *viz*; (i) Transfer; (ii) Promotion; (iii) Personal Record and skills Banks; (iv) Job posting and Bidding; and (v) Informal Methods.

(i) ***Transfer:*** It involves the shifting of an employee from one job to another. At the time of transfer it is ensured that the employee to be transferred to the new job is capable of performing it. In fact transfer does not involve any drastic change in the responsibilities and status of the employee.

(ii) ***Promotion:*** Promotion leads to shifting an employee to a higher position carrying higher responsibilities, facilities, status and pay. Most of the companies follow the practice of filling higher jobs by promoting employees who are considered for such positions. Filling vacancies in higher jobs from within the organization has the advantages of stimulating and preparing the employees for possible transfers or promotions increasing the morale of the employees and simplifying the selection and placement problems.

(iii) ***Personnel Record and skills Banks:*** Examining personnel records may uncover employees who are working in jobs below their educational or skills level. Computerized systems can help to ensure that qualified internal candidates are identified and considered for the opening.

(iv) ***Job posting and Bidding:*** The entrepreneur can post or otherwise circulate and notify listings of available job openings and let the current employees bid for the same, should they be interested.

(v) ***Informal Methods:*** For a short-term labour shortage or for a limited amount of additional work, the organization can use inside moonlighting (Moonlighters: who work part-time and are especially useful if the organization can provide flexible works hours). There are many organization that follow informal methods. An indication of interest by an employee through the use of 'important' channels may result in his or her screening that position.

The decision to recruit internally can, thus cause much debate. While, promoting from within policy can serve as an effective reward, it also commits a firm to providing training and career development opportunities if the promoted employees are to perform well, and are truly competitive for positions and do not perceive internal recruitment for higher level positions as 'mere talk' on the part of management.

(2) *External Sources of Recruitment:* Every new enterprise has to tap external sources for various positions. Running enterprises have also to recruit employees from outside, for filling the positions whose specifications cannot be met by the present employees. An important source of recruitment is direct recruitment by placing a notice on the notice board of the enterprise specifying the details of the jobs available. Another name for this type of recruitment in "Recruitment at Factory gate". Very common external sources of recruitment are as follows:

(i) ***Unsolicited Applications:*** This type of recruitment serves as valuable sources of manpower. If adequate attention is paid to maintain pending application folders for various jobs, the personnel department may find the unsolicited applicants useful in filling the vacancies whenever they arise.

(ii) ***Advertisement:*** Advertisement in newspaper or trade and professional journals is generally used when qualified or experienced personnel are not available from other sources. Most of the senior positions in industry as well as others are filled by this method.

(iii) ***Employment Agencies:*** Employment exchanges run by the Government are regarded as a good source of recruitment for skilled, semi-skilled and skilled operative jobs. In some cases, compulsory notification of vacancies to the employment exchange is required by law. Thus, the employment exchanges brings in contact with the job-seekers.

(iv) ***Educational Institutions:*** Jobs in commerce and industry have become increasingly technical and complex to the point where school and college degrees are widely required. Consequently, many big organizations maintain a close liaison with the Universities vocational institutes and management institutes for recruitment to various jobs. Recruitment from educational institutions is the well-established practice of thousands of business and other organizations.

(v) ***Recommendations:*** Applicants introduced by friends and relatives may prove to be a good sources of recruitment and indeed many employers prefer to take such persons because something about their background is known. When a present employee or a business friend recommends a person, a type of preliminary screening takes place.

(vi) ***Labour Contractors:*** Labour Contractors are one of the important source of recruitment in many industries in India. Workers are recruited through labour contractors who are themselves employees of the organization. But, nowadays this sytem of recruitment is losing popularity.

(vii) ***Head Hunters:*** The term "Head hunters" refers to the tribe that beheaded its enemies and kept their heads as trophies. Now, it symbolizes a method of recruiting for top-level positions through informal channels or personal contacts. Normally the firm is asked to get a person for the client organization at any cost. The executive search firms may provide high quality latent by luring away employees from other organizations.

(viii) ***Direct Applications:*** For hourly workers, "walks-ins" is a major source of applicants. For blue-collar jobs, walk-ins are often called gates-hires.

(ix) ***Employee Data Bases:*** Employers are increasingly turning to computerized resume registries to identify candidates. The reason - organizations can quickly and efficiently gain access to national samples of prospective applicants by using databases.

(x) ***Campus Recruiting:*** Many entry - level professional and managerial jobs require a college degree. In college recruiting, the organization sends a recruiter or a recruiting team to a campus to interview candidates and describe the organization to them. Good recruiters convey an image and appearance that reflects favourably on the organization.

(xi) ***Former Employees:*** Those executives who resigned and left in search for greener Pasteur's may be re-employed by the organization should they want to come back home. It only makes sense for companies to lay-out the welcome mat for valuable employees, who want to return to the fold.

A number of methods are available for external recruiting. There is no single combination of resources and methods that will work well for all organizations, or for that matter, across all types of jobs and labour market, or even within a labour market. Research and experience indicates that there are particulars methods that are more effective for some types of jobs and potential applicants than for others.

Training and Development

Although training helps employees do their current jobs, the benefits of training may extend throughout a person's career and help develop that person for future responsibilities. Development, by contrast, helps the individual handle future responsibilities, with little concern for current job duties. The term "Development" can be defined as the nature and direction of change taking place among personnel through educational and training processes.

According to **Dunn** and **Stephens**, *"training refers to the organization's efforts to improve an individual's ability to perform a job or organizational role, whereas development refers to the organizations efforts (and the individual's own efforts) to enhance an individual's abilities to advance in his organization to perform additional job duties."* Thus, training provides knowledge and skills required to perform the job. It can be viewed as job-oriented leading to an observable change in the behavior of the trainee in the form of increased ability to perform the job. On the other hand, although development is still job-related, it is much broader in scope. It enhances general knowledge related to a job as well as the ability to adopt to change.

Earlier, training programmes stressed preparation for an improved performance in largely specific rank-and-file jobs. With the growth of organizations, several problems developed. Therefore, development programmes were started for middle managers as well as top management. Thus, training appeared to be an improper designation for learning a variety of complex, difficult and intangible functions of personnel management. Development of an individual is due to his daytoday experience on the job. Therefore, one must emphasize the development is highly individual and is self-development too. It must be generated within the man himself. No amount of coercion can produce development in a hostile or apathetic manager.

Since the distinction between training (now) and development (future) is often blurred and is primarily one of intent, both are combined together for developing skills as well as basic attitudes, leading to continued personnel growth. These programmes purport to improve job performance, minimize waste and scrap, prepare individuals for promotions, reduce labour turnover/absenteeism, enable individuals to accept organizational changes, facilitate understanding of organizational goals and attain allied behavioral objectives.

The special problems of the developing countries which have a planned economy with emphasis on rapid industrial and business development, has given to this subject a particular significance. For these countries, a continuous supply of competent managers for every sector on industrial and business activity is a vital requisite for economic growth.

Training and Development

- Knowledge, skills and teaching abilities manifested by academic world.
- Experience, exercise and resources provided by organization.
- Trainee himself.
- Any management development programme should have five objectives:
  - To improve the job performance of managers currently in post.
  - To provide adequate cover in the extent of unexpected short-term changes such as deaths, transfers, resignations or unanticipated developments.

- To raise the general level of management thinking and understanding in all branches and at all levels in the organization.
- To provide supply of managerial talent which will meet the needs of the future development of the organization in terms of environmental change and growth.
- To extend the frontiers of knowledge in the understanding of the management function.

An eagerness to learn at all levels is a pre-requisite for the success of management development programmes. Education, training and personal development are all parts of the pattern of management development leading to an organization-wide atmosphere of learning in which everybody has a part to play. The management development process ensures that the organization has the effective managers; it needs to accomplish its present and future requirements. It develops capabilities of managers accomplish organization's business strategies in the context of critical success factors such as innovations, quality and cost leadership. There are three activities involved in the process of management development– analysis of needs, evaluation of skills and competencies, and meeting the needs. Attempt should be made to combine self-development, organization-derived development and boss-derived development to evolve an effective management development system.

Summing up

Meaning

Human resource management is the organization function that deals with issues related to people such as compensation, hiring, performance management, safety, wellness, benefits, employee motivation, communication, administration, and training.

Basic Principles of Human Resource Management

Human Resource Management (HRM) is an approach to the management of people based on four basic principles.

Firstly, human resources are the most important assets an organization has and their effective management is the key to its success.

Secondly, this success is most likely to be achieved if the personnel policies and procedures of the enterprise are closely linked with, and make a major contribution to, the achievement of corporate objectives and strategic plans.

Thirdly, the corporate culture and the values, organizational climate and managerial behavior that emanate from that culture will exert a major influence on the achievement of excellence. This culture must, therefore, be managed, which means that organizational values may need to be changed or reinforced and continuous efforts from the top to the bottom of the organizational hierarchy, will be required to get them accepted and acted upon.

Finally, HRM is concerned with integration, getting all the organizational members involved so as to make them work together with a sense of common purpose.

Recruitment

Meaning and Definition

According to **Dales S. Beach** - *"Recruitment is the development and maintenance of adequate manpower resources. It involves the creation of a pool of available labour upon whom the organization can depend when it needs additional employees."*

According to **Edwin B. Flippo**- *"Recruitment is the process of searching for prospective employees and stimulating them to apply for jobs in the organization."*

Further, **Roger H.Hawk** has written that *"the purposes of a recruitment function are primarily straightforward; to seek out, to evaluate, to obtain commitment from, place and orient the employees to fill positions required for the successful conduct of the work of an organization."*

Importance of Recruitment Method

The method of recruitment that an organization uses directly affects the efficiency of its selection and placement of programme is at least three ways:

(i) It determines the number of qualified applicants applying for a particular position.

(ii). It influences how well the organization meets its obligations to hire minority group members and women.

Sources of Recruitment

Sources of manufacture supply can be classified into two broad categories:

1. ***Internal Sources of Recruitment:*** The very important internal sources of recruitment, *viz;* (i) Transfer; (ii) Promotion; (iii) Personnel Record and skills Banks; (iv) Job posting and Bidding; and (v) Informal Methods.

2. ***External Sources of Recruitment:*** Very common external sources of recruitment are as follows: (i) Unsolicited Applications; (ii) Advertisement; (iii) Employment Agencies; (iv) Educational Institutions; (v) Recommendations; (vi) Labour Contractors; (vii) Head Hunters; (viii) Direct Applications; (ix) Employee Data Bases; (x) Campus Recruiting; and (xi) Former Employees.

There is no single combination of resources and methods that will work well for all organizations.

Training and Development

According to **Dunn and Stephens**, *"training refers to the organization's efforts to improve an individual's ability to perform a job or organizational role, whereas development refers to the organizations efforts (and the individual's own efforts) to enhance an individual's abilities to advance in his organization to perform additional job duties'.* Thus, training provides knowledge and skills required to perform the job.

Training appeared to be an improper designation for learning a variety of complex, difficult and intangible functions of management personnel. Development of an individual is due to his day to day experience on the job.

Since the distinction between training (now) and development (future) is often blurred and is primarily one of intent, both are combined together for developing skills as well as basic attitudes, leading to continued personnel growth. These programmes purport to improve job performance, minimize waste and scrap, prepare individuals for promotions, reduce labour turnover/absenteeism, enable individuals to accept organizational changes, facilitate understanding of organizational goals and attain allied behavioral objectives.

18 ENTREPRENEURIAL FINANCE

Financial Management: Meaning and Definition, Fixed Capital: Introduction, Sources of Fixed Capital, Factors Determining Fixed Capital, Management of Fixed Capital, Working Capital: Introduction, Factors Determining Working Capital, Need for Working Capital, Sources of Working Capital Finance, Management of Working Capital, Summing Up.

Financial Management

Meaning

The term business finance mainly involves raising of funds and their effective utilization keeping in view the overall objectives of the firm. This requires great caution and wisdom on the part of management. The management makes use of various financial techniques, devices, etc., for administering the financial affairs of the firm in the most effective and efficient way. **Financial management,** therefore, *means the entire gamut of managerial efforts devoted to the management of finance - both its sources and uses - of the enterprise.*

Definition

Financial management is mainly concerned with the proper management of funds. The finance manager must see that the funds are procured in a manner that the risk, cost and control considerations are properly balanced in a given situation and there is optimum utilization of funds.

According to **Solomon**, *"Financial management is concerned with the efficient use of an important economic resource, namely, Capital Funds,"* **Phillippatus** has given a more elaborate definition of the term financial management. According to him *"Financial management is concerned with the management decisions that result in the acquisition and financing of long and short-term credits for the firm.* As such it deals with the situations that require selection of specific assets (or combination of liabilities) as well as the problem of size and growth of an enterprise. The analysis of these decisions is based on the expected inflows and outflows of funds and their effects upon managerial objectives".

Fixed Capital

Introduction

Fixed capital is important for every business unit. It is the preliminary need for starting an enterprise. Adequate fixed capital lays down foundation for the stable life and also provides strength and stability to the enterprise. The launching of business activity is just not possible unless there is a provision for adequate fixed capital. Modern business is capital intensive and naturally the importance of fixed capital cannot be overemphasized. It acts as a cornerstone of the capital structure of a business unit. It is necessary for the stability, modernization and expansion of business activities. Promoters have to make accurate estimate of fixed capital requirement and collect it through suitable sources like equity and preference share. In brief, adequate fixed capital provides strength and stability to a business unit. It also facilitates the process of growing technology, replacement of assets which become obsolete; acquisition of new fixed assets and the expansion of business operation are just not possible unless adequate fixed capital is arranged for meeting new capital expenditure. It also ensures continuous working of a business unit.

Sources of Fixed Capital

A company can raise fixed capital from the following sources:

(1) ***Issue of equity and preference shares:*** Majority companies collect initial fixed capital through the issue of share. They represent ownership securities. Shares are popular with the investing class, and rich as well as middle class people purchase shares of companies and provide crores of rupees as fixed capital to corporate sector. Companies issue equity and preference shares for the convenience of investors.

(2) ***Ploughing back of profits:*** Fixed capital can be collected out of accumulated profits. Such profit is converted into share capital and invested in the business. This source is available only to big and profitable companies. It is an internal method useful for collecting fixed capital. This source is generally used for modernization or expansion programmes of a company. This method of self-financing is popular among large companies.

(3) ***Loans from financial institutions:*** Financial institutions like IDBI and ICICI offer long-term loans to industrial units. Such loans are repayable after a long period and hence they can be used for purchasing fixed assets. Such loans are also useful for financing expansion and development programmes of the company.

(4) ***Debentures and bank loans:*** Many companies issue long period debentures for collecting fixed capital required. Even irredeemable debentures are also issued. In addition, long-term loans are taken from banks to meet the long term financial needs. Even short-term loans are renewed often and again for meeting long-term capital needs. It may be pointed out that debentures and bank loans are used only to a limited extent for meeting the long-term capital needs whereas equity and reference shares are used extensively for raising long-term capital.

Factors Determining Fixed Capital

The amount of fixed capital requirements of a business depends on the following factors:

(i) ***Nature of the business:*** The nature of the business to a great extent determines the amount of fixed capital required by the business. For example, public utility concerns like electricity supply companies, water supply undertakings or railway companies would require heavy investment in fixed assets; on the other hand, a trading concern would require relatively much less investment in fixed assets.

(ii) ***Size of the business:*** Size of the business has also its impact on the fixed capital requirements of the business. It can generally be said that larger the size of the business, the heavier would be the investment in fixed capital.

(iii) ***Types of products:*** A company manufacturing simple consumer articles like soap, oil, etc., will require a smaller amount of fixed capital as compared to a company manufacturing complicated industrial goods such as heavy machinery, tractors, etc.

(iv) ***Diversity of production lines:*** More fixed capital will be required in case of companies which have diversity of production lines as compared to companies which do not have much of diversification. For example, a company producing ancillary products or by-products together with main product will require greater amount of fixed capital as compared to companies which manufacture only main products.

(v) ***Method of production:*** A company manufacturing each part of finished product by itself requires a greater amount of fixed capital as compared to a company which gets the parts manufactured from outside and merely assembles them in its own factory premises.

(vi) ***Method of acquisition of fixed assets:*** A company which purchases fixed assets against immediate cash payment or ownership basis requires a greater amount for fixed capital as compared to a company which acquires fixed assets on hire-purchase system or lease system.

Management of Fixed Capital

Management of fixed capital is concerned with the raising of required fixed capital at minimum cost and its effective utilization. The following principles should be observed in order to have an efficient management of fixed capital:

(i) Generally only such fixed assets should be purchased which are likely to increase the earning capacity of the business.

(ii) Where feasible, fixed assets should be purchased on rental or hire purchase system. This would result in releasing pressure on bulk funds.

(iii) Obsolete or outmoded fixed assets should not be brought even though they may be available at lower prices.

(iv) There should not be any idle capacity. This would increase the overhead burden. In words, new fixed assets should be bought only when there is already full utilization of the existing fixed assets.

(v) Fixed assets should be maintained properly. Periodical inspection, overhaul and scheduled repairs would considerably increase the working life of the assets.

(vi) Proper depreciation should be provided out of profits to enable times replacement of the fixed assets.

(vii) Investment in fixed assets should have a proper relationship with sales and profits. Fixed assets turnover ratio for different years can be found out to determine whether investment in fixed assets has been judicious or not.

(viii) The requirements of fixed capital should be met out of long-term funds such as share capital, debentures, loans from financial institutions, etc.

Working Capital

Introduction

Every industrial or commercial unit requires working capital along with fixed capital. It is that part of total capital which required for purchased current assets, i.e., for meeting regular day to day needs of a business unit. Working capital or circulating capital is required for purchasing raw materials, spare parts, components, and payment of wages, rent and other recurring expenses of a business unit. Working capital indicates revolving a circular flow of cash starting with cash paid for purchase of material and ending with cash receipt after the sale of finished goods. This is how working capital is a circular cash flow from cash to inventories and back to cash. A diagram showing circular flow of funds within a firm is given below:

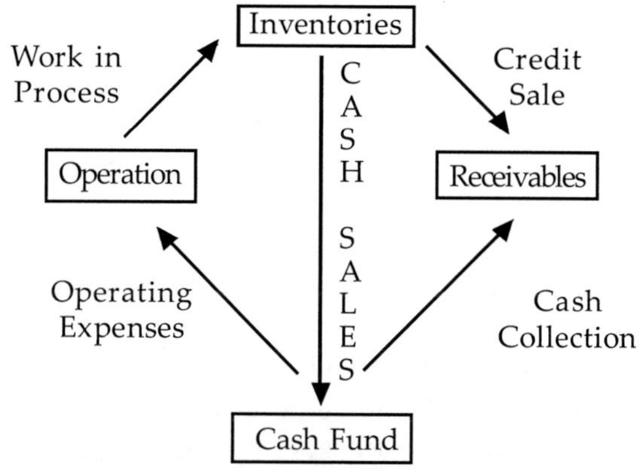

Fig: Circular Flow of Funds (Working Capital)

A business unit requires adequate working capital for its regular and smooth working. Adequate working capital creates goodwill and prestige for the company. It enables a company to make all payments on due dates. It also raises efficiency and general morale of employees. Working capital is required only for a short period as it is recovered from the purchasers out of the price paid. Thus, working capital is of short duration but is recurring in character. In addition, a part of the working capital is treated as regular as fixed working capital and the remaining part is known as variable or fluctuating working capital. Working capital is defined as excess of current asses over current liabilities. Distinction is also made between the gross and net working capital.

According to **Shubin**, *"working capital is the amount of funds necessary to cover the cost of operating the enterprise. Working capital in a going concern is a revolving fund, it consists of cash receipts from sales which are used to cover the cost of current operations".*

The company promoters have to make an estimate of working capital requirements of the company and collect the same from convenient sources. It is treated as the controlling nerve centre of a business unit. Working capital is also called circulating capital. In modern business, production is conducted in anticipation of demand and hence, payment has to be made in advance for purchasing raw materials, stores, etc. Working capital is needed for meeting such financial needs in order to preserve the continuity of production. It is also needed in order to meet all normal as well as abnormal cash needs of the company.

Factors Determining Working Capital

The following factors determine the amount of working capital requirements:

(1) ***Nature and size of business:*** A company's working capital requirements are related to the kind of business it conducts. Public utilities need not maintain inventories as they sell services instead of commodities. They conduct their business on cash basis and hence, they require extremely limited working capital. On the contrary, trading concerns and service industries require huge working capital as they have to carry stock-in-trade, accounts receivable and liquid cash. Manufacturing units stand in between the two extremes regarding their working capital requirements. Size of the concern also determines the amount of working capital. Large sized units require more working capital while small units require less working capital. Similarly, growth-oriented companies need more working capital as compared to static companies.

(2) *Production policies:* Working capital requirements depend upon the production policies of a business unit. Production schedules are adjusted to market deliveries or stock of inventories are built up during off-season periods. Both will entail higher investment in working capital either to hold the stocks of raw materials or to hold the stocks of finished goods.

(3) *Time consumed in manufacturing process:* When manufacturing process is lengthy and complex in character, more working capital is required. Companies producing heavy machinery and equipment require more working capital. Similarly, if the manufacturing cost is high, more working capital will be necessary. Thus, the working capital required by an automobile manufacturing unit will be quite substantial whereas the working capital required by a soap manufacturing unit will be comparatively limited as the process of production is rather simple and quick.

(4) *Turnover of circulating capital:* The speed with which the circulating capital completes its round plays an important role in judging the adequacy of working capital. If the sale or turnover is quick, limited working capital is adequate. Thus, the faster the sales, the lesser will be the working capital requirements and *vice versa.* The cash requirement also determines the amount of working capital. If more cash is needed for meeting regular needs, the amount of working capital required will be more. A credit commanding company may require less working capital.

(5) *Business cycle:* Requirements of working capital of a company vary with the business variations. During boom period, the management is induced to pile up big stock of raw materials and other goods likely to be used in the business operations to take advantage of favorable prices. During depression, big amounts are locked up in the working capital as the inventories remain unsold and book-debts uncollected. In both the cases, the requirement of working capital increases.

(6) *Terms of purchase and sale:* A business unit, making purchases of raw materials, etc., on credit basis and selling goods on cash basis will require lower amount of working capital. On the contrary, a concern having no credit facilities and at the same time forced to grant credit to its customers may require larger amount of working capital.

(7) *Dividend policy:* Every company takes into consideration the effects of dividend policy on cash position. A shortage of working capital often acts as a powerful reason for reducing the rate of dividend. On the other hand, a strong position on the working capital front may justify continuing high dividend payment even though earnings of the company are not sufficient to cover the payment.

(8) *Cost of raw materials and importance of labour:* A business unit requires more working capital if the raw material required is more in quantity and higher in cost. Similarly, labour intensive business unit requires more working capital as the wage bill is more. For example, small-scale industries need more working capital as they are labour intensive. On the contrary, a capital intensive industrial unit needs less amount of working capital.

(9) *Seasonal variation:* The working capital requirements have seasonal variations. During the busy season, more working capital is required while the amount required will be less during the slack season. For example, in the case of sugar factory, working capital required will be more during the busy season whereas the amount required during the slack season will be very limited, as production of sugar is not possible during the slack season.

(10) *Banking connections:* A company with good banking connections requires limited working capital but working capital required will be more in the absence of such connection.

(11) *Cash requirement:* The working capital requirements are influenced by the amount of cash required for meeting various payments like salaries, rent, taxes, etc. The greater the requirement of cash, the higher will be the working capital needs of a business unit.

Need For Working Capital

The basic objective of financial management is to maximize shareholders wealth. This is possible only when the company earns sufficient profit. The amount of such profit largely depends upon the magnitude of sales. However, sales do not convert into cash instantaneously. There is always a time gap between the sale of goods and receipt of cash. Working capital is required for this period if not available for this period, the company will not be in a position to sustain the sales since it may not be in a position to purchase raw material, pay wages and other expenses required for manufacturing the goods to be sold.

Operating Cycle

From the above it is clear that the working capital is required because of the time gap between the sales and their actual realization in cash. This time gap is technically termed as "operating cycle" of the business. In case of a manufacturing company, the operating cycle is the length of time necessary to complete the following cycle of events:

(i) Conversion of cash into raw materials;

(ii) Conversion of raw materials into work-in-process;

(iii) Conversion of work-in-process into finished goods;

(iv) Conversion of finished goods into accounts receivable; and

(v) Conversion of accounts receivable into cash.

This cycle will be repeated again and again.

Sources of Working Capital Finance

The two segments of working capital, *viz.*, regular or fixed or permanent and variable are financed by the long and short-term sources of funds respectively. The main sources of long-term funds are shares debenture, term-loans, retained earnings etc.

The sources of short-term funds used for financing variable part of working capital mainly include the following:

(1) Loans from commercial banks.
(2) Public deposits.
(3) Trade credit.
(4) Factoring.
(5) Discounting bills of exchange.
(6) Bank overdraft and cash credit.
(7) Advances from customers.
(8) Accrual accounts.

(1) *Loans from Commercial Banks:* Small scale industries can raise loans from the commercial banks with or without security. This method of financing does not require any legal formality except that of creating a mortgage on the assets. Loan can be paid in lump sum or in parts. The short term loans can also be obtained from banks on the personal security of the directors of a company. Such loans are known as clean advances.

Bank finance is made available to small scale industries at concessional rate of interest. Hence it is generally a cheaper source of financing working capital requirements of enterprises. However, this method of raising funds for working capital is a time-consuming process.

(2) *Public Deposits:* Often companies find it easy and convenient to raise, short-term funds by inviting shareholders, employees and the general public to deposit their savings with the company. It is a simple method of raising funds from public for which the company has only to advertise and inform the public that it is authorized by the Companies Act to accept public deposits. Public deposits can be invited by offering a higher rate of interest than the interest allowed on bank deposits. However, the companies can raise funds through public deposits subject to a maximum of 25% of their paid up capital and free reserves.

But, the small-scale industries are exempted from the restrictions of the maximum limit or public deposits if they satisfy the following conditions.

(1) The amount of deposits does not exceed ₹ 8 lakh or the amount of paid up capital whichever is less.

(2) The paid up capital does not exceed ₹ 12 lakh.

(3) The number of depositors is not more than 50 per cent.

(4) There is no invitation to the public for deposits.

The main merit of this source of raising funds is that it is simple as well as cheaper. But the biggest disadvantage associated with this source is that it is not available during depression and financial stringency.

(3) *Trade Credit:* Just as the companies sell the goods on credit, they also buy raw materials, components and other goods on credit from their suppliers. Thus, outstanding amounts payable to the supplier's, i.e., trade creditors for credit purchases are regarded as sources of finance. Generally, supplies grant credit to their clients for a period of 3 to 6 months. Thus, they provide in a way of short-term finance to the purchasing company. As a matter of fact, availability of this type of finance largely depends upon the volume of business. More the volume of trade credit available also depends upon the reputation of the buyer company, its financial position, degree of competition in the market, etc. However, availing of trade credit involves loss of cash discount which could be earned if payments were made within 7 to 10 days from the date of purchase of goods. This loss of cash discount is regarded as implicit cost of trade credit.

(4) *Factoring:* Factoring is a financial service designed to help firms in managing their book debts and receivables in a better manner. The book debts and receivables are assigned to a bank called the 'factor' and cash is realized in advance from the bank. For rendering these services, the fee or commission charged is usually a percentage of the value of the book debts/ receivables factored. This is a method of raising short-term capital and known as 'factoring'. On the one hand, it helps the supplier companies to secure finance against their book debts. The disadvantage of factoring is that customers who are really in genuine difficulty do not get the opportunity of delaying payment which they might have otherwise got from the supplier company.

In the present context there industrial sickness is spreading like an epidemic, the reason for which particularly in SSI sector being delayed payments from their suppliers, there is a clear-up rationale for introduction of factoring system. There has been some progress also on this front. The recommendations of Study Group to examine the feasibility of setting up of factoring organizations in the country, under the Chairmanship of **Shri C.S Kalyansundaram** have been accepted by the Government of India. The group is of the view that factoring for SSI units could prove to be mutually beneficial to both factors and SSI units and Factors should make every effort to orient their strategy to crystallize the potential demand from the sector.

(5) *Discounting Bills of Exchange:* When goods are sold on credit, bills of exchange are generally drawn for acceptance by the buyers of goods. The bills are generally drawn for a period of 3 to 6 months. In practice, the writer of the bill, instead of holding the bill till the date of maturity, prefers to discount them with commercial banks on payment of a charge known as discount. The term 'discounting of bills' is used in case of time bills whereas the term, 'purchasing of bills' is used in respect of demand bills. The rate of discount to be charged by the bank is prescribed by the Reserve Bank of India form time to time. It generally amounts to the interest for the period from the date of discounting to the date of maturity of bills. If a bill is dishonored on maturity, the bank returns the dishonoured bill to the company who then becomes liable to pay the amount to the bank. The cost of raising finance by this method is the amount of discount charged by the bank. This method is widely used by companies for raising short-term finance.

(6) ***Bank Overdraft and Cash Credit:*** Overdraft is a facility extended by the banks to their current account holders for a short period generally a week. A current account holder is allowed to withdraw from its current deposit account upto a certain limit over the balance with the bank. The interest is charged only on the amount actually overdrawn. The overdraft facility is also granted against securities.

Cash credit is an arrangement whereby the commercial banks allow the company to borrow money upto a specified limit known as 'cash credit limit'. The cash credit facility is allowed against the security. The cash credit limit can be revised from time to time according to the value of securities. The money so drawn can be repaid as and when possible. The interest is charged on the actual amount drawn during the period rather on limit sanctioned.

The rate of interest charged on both overdraft and cash credit is relatively higher than the rate of interest given on the bank deposits. Arranging overdraft and cash credit with the commercial banks has become a common method adopted by companies for meeting their short-term financial\working capital requirements.

(7) ***Advances from Customers:*** One way of raising funds for short-term requirement is to demand for advance from one's own customers. Examples of advances from the customers are advanced at the time of booking a car, a telephone connection, a flat, etc., this has become an increasingly popular source of short-time finance among the companies mainly due to two reasons. First, the companies do not pay any interest on advances from their customers. Second, if any company pays interest on advances, that too at a nominal rate. Thus, advances from customers become one of the cheapest source of raising funds for meeting working capital requirements of companies.

(8) ***Accrued Accounts:*** Generally, there is a certain amount of time gap between an income is earned and is actually received or an expenditure becomes due and is actually paid. Salaries, wages and taxes, for example, become due at the end of the month but are usually paid in the first week of the next month. Thus, the outstanding salaries and wages, say, expenses for a week help the enterprise in meeting their working capital requirements. This source of raising funds does not involve any cost.

Management of Working Capital

By now, you know that working capital refers to the funds required to meet the day to day obligations of business operations. Hence, working capital is said to be the life-blood of an enterprise. The fact remains that it is working capital that keeps the wheel on. Working capital, therefore, needs to be maintained at an adequate level because, both excessive and inadequate working capitals are harmful for an enterprise. For example, if the current assets are inadequate to meet the current liabilities, it will tell upon the liquidity position of the business. In case, the current assets are in excessive volume, the profitability of the business will be adversely affected due to some assets lying idle.

Management of working capital means managing different components of current assets and current liabilities. These are discussed hereunder:

(a) ***Management of Cash:*** Every enterprise irrespective of its scale requires certain amount of cash to meet its daytoday obligations. Hence, the enterprise needs to decide carefully how much should be carried in cash. Management of cash aims at striking a balance between two contradictory objectives of meeting the cash disbursement needs and minimizing the amount locked up as cash balance. For this purpose, cash management addresses to the following four problems:

- Controlling the level of cash.
- Controlling inflows of cash.
- Controlling outflows of cash.
- Optimum use of surplus cash.

(b) *Management of Inventory:* Inventories refer to raw material, work-in-progress and finished goods. These constitute a major portion, about 60%, of total current assets. There are three major motives for holding inventories in a firm, namely, transaction motive, precautionary motive and speculative motive. But, holding inventories involves costs, i.e., ordering costs and carrying costs. Hence, inventories need to be maintained at an optimum size inventory management is a trade-off between cost of acquiring and cost of holding inventories. Among various models evolved for managing inventories, the commonly used model is Economic Ordering Quantity (EOQ) Model based on Baumol's cash management model. The other model of inventory management is ABC Analysis also known as Control by Importance and Exception (CIE). This method controls expensive inventory items more closely than less expensive items.

(c) *Management of Accounts Receivable:* Accounts receivable represent the amount of goods sold on credit with a view to increase the volume of sales. Accounts receivable constitute major portion of current assets. According to the Indian Chamber of Commerce and Industry (ICCI) study of 417 companies, the ratios of accounts receivable to total assets, current assets and sales were, on average, 17%, 30% and 14-15% respectively. The main objective of maintaining accounts receivable are achieving growth in sales, increasing profits and meeting competition. Like inventories, maintaining accounts receivable also involves certain costs such as capital costs, administrative costs, collection costs and defaulting costs, i.e., bad debts.

The size of accounts receivable depends on the level of sales, credit policy, terms of trade, efficiency of collection, etc. A larger size of accounts receivable increases profitability and reduces liquidity and *vice versa.* Therefore, accounts receivable need to be maintained at an optimum size.

The optimum size of accounts receivable occurs at a point where there is a "trade-off" between profitability and liquidity. This is depicted in figure above.

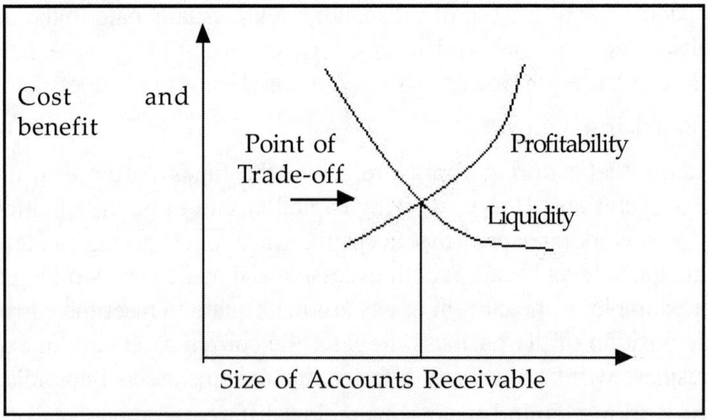

Trade-off between profitability and liquidity

(d) *Management of Accounts payable:* Accounts payable are just reverse to accounts receivable. Accounts payable emerge due to credit purchase. This refers to a loaning of goods and inventories to the buyer. This is also called 'buy-now, pay-later'. The underlying objective of accounts payable is to slow down the payments process as much as possible. But, it should be noted that the saving of interest cost should be offset against loss of credit standing of the enterprise. The enterprise has, therefore, to ensure that the payments to the creditors are made at the stipulated time periods after obtaining the best credit terms possible.

The salient points to be noted on effective management of accounts payable are:

- Obtain most favourable credit terms with the prevailing credit practice.
- Make payments on maturity or due dates.
- Keep good track record of past dealings with the suppliers.
- Avoid tendency to divert payables.
- Provide full information to the suppliers.
- Keep a constant check on incidence of delinquency.

Summing Up

Financial Management

Meaning

The term business finance mainly involves raising of funds and their effective utilization keeping in view the overall objectives of the firm. This requires great caution and wisdom on the part of management. The management makes use of various financial techniques, devices, etc., for administering the financial affairs of the firm in the most effective and efficient way. *Financial management, therefore, means the entire gamut of managerial efforts devoted to the management of finance - both its sources and uses - of the enterprise.*

Definition

Financial management is mainly concerned with the proper management of funds. The finance manager must see that the funds are procured in a manner that the risk, cost and control considerations are properly balanced in a given situation and there is optimum utilization of funds.

According to **Solomon**, *"Financial management is concerned with the efficient use of an important economic resource, namely, Capital Funds,"* **Phillippatus** has given a more elaborate definition of the term financial management. According to him *"Financial management is concerned with the management decisions that result in the acquisition and financing of long and short-term credits for the firm.* As such it deals with the situations that require selection of specific assets (or combination of liabilities) as well as the problem of size and growth of an enterprise. The analysis of these decisions is based on the expected inflows and outflows of funds and their effects upon managerial objectives".

Fixed Capital

Adequate fixed capital lays down foundation for the stable life and also provides strength and stability to the enterprise. The launching business activity is just not possible unless there is a provision for adequate fixed capital. Modern business is capital intensive and naturally the importance of fixed capital cannot be overemphasized. It acts as a cornerstone of the capital structure of a business unit. It is necessary for the stability, modernization and expansion of business activities. Promoters have to make accurate estimate of fixed capital requirement and collect it through suitable sources like equity and preference share.

Sources of Fixed Capital

A company can raise fixed capital from the following sources: Issue of equity and preference shares; Ploughing back of profits; Loans from financial institutions; and Debentures and bank loans;

Factors Determining Fixed Capital

The amount of fixed capital requirements of a business depends on the following factors: Nature of the business; Size of the business; Types of products; Diversity of production lines; Method of production; and Method of acquisition of fixed assets

Management of Fixed Capital

Management of fixed capital is concerned with the raising of required fixed capital at minimum cost and its effective utilization. The following principles should be observed in order to have an efficient management of fixed capital:

(i) Generally only such fixed assets should be purchased which are likely to increase the earning capacity of the business.

(ii) Where feasible, fixed assets should be purchased on rental or hire purchase system. This would result in releasing pressure on bulk funds.

(iii) Obsolete or outmoded fixed assets should not be brought even though they may be available at lower prices.

(iv) There should not be any idle capacity. This would increase the overhead burden. In words, new fixed assets should be bought only when there is already full utilization of the existing fixed assets.

(v) Fixed assets should be maintained properly. Periodical inspection, overhaul and scheduled repairs would considerably increase the working life of the assets.

(vi) Proper depreciation should be provided out of profits to enable times replacement of the fixed assets.

(vii) Investment in fixed assets should have a proper relationship with sales and profits. Fixed assets turnover ratio for different years can be found out to determine whether investment in fixed assets has been judicious or not.

(viii) The requirements of fixed capital should be met out of long-term funds such as share capital, debentures, loans from financial institutions, etc.

Working Capital

Working capital or circulating capital is required for purchasing raw materials, spare parts, components, and payment of wages, rent and other recurring expenses of a business unit. Working capital indicates revolving a circular flow of cash starting with cash paid for purchase of material and ending with cash receipt after the sale of finished goods. This is how working capital is a circular cash flow from cash to inventories and back to cash.

According to **Shubin,** *"working capital is the amount of funds necessary to cover the cost of operating the enterprise. Working capital in a going concern is a revolving fund, it consist of cash receipts from sales which are used to cover the cost of current operations".*

Factors Determining Working Capital

The following factors determine the amount of working capital requirements: Nature and size of business; Production policies; Time consumed in manufacturing process; Turnover of circulating capital;

Business Cycle; Terms of Purchase and Sale; Dividend policy; Cost of raw materials and importance of labour; Seasonal variation; Banking connections; and Cash requirement.

Need for Working Capital

Working capital is required for this period if not available for this period, the company will not be in a position to sustain the sales since it may not be in a position to purchase raw materials, pay wages and other expenses required for manufacturing the goods to be sold.

Sources of Working Capital Finance

The two segments of working capital, *viz.*, regular or fixed or permanent and variable are financed by the long-term and the short-term sources of funds respectively. The main sources of long-term funds are shares debenture, term-loans, retained earnings etc.

The sources of short-term funds used for financing variable part of working capital mainly include the following:

(1) Loans from commercial banks.
(2) Public deposits.
(3) Trade credit.
(4) Factoring.
(5) Discounting bills of exchange.
(6) Bank overdraft and cash credit.
(7) Advances from customers.
(8) Accrual accounts.

Management of Working Capital

Management of working capital means managing different components of current assets and current liabilities. These are hereunder:

Management of Cash; Management of Inventory; Management of Accounts Receivable; and Management of Accounts payable.

19 ENTREPRENEURIAL MARKETING

Marketing Management: Introduction, Functions, Market Research: Meaning, What is a Market Survey? Why Need Market Survey? Techniques of Market Survey, Distribution Channels: Meaning, Types of Distribution Channels for Consumer Goods, Types of Distribution Channels for Industrial Goods, Choice/Selection of Distribution/Marketing Channel, Problems of Marketing, Institutionalized Marketing for Entrepreneurs, Summing Up.

Marketing Management

Introduction

Marketing management is one component of total business management. It is a specialized area of management which deals with the marketing aspect of business. Marketing management means managing the marketing function efficiently. It represents marketing concept in action. According to **Philip Kotler**, *"Marketing management is the analysis, planning, implementation and control of programmes designed to create, build and maintain beneficial exchanges and relationships with target markets for the purpose of achieving organizational objectives"*. Marketing management deals with planning, implementation and control of the entire marketing, programmes of a firm. It includes various managerial functions such as determining marketing objectives and so on. Thus, marketing management is concerned with that area of total management which deals with the broad problem of sales. Marketing management may be defined as the process of managements of marketing programmes in order to accomplish corporate objectives. The marketing management process is quite comprehensive. It is looked after by a manager called marketing manager. The basic functions of management (e.g., planning, organizing, directing) are required to be conducted by all categories of managers. A marketing manager has to perform similar managerial functions while performing regular marketing operations and activities. A marketing manager needs capacity to perform all managerial functions in the field of marketing in an efficient and orderly manner.

Functions

The functions covered by marketing management are as explained below:

(1) ***Determining Marketing Objectives:*** A marketing manager has to decide marketing objectives in the context of overall business objectives of the firm. Objectives must be decided in an accurate manner as they give clear direction to the activities, plans and programmes of the marketing organization. The marketing objectives may be varied and may be expressed in terms of sales, profit, and consumer support market standing and so on. Marketing planning is for achieving such marketing objectives.

Thus, clearly defined objectives act as a base for other management functions. Marketing objectives may be short or long-term. However, objectives should be based on hard realities and detailed study of prevailing marketing environment. In brief, setting the objectives is the primary function of marketing management and the whole management process moves smoothly once the objectives are decided and communicated clearly to concerned persons and departments.

(2) *Planning:* Planning as a managerial function comes next to setting up of marketing objectives. A plan is for achieving the objectives decided. It suggests the course of action needed for achieving the objectives. It involves various broad decisions regarding future course of action. Plan may be for a short period or long period. Similarly, alternative plans are kept ready and a suitable one is selected for actual execution. A plan gives various details regarding the marketing activities of a firm. It gives clear direction to the marketing activities and facilitates the use of marketing strategies as per the need of the situation. Planning creates proper background for the conduct of other managerial functions namely, organizing, directing and so on. Marketing management is concerned with the formulation of marketing plans, policies and procedures.

(3) *Organizing:* Organizing is next to planning. Organizing means a creative suitable administrative structure for orderly execution of marketing plan. Without suitable organization, execution of the plan will not be possible. Efficient organization is necessary for dividing the activities and for utilizing material and human resources to the fullest extent. A marketing manager has to create suitable internal organizational structure for the execution of his marketing plan. Such structure avoids duplication of efforts, misdirection of activities and creates proper atmosphere for the implementation of marketing plan.

(4) *Directing:* Directing function involves giving guidance and instructions to subordinates in regard to steps to be taken for the execution of a plan. Directing also includes leading and motivating as two supplementary functions. Effective communication is also one sub-function of directing. The purpose of directing is to execute the plan in an orderly manner. Mistakes, wastages, misuse of resources, etc., will be avoided due to directing function.

(5) *Co-ordinating:* Co-ordination is the essence of management process. A marketing manager has to co-ordinate his marketing plan with the plans of other departments. He needs support and cooperation from other departments and for this co-ordination is essential. Even within the marketing department, internal coordination among the sections and staff is necessary. The entire marketing organization will function smoothly and move in one direction due to such co-ordination. Co-ordination will not come easily and automatically and hence, special efforts are necessary on the part of marketing manager.

(6) *Controlling:* Controlling function is important as it avoids mistakes and errors during the process of execution of marketing plan. Expected results may not be available if proper controlling mechanism is not introduced. Preparing marketing plan is not adequate. It is necessary to see that it is executed properly and for this controlling is necessary. For effective controlling, performance standards must be decided and actual performance must be evaluated for the introduction of suitable remedial measures, if necessary. Follow-up steps are possible if the controlling system is effective. In brief, proper control and co-ordination of all marketing functions is one area covered by marketing management.

(7) *Staffing:* In this managerial function, the manpower requirement of the sales organization is estimated and arrangements are made for the recruitment, selection, training, etc., of the staff/manpower. Many personnel functions are covered under staffing. Plan is to be executed with the co-operation and support of staff and hence manpower selected should be properly qualified, trained and efficient. Failure of a promising plan is possible if the persons connected with the execution are not competent.

Market Research

Meaning

Small firms are over and over again reluctant to invest in market research exercise as it seems to be an expensive proportion. Moreover, it is a time-taking process, and an entrepreneurial business enterprise is usually in urgency.

Many entrepreneurial ventures take a middle path and decide to undertake market research when there is a big decision to be taken. This is not necessarily the right approach. The question of when to resort to market research can be answered by a cost-benefit analysis. The costs of doing market research are the direct expenses of doing research as well as the likely loss in sales due to delaying decision. A delay in the decision caused by waiting for the results of the market research can give an opportunity to competitors to capture market share at your cost.

Market research is not to be confused with field survey. A field survey is just one of the techniques used in market research. **Any dependable information that improves the marketing decision is market research.**

What is a Market Survey?

The firm market survey is used by some as synonymous with market research or market analysis. This is incorrect. Market survey is only a technique or method of market research or market analysis. Its purpose is to collect specific data concerning the market that cannot be had from the company's internal records or from external published sources of data. When a market survey is used for generating relevant market information and such information forms the basis of the sales forecasts, the forecasting method is referred to as the market survey method of sales forecasting.

Why Need Market Survey?

Normally, when an enterprise wants to introduce a new product or an improved product, it resorts to a market survey to assess the likely demand for the product. Marketing a new product is not an easy job and a novice can very easily be thrown out by other competitors. To chalk out a programme for marketing a new product is therefore, necessary. A new article is one which has not been previously marketed by any other business concern, e.g., new drink, new toilet soap, new hair oil, new type of cloth and a new machine, etc. Whereas a new brand is simply a competitor among other products of that type already available on the market. For a new brand it is necessary to find out merely whether the market is being adequately served or whether there is room for another brand. For a new product it is necessary to find out whether a market does exist and if it does not, whether it is possible to create a market for the product. Likewise, any new enterprise entering the market for the first time, resort to the market survey method for forecasting its demand/sales.

This is quite natural. The enterprise does not have any data of past sales demand patterns to fall back upon. It has to gather the information from the market and take decisions. Usually, the enterprise conducts a survey among a sample of consumers and gauges their attitude, likely purchase, purchase habits, etc. The merit of the market survey method lies in the fact that the method facilitates gathering of original or primary data, i.e., specific to the problem on hand. The main demerit is that it is time-consuming and expensive.

Techniques of Market Survey

Usually the following techniques are used to collect factual data, less so when used to gain insight into respondent's interpretations. The market survey techniques may be of the following types:

(1) *Product-oriented:* A product needs proper planning by the entrepreneur before its introduction in the market. The purpose is to offer better service and satisfaction to customers. Today's marketing firms are selling product's benefits and image rather than the product itself.

Product-oriented survey techniques help in gathering essential facts about the product. It entails finding answers to the following:

(1) What fundamental human instincts does the use or consumption of the product satisfy?
(2) What interests and desires does it appeal to?
(3) How well does it meet the requirement of the user or consumer?
(4) Can any improvements or modifications be made which would strengthen its appeal?
(5) Are there any use for it not hither to thought of?
(6) What are its selling points?
(7) What should be the unit or unit of sale?

Even while selecting the methods of marketing and the channels of distribution the following question certainly will do a impressive job:

(1) Will it be better to employ salesmen alone?
(2) Should it use advertising alone?
(3) To use a combination?
(4) What subsidiary forms of selling should be used?
(5) What will be the relative costs of marketing by these methods?
(6) Should the product be sold to the consumer or user through the manufacturer's organisation?
(7) Through retailers?
(8) Would the employment of wholesalers be advantageous?
(9) What would be the benefits of using special selling agents?
(10) What are the relative costs and net profits likely to be as a result of using each of these methods?

(2) *Market-oriented:* Now, the customers were not ready to buy whatever was offered to them by the entrepreneurs. They started to buy the goods or service that was more beneficial to them in terms of quality, price, satisfaction, durability, look and soon. Therefore, the entrepreneurs were compelled to produce what the customers want.

An entrepreneur should seek answer to the following raised questions in order to have strong standing in the market.

(1) Who are its logical consumers?
(2) Who are its marginal consumers?
(3) Where arc thcy to be found?
(4) Who are its logical distributors?

Expected investigation

(1) What type of investigation will suit the product?
(2) By whom will it be conducted?
(3) Exactly what information should be sought for?
(4) What size of sample should be considered as sufficiently indicative?
(5) Are there any existing product which might give some indication of size of the market and volume of sales to be expected?

(6) How should the product be packed?
(7) What prices should it be sold?
(8) What terms would be most satisfactory to dealers and manufacturers?
(9) What class of dealers should handle the product?

(3) *Desk research:* The terms 'Desk Research' denotes all marketing researches done by a marketing expert/entrepreneur with the help of published and other written sources of information. It is a table work involving the analysis of data available in directories, journals and magazines and in the internal records of the firms such as final statements, sales reports and so on.

Advantages

(1) Information is available without much effort.
(2) The method is least expensive.
(3) The data are free from investigator's bias.
(4) It keeps the marketing manager free from botheration of field investigation.
(5) The data available from government, stock exchange, chamber of commerce and industry and other organized bodies is also reliable to a great extent.

Disadvantages

(1) This is based on secondary data, therefore limitations of secondary data is involved in them.
(2) Published information will have to be modified to meet the requirement of the entrepreneur/researcher before using it.
(3) It is less reliable and results are doubtful unless tested by field investigation.

(4) *Field Investigation:* Field investigation is a very reliable technique as it is based on primary data collected directly by the researcher/entrepreneur from the field. Sometimes, the primary data is supplemented with secondary or published data too. There are three field research techniques.

(a) ***Mail Order Surveys:*** A mail order survey is a complete antithesis of the personal interviews. Under this method, a questionnaire which is sent to him by mail is completed by informant completely unaided and unguided. Under this method, the questionnaire should be carefully compiled, structured and pre-tested, as it will have to be filled in by the informant himself. The names and addresses of people to whom questionnaire are sent by post are obtained by various means. There are agencies which specialize in providing list of different kinds of people such as lawyers, doctors, engineers, government officers, professors and so forth. The simplest list is of course the telephone directory. But it cannot be an exhaustive list.

(b) ***Telephone Surveys:*** Telephone interviewing is the second type of field research. This technique has been used in particular for the estimation of the number of persons who have just finished watching a television programme or listening to a radio broadcast. This is also used to estimate quickly to ascertain the ownership of different types of product. Though this method is very convenient for industrial surveys, it is not widely used in this country.

(c) ***Personal Interviews:*** The third technique of field investigation is personal interviewing. Under this technique, the interviewer follows a rigid procedure in asking question in prescribed form and order. A structured questionnaire is prepared and the interviewer fills it on the basis of answers supplied by the informant. The interviewer may, however, be allowed varying degrees of freedom in conducting the interview. The greater the freedom allowed, the higher is the skill required in the interviewer and the more complex are the problems of analysis of the results. These interviews may be of various type-structured, semi- structured, unstructured, the free interview, the focus interview, depth interview and so on. Every type of interview has its own merits and demerits. Interviewing method is quite popular in conducting marketing researches in India and abroad.

(5) ***The Delphi Technique:*** The Delphi Technique was originally conceived as a way to obtain the opinion of experts without necessarily bringing them together face to face. In recent times, however, it has taken on an all new meaning and purpose. The Delphi Technique is the method being used to squeeze citizens out of the process, affecting a left-wing takeover of the schools.

The change agent or facilitator goes through the motions of acting as an organizer, getting each person in the target group to elicit expression of their concerns about a program, project, or policy in question. The facilitator listens attentively, forms "task forces," "urges everyone to make lists," and so on. While she/he is doing this, the facilitator learns something about each member of the target group. She/he identifies the "leaders," the loud mouths," as well as those who frequently turn sides during the argument - the "weak or noncommittal". This technique is a very unethical method of achieving consensus on a controversial topic in group settings. It requires well-trained professionals who deliberately escalate tension among group members, pitting one faction against the other, so as to make one viewpoint appear ridiculous so the other becomes "sensible" whether such is warranted or not.

The Delphi technique is one more way of obtaining group input for ideas and problem-solving. Unlike the nominal group process, the Delphi does not require face to face participation. It uses a series of carefully designed questionnaires interspersed with information summaries and feedback from preceding responses.

In a planning situation, the Delphi can be used to:

- Develop a number of alternatives;
- Assess the social and economic impacts of rapid community growth;
- Explore underlying assumptions or background information leading to different judgments;
- Seek out information on which agreement may later be generated;
- Correlate informed judgments on a subject involving many disciplines; and
- Educate respondents on the diverse and interrelated elements of a topic.

The Delphi begins with the initial development of a questionnaire focusing on the identified problem. An appropriate respondent group is selected, and then the questionnaire is mailed to them. Each participant answers the questionnaire independently and returns it. The initiators of the questionnaire summarize responses, and then develop a feedback summary and a second questionnaire for the same respondent group. After reviewing the feedback summary, respondents independently rate priority ideas included in the second questionnaire, then mail back the responses. The process is repeated until investigators feel positions are firm and agreement on a topic is reached. A final summary report is issued to the respondent group. The Delphi can be modified in many ways.

In assessing community needs, the Delphi technique could be used for many of the same things as the nominal group process-determining and prioritizing community problems; setting goals; designing needs assessment strategies; planning a conference or community forum; developing improved community services; evaluating alternative plans for community development; or aggregating judgments of special-interest or mutually hostile group.

Advantages and Disadvantages of the Delphi Technique for community need assessment.

Advantages

- Allows participants to remain anonymous.
- Inexpensive.
- Free of social pressure, personality influence and individual dominance.
- A reliable judgment or forecast results.
- Allows sharing of information and reasoning among participants.

- Conducive to independent thinking and gradual formulation.
- A well-selected respondent panel - a mix of local official, knowledgeable individuals, members of impacted community regional officials, academic social officials academic social scientists.etc. - can provide a broad analytical perspective on potential growth impacts.
- Can be used to reach consensus among groups hostile to each other.

Disadvantages

- Judgements are those of a selected group of people and may not be representative.
- Tendency to eliminate extreme positions and force a middle-of-the-road consensus.
- More time-consuming than the group process method.
- Should not be viewed as a total solution to forecasting.
- Requires skill in written communication.
- Requires adequate time and participant commitment (about 30-45 days).

Distribution Channels

Meaning

Goods move from manufacturer to final consumer through a specific route is called channel. Goods are distributed or sold out over wide geographical area through such channels called channels of distribution. Manufacturer-Wholesaler-Retailer-Consumer is one popular and extensively used channel of distribution, particularly for the distribution of consumer goods of daily use. In brief, distribution channel is the route taken by goods on their journey from the producer to the ultimate consumer. It is the system/mechanism used for funneling goods and services from producers to consumers. Distribution channels are also called trade channels or marketing channels. Every distribution channel starts with the producer and ends with consumers. There may be one or more middlemen in between the two ends. Such middlemen may be mercantile agents or merchant middlemen. According to **Richard M. Clewett**, *"A channel is the pipeline through which a product flows on its way to the consumer. The manufacturer puts his product into the pipe line or marketing channel and various marketing people move it along to the consumer at the other end of the channel"*. In addition, **Louis P. Bucklin** has defined distribution channel as *"the set of institutions which participate in the distribution of goods from the point of production to the point of consumption"*. Finally, in the words of **William Stanton**, *"A channel of distribution (sometimes called a trade channel) for the product is the route taken by the title to the product as it moves from the producer to the ultimate consumer or individual user"*. Marketing channels are necessary for large scale distribution of goods in an economically manner. These channels also perform the role of salesmanship. Mass production means mass distribution which is possible through extensive use of various distribution channels. These channels perform various functions and offer useful services to manufacturers and consumers. Distribution channels bring large scale distribution of goods and provide such goods to consumers regularly. These channels facilitate expansion of trade. They also act as line of communication in the distributive system. Even new products can be introduced in the market easily, quickly uneconomically through such channels.

Types of Distribution Channels for Consumer Goods

Channels of distribution are many and varied in nature. Broadly speaking, there are six important channels used for the distribution of consumer goods. These channels are as noted below:

(1) Manufacturer - Wholesaler - Retailer - Consumer Channel.
(2) Manufacturer - Sole Selling Agent - Wholesaler - Retailer - Consumer Channel.
(3) Manufacturer - His own depots - Retailer - Consumer Channel.

(4) Manufacturer - Retailer - Consumer Channel.
(5) Manufacturer -His chain shops - Consumer Channel.
(6) Manufacturer - Consumer Channel.

Let us, now, consider the details of these channels of distribution for consumer goods.

(1) ***Manufacturer - Wholesaler - Retailer - Consumer Channel :*** This is one popular and extensively used marketing channel. It is rightly called 'traditional channel' for the distribution of goods. In this channel, the manufacturer utilizes the services of two middlemen for the distribution of goods. The wholesalers and retailers render valuable services in the distribution of goods. In fact, manufacturer sells goods through them only. However, he has to be very careful while selecting the wholesalers. The wholesalers selected should have better contacts with the retailers. They must have adequate warehousing facility and should be able to perform some other marketing functions such as transporting, advertising and sales promotion. In addition, they should also be able to give financial support to manufacturer in the case of need. As far as possible the manufacturer should select wholesalers who do not deal in the product/products which directly compete with his own product/products. This lengthy channel has certain advantages. For example, this channel is convenient from the view point of the manufacturer as it brings about division of labour. It enables the manufacturer as to concentrate fully on production and not to bother about distribution. He is also relieved from the anxiety regarding selling of goods. This marketing channel widens the scope of marketing. Finally, it reduces the need of extensive advertising and publicity programmes. Thus manufacturer enjoys a number of advantages from this channel. However there are certain limitations as well. The serious drawback of this channel is that due to the existence of middlemen and their commission, goods become costlier to consumers. Similarly, the middlemen resort to various malpractices such as adulteration, artificial scarcity and price rise. This affects sales and profit of the manufacturer. The manufacturer also loses his control over the marketing of his products soon after the delivery of goods to wholesales. The manufacturer has to depend fully on the middlemen for marketing his products. This lengthy channel is suitable for large scale distribution of large number of consumer goods like soaps, detergents and cosmetics. Such goods are usually supplied to consumers through this traditional channel. For instance; Hindustan Lever Ltd., makes use of this channel extensively for the sale of its products. The same is the case with many other leading manufacturers of consumer goods.

(2) ***Manufacturer- Sole Selling Agent- Wholesaler- Retailer- Consumer Channel:*** In this lengthy marketing channel, the manufacturer appoints some dealers as sole distributors for his goods in a particular region or territory. The sole distributor accepts the entire responsibility of marketing of products within his area. He is paid commission for his services. The sole distributors selected must have considerable marketing influence in a concerned territory. They must have efficient sales organization and sufficient financial backing at their disposal. The appointment of sole selling agents facilitates planned production and control over the sale of product. It also lowers overhead expenditure and provides incentive to distributors. The manufacturer gets the benefit of the reputation of sole distributors. Thus, in this channel, goods flow from manufacturer to sole distributors and finally to consumers through wholesalers and retailers. Naturally, this channel is lengthy with three marketing middlemen.

The advantages and limitations of the first channel are equally applicable to this channel of distribution. Consumer goods as well as capital goods are distributed through this channel. For example, Kelvinator has appointed Blue star as their selling agents. Blue Star sells Leonard refrigerators to large number of dealers in different towns and cities. Finally, consumers purchase them from local dealers. This channel is longer as compared to the previous one as three middlemen are involved in the distributive process.

Manufacturers of mass consumption goods having a nationwide market do not want to deal directly with large number of wholesalers. They appoint sole selling agents for various regions who sell to wholesalers, who in turn sell to retailers.

(3) *Manufacturer- His own depots- Retailer- Consumer Channel:* In this marketing channel, an attempt is being made to eliminate one middleman (wholesaler) from the distributive process. Here, the manufacturer supplies goods directly to retailers through his own marketing organization. For regular supply to large number of retailers, the manufacturer opens this own depots at important commercial centres. Goods are directly supplied to retailers through his own marketing organization. For regular supply to large number of retailers, the manufacturer opens his own depots at important commercial centres. Goods are directly supplied to retailers from these depots. The manufacturer keeps stocks in these deposits as per the requirements of the area. In addition, the manufacturer collects orders from the retailers through his salesmen and supplies goods to them. Sometimes, large retail trading organizations such as departmental stores and super markets purchase directly from the manufacturer. This channel is now, popular in business world. This is because efforts are being made by the manufacturers and retailers to eliminate wholesalers from the system of distribution.

This marketing channel has the following advantages:

- The wholesaler and his commission are eliminated.
- This channel is a shorter channel and there is no scope for malpractices (of wholesalers) in this channel.
- The manufacturer has effective control on the whole marketing process and hence he prefers this channel.
- The profit of the manufacturer is likely to increase as commission is not required to be paid to the wholesalers.
- In this channel, a manufacturer has close contact with the market situation. This enables him to adjust his production and marketing plans and policies as per the need of the situation.

This Marketing channel has the following Limitations:

- In this channel, the manufacturer has to shoulder the responsibility of production as well as marketing of goods.
- The manufacturer has to maintain depots at different places and engage staff for collecting orders from retailers. This puts heavy financial and administrative burden on the manufacturer.
- The manufacturer has to give attention to various marketing functions including warehousing pricing, packaging, and transportation, advertising and risk-bearing. Naturally, this channel puts heavy burden on the manufacturer.
- Small manufacturers with limited financial support find it difficult to use this channel of distribution. They naturally prefer to use the services of wholesalers for the distribution of goods.

This lengthy and time consuming marketing channel is convenient and is used mainly by large scale manufacturers with huge financial backing. Tata's and Hindustan Lever have their own distributive system. Tea companies use this marketing channel for large-scale distribution. They have their depots in all major towns for the supply of tea to thousands of retailers directly. These organizations supply their products directly to retailers regularly and thereby eliminate wholesalers.

(4) *Manufacturer - Retailer- Consumer Channel:* This shorter marketing channel is rather similar to the previous channel as wholesalers are eliminated in both. Here, the goods move directly from the manufacturer to retailers and finally to consumers. There is only one middleman in the distributive process. The manufacturer keeps close contact with retailers and supplies them goods regularly for onward distribution to consumers. He has to keep huge sales organization for supplying goods regularly to large number of retailers. Sometimes, even retailers keep direct contact with the manufacturer, keeps close contact with retailers and supplies them goods regularly for onward distribution to consumers. Large retail shops like co-operative stores, chain shops and departmental stores purchase goods in large quantities directly from the manufacturers and supply them to consumers. In brief, manufacturers and retailers find this shorter marketing channel convenient and economical. This channel is used for the distribution of consumer goods (shoes, clothing and food items) as well as machinery, automobiles and other durable products. The wholesalers are bypassed in this channel and naturally their functions are undertaken by manufacturers.

Advantages

(1) It is a short channel as the wholesalers are eliminated. The commission to them is also eliminated. This gives benefit to manufacturers and consumers.

(2) The cost of distribution is brought down considerably in this channel.

(3) The malpractices of wholesalers are also eliminated.

(4) In this channel, the distribution is done quickly and hence it can be used even for the distribution of perishable goods within a small area.

(5) Consumers get goods at lower prices as they have not to share the burden of commission of the wholesaler.

Limitations

(1) The manufacturer has to look after the production and marketing at one and the same time. This puts heavy financial and administrative pressure/burden on him.

(2) The manufacturer has to maintain huge marketing organization and naturally he has to invest more capital in the business.

(3) The wholesaler is eliminated in this channel but not his functions. They are shared by the manufacturer himself.

(4) This channel is not convenient for the distribution of perishable commodities which need quick marketing and shortest channel.

(5) *Manufacturer- His chain shops- Consumer Channel:* In this shorter marketing channel both the wholesalers and retailers are eliminated. The functions of the wholesalers and retailers are performed by the manufacturer himself. Here, the manufacturer's opens his own retail shops/Branches in different parts of the country and sells his goods directly to consumers. The services of middlemen are not necessary in this shorter channel. The manufacturer looks after manufacturing and retailing. He keeps direct contact with the consumers. The branch managers are appointed for managing sales operations at the branch local level. They work as per the instructions of the head office. The manufacturers of textile, leather goods, readymade garments, ice creams and bakery products have opened their retail shops in big cities for effective distribution. The pricing policy is under their control. The prices are lowered due to the elimination of middlemen. The manufacturer will know the market reactions and will be able to incorporate necessary changes in the marketing policies at the right time. However, his attention will be diverted from manufacturing activities as he has to perform all marketing functions along with manufacturing proper. The cost of operation will also increase considerably. This channel can be used by large manufacturers who are financially sound and stable. In India, this channel of distribution is used by many manufacturers. Bata Shoe Company, for example, sells shoes to consumers directly through its branches. Similarly, Bombay Dyeing, Raymonds and other companies have their retail shops for selling cloth.

(6) *Manufacturer- Consumer Channel:* This is the shortest marketing as there is a no middleman in the distributive process. It is an example of a simple, direct and economical channel. In fact, it need not be treated as a channel at all as there is no middleman involved in the process of distribution. In this case, the manufacturer establishes direct contact with the consumers and supplies them goods. The goods are directly supplied to consumers either by establishing mail order house or through travelling salesmen or through retail shops. Bata, DCM (Delhi Cloth and General Mills), Binny and NTC (National Textile Corporation) sell their products directly to consumers. In mail order business, goods are sold through the medium of post office. In this channel, orders are collected by post and goods are sent to customers by V.P.P (Value payable by post). The other method is to appoint a large number of salesmen for canvassing and sales promotion. The salesmen go from door to door and convince the prospects about the utility of the products. The salesmen are usually paid commission on the basis of their sales. Hence they do their best to promote sales. Small manufacturers sell their production in the local market directly. In villages, village artisans sell goods directly to local people. Small business establishments like bakeries, dairies, hotel and sweetmeat stalls use this direct marketing channel. Even farmers sometimes sell their products directly to consumers. However, this channel is not convenient for a wide market. In advances countries, goods like cold drinks, milk and ice creams are sold through automatic machines. Machines are installed at convenient places like gardens, petrol pumps and picnic spots. The buyer has to insert coins in the machines and collect the required commodity. Neither salesmen nor dealers are required to push the sales. Direct sale to consumers through retail shops is also possible under this channel. Similarly industrial goods may be sold directly to industrial buyers. In addition, services like water, electricity, gas, etc., are distributed by using this direct channel.

Manufacturer- Consumer channel has certain advantages. The manufacturer gets complete control over the process of distribution and gets first hand information about market trends. The middlemen are eliminated from the distributive process. This gives more profit to the manufacturer without charging high price to consumers. Along with this, there are certain Disadvantages of this marketing channel. For instance, there will be increase in the cost of operation. A manufacturer will also have to maintain a large sales force for conduction of door-to-door campaign. The manufacturer will also have to spend on advertisement and publicity. He will have to spend large amount of money on his sales organization. In brief, this channel is rather costly and not suitable for wider market.

Manufacturer- Consumer channel of distribution is suitable under the following circumstances:

(1) When the market is local in character.

(2) When the goods to be distributed are perishable in character.

(3) When the manufacturer has financial support to establish his own distributive system.

(4) When the goods to be distributed are costly and after-sales sevice is necessary.

(5) When the goods are to be distributed in a selected market or area.

(6) When the manufacturer desires to have effective control on the entire marketing mechanism.

Manufacturer- Consumer channel is a direct one. However, it is very difficult to use it in the present day complicated marketing system. This is because a manufacturer finds it difficult to keep direct contact with growing number of consumers and also to give attention to other aspects of marketing including advertising, warehousing and actual retail selling.

It may be noted that every marketing channel has its own feature, advantages and limitations. Every channel is suitable for marketing under certain circumstances. A manufacturer can use one or more channels for the distribution of his products. In fact, the use of more than one channel is quite common in case of large manufacturers. There is no hard and fast rule as regards the selection and use of a channel of distribution. The selection of marketing channel is entirely at his discretion. In general, shorter channel is better as it is quick and economical. The longer channel is always costly and time consuming. However, it is useful for large-scale distribution of goods.

Types of Distribution Channels for Industrial Goods

The usual channels for the distribution of industrial goods are as noted below:

(1) Manufacturer- Customer(industrial user) channel.

(2) Manufacturer- Distributor - Customer Channel.

(3) Manufacturer- Agent - Distribution- Customer Channel.

(4) Manufacturer- Agent- Customer Channel.

Let us, now, consider brief details of these channels for the distribution of industrial goods:

(1) *Manufacturer- Customer/Consumer Channel:* This direct channel is most appropriate for marketing high priced complex products like locomotives, generators and computers. The purchases are limited and naturally manufacturer can sell as well as provide various services including after-sales services directly to the actual user of the product. Moreover, such direct contact between the manufacturer and user is necessary for negotiations regarding price, terms and conditions of sale, extra facilities required and so on. The middleman may not be able to do this job properly due to lack of technical knowledge, etc. This channel is also quick and economical in operation. It is convenient to both the parties and hence used extensively.

(2) *Manufacturer- Distributor- Customer Channel:* This channel is normally used for the marketing of accessories, multi-purpose standardized machines, machine tools, metal and so on. Here, manufacturers frequently use distributors (called industrial distributors) in order to establish contacts with potential purchasers. The purchasers are quite large in number and manufacturers find it expensive to keep contact with them. It is also profitable to promote sale through distributors rather than establishing separate sales organization or using the existing one. It is a little costly channel as the services of middleman are used on commission basis. The distributor is given title to the goods which they handle.

(3) *Manufacturer- Agent- Distribution- Customer Channel:* In this lengthy channel, one more middleman (i.e., agent) is added. Manufacturers of new industrial products (particularly without sales organization) prefer to appoint agents and use their services for promoting sales. Such agents are appointed on regional basis and they take interest in promoting sales. Such agents are appointed on regional basis and they take interest in promoting sales within the territory assigned to them. The agent stands as link between manufacturer and distributor. He acts as manufacturer's agent. This channel is also convenient to small manufacturers of industrial goods.

(4) *Manufacturer - Agent- Customer Channel:* In this short channel, the agents are appointed for sales promotion. The agents act as a manufacturer's sales force. This channel is useful for marketing industrial products with high price and where personal contact with the customer is necessary. The agent is paid commission for his services. A manufacturer may prefer this channel in order to make entry in a new market.

Choice/Selection of Distribution/Marketing Channel

Selection of appropriate distribution/ marketing channel is an important consideration in the marketing management. It is rather a knotty and ticklish problem in the marketing mix. It may be pointed out that there is not hard and fast rule for deciding which channel of distribution is to be selected for successful marketing. A manufacturer has to study all available channels and select one channel which would give the best results under the given circumstances. While selecting one or two channels, certain considerations like product considerations, market considerations, consumer considerations, enterprises considerations, etc. should be given adequate attention. Important factors which need careful consideration while selecting the channel of distribution is as noted below:

(1) *Nature of Product:* The nature of product is one significant factor influencing the selection of the distribution channel. The nature of product means the characteristics of the product. The product for marketing may be a new product or an established one. It may be a cheap or costly and finally it may be perishable or durable. If it is perishable like fruits or vegetables, it will be better to sell it directly to consumers. Similarly, costly products requiring after sale service should pass on through few hands. Thus consumer durables like sewing machines, automobiles, television sets and scooters are sold either directly by the manufacturer or through one area distributor. An industrial product is usually sold directly to the industrial user. If a product is new, active support of middlemen is necessary. Once it is established in the market, some middlemen can be eliminated. Standardized products like machine tools are commonly handled by wholesale distributors. In the case of local market, direct sale is possible and also preferred.

(2) *Nature of the Market:* The size and location of the market also influence the choice, regarding the distribution channel. In the case of national markets, the producer may be compelled to avail the services of intermediaries for effective marketing of goods. Similarly, if the number of customers is very large and if they are widely scattered, the services of middlemen are essential. On the contrary, in the case of local market and a small number of customers, the manufacturer may resort to direct channel. For example, in the marketing of consumer items, wholesalers and retailers are inevitable but they are not essential for marketing industrial goods. Finally, for mass distribution of goods, the services of middlemen are required but for selective or exclusive distribution one or two dealers are adequate.

(3) *Nature of Market Competition and Marketing Environment:* The nature and intensity of market competition is another factor connected with the selection of distribution channel. In the case of keen competition, the manufacturer has to seek active support of middlemen. Similarly, in the case of certain products like medicines, a manufacturer has to follow the same channel as used by his competitors. A manufacturer can use a shorter channel if the market competition is limited. Similarly, shorter channel can be used during the recession when the demand is less. Longer channel will be more useful during the period of prosperity when demand is more and also increasing. Along with market competition, marketing environment needs careful consideration while selecting the marketing/distribution channel. Such environment is the net result of various factors such as market competition, entry of new products in the market policies of competitors, government policies and so on. The channel should be selected after due consideration of market environment -present and future.

(4) *Nature and Features of Customers:* While selecting distribution channel, the convenience of the prospective customers should be taken into consideration. Selecting channel from the view point of customers requires information of regarding prospective customers age , income group, sex, etc. The buying habits of customers should also be taken into consideration while selecting a marketing/distribution channel.

(5) *Financial Resources and Cost of Distribution:* Another significant factor influencing selection of marketing/distribution channel is a financial resources at the disposal of the manufacturer and the cost of distribution in relation to the product. A manufacturer with limited financial support has to use a longer channel as he needs the services of middlemen for the distribution of goods. He can use shorter channel or can sell his goods directly to consumers if he is financially strong and capable to establish his own sales organization. Similarly, if the market is local, direct sale to consumers is possible. However, a longer channel is required if the market is too wide. This is natural as a manufacturer finds it difficult (financially) to establish his own sales organization. New companies depend heavily on the middlemen for distribution due to lack of finance but established companies try to sell their products with minimum number of middlemen. The company's product mix influences the selection of marketing channel. Here, the broader the product line, shorter will be the dealerships. Finally, a company interested in keeping greater control over the marketing channels prefers a shorter marketing channel.

(6) ***Availability of Middlemen:*** The manufacturer of a particular product may need a large number of middlemen for efficient distribution of his product. He may also be willing to pay them attractive commission. However, he may not get the services of middlemen on fair terms and conditions. Under such circumstances, he has no alternative but to establish his own sales organization for marketing. This is because of non-availability of suitable middlemen. In brief, availability of middlemen, willingness of middlemen and the services which the middlemen are willing to provide are three broad factors connected with the middlemen in the distribution channels.

(7) ***Miscellaneous Factors:*** In addition to the factors noted above, there are other miscellaneous factors which influence the selection of distribution channel. Such factors are: proportion of credit sales, risk-bearing in business, additional services offered by the middlemen, size of sales organization, desire for control over distribution channel and number of potential consumers.

Problems of Marketing

Production is meaningless without market. Therefore, the very purpose of an enterprise is to produce what the customer will buy. All industries, whether small or large, face problems in marketing their products or services. But, small scale enterprises are more plagued by the marketing of their products is commonly noticed over time and clime. Notwithstanding, there are two main reasons conditioning the marketing of products produced by small enterprises. **First,** small enterprise cannot withstand with cut-throat competition in respect of quality, cost, and standardization of the products with medium and large scale industries. In fact, the same is attributed to one of the major reasons limiting the fuller utilization of their production capacity. **Second,** the small enterprises of our country neither have the full appreciation of the importance of marketing not had they employed and implemented effective marketing techniques in their enterprises.

In this regards, the observation made by the **Ford Foundation** seems worth quoting *"In spite of an extensive potential market, the Indian small entrepreneurs were most reluctant towards efficient marketing technique and consequently have met with failure on the front of marketing of their products. When it comes to the question of markets for which the products are produced, most of the small entrepreneurs appear to be as much anchored to the past as they are in the methods of manufacturing. Types and areas of consumption are shifting but only few products try to follow them. This, in part at least, is due to the prevailing system of distribution. Few channels of communication exits between the small manufacturer and the ultimate customer. In many cases, the manufacturer does not even know in what part of the country his wires are used, or who buys them"*

The Japanese delegation on small-scale industries in India also gave similar view that the most knotty point in the operation of small-scale enterprises and cottage industries is that the industry is isolated from the market and unable to understand quickly and accurately the prevalent trend of the market.

Major problems of marketing of small industry products are:

(1) ***Competition with Modern Sector:*** The market competition of the small enterprises with the modern sector has aggravated due to several factors over the years. Although the traditional hallmarks of the small-scale industries are slowly yet steadily changing. There is an implicit assumption of poor quality for goods manufactured in small enterprises. This sector needs to cater to wide diversity and changing tastes and preferences of their clientele which they do fail.

(2) *Lack of Sales Promotion:* Advertisement of the products through the elaborate sales promotion methods such as cadres of trained salesmen, advertisement in cinema slides, Posters, papers, magazines and soon have become increasingly fashionable particularly in the case of medium and large scale industries. But, small scale industries lack in the required resources as well as knowledge to practice the methods or sales promotion. As a result, the former usually have patented names which facilitate the dealers in selling their products without making much effort. It can also be postulated that in the case of the products of small scale industries, at least at their initial stage, persuasive capacity of the dealer plays on important role in influencing their sales. In such case, the dealers demand and producers are bound to pay a relatively higher rate of commission than those paid by the large-scale producers. This reckets high unit cost and, thus, impinges on their capacity to compete with the large sector. In this way the small enterprises are unstirred. If these small enterprises make a modest start too, it is stagnated and dies out or devoured by the successful bigger enterprises.

(3) *Weak in Bargaining Power:* In case of handicraft units such as copper smithy and carpet weaving units, the price realized is usually better then the sales are made at the place of production itself than when these products are marketed in the fairs. It looks that, very possibly, the manufacturers are in a better bargaining position at home than in other locations like fairs where they take their products for selling. Other studies also support this finding. One can add some other problems depending upon the type of enterprise, yet these are the major ones encompassing various problems in one way or other.

(4) *Financial Weakness:* Due weak financial base, a small industrialist cannot afford to spend as heavily as a large unit does while marketing his products. A rare exception is the pharmaceutical industry, in which the gap between the manufacturing cost and the selling price is very large. This is a special situation, in which marketing techniques are different, and therefore the cost of marketing is very high, particularly the marketing cost of those drugs for which there is stiff competition. The small industrialists in this line have to follow this trend in order to survive.

(5) *Absence of Own Marketing Channel:* In the absence of a marketing channel of their own, many small units sell their products to large selling houses. Voltas, for instance, markets a number of products produced by small units. Similarly, the Bata Shoe Company sells the shoes manufactured by the small sector. As a result, small units invariably get a raw deal. The large companies make handsome profits from marketing the products of small units by charging a much higher price from the consumer. In this respect, there is a need for a large number of marketing consortia, whose primary responsibility will be to assist small units.

Institutionalized Marketing for Entrepreneurs

Before they come up and for their sustenance, small industries need various supporting services, efficiently organized and promptly extended. Marketing guidance and assistance is one such service, which is increasingly expected by newly established small units in areas which are far away from developed metropolitan cities. These industries are often not in a position to carry on market research, which is an essential pre-requisite in the marketing process. To encourage the small entrepreneur to take up the production and marketing of new products, the governments in the developing countries and their specialized institutions collect, collate and disseminate up to date and reliable market intelligence on a regular basis in the absence of which an entrepreneur would often operate either in the dark or wander on an uncharted sea. As a matter of fact, manufacturing units should be guided into the unexplored areas of assumed profit. This is the rationale behind the Market Intelligence Bureau, which collects and disseminates relevant information about potential and profitable market areas.

The production and financial capacity of small industries are limited; so are their sustaining power and competitive strength. They can compete individually if the product is special, and demand outstrips supply. In the case of products which are not special, and in lines where competition, particularly from the large-scale sector, is fierce, individual marketing becomes difficult. To contend against established large and even small units is not easy job. The very small size of operations is then a handicap. But if several small units decide to pool their resources, their combined aggregate capacity would be larger than even the largest industrial unit. In fact, in some lines of production, the total installed capacity in the small scale sector is higher than that in the large sector small units can then compete collectively and secure a share of the market, which is legitimately theirs. However, a collective of this type can succeed only if the participants are prepared to sacrifice a part of their individuality. This is more true of foreign markets, where one has to contend not only against all the other countries, but also against a vast, domestic market. Extensive organization is needed to reach potential areas, and to hold one's own against the unfair competition from the large-scale sector. It is in this context that the consortium idea, which is still is an embryonic stage in India, is relevant. Government purchase from small industries would also go up tremendously if small entrepreneurs adopt this consortium approach. They would eliminate to a great extent competition amongst themselves in their own sector and face confidently and successfully competition from other quarters.

Some small industries have good prospects of selling their products in international markets. If they cannot develop a consortium for the export of their products, they should at least associate with and support an export house. If marketing is a war, it is the fiercest in the international fields.

Summing Up

Marketing management is a specialized area of management which deals with the marketing aspect of business. Marketing management means managing the marketing function efficiently. It represents marketing concept in action. According to **Philip Kotler**, *"Marketing management is the analysis, planning, implementation and control of programmes designed to create, build and maintain beneficial exchanges and relationships with target markets for the purpose of achieving organizational objectives"*.

Functions

The functions covered by marketing management are as below:

Determining Marketing Objectives; Planning; Organizing; Directing; Co-ordinating; Controlling; and Staffing

Market Research

Market research is not to be confused with field survey. A field survey is just one of the techniques used in market research. **Any dependable information that improves the marketing decision is market research.**

What is a Market Survey?

The firm market survey is used by some as synonymous with market research or market analysis. This is incorrect. Market survey is only a technique or method of market research or market analysis. Its purpose is to collect specific data concerning the market that cannot be had from the company's internal records or from external published sources of data. When a market survey is used for generating relevant market information and such information forms the basis of the sales forecasts, the forecasting method is referred to as the market survey method of sales forecasting.

Why Need Market Survey?

Marketing a new product is not an easy job and a novice can very easily be thrown out by other competitors. A new article is one which has not been previously marketed by any other business concern, e.g., new drink, new toilet soap, new hair oil, new type of cloth and a new machine, etc., whereas a new brand is simply a competitor among other product of that type already available on the market. For a new brand it is necessary to find out merely whether the market is being adequately served or whether there is room for another brand. For a new product it is necessary to find out whether a market does exist and if it does not, whether it is possible to create a market for the product. Likewise, any new enterprise entering the market for the first time, resort to the market survey method for forecasting its demand/sales.

This is quite natural. The enterprise does not have any data of past sales demand patterns to fall back upon. It has to gather the information from the market and take decisions. Usually, the enterprise conducts a survey among a sample of consumers and gauges their attitude, likely purchase, purchase habits, etc. The merit of the market survey method lies in the fact that the method facilitates gathering of original or primary data, i.e., specific to the problem on hand. The main demerit is that it is time-consuming and expensive.

Techniques of Market Survey

Usually the following techniques are used to collect factual data, less so when used to gain insight into respondent's interpretations. The market survey techniques may be of the following types:

Product-oriented: A product needs proper planning by the entrepreneur before its introduction in the market. The purpose is to offer better service and satisfaction to customers. Today's marketing firms are selling product's benefits and image rather than the product itself.

Product-oriented survey techniques help in gathering essential facts about the product.

Market-oriented: They started to buy the goods or service that was more beneficial to them in terms of quality, price, satisfaction, durability, look and soon. Therefore, the entrepreneurs were compelled to produce what the customers want.

Desk research: The terms 'Desk Research' denotes all marketing researches done by a marketing expert/entrepreneur with the help of published and other written sources of information. It is a table work involving the analysis of data available in directories, journals and magazines and in the internal records of the firms such as final statements, sales reports and so on.

Field Investigation: Field investigation is a very reliable technique as it is based on primary data collected directly by the researcher/entrepreneur from the field. Sometimes, the primary data is supplemented with secondary or published data too. There are three field research techniques. Mail Order Surveys; Telephone Surveys; and Personal Interviews

The Delphi Technique: The Delphi Technique was originally conceived as a way to obtain the opinion of experts without necessarily bringing them together face to face. This technique is a very unethical method of achieving consensus on a controversial topic in group settings. The Delphi technique is a way of obtaining group input for ideas and problem-solving. The Delphi can be modified in many ways.

Meaning of Distribution Channels

Goods are distributed or sold out over wide geographical area through such channels called channels of distribution. It is the system/mechanism used for funneling goods and services from producers to consumers. Distribution channels are also called trade channels or marketing channels. Every distribution channel starts with the producer and ends with consumers. There may be one or more middlemen in between the two ends. Such middlemen may be mercantile agents or merchant middlemen. According to **Richard M. Clewett**, *"A channel is the pipeline through which a product flows on its way to the consumer. The manufacturer puts his product into the pipe line or marketing channel and various marketing people move it along to the consumer at the other end of the channel"*. In addition, **Louis P. Bucklin** has defined distribution channel as *"the set of institutions which participate in the distribution of goods from the point of production to the point of consumption"*. Finally, in the words of **William Stanton**, *"A channel of distribution (sometimes called a trade channel) for the product is the route taken by the title to the product as it moves from the producer to the ultimate consumer or individual user"*.

Types of Distribution Channels for Consumer Goods

Channels of distribution are many and varied in nature. Broadly speaking, there are six important channels used for the distribution of consumer goods. These channels are as noted below:

(1) Manufacturer - Wholesaler - Retailer - Consumer Channel.
(2) Manufacturer - Sole Selling Agent - Wholesaler - Retailer - Consumer Channel.
(3) Manufacturer - His own depots - Retailer - Consumer Channel.
(4) Manufacturer - Retailer - Consumer Channel.
(5) Manufacturer -His chain shops - Consumer Channel.
(6) Manufacturer - Consumer Channel.

Types of Distribution Channels for Industrial Goods

The usual channels for the distribution of industrial goods are as noted below:

(i) Manufacturer- Customer(industrial user) Channel.
(ii) Manufacturer- Distributor - Customer Channel.
(iii) Manufacturer- Agent - Distribution- Customer Channel.
(iv) Manufacturer- Agent- Customer Channel.

Choice/Selection of Distribution/Marketing Channel

Selection of appropriate distribution/ marketing channel is an important consideration in the marketing management. A Manufacturer has to study all available channels and select one channel which would give the best results under the given circumstances. While selecting one or two channels, certain considerations like product considerations, market considerations, consumer considerations, enterprises considerations, etc., should be given adequate attention.

Important factors which need careful consideration while selecting the channel of distribution are as noted below: Nature of product; Nature of the Market; Nature of Market Competition and Marketing Environment; Nature and Features of Customers; Financial Resources and Cost of Distribution; Availability of Middlemen; and Miscellaneous Factors.

Problems of Marketing

The Japanese delegation on small scale industries in India also gave similar view that the most knotty point in the operation of small-scale enterprises and cottage industries is that the industry is isolated from the market and unable to understand quickly and accurately the prevalent trend of the market.

Major problems of marketing of small industry products are: Competition with Modern Sector; Lack of Sales Promotion; and Weak in Bargaining Power; Financial weakness and Absence of own marketing channel.

Institutionalized Marketing for Entrepreneurs

Marketing guidance and assistance is one such service, which increasingly expected by newly established small units in areas which are far away from developed metropolitan cities. These industries are often not in a position to carry on market research, which is an essential pre-requisite in the marketing process. To encourage the small entrepreneur to take up the production and marketing of new products, the governments in the developing countries and their specialized institutions collect, collate and disseminate up to date and reliable market intelligence on a regular basis in the absence of which an entrepreneur would often operate either in the dark or wander on an uncharted sea. As a matter of fact, manufacturing units should be guided into the unexplored areas of assumed profit. This is the rationale behind the Market Intelligence Bureau, which collects and disseminates relevant information about potential and profitable market areas.

20 INDUSTRIAL SICKNESS

Introduction, Definition, Symptoms of Industrial Sickness, Causes of Industrial Sickness, Consequences of Industrial Sickness, Remedial Measures to Overcome and Avoid Industrial Sickness, Summing Up.

Introduction

The problem of sickness in industries has become very acute in India. It has adversely affected the 'health' of the industrial sector in particular and the economy in general.

Definition

Prior to the enactment of the Sick Industrial Companies (Special Provision) Act, 1985, there was no unanimity regarding the definition of industrial sickness. Reserve Bank of India, term lending institutions and State Bank of India all defined sick industries in different ways. However, enactment of the **Sick Industrial Companies (Special Provisions) Act, 1985,** settled the issue. According to this Act, a sick unit was defined as *"an industrial company (being a company registered for not less than seven years) which has at the end of any financial year accumulated losses equal to or exceeding its entire net worth and has also suffered cash losses in such financial year and the financial year immediately preceding such financial year"*. In December 1991, public sector companies were also brought under the purview of the Act. The 1992 amendment (introduced in February 1994) altered the criterion somewhat: firms only need to be registered for five years, and the criterion of cash losses for two successive years was eliminated.

As far as small-scale sector is concerned, that small-scale industrial unit was considered to be sick that had:

(a) incurred a cash loss in the previous accounting year and was likely to continue with losses in the current accounting year and erosions on account of cumulative cash losses to the extent of 50 per cent or more of its peak net worth during the last five years; and/or

(b) Continuously defaulted in meeting four consecutive installments of interest or two-half yearly installments of principal on term loan and there were persistent irregularities in the operation of its credit limits with the bank. While both (a) and (b) were required to be satisfied in the case of larger small-scale units, it was to suffice if either alternative (a) or (b) was satisfied in the case of tiny and decentralized sector units.

Symptoms of Industrial Sickness

The persistence of various signals over a long period of time becomes symptoms of sickness. The various symptoms ultimately reflect on plant performance, capacity utilization, financial ratios, share market price and practices in the diverse areas of finance, production, marketing and labour relations in the industry. Some of the important symptoms which characterize industrial sickness are given below:

(i) Persisting Shortage of Cash;
(ii) Deteriorating Financial Ratios;
(iii) Widespread Use of Creative Accounting;
(iv) Continuous Tumble in the Prices of the Shares;
(v) Frequent Request to Banks and Financial Institutions for Loans;
(vi) Delay and Default in the Payment of Statutory Dues;
(vii) Delay in the Audit of Annual Accounts; and
(viii) Morale Degradation of Employees and Desperation Among the Top and Middle Management Level.

However, the financial ratios, in all cases, cannot be considered as true symptoms of industrial sickness mainly due to two reasons. **First**, the sickness prone units, in order to present a better and sound image do a lot of window dressing. **Second,** the financial data is available after a gap of one year. However, an early identification of signals and symptoms of industrial sickness makes the task of detecting sickness easier.

Causes of Industrial Sickness

Causes of industrial sickness are usually divided into two categories:

(i) External; and
(ii) Internal.

The former include factors which originate outside the unit and, therefore, are not under the control of the unit such as power cuts, demand (or market) recession, erratic availability of inputs, government policies, etc. The latter include factors which originate within the unit and can, therefore, be said to be under the control of the unit such as production, management, finance etc.

External Causes

(1) ***Power Cuts:*** A large number of industrial units face power cuts from time to time. These power cuts are imposed by the state governments as the generation of power is considerably below its actual requirements. Drought situation during some years in a number of states further aggravated the problem and acute power shortage resulted in frequent power cuts.

(2) ***Erratic Supply of Inputs:*** Some units depend on scarce raw materials whose supply is erratic. This results in disturbing the production schedule causing losses to the unit. This often happens in the case of units depending upon the supply of imported inputs. Insufficient availability of transport facilities (like shortage of wagons etc.) can also upset the supply schedule of inputs.

(3) ***Demand and credit restraints:*** At times, recession in the market causes a steep decline in the demand resulting in unsold stocks and losses to individual units. Products with high prices for example tractors, trucks, buses, cars, etc. depend for their sustained demand on easy availability of credit to purchasers. If credit restraints are imposed so that the purchasers are not able to arrange finance, the demand for these products are bound to suffer.

This is likely to leave the manufacturers with unsold stocks inflicting losses on them. If this situation persists for quite some time, the producing units are prone to turn sick. This problem can emerge in a serious way for ancillary units. If the demand of the principle buyer of the output of ancillary units falls due to any reason whatsoever, these units are put in a precarious position. They are bound to turn sick and may even face closure.

(4) ***Government Policy:*** Sudden changes in the government policy relating to imports, exports, industrial licensing, and taxation etc., can make viable units sick overnight. For instance, liberal import policy for a particular product can inflict serious damage on the domestic unit(s) producing similar/substitute products. The very existence of these domestic units are likely to be threatened particularly if the imported product is cheaper and is of a better quality as compared to their products. In a similar way, granting of liberal licenses to big industrial houses in the production lines reserved exclusively for the small-scale sector is bound to affect the prospects of the units in the latter sector adversely. The opening up of the internal market to foreign competition in recent years in line with India's commitments to the World Trade Organisation (WTO) is making it difficult for many industrial units to survive. The most difficult problems are being faced by the small-scale industries that are now facing tough competition from cheap imports (particularly from China) on the one hand, and from large-scale industries (due to dereservation) on the other hand.

Internal Causes

(1) ***Faults at the Planning and Construction Stage:*** Faults can occur at the planning and construction stage itself. The first fault can be the wrong location of an industrial unit. If the place where the unit has been set up lacks infrastructural facilities, the unit is likely to face difficulties. The second fault can be the absence of market analysis. Some small-scale entrepreneurs plunge into production without bothering to find out the market potential of their product and this pushes them into difficulties later. At times, these small units do not 'plan' production properly. Some units start with an unbalanced capital structure some underestimate the project cost while some spend recklessly on unproductive assets. In all these cases either the implementation of the small-scale project is delayed or production is started under severe handicaps. A slight disturbance in the normal functioning of these units is sufficient to disturb their 'balance' and turn them into sick units.

(2) ***Defective Plant and Machinery:*** Many entrepreneurs in the small scale sector do not seek professional and technical guidance from competent authorities in choosing correct machinery. If the plant and machinery finally selected and installed by them turns out to be defective, their units are bound to suffer losses and will in all probability turn sick.

Not only this, at times, the technology adopted by the entrepreneur obsolete and inappropriate. Production with the help of such technology is bound to be inferior in quality as compared to the production using modern and appropriate technology. Units employing obsolete and inappropriate technology are also likely to suffer a cost and price disadvantage *vis-à-vis* units employing modern technology.

(3) ***Financial Problems:*** A number of units face acute financial problems right from the stage of planning and construction to the stage of implementation and beyond. The equity base of many small scale units is very weak and slight disturbances in the market put them under acute financial strain. Often small scale units borrow from banks and financial institutions but are unable to meet the repayment schedules. The burden of unpaid debt accumulates and they turn sick. In some cases, lack of support from banks causes a failure of small scale units as the banks insist on 'proven performance' either to restore working capital limits or to enhance existing limits.

(4) ***Entrepreneurial Incompetence:*** Many persons setting up small-scale units are 'incompetent entrepreneurs' in the sense that they do not possess basic technical knowledge of the product they intend manufacturing, lack basic business acumen, do not know the costing of their products, have no knowledge of business accounts, marketing etc. No wonder then that units set up by such people turn sick.

(5) *Management Problems:* The most important internal cause of sickness is management problems. Faculty managerial decisions in the fields of production, marketing, finance, personnel management etc., can ruin a business. For instance, lack of inventory and materials management, inadequate attention towards maintenance management (leading to frequent breakdowns and consequent lower capacity utilization), absence of quality control systems etc. are some examples of mis-management in the sphere of production. Insufficient sales promotion activities and improper pricing policies can create problems in the field of marketing. Inefficient use of working capital can cause financial mismanagement. Faults in personnel management include improper wage, increment and promotion policies, and lack of manpower planning and bad industrial relations.

(6) *Labour Problems:* In some cases, acute labour have resulted in strikes, lock-outs and even closure of industrial units. These problems may emanate from differences with management over the issue of wages, bonus, suspensions and retrenchment, inter-union rivalry, etc. If not tackled in time satisfactorily such problems can cause sickness.

Consequences of Industrial Sickness

In a planned and underdeveloped labour surplus economy like India, industrial sickness can have serious consequences as would be clear from the discussion below:

(1) *Setback to Employment Prospects:* India is a labour surplus economy where avenues of employment are very much restricted in relation to the number of people seeking employment. Accordingly, closure of industrial units is likely to render workers unemployed. The implications are likely to be particularly serious if the sick industrial unit is a large one employing a large number of people (say, for instance, a huge cotton textile mill).

(2) *Fear of Industrial Unrest:* Closure of a sick industrial unit (particularly if it is a large one) not only causes substantial unemployment, it also causes wide spread labour unrest. Trade unions of other industries are likely to oppose retrenchment of labour of the closed unit and resort to widespread industrial strikes. The peace and tranquility of the industrial environment will be threatened resulting in industrial losses and setback to production in a number of units.

(3) *Wastage of Resources:* Resources are scarce in an underdeveloped economy and if an industrial unit turns sick and is closed down on this account, resources invested in that unit are wasted. This problem is particularly serious for large scale sick units where substantial investments have been made in plant and machinery. Stoppage of production in these units not only results in a decline in production of the industry as a whole, it also implies the blocking up of valuable savings and capital equipment.

(4) *Adverse Impact on Related Units:* Frequently an industrial unit is linked up with a number of other industrial units through backward and forward linkages. Therefore, sickness in one unit is likely to affect adversely a number of other units. For instance, iron and steel industry is linked up with a number of other industries via backward and forward linkages. Accordingly, sickness in a large unit manufacturing iron and steel is likely to have adverse repercussions on a number of other units.

(5) *Adverse Effect on Investors and Entrepreneurs:* Closure or liquidation of a large sick unit creates a psychology of despair amongst investors. The share price of that unit will tumble down and the prevalence of gloomy market conditions can adversely affect the entire stock market. Not only this. Failure of a unit acts as a disincentive to other entrepreneurs who were planning to launch production in the same lines. Such industrial climate is not conducive for industrial development.

(6) *Losses to Banks and Financial Institutions:* Closure of industrial units causes substantial financial losses to banks and financial institutions which had granted loans to these units to set up their plant and machinery and commence production. Locking up of funds in the sick units also affects adversely the future lending programmes of banks and financial institutions as shortage of resources emerges. Data given earlier shows that the amount of bank credit outstanding against the large and medium sick industrial units amounted to ₹ 33,838 crore at end March 2006, while the amount of bank credit outstanding against the small scale sick industrial units touched ₹ 4,981 crores. While banks and financial institutions do initiate legal proceedings against defaulters after giving them reasonable time for repayment, the recovery of over dues takes a very long time and, in some cases, the recovered amount falls short of actual overdue.

(7) *Loss of Revenue to Government:* The Central, State and local governments raise substantial revenue from industrial units by way of various levies. Therefore, sickness in industrial units results in loss of revenue to these levels of government.

Remedial Measures to Overcome and Avoid Industrial Sickness

On account of the above consequences of industrial sickness, it was for long regarded as a 'social' problem' in our country, accordingly, various concessions and incentives were offered to sick units to help them regain their 'health' and stand on their feet once again. Some of measures undertaken for the revival and rehabilitation of sick industrial units were as follows:

(1) *Steps taken by banks:* The commercial banks granted various concessions to sick industrial units like:

(i) Grant of additional working capital facilities to overcome the shortage of working capital faced by such units;
(ii) Recovery of interest at reduced rates;
(iii) Suitable moratorium on payment of interest;
(iv) Freezing a portion of the outstanding in the accounts, etc.

A number of steps were also undertaken on the organizational front like:

(i) setting up a sick industrial undertakings cell in Reserve Bank of India to function as a clearing house for information relating to sick units and to act as a co-coordinating agency between the government, banks, financial institutions and other agencies for tackling the various related issues;
(ii) setting up of State level inter-institutional committees at all the regional offices of the Department of Banking Operations and Development of the Reserve Bank of India for ensuring better co-ordination between the banks, State governments, Central and State level financial institutions and other agencies;
(iii) constitution of a standing co-ordination committee by Reserve Bank to consider the issues relating to co-ordination between commercial banks and term-lending institutions on an ongoing basis; and
(iv) setting up of a special cell within the rehabilitation finance division of Industrial Development Bank of India for attending to references from banks in respect of their sick and problem areas. As regards the small-scale industries, Reserve Bank issued guidelines to the banks with a view to ensuring that the potentially viable sick units in small-scale industries sector receive due attention and timely support.

(2) *Policy Framework of the Government:* The policy framework in respect of measures to deal with the problem of industrial sickness was laid down in the guidelines issued in October 1981 (which were subsequently modified in February 1982) for guidance of Administrative Ministries of the Central Government, State Government and financial institutions. Under these guidelines, the Administrative ministries in the government were given specific responsibility for prevention and remedial action in relation to sickness in industrial sector within their respective charge. They were required to monitor sickness and co-ordinate action for revival and rehabilitation of sick units. The financial institutions were asked to strengthen the monitoring system so that timely corrective action could be taken to prevent incipient sickness. To restore the sick unit to 'health', the financial institutions could even consider assuming managerial responsibility. However, where the banks and financial institutions felt that a sick unit cannot be revived, they could deal with their outstanding dues to the unit in accordance with the normal banking procedures. Before doing so, they were required to report the matter to the government who was then to decide whether some measures (like nationalization or workers' participation in management) could revive the unit. If the government decided to nationalize the unit its management could be taken over under the provisions of the Industries Development and Regulation Act 1951, for a period of six months to enable government to take necessary steps for nationalization. The government could also consider steps such as restructuring, merger with healthy units etc. to rehabilitate the sick. Where revival did not seem possible, the government could denotify the unit resulting in its closure.

(3) *Concessions by Government:* Certain concessions were also provided by the government to assist revival of sick units without intervention. For instance, the Income Tax Act was amended in 1977 by addition of Section 72 A which provided for the grant of tax benefit to healthy units when they took over the sick units by amalgamation with a view to reviving them. On January 1, 1982 a scheme for provision of margin money to sick units in the small scale sector at soft terms was introduced to enable them to obtain necessary funds from banks and financial institutions to implement their revival scheme. This was followed by the introduction of a liberalized margin money scheme in June 1987 to supplement the efforts of the state governments in reducing sickness in the small scale sector. In October 1989, the government announced a scheme for the grant of excise loan to sick/weak industrial units. Under this scheme, selected sick units were eligible for excise loan not exceeding 50 per cent of the excise duty actually paid for 5 years.

(4) *Steps for Detecting Sickness Early:* Importance of detecting sickness in incipient stage is crucial as corrective steps can then be taken early and well in time. With this end in view, the Reserve Bank advised banks to take necessary remedial steps in respect of industrial units which do not come under the purview of Sick Industrial Companies (special Provisions) Act, 1985, at the stage of 50 per cent erosion of their net worth. The Reserve Bank has also closely monitored certain specific industries where sickness is more widespread.

(5) *The Industrial Investment Bank of India:* The government established the Industrial Reconstruction Corporation of India (IRCI) with a view of reviving and rehabilitating sick units. The authorized capital and paid up capital of IRCI were ₹ 25 crore and ₹ 2.5 crore, respectively. Its share capital was subscribed by IDBI, IFCI, ICICI, LIC, State Bank of India and commercial banks. It also received a ₹ 10 crore interest free loan from the government of India. Functions assigned to IRCI were as follows:

(i) to provide financial assistance to sick industrial units;
(ii) to provide managerial and technical assistance to sick industrial units;
(iii) to secure assistance of other financial institutions and the government agencies for ensuring the revival and rehabilitation of sick industrial units;
(iv) to provide merchant banking services for amalgamation, merger etc; and
(v) to provide consultancy services to banks in matters relating to sick industrial units.

By a notification issued on March 20,1985, the government converted the IRCI (which was a company registered under the Companies Act) into a statutory corporation & it was given the name Industrial Reconstruction Bank of India (IRBI) with a view to overcoming the inherent difficulties which had been faced by the IRCI in its efforts to rehabilitate sick industrial units. IRBI was reconstituted into a full-fledged all purpose development financial institution with effect from March 27, 1997 & its new name is Industrial Investment Bank of India Ltd.(IIBI).

(6) *Board of Industrial and Financial Reconstruction:* In terms of the Sick Industrial Companies (Special Provisions) Act, 1985 (SICA), the government of India setup the board for Industrial and Financial Reconstruction (BIFR) in January 1987 (which became operational on May 15, 1987) for determining the preventive, ameliorative, remedial and other measures which are required to be taken in respect of sick industrial companies and for expeditious enforcement of the measures determined. Industrial Companies whose net-worth had been eroded completely and those which had net-worth eroded by 50 per cent or more were required to make a reference to the BIFR under sections 15 and 23 of the Act, respectively. While references received under section 15 were required to be enquired into, there was no such requirement in respect of references received under section 23. Public sector enterprises were brought within the purview of BIFR through an amendment of the Sick Industrial Companies (Special Provisions) Act in December 1991.

The Board could, if it deemed necessary, require by order, an operating agency to enquire into and make a report with respect to such matters as may be specified in the order. In case, where sickness was confirmed, BIFR was asked to determine the course of action to be followed with regard to the company. This course of action could be:

(a) Allowing the company time on its own, i.e. as per the scheme already initiated by the banks/ institutions to make its net-worth positive within a reasonable period;

(b) Having a scheme prepared through the operating agency in respect of the company; or

(c) Deciding on the winding up of the company.

The subject matters that could be covered were wide ranging and the powers of the Board extended to the framing of the scheme of amalgamation and reconstruction, financial and otherwise. Where the scheme related to preventive, remedial and other measures with respect to any Sick Industrial Company, the scheme could provide for financial assistance by way of loans, advances, guarantees, reliefs or concessions from official agencies. Where the Board after making enquiry and after consideration of all the relevant facts felt that it was just and equitable for the Sick industrial company to wind up its operations, it could record and forward its opinion to the concerned High Court.

Since its inception in May 1987 till the end of December 2007, BIFR had received 7,158 references under SICA, 1985. These references included 297 references from central and State Public Sector Undertakings. Out of the total references received, 5,471 were registered under section 15 of SICA. While 1,857 references were dismissed as non-maintainable under the Act, 825 rehabilitation schemes were sanctioned: and, 1,337 companies were recommended to be wound up.

The working of BIFR has been a subject of much debate and criticism. This is due to the reason that there are considerable delays in the BIFR process. In many cases the delay can extend to two years or even more. Such inordinate delays make it very difficult for a sick company (Which already reports negative net-worth on the current definition of SICA) to turnaround successfully and rehabilitate itself. The Committee on Industrial Sickness and Corporate Restructuring which submitted its Report in July 1993, stated that the quasi-judicial nature of BIFR proceedings further compounded the problems as it depends on consensus at almost all stages. "Consensus gives any claimant the right to veto, and implies that the BIFR process can be only as fast as the slowest party" The Committee also noted the absence of 'credible threats' to expedite negotiations and criticized BIFR for its clear preference for rehabilitation over winding up.

Summing Up

The problem of sickness in industries has become very acute in India. It has adversely affected the 'health' of the industrial sector in particular and the economy in general.

Definition

Prior to the enactment of the Sick Industrial Companies (Special Provision) Act, 1985, there was no unanimity regarding the definition of industrial sickness. Reserve Bank of India, term lending institutions and State Bank of India all defined sick industries in different ways. However, enactment of the **Sick Industrial Companies (Special Provisions) Act, 1985,** settled the issue. According to this Act, a sick unit was defined as *"an industrial company (being a company registered for not less than seven years) which has at the end of any financial year accumulated losses equal to or exceeding its entire net worth and has also suffered cash losses in such financial year and the financial year immediately preceding such financial year"*. In December 1991, public sector companies were also brought under the purview of the Act. The 1992 amendment (introduced in February 1994) altered the criterion somewhat: firms only need to be registered for five years, and the criterion of cash losses for two successive years was eliminated.

As far as small-scale sector is concerned, that small-scale industrial unit was considered to be sick that had:

(a) incurred a cash loss in the previous accounting year and was likely to continue with losses in the current accounting year and erosions on account of cumulative cash losses to the extent of 50 per cent or more of its peak net worth during the last five years; and/or

(b) Continuously defaulted in meeting four consecutive installments of interest or two - half yearly installments of principle on term loan and there were persistent irregularities in the operation of its credit limits with the bank. While both (a) and (b) were required to be satisfied in the case of larger small-scale units, it was to suffice if either alternative (a) or (b) was satisfied in the case of tiny and decentralized sector units.

Symptoms of Industrial Sickness

The persistence of various signals over a long period of time becomes symptoms of sickness. The various symptoms ultimately reflect on plant performance, capacity utilization, financial ratios, share market price and practices in the diverse areas of finance, production, marketing and labour relations in the industry. Some of the important symptoms which characterize industrial sickness are given below:

(i) persisting shortage of cash;

(ii) deteriorating financial ratios;

(iii) widespread use of creative accounting;

(iv) continuous tumble in the prices of the shares;

(v) frequent request to banks and financial institutions for loans;

(vi) delay and default in the payment of statutory dues;

(vii) delay in the audit of annual accounts; and

(viii) morale degradation of employees and desperation among the top and middle management level.

However, the financial ratios, in all cases, cannot be considered as true symptoms of industrial sickness mainly due to two reasons. First, the sickness prone units, in order to present a better and sound image do a lot of window dressing. Second, the financial data is available after a gap of one year. However, an early identification of signals and symptoms of industrial sickness makes the task of detecting sickness easier.

Causes of Industrial Sickness

Causes of industrial sickness are usually divided into two categories:

(i) **External Causes;** and

(ii) **Internal Causes.**

The former include factors which originate outside the unit and, therefore, are not under the control of the unit such as power cuts, demand (or market) recession, erratic availability of inputs, government policies, etc. The latter include factors which originate within the unit and can, therefore, be said to be under the control of the unit such as production, management, finance etc.

External Causes

Power cuts; erratic supply of inputs; Demand and credit restraints; and Government policy.

Internal Causes

Faults at the planning and construction stage; Defective plant and machinery; Financial problems; Entrepreneurial incompetence; Management problems; and Labour problems.

Consequences of Industrial Sickness

In a planned and underdeveloped labour surplus economy like India, industrial sickness can have serious consequences as below: Setback to employment prospects; Fear of industrial unrest; Wastage of resources; Adverse impact on related units; Adverse effect on investors and entrepreneurs; Losses to banks and financial institutions; and Loss of revenue to government.

Remedial Measures to Overcome and Avoid Industrial Sickness

On account of the above consequences of industrial sickness, it was for long regarded as a 'social' problem' in our country, accordingly, various concessions and incentives were offered to sick units to help them regain their 'health' and stand on their feet once again. Some of measures undertaken for the revival and rehabilitation of sick industrial units are steps taken by banks; Policy framework of the government; Concessions by government; Steps for detecting sickness early; The Industrial Investment Bank of India; and Board of industrial and Financial Reconstruction.

21 INNOVATION IN ENTREPRENEURSHIP

Introduction, Purposeful Innovation, Seven Sources for Innovative Opportunity, The Characteristics of Knowledge-based Innovation, What knowledge-based Innovation Requires? Principles of Purposeful Innovation, Summing Up.

Introduction

Innovation is the specific instrument of entrepreneurship. It is the act that endows resources with a new capacity to create wealth. Innovations indeed, create a resource. There is no such thing as a 'resource' until man finds a use for something in nature and thus endows it with economic value and there is no greater resource in an economy than 'purchasing power'. But purchasing power is the creation of the innovating entrepreneur.

Purposeful Innovation

The American farmer had virtually no purchasing power in the early nineteenth century; he therefore could not buy farm machinery. There were dozens of harvesting machines on the market, but, however, much he might have wanted them, the farmer would not pay for them. Then one of the many harvesting machine inventors, **Cyrus McCormick**, invented installment buying. This enabled the farmer to pay for a harvesting machine out of his future earnings rather than out of past savings-and suddenly the farmer had 'purchasing power' to buy farm equipment. Innovation does not have to be technical, does not indeed have to be a 'thing' altogether. Few technical innovations can compete in terms of impact with social innovation. For instance, from the time Japan opened her doors to the modern world in 1867, Japan has been consistently underrated by westerners, despite her successful defeats of China and then Russia in 1894 and 1905, respectively; despite Pearl Harbor; and despite her sudden emergence as an economic superpower and the toughest competition in the world market of the 1970s and 1980s. A major reason, perhaps the major one, is the prevailing belief that innovation has to do with things and is based on science or technology. And the Japanese, so the common belief has held, are not innovators but imitators, for the Japanese have not, by and large, produced outstanding technical or scientific innovations. Their success is based on social innovation. The Japanese made a deliberate decision a hundred years ago to concentrate their resources on social innovations, and to imitate, impart and adopt technical innovations with starting success.

We cannot yet develop a theory of innovation. But we already know enough to say when, where and how one looks systematically for innovative opportunities, and how one judge the chances for their success or the risks of their failure. We know enough to develop, though still only in outline farm, the practice of innovation.

Seven Sources for Innovative Opportunity

Entrepreneur will have to learn to practice systematic innovation. Specifically, systematic innovation means monitoring seven sources for innovative opportunity.

The **first four** sources lie within the enterprise, whether business or public-service sector. They are therefore visible primarily to people within that industry or service sector. They are basically symptoms. But they are highly reliable indication of changes that have already happened or can be made to happen with little effort. The second set of sources for innovative opportunity, a set of **three**, involves change outside the enterprise or industry. These **seven** source areas are:-

I. The unexpected–the unexpected success, the unexpected failure, the unexpected outside event;
II. The incongruity–between reality as it actually is and reality as it is assumed to be or as it 'ought to be';
III. Need as a source of innovation;
IV. Changes in industry structure or market structure that catches everyone unawares;
V. Demographic (population changes);
VI. Changes in perception, mood and meaning; and
VII. New knowledge, both scientific and non-scientific.

I. The Unexpected

(a) ***The unexpected success:*** The unexpected success is a challenge to management's judgment. One reason why it is difficult for management to accept unexpected success is that all of us tend to believe that anything that has lasted a fair amount of time must be 'normal' and go on 'forever'. Anything that contradict what we have come to consider a law of nature is then rejected as unsound, unhealthy, and obviously abnormal.

This explains for instance, why one of the major U.S. steel companies around 1970, rejected the mini-mill. Management knows that its steelworks were rapidly becoming obsolete and would need billions of dollars of investment to be modernized. It also known that it could not obtain the necessary firms. A new, smaller "mini-mill" was the solution.

Almost by accident, such a "mini-mill" was acquired. It soon began to grow rapidly and to generate cash and profits some of the younger men within the steel company, therefore proposed that the available investment funds be used to acquire additional 'mini-mills' and to build new ones. Top management vetoed the proposal. But ten years later the only parts of the steel industry in America that were still healthy, growing and reasonably prosperous were 'mini-mills.

The expected success is not just an opportunities for innovation; it demands innovation. It forces us to ask, what basic changes are now appropriate for the organization in the way it defines its business, its technology, its markets. If these questions are faced up to, then unexpected success is likely to open up the most rewarding and least risky of all innovative opportunities.

(b) ***The unexpected failure:*** Failure, unlike successes, cannot be rejected and rarely go unnoticed. A good many failures are of course, nothing but mistakes the results of greed, stupidity thoughtless bandwagon-climbing, or incompetence whether in design or execution. Yet it something fails despite being carefully planned, carefully designed, and conscientiously executed, that failure often bespeaks underlying change and, with it, opportunity.

The unexpected failure demands that you go out, look around and listen. Failure should always be considered a symptom of an innovative opportunity, and taken seriously as such. For instance the result of **Ford's** decision to go out and investigate was the one genuine innovation in the American automobile industry since **Alfred P. Sloan**, in the 1920s, had defined the socio-economic segmentation of the American market into 'low', 'lower-middle', 'upper-middle', and 'upper' segments, the insight on which he then built the General Motors company. When the Ford people went out, they discovered that this segmentation was rapidly being replaced or at least paralleled by another quite different one, the one we would now call lifestyle segmentation. The result, within a short period after the **Edsel's** failure, was the appearance ford's Thunderbird, the greatest success of any American car since **Henry Ford, Sr**. had introduced his Model T in 1908. The Thunderbird established Ford again as a major producer in its own right, rather than as General Motor's Kid brother and a perennial imitator.

(c) *The unexpected outside event:* Unexpected success and unexpected failure occurs within a business or an industry. But outside events are the events that are not recorded in the information. The unexpected outside event may be an opportunity to apply already existing expertise to a new application. But to an application that does not change the nature of the 'business we are in'. It may be extension rather than diversification. For instance, the United States has never been a book buying country, in part because of the ubiquitous free public library. When TV appeared in the early fifties and more and more American's began to spend more and more of their time in front of the tube–particularly people in their prime book-reading years, that is people of high school and college-age 'everyone knew' that book sales would drop drastically. Book publishers frantically began to diversify into 'high-tech media': educational movies or computer programs. But instead of collapsing, book sales in the United States have soared since TV first came in. They have grown several times as every indication had predicated, whether family incomes, total population in the 'book-reading years' or even people with higher degrees.

Both the publishers and the existing book stores knew of course all along those book sales were soaring. Neither, however, did anything about it. The unexpected event was exploited instead, by a few mass retailers such as department stores in Minneapolis and Los Angeles. Traditionally, book sellers were themselves 'Literary types' and tried to hire people who 'love books'. The managers of the new bookstores are former cosmetics salespeople. For ten years now these new bookstore chains have been among the most successful and fastest growing segments in American retailing and among the fastest-growing new business in this country altogether.

II. Incongruities

An incongruity is a discrepancy, a dissonance, between what is and what 'ought' to be, or between what is and what everybody assumes it to be. It bespeaks an underlying 'fault' to use the geologists term, such a fault is an invitation to innovate. Incongruities are qualitative rather than quantitative.

Like the unexpected event, whether success or failure, incongruity is a symptom of change, either change that has already occurred or change that can be made to happen. Like the changes that underlie the unexpected event, the changes that underlie incongruity are changes within an industry, a market, a process.

There are several kinds of incongruity:

- Incongruous economic realities.
- Incongruity between reality and the assumptions about it.
- Incongruity between perceived and actual customer values and expectations.
- Incongruity within the rhythm or logic of a process.
- ***Incongruity between Economic Realities:*** If the demand for a product or a service is growing steadily, its economic performance should steadily improve, too. It should be easy to be profitable in an industry with steadily rising demand. A lack of profitability and results in such an industry bespeaks an incongruity between economic realities.

- ***The Incongruity between Reality and the Assumptions about it:*** Whenever the people in an industry or a service misconceive reality, whenever they therefore make erroneous assumptions about it, their efforts will be misdirected. They will concentrate on the area where results do not exist. Then there is an incongruity between reality and behaviour, an incongruity that once again offers opportunity for successful innovation to whoever can perceive and exploit it.
- ***The Congruity between Perceived and Actual Customer Values and Expectations:*** Producer and suppliers almost always misconceive what it is the customer actually buys. They must assume that what represents 'value' to the producer and supplier is equally 'value' to the customer. People who make cosmetics must believe in them; otherwise 'they turn out interior quality of products and soon lose their customers. People who sees a hospital must believe in health care as an absolute 'good' or the quality of medical and patient care will deteriorate fast.
- ***Incongruity within the Rhythm or Logic of a Process:*** The incongruity within a process, its rhythm or its logic, is not a very subtle matter. Users are always aware of it. Every eye surgeon knew about the discomfort he felt when he had to cut eye muscle-and talked about the frustration of his lawn customers-and talked about it. What was lacking, however, was someone willing to listen, somebody who took seriously what everybody proclaims: 'the purpose of a product or a service is to satisfy the customer.' If this axiom is accepted and acted upon, using incongruity as an opportunity for innovation becomes fairly easy and highly effective.

III. Process Need

Process need, is not like the other sources of innovation, does not start out with an event in the environment, whether internal or external. It starts out with the job to be done. It is task focused rather than situation-focused. It perfects a process that already exists replaces a link that is weak, redesigns an existing old process around newly available knowledge. Sometimes it makes possible a process by supplying the 'missing link.'

Opportunity is the source of innovation. Opportunity for innovation based on process needs can be found systematically. But once a process needs has been found, it has to be tested against the five basic criteria:

- A self-contained process;
- One 'weak' or 'missing' link;
- A clear definition of the objective;
- That the specifications for the solution can be defined clearly; and
- Widespread realization that 'there ought to be a better way', that is, high receptivity.

Then, finally, the process need opportunity has to be tested also against the three constraints

- Do we understand what is needed?
- Is the knowledge available or can it be procured within the 'State-of-the-art?' and
- And does the solution fit, or does it violate the morals and values of the intended users?

IV. Industry and Markct Structures

A change in market or industry structure is a major opportunity for innovation. In industry structure, a change requires entrepreneurship from every member of the industry. A change in industries structure offers exceptional opportunities, highly visible and quite predictable to outsiders. But the insiders perceive these same changes primarily as threats.

Innovations that exploit changes in industry structure are particularly effective if the industry and its markets are dominated by a one very large manufacturer or supplier or by a very few. Even if there is no true monopoly, these large, dominant producers and suppliers, having been successful and unchallenged for many years, lend to be arrogant.

V. Demographics

Demographics changes defined as changes in population, size, age structure, composition, employment, education, status, and income. They are unambiguous. They have the most predictable consequences.

Demographics have major impact on what will be bought, by whom and in what quantities. For instance, American teenagers buy a good many pairs of cheap shoes a year; they buy for fashion, not durability, and their purpose are limited. The same people, ten years later, will buy very few pairs of shoes a year-a sixth as many as they bought when they were seventeen- but they will buy them for comfort and durability first and for fashion second.

Demographics alone, the combined effects of the sharp drop in birth rates and of the 'education explosion' makes it near certain that traditional manual blue-collar employment in manufacturing in developed countries, by the year 2010, cannot be more than one-third or less than what it was in 1970.

What makes demographic a rewarding opportunity for the entrepreneur is precisely its neglect by decision makers, whether business men, public service staffs or governmental policymakers. They still cling to the assumption that demographics do not change or do not change fast. Indeed, they reject even the plainest evidence of demographic changes. Changing demographics is both a highly productive and highly dependable innovative opportunities genuinely for those willing to go out into the field, to look and to listen.

VI. Changes in Perception

Change in perception has created substantial innovative opportunities. For instance, a market for new health care magazines; one of them, American Health, reached a circulation of a million within two years. It created the opportunity for a substantial number of new and innovative businesses to exploit the fear of traditional foods causing irreparable damage.

Traditionally, the way people feed themselves was very largely a matter of income group and class. Ordinary people 'ate'; the rich 'dined'. This perception has changed within the last twenty years. Now the same people both 'eat' and 'dine '.

Whether sociologists or economists can explain the perceptional phenomenon is irrelevant. It remains a fact. Very often it cannot be quantified; or rather, by the time it can be quantified it is too late to serve as opportunity for innovation. But it is not exotic or intangible. It is concrete: it can be defined, tested and above all exploited.

VII. New Knowledge

Knowledge-based innovation is the 'super-star' of entrepreneurship. It is temperamental, capricious and hard to manage. It gets the publicity. It is what people normally mean when they talk of innovation. Of course, not all knowledge-based innovations are important. But amongst the history making innovation, Knowledge-based innovations rank high. The knowledge, however, is not necessarily scientific or technical. Social innovations based on knowledge can have equal or even greater impact. Knowledge-based innovation differs from all other innovation in its basic characteristics: time span, casualty rate, predictability, and in the challenges it poses to the entrepreneur.

The Characteristics of Knowledge-based Innovation

(1) *Longest Lead Time:* Knowledge-based information has the longest lead time of all innovations. There is first, a long time span between the emergence of new knowledge and its becoming applicable to knowledge. And then there is another long period before the new technology turns into products, processes, or services in the market place. The long lead time for knowledge-based innovations is by no means confined to science or technology. It applies equally to innovations that are based on non-scientific and non-technological knowledge.

(2) *Convergence:* The second characteristic of knowledge-based innovations and a truly unique one is that they are almost never based on one factor but on the convergence of several different kinds of knowledge, not all of them scientific or technological.

(3) *The Unique Risks:* Even when it is based on meticulous analysis, endowed with clear focus, and conscientiously managed, knowledge-based innovation still suffers from unique risks and worse an innate unpredictability. Which one will survive, which one will die and which one will become permanently crippled–able neither to live nor to die is unpredictable. So, there is the need to plough more and more money back into research, technical development, and services to stay in the race. There is no way to eliminate the element of risk no way even to reduce it. Market research does not work–one cannot do market research on something that does not exist. Opinion research is probably not just useless but likely to do damage. At least this is what the experience with 'expert opinion on the receptivity to knowledge-based innovation would indicate. Yet there is no choice. If we want knowledge-based innovation, we must gamble on receptivity to it.

What Knowledge-based Innovation Requires?

Its characteristics give knowledge-based innovation specific requirements. And these requirements differ from those of any other kind of innovation.

In the **first** place, knowledge-based innovation requires careful analysis of all the necessary factors whether knowledge itself, or social, economic or perpetual factors.

The **second** requirement of knowledge-based innovation is a clear focus on the strategic position.

Finally the knowledge-based innovation and especially the one whose innovation is based on scientific or technological knowledge needs to learn and to practice entrepreneurial management.

Principles of Purposeful Innovation

The purposeful innovation resulting from analysis, system, and hard work is all that can be discussed and presented as the practice of innovation. But this is all that need be presented since it surely covers at least 90 per cent of all effective innovations. And the extraordinary performer in innovation, as in every other area, will be effective only if grounded in the discipline and master of it.

What then, are the principles of innovation, representing the hardcore of the discipline? There are a number of 'dos–things that have to be done. There are also a few 'don'ts–things that had better not be done, and then there are what that would call 'conditions'.

The Dos

(1) ***Analysis of opportunities:*** Purposeful, systematic innovation begins with the analysis of the opportunities. An opportunity is the external force in the business environment. Opportunities are created out of sudden or deliberate changes. An entrepreneur should travel around for right opportunities while establishing a new enterprise. He has to begin with his new enterprise by selecting an appropriate opportunity out of obtainable options. It begins with the thinking of innovation which is called as the sources of innovative principles. But if he fails to do so, if he diverts himself from best opportunity, he has to undergo a number of hindrances coming in his way. Entrepreneur must make the use of available sources/data to take the opportunity. For instance; Chamber of Commerce and Industry, Government Agencies and Ministries publishes detailed information related to different schemes and export opportunity.

(2) ***Innovation is both conceptual and perpetual:*** The second imperative of innovation is to go out and look at the customers, the users, to see what their expectations, their values, and their need are. An innovation which can able to meet customer's expectation must be preferred. Innovator must designed the product as per the need, desire of the customers and must be user-friendly.

(3) ***Simple:*** An innovation has to be simple, should do only one thing, directed towards a specific target, clear and designed application. Innovator should never try to dump all things into one basket and repent later on while taking decision. There has to be consistency in the work. Objective must be well clear and easy to execute. For an effective innovation, it must be simple and focused. Work should be done in single, otherwise confusions would be created. Because it won't work if it is not simple.

(4) ***Start with small:*** Effective innovation is that innovation which starts with small. Small unit requires relatively low – capital cost, simple organisation, easy formation, efficient working, limited requirements and social benefits. Small units can facilitate a wide range of consumer, simple produced goods; and can economically produce domestically on a small scale basis. Hence, effective innovations starts small, *viz.*, few people and only a small and limited market.

(5) ***Achieve leadership from within environment:*** Leadership includes maintenance of smoothness and peacefulness in the business environment. Innovator must able to achieve leadership within a given environment in order to exploits an innovation. Otherwise, they will simply create an opportunity for the competitors. Entrepreneurship can be developed in a society where its culture permits a variety of choice and where social processes are not rigid. A successful innovation aims at leadership.

The Don'ts

(1) ***Cleverness:*** The first is simply not to try to be clever. Innovation is to be handled by human beings. Anything too clever, whether in design or execution, is almost bound to fail.

(2) ***Diversification:*** Don't diversify, don't splinter, and don't try to do too many things at once. Innovations that stray from a core are likely to become diffuse.

(3) ***Innovation for the future:*** Finally, don't try to innovate for the future. Innovate for the present. Demand for future Innovation is uncertain and the probability for the future demand is unknown. Hence it is baseless to work for unpredictable market.

Three Conditions

Three conditions are to be fulfilled. All three are obvious but often go disregarded.

(1) ***Innovation is Work:*** It requires knowledge. It often requires great ingenuity. When all is said and done, innovation becomes hard, focused on purposeful work, making very great demands on persistence and commitment.

(2) ***Innovation Means Strength:*** To survive in such hypercompetitive market, entrepreneur must undertake innovative project. Entrepreneur must be able to prove his potentiality with the help of strength of innovativeness. He must not forget that innovation is the need of the hour. To succeed, innovators must build on own their strengths.

(3) ***Market Focused:*** Innovation has to be close to the market, focused on the market, indeed market driven. Innovations have an effect on economy, society, customer's behaviour, and teachers.

Summing Up

Innovation is the specific instrument of entrepreneurship. It is the act that endows resources with a new capacity to create wealth. Innovations indeed, create a resource. There is no such thing as a 'resource' until man finds a use for something in nature and thus, endows it with economic value and there is no greater resource in an economy than 'purchasing power'. But purchasing power is the creation of the innovating entrepreneur.

Purposeful Innovation

Innovation does not have to be technical, does not indeed have to be a 'thing' altogether. Few technical innovations can compete in terms of impact with social innovation. The Japanese made a deliberate decision a hundred years ago to concentrate their resources on social innovations, and to imitate, impart and adopt technical innovations with starting success.

Seven Sources for Innovative Opportunity

Entrepreneur will have to learn to practice systematic innovation. Specifically, systematic innovation means monitoring seven sources for innovative opportunity.

The first four sources lie within the enterprise, whether business or public-service sector. They are therefore visible primarily to people within that industry or service sector. They are basically symptoms. But they are highly reliable indication of changes that have already happened or can be made to happen with little effort. The second set of sources for innovative opportunity, a set of three, involves change outside the enterprise or industry. These seven source areas are:-

I. The unexpected–the unexpected success, the unexpected failure, the unexpected outside event;
II. The incongruity–between reality as it actually is and reality as it is assumed to be or as it 'ought to be';
III. Need as a source of innovation;
IV. Changes in industry structure or market structure that catches everyone unawares;
V. Demographic (population changes);
VI. Changes in perception, mood and meaning; and
VII. New knowledge, both scientific and non-scientific.

I. The Unexpected

(a) ***The unexpected success:*** The unexpected success is a challenge to management's judgment. Anything that contradicts what we have come to consider a law of nature is then rejected as unsound, unhealthy, and obviously abnormal.

This explains for instance, why one of the major U.S. steel companies around 1970, rejected the mini-mill. Management knows that its steelworks were rapidly becoming obsolete and would need billions of dollars of investment to be modernized. It also known that it could not obtain the necessary firms. A new, smaller "mini-mill" was the solution.

(b) ***The unexpected failure:*** The unexpected failure demands that you go out, look around and listen. Failure should always be considered a symptom of an innovative opportunity, and taken seriously as such. For instance the result of Ford's decision to go out and investigate was the one genuine innovation in the American automobile industry since Alfred P. Sloan, in the 1920s, had defined the socio-economic segmentation of the American market into 'low', 'lower-middle', 'upper-middle', and 'upper' segments, the insight on which he then built the General Motors company. When the Ford people went out, they discovered that this segmentation was rapidly being replaced-or at least paralleled by another quite different one, the one we would now call 'lifestyle segmentation. The result, within a short period after the Edsel's failure, was the appearance Ford's Thunderbird, the greatest success of any American car since Henry Ford, Sr. had introduced his Model T in 1908. The Thunderbird established Ford again as a major producer in its own right, rather than as General Motor's Kid brother and a perennial imitator.

(c) *The unexpected outside event:* Outside events are the events that are not recorded in the information. The unexpected outside event may be an opportunity to apply already existing expertise to a new application, But to an application that does not change the nature of the 'business we are in'. When TV appeared in the early fifties and more and more American's began to spend more and more of their time in front of the tube-particularly people in their prime book-reading years, that is people of high school and college-age 'everyone knew' that book sales would drop drastically. Book publishers frantically began to diversity into 'high-tech media': educational movies, or computer programs. But instead of collapsing, book sales in the United States have soared since TV first came in. They have grown several times as every indication had predicated, whether family incomes, total population in the 'book-reading years' or even people with higher degrees.

II. Incongruities

An incongruity is a discrepancy, a dissonance, between what is and what 'ought' to be, or between what is and what everybody assumes it to be.

There are several kinds of incongruity:

- ***Incongruity between Economic Realities:*** A lack of profitability and results in such an industry bespeaks an incongruity between economic realities.
- ***The Incongruity between Reality and the Assumptions about it:*** Whenever the people in an industry or a service misconceive reality, whenever they therefore make erroneous assumptions about it, their efforts will be misdirected. They will concentrate on the area where results do not exist.
- ***The Congruity between Perceived and Actual Customer Values and Expectations:*** Producer and suppliers almost always misconceive what it is the customer actually buys. They must assume that what represents 'value' to the producer and supplier is equally 'value' to the customer.
- ***Incongruity within the Rhythm or Logic of a Process:*** The incongruity within a process, its rhythm or its logic, is not a very subtle matter. Users are always aware of it.

III. Process Need

Process need, is not like the other sources of innovation, and does not start out with an event in the environment, whether internal or external. It starts out with the job to be done. It is task focused rather than situation-focused. It perfects a process that already exists replaces a link that is weak, redesigns an existing old process around newly available knowledge. Sometimes it makes possible a process by supplying the 'missing link.'

IV. Industry and Market Structures

A change in industries structure offers exceptional opportunities, highly visible and quite predictable to outsiders. But the insiders perceive these same changes primarily as threats. Innovations that exploit changes in industry structure are particularly effective if the industry and its markets are dominated by a one very large manufacturer or supplier or by a very few.

V. Demographics

Demographics changes defined as changes in population, size, age structure, composition, employment, education, status, and income. They are unambiguous. They have the most predictable consequences.

Demographics have major impact on what will be bought, by whom and in what quantities. For instance, American teenagers buy a good many pairs of cheap shoes a year; they buy for fashion, not durability, and their purpose are limited. The same people, ten years later, will buy very few pairs of shoes a year–a sixth as many as they bought when they were seventeen– but they will buy them for comfort and durability first and for fashion second.

VI. Changes in Perception

Changes in perception has created substantial innovative opportunities. For instance, a market for new health care magazines; one of them, American Health, reached a circulation of a million within two years. It created the opportunity for a substantial number of new and innovative businesses to exploit the fear of traditional foods causing irreparable damage.

Whether sociologists or economists can explain the perceptional phenomenon is irrelevant. It remains a fact. Very often it cannot be quantified; or rather, by the time it can be quantified it is too late to serve as opportunity for innovation.

VII. New Knowledge

Knowledge-based innovation is the 'super-star' of entrepreneurship. It is temperamental, capricious and hard to manage. It gets the publicity. It is what people normally mean when they talk of innovation. The knowledge, however, is not necessarily scientific or technical. Social innovations based on knowledge can have equal or even greater impact. Knowledge-based innovation differs from all other innovation in its basic characteristics: time span, casualty rate, predictability, and in the challenges it poses to the entrepreneur.

The Characteristics of Knowledge-based Innovation

Longest Lead Time: There is first, a long time span between the emergence of new knowledge and its becoming applicable to knowledge. And then there is another long period before the new technology turns into products, processes, or services in the market place. The long lead time for knowledge-based innovations is by no means confined to science or technology. It applies equally to innovations that are based on non-scientific and non-technological knowledge.

Convergence: The second characteristic of knowledge-based innovations and a truly unique one is that they are almost never based on one factor but on the convergence of several different kinds of knowledge, not all of them scientific or technological.

The Unique Risks: Which one will survive, which one will die and which one will become permanently crippled-able neither to live nor to die is unpredictable.

What knowlege-baced Innovation Requires?

- Careful analysis of all the necessary factors; and
- clear focus on the strategic position.

Principles of Purposeful Innovation

The purposeful innovation resulting from analysis, system, and hard work is all that can be discussed and presented as the practice of innovation. What then, are the principles of innovation, representing the hardcore of the discipline? There are a number of 'dos-things that have to be done. There are also a few 'don'ts-things that had better not be done, and then there are what that would call 'conditions'.

22 BUSINESS INCUBATION

Introduction, Evolution of Business Incubators Definition, Historic Development of Business Incubators, Establishing Business Incubator, Types of Incubators, Value Framework of Business Incubator, Performance of Business Incubator in Industrially Developed Countries, What makes a Business Incubator Successful?, Business Incubators and Facilitators in India, How do Incubators help start-ups get funding?, Role of Business Incubator in the Present Scenario, Summing Up, Case Study, Annexure.

Introduction

The concept of an incubation was first initiated in the early 20th century itself at the Stanford University, California, USA, when the University President **David Starr Jordan** urged his staff to make personal investments in a company founded in the early nineties by **Cyril Elewell**, an engineering school graduate who worked on the first round of 'wireless' technologies, ship-to-shore radio communications where later many Stanford graduates began their career. The Stanford University staff knew that if they did not work hard and support to build industry infrastructure around **Stanford**, they would lose an advantage of making an early alliance with companies and thus, not have a mechanism in place where they could send their graduate to cut their teeth.

It was not too long after that time when **Stanford's** then President **Ray Lyman Wilber**, in return for half of the royalties on any patents developed, agreed to provide lab space and US$ 100 in parts to two brothers **Sigurd** and **Russel Varian**, thus, giving them a chance to develop what turned out to be the **Klystron** tube. **Russel** had a PhD. in physics and **Sigurd** was a pilot for Pan Am, interested in building a landing system that would work in fog and bad weather. The technology that the two brothers developed led to the possibility of building Radar system that was critical to the Battle of Britain and winning World War II!

About the same time, Professor **Fred Terman** brought together **Bill Hewlett** and **David Packard**, the names behind **Hewlett Packard**, together. Prof. **Terman** was concerned that electronics engineering graduates of **Stanford** could not find employment on the West Coast. As a solution, he encouraged his students and others to form companies in the **San Francisco** bay area and **Stanford** faculty to consult with them to help to create products. Prof.**Terman** made a personal investment of US$ 500 to the start-up efforts to **Hewlett Packard** apart from lending his expertise. Recently, **William** and **Flora Hewlett** Foundation gave US$ 400 million to **Stanford** who had no rights to anything created by HP (**Richards** 2002).Thus, technology grew in 60 square miles around Stanford University rapidly through the establishment of a strong 'entrepreneurial culture'.

Block Schematic Highlighting the Four Basic Elements that are Essential for Establishing BI

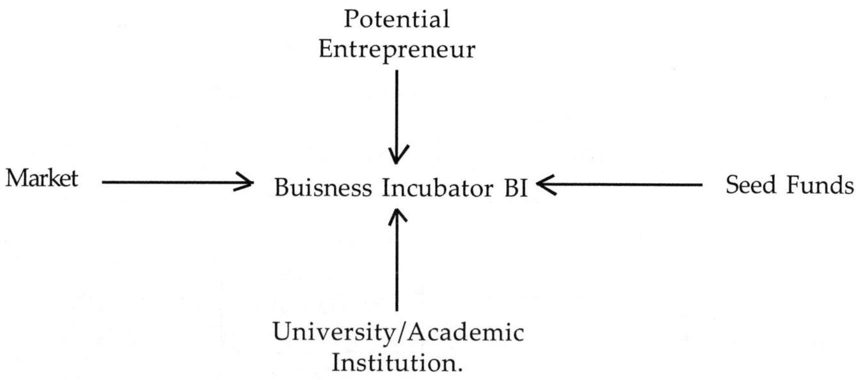

Evolution of Business Incubators–Definition

The term incubator literally means a climate-controlled environment that supports the early development, sometimes even saving the life of a 'new born'. In the economic development context, 'incubators' support the transformation of selected early stage business with high potential, into self-sufficient, growing and profitable enterprise. By reducing the risks during the early period of business formation, the incubator is intended to contribute to economic growth through sustaining new enterprises. *An incubator can also be defined as 'a facility that provides affordable space, shared office services and business development assistance in an environment conducive to new venture creation, survival and early stage growth'.*

Historic Development of Business Incubators (BIs)

In a rapidly changing global economy, small enterprises (SEs) are increasingly a force for national economic growth. Since 1980s, SEs and the entrepreneurs who drive them–have received serious attention by planners, legislators and development practitioners the world over. New structures and strategies are being explored that will help small businesses to start, survive and grow. In this quest, the business incubation centre has emerged as a recent innovation, harboring great potential as a tool for economic development. The new global economy is increasingly characterized by three processes: the overall lowering of trade barriers and concurrent emergence of regional trading blocs; the shift towards information and service-oriented activities, in order to create new competitive advantages in the world market and the downsizing of large organizations, together with mergers and acquisitions, in the face of this restructuring. These factors are in turn, shrinking opportunities for people to join labour force. Thus, those unemployed who are able are increasingly turning to the creation of entrepreneurial small business. Thus, there is a pressing need to build an entrepreneurial society which would facilitate smooth establishment and operation of enterprises.

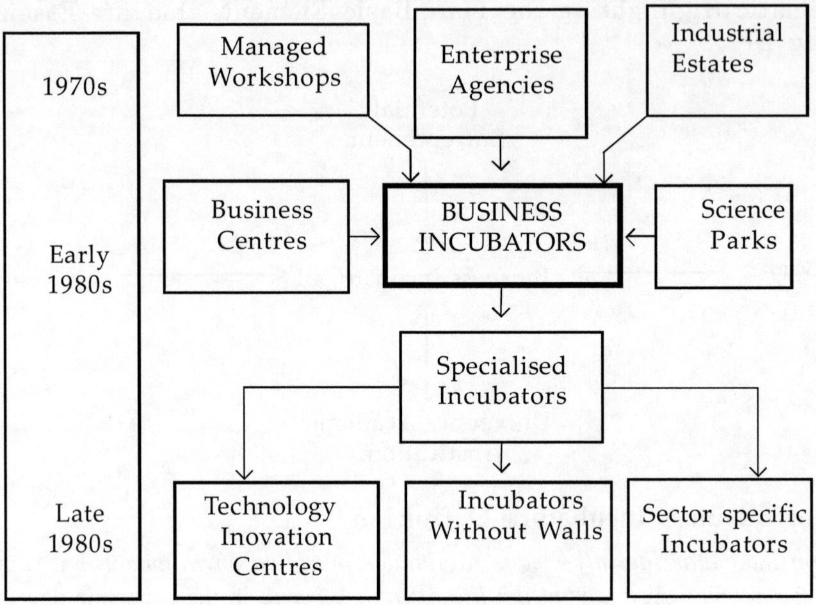

Early focus of many entrepreneurship development programmes was in creating awareness and training in the essentials of business operation, often for individual entrepreneurs. With the increasing need to understand technology, business strategies, forming the right management teams and management practices, emphasis is more on 'technical' and 'managerial' mentoring. Thus, Business Incubators (BIs) emerged in the early eighties out of precursor to SE programmes developed over two decades earlier.

Establishing Business Incubator

Business incubator (BI) focuses on nurturing the process of SE development. This kind of business development requires the provision of workspace and value-adding technical and managerial support. While establishing an incubator, the following aspects have to be considered:

(a) Mobilizing government support through funding, fully or partly, to initiate the concept, implement the operations plan and cover initial operations.

(b) Promoting active community participation and private industry membership of the governing and advisory boards, and their involvement as mentors, suppliers and customers.

(c) Organizing tenant support by a small but experienced management staff.

(d) Implementing the selection and graduation criteria, because the essential feature of the incubator is the development of viable tenant business within a relatively short period of time.

(e) Ensuring the financial stability of the incubator itself.

The fiscal discipline by management is a must, to enable the incubator to survive changes in the climate of government support and to set a proper example for entrepreneurs in reaching sustainability themselves.

Types of incubators

Developing a theme for an incubator involves creating special programmes directed towards specific kinds of businesses. During the past decade, a variety of themes have emerged to serve specific kinds of business needs:

(1) ***Targeted Population Incubator:*** A targeted population incubator enhances conventional incubation programme with specific features to support empowerment of specific populations, for example, women, fresh graduates and minorities.

(2) ***International Incubator:*** An international incubator encourages foreign investment, both financial and technology. Such as incubator often includes a range of services for international and expatriate professionals.

(3) ***Industrial Subcontracting:*** An industrial subcontracting orientation is built on linkages to large enterprises, supporting the development of new businesses as vendors, key features include quality control and scheduling.

(4) ***Single Business Incubators:*** Single business incubators will have programmes specifically tailored to the needs of a particular class of industrial products/services, for example, IT services, biotechnology, handicrafts, and so forth.

(5) ***University Incubators:*** University incubators specialize in supporting the development technologyor new process initiated by the faculty and staff of the university or based on some relationship to the university.

(6) ***Technology Business Incubators:*** Technology business incubators focusing on an overall local or national economic development programme, providing the expectation of highly paid, environmental-friendly, employment opportunities, although direct job creation may be modest, yet the ripple effect of their actions can extend the positive range of their impact.

(7) ***Hub Incubator:*** A hub incubator, with a full management team, can support a number of satellite incubators with a minimal staff and greater outreach possibilities. Such as incubator can reduce operational costs and increase impact of the incubator.

(8) ***Virtual Incubator:*** Virtual incubator of the incubator without walls has recently emerged, focusing on the provision of counseling to client businesses.

(9) ***Regional or Rural Incubator:*** Regional or rural incubator is focused on stimulating businesses which utilize local material and other resources, including local skill sets, primarily serving specified geographical areas.

Value Framework of Business Incubator

Indicates how when a BI is established, taking into account the key aspects explained early, it creates a value by ensuring balance between business ecosystem and social ecosystem:

(1) ***Entrepreneurship Development:*** Entrepreneurship development is the key value process that any government is looking at in the absence of growth in jobs, as this process would have greater possibility of job creation in the society.

(2) ***Mentoring Relationship:*** Mentoring relationship will play a key role in ensuring the success rate of the formation of an enterprise. India has a large pool of experienced academia and professionals who have either retired voluntarily or after attaining the superannuating age. This resource could be used for handholding the entrepreneurs in the initial stages with suitable soft skills training as well as technical support.

(3) ***Opportunities Assessment and Risk Evaluation:*** Opportunities assessment and risk evaluation is an area that normally an individual entrepreneur finds difficult to tackle. With the experience of screening committee members and business networking support, business incubators can add value to this activity.

(4) ***Seed Funding:*** Seed funding assumes importance once the business model and feasible business plan are in place. If the initial funding is tied up quickly, early launching of enterprise is possible, this will reduce the time to market the new product or service of the start-up. This is an area which rural entrepreneurs especially would find difficult to handle and the BI can play a significant role.

(5) ***Business Networks:*** Business networks of the incubator should help the entrepreneurs in finding a market for their product or service to an extent. Sometimes the entrepreneurs can find a market even in the cotenants of the incubator.

Thus, business incubators through their 'value frame work' bring about a fine balance between social ecosystem of creating jobs in the society, contributing to the economic growth and 'business ecosystem' of creating customers and suppliers for new products/services to meet the market needs utilizing the funds that are available in the public/private organizations

Performance of Business Incubator (BIs) in Industrially Developed Countries

The National Business Incubation Association (NBIA) reports that throughout the United States, small businesses generate approximately two out of every three new jobs. At almost any time, roughly seven million people are starting new businesses. All across the country, business incubators are providing entrepreneurs with tools that encourage technology transfer, enhance the local economy and create new jobs. NBIA has estimated recently that roughly 500 business incubators are operating in the United States alone.

The average single-site unit houses 19 tenant companies and incubates each one for around three years. In the UK, the survival rate of incubated businesses is around 80 per cent compared with around 50 per cent for those businesses based outside a unit. This is attributed to the level of support incubators offer (Whetting steel, 2000).

What makes a business incubator successful?

Incubator developers must first invest time and money in a feasibility study to lay the groundwork for a successful incubation programme. An effective feasibility study will help determine whether the proposed project has all the factors crucial to an incubator's success - a solid market, a sound financial base and strong community support.

Once established, model business incubation programmes commit to industry best practices such as structuring for financial sustainability, recruiting and appropriately compensating management with company-growing skills, building an effective board of directors, and prioritizing management's time to place the greatest emphasis on resident assistance.

Business Incubators and Facilitators in India

A Business Incubator is a facility designed to assist businesses to become established and sustainable during their start up phase. Typically, they do this by providing- shared premises, business advice, business services, access to investor, market and international networks, mentoring and a full-time, hands-on management team. Business incubators are programs designed to accelerate the successful development of entrepreneurial companies through an array of business support resources and services, developed and orchestrated by incubator management and offered both in the incubator and through its network of contacts. Incubators vary in the way they deliver their services, in their organizational structure, and in the types of clients they serve. Successful completion of a business incubation program increases the likelihood that a start-up company will stay in business for the long term.

The main goal of most business incubation programmes is to produce companies that create jobs and wealth in their communities. Business incubators nurture the development of entrepreneurial companies, helping them survive and grow during the start-up period, when they are most vulnerable.

Business incubators provide their resident companies with business support services and resources such as guidance, assistance with business planning and help obtaining financing. Incubators usually also offer companies rental space with flexible leases, shared basic office services and access to equipment all under one roof.

Business Incubator Framework for Value Creation

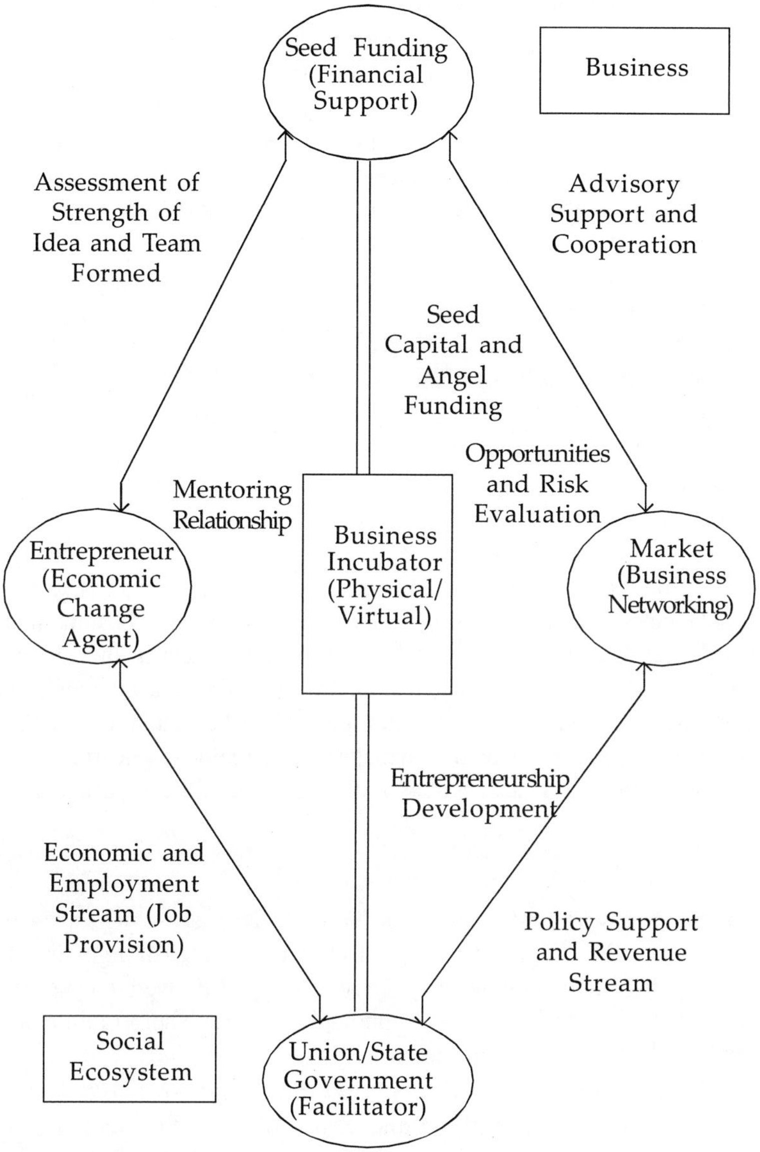

How do incubators help start-ups get funding?

Incubators help resident companies secure capital in a number of ways, including:

- Connecting companies with angel investors (high-net-worth individual investors).
- Working with companies to perfect venture capital presentations and connecting them to venture capitalists.
- Assisting companies in applying for loans.
- Assisting companies in accessing government agency (e.g. NZTE, Technology NZ) business assistance grant programmes.

Role of Business Incubator in the Present Scenario

Business incubator (BI) is an entity, which helps start-up businesses with, all the necessary resources/ support that the start-up needs to evolve and grow as a mature business. Typically, BIs provide incubatees, the start-up businesses supported by incubator, with necessary infrastructure support, technology/ prototype development support, research assistance, help in getting funding, business consulting assistance and do whatever is necessary to make the start-up a success. Business incubators are organizations that support the entrepreneurial process, helping to increase survival rates for innovative startup companies. Entrepreneurs with feasible projects are selected and admitted into the incubators, where they are offered a specialized menu of support resources and services. Resources and services open to an entrepreneur might include such diverse elements as:

- Provision of Physical Space (offices, labs);
- Management Coaching;
- Help in Preparing an Effective Business Plan;
- Administrative Services;
- Technical Support;
- Business Networking;
- Advice on Intellectual Property; and
- Help in Finding Sources of Financing.

An incubator houses a number of new, small businesses that share space and administrative support. Management assistance is usually available and financial assistance is sometimes provided. Incubator managers can aid tenants also by encouraging and assisting them in their planning efforts. However, this study found a wide variance among incubators regarding the amount of planning by tenant firms. Further, the amount of planning by tenants appears to be a function of the amount of planning that is required or encouraged by incubator managers. The major implication is that planning can be affected by incubator managers. Thus, incubator managers should see part of their role as a planning facilitator.

Summing Up

The concept of an incubation was first initiated in the early 20th century itself at the Stanford University, California, USA, when the University President David Starr Jordan urged his staff to make personal investments in a company founded in the early nineties by Cyril Elewell, an engineering school graduate who worked on the first round of 'wireless' technologies, ship-to-shore radio communications where later many **Stanford** graduates began their career.

Prof.**Terman** made a personal investment of US$ 500 to the start-up efforts Hewlett Packard apart from lending his expertise. Recently, **William** and **Flora Hewlett** Foundation gave US$ 400 million to **Stanford** who had no rights to anything created by HP (**Richards** 2002).Thus, technology grew in 60 square miles around **Stanford** University rapidly through the establishment of a strong 'entrepreneurial culture'.

Evolution of Business Incubators Definition

The term incubator literally means a climate-controlled environment that supports the early development, sometimes even saving the life of a 'new born'. In the economic development context, 'incubators' support the transformation of selected early stage business with high potential, into self-sufficient, growing and profitable enterprise. *An incubator can also be defined as 'a facility that provides affordable space, shared office services and business development assistance in an environment conducive to new venture creation, survival and early stage growth'.*

Historic Development of Business Incubators (BIs)

Since 1980s, SEs and the entrepreneurs who drive them-have received serious attention by planners, legislators and development practitioners the world over. New structures and strategies are being explored that will help small businesses to start, survive and grow. The new global economy is increasingly characterized by three processes: the overall lowering of trade barriers and concurrent emergence of regional trading blocs; the shift towards information and service-oriented activities, in order to create new competitive advantages in the world market and the downsizing of large organizations, together with mergers and acquisitions, in the face of this restructuring.

Establishing Business Incubator

While establishing an incubator, the following aspects have to be considered:

(a) Mobilizing government support through funding, fully or partly, to initiate the concept, implement the operations plan and cover initial operations.

(b) Promoting active community participation and private industry membership of the governing and advisory boards, and their involvement as mentors, suppliers and customers.

(c) Organizing tenant support by a small but experienced management staff.

(d) Implementing the selection and graduation criteria, because the essential feature of the incubator is the development of viable tenant business within a relatively short period of time.

(e) Ensuring the financial stability of the incubator itself.

Types of Incubators

During the past decade, a variety of themes have emerged to serve specific kinds of business needs: Targeted population Incubator; International Incubator; Industrial Subcontracting; Single Business Incubators; University Incubators; Technology Business Incubators; Hub Incubator; Virtual Incubator; and Regional or Rural Incubator.

Value Framework of Business Incubator (BI)

Business incubators through their 'value framework' bring about a fine balance between social ecosystem of creating jobs in the society, contributing to the economic growth and 'business ecosystem' of creating customers and suppliers for new products/services to meet the market needs utilizing the funds that are available in the public/private organizations. Value Framework of Business Incubator meanly include: Entrepreneurship Development, Mentoring Relationship, Opportunities Assessment and Risk Evaluation, Seed Funding and Business Networks.

Performance of Business Incubator (BIs) in Industrially Developed Countries

The National Business Incubation Association (NBIA) reports that throughout the United States, small businesses generate approximately two out of every three new jobs. NBIA has estimated recently that roughly 500 business incubators are operating in the United States alone.

In the UK, the survival rate of incubated businesses is around 80 per cent compared with around 50 per cent for those businesses based outside a unit.

What makes a Business Incubator Successful?

An effective feasibility study will help determine whether the proposed project has all the factors crucial to an incubator's success - a solid market, a sound financial base and strong community support.

Business Incubators and Facilitators in India

A Business Incubator is a facility designed to assist businesses to become established and sustainable during their start up phase. Business incubators are programs designed to accelerate the successful development of entrepreneurial companies through an array of business support resources and services, developed and orchestrated by incubator management and offered both in the incubator and through its network of contacts. Successful completion of a business incubation program increases the likelihood that a start-up company will stay in business for the long term. Business incubators provide their resident companies with business support services and resources such as guidance, assistance with business planning and help obtaining financing. Incubators usually also offer companies rental space with flexible leases, shared basic office services and access to equipment all under one roof.

How do Incubators help start-ups get funding?

Incubators help resident companies secure capital in a number of ways, including: Connecting companies with angel investors; Working with companies to perfect venture capital presentations and connecting them to venture capitalists; Assisting companies in applying for loans; and Assisting companies in accessing government agency.

Role of Business Incubator in the Present Scenario

Resources and services open to an entrepreneur might include such diverse elements as:

- Provision of Physical Space (offices, labs);
- Management Coaching;
- Help in Preparing an Effective Business Plan;
- Administrative Services;
- Technical Support;
- Business Networking;
- Advice on Intellectual Property; and
- Help in Finding Sources of Financing.

Case 6- Tech Co.s Adopt Venture Capital Model

Indian technology companies are donning the venture capital hat to inculcate business ideas generated by employees. With the industry maturing beyond process-oriented cost arbitrage solutions, it has become imperative for these companies to be innovative.

Some want to inculcate ideas that could help them enter areas they are not present in, others to create intellectual property–based frameworks and service offerings that are complementary to their existing offerings.

Internal funding of ideas is useful also to retain talented employees who otherwise look to start their own ventures. Mphasis, which does not have a play in the fast growing product engineering space, has just sanctioned funds to a team that is incubating projects in this area. The company is also incubating a team in the payments solutions space, which could strengthen its core focus in banking, insurance and capital markets. "We are looking to develop mini-CEOs who have the flexibility and freedom to grow the business. The plan is to integrate them into the company at a later stage," Ganesh Ayyar, CEO of Mphasis said. Cognizant calls its VC model Cognizant Capital, where employees are encouraged to suggest innovative business.

The company has a fund dedicated for this but did not disclose the size. There is an internal board that vets business plans and allocates funds in a staged model patterned after Silicon Valley VC firms.

The company's Cognizant 2.0 platform, a knowledge management and web 2.0 platforms with social computing characteristics, was incubated from an employee's idea. "We have spent over 1000 person years in building and managing this platform, which would translate to well over $10 million of spend on it," said Sukumar Rajagopal, global head of innovation in Cognizant. He added that innovation had become key for customers as they undergo structural shifts because of globalization, consolidation and virtualization.

Infosys Technologies has incubated companies like On Mobile in the past, but this was proposed from an external party and there was no formalized process in place then. Now the company has established a structure where vertical heads would mentor employees with investable ideas. These would be passed through an Intellectual Property commercializing wing and funded at a later stage if found viable.

Infosys also plans to go a step further in adopting a Google ventures like model where it will take stakes in external start-ups with innovative ideas. Even global companies like SAP are following the incubation model in their India operations.

ANNEXURE VI

List of Business Incubators in India

Name	Contact Person	Address	Contact Information
Centre for Innovation, Incubation and Entrepreneurship (CIIE)	Mr. Kunal Upadhyay– CEO	Indian Institute of Mana gement, Vastrapur, Ahmadabad- 380015	91-79-26324203/ 079 - 26308357 kunal@iimahd.ernet.in www.iimahd.ernet.in/ciie
Society for Innovation and Entrepreneurship (SINE)	Prof. N.L. Sarda-Professor in Charge	IIT Bombay, Powai, Mumbai - 400076	91- 22- 25767072 Direct: 25767710 nls@csc.iitb.ac.in www.sineiitb.org
TBI ON EMBEDDED SYSTEMS AND VLSI DESIGN	Prof.S, Gurunarayanan Co-ordinator, TBI	Birla Institute of Technology and Science, Pilani -333031 Rajasthan.	91-1596-245073 Extn: 252 sguru@bits-pilani.ac.in www.bits-pilani.ac.in
TBI for Composites	Dr.R. Gopalan, Executive Director	Composites Technology Park, 205, Bande Mutt, Kengeri Satellite Township Bangalore-560060	91-80-56997605, 56681005 drgopal@blr.vsnl.net.in
Centre for Biotechnology	Dr. S. Meenakshi sundaram Business Manager	Centre for Biotechnology, Anna University Chennai - 600025	91-44-22350772, 9840348173 eenakshi@annauniv.edu www.annauniv.edu/ biotech
MITCON Biotechnology Centre	Mr. Kulkarni - Chief Executive	MITCON Biotechnology Centre, BAIF Campus Mr. Manibhai Desai Nagar Pune - 411052	91-20-66289451 kulkarni@mitconbt.com www.mitconindia.com
National Design Business Incubator	Mr. Mahesh. K Rovvidi - Chief Operating Officer	National Institute of Design (NID), Paldi, Ahmedabad - 380007	91-79-2662 3692 Extn 5001 ndbi@nid.edu www.ndbiindia.org
Vellore Institute of Technology	Mr. A. Balachandran, Manager- TBI	VITTBI, Vellore Institute of Technology, Vellore-632014	91-416-2243097 - Direct vittbi@vit.ac.in www.vittbi.com
National Institute of Technology, Calicut	Mr. A.V. Francis, Officer on Special Duty, TBI	National Institute of Technology, Calicut - 673601 kerala	91-0495-2286162,Direct - 2286604 avf@nitc.ac.in
J.S.S. Mahavidya peetha	Prof. R. Raghuna - nadan Chief Executive	J.S.S. Academy of Technical Education, C-20/1, Sector -62 Noida 201301	91-120-2401442 ce@jssstepnoida.org www.jssstepnoida.org
ICRISAT	Mr. S. Karuppanchetty - Deputy COO, Mr. Abdul Rahman Ilyas - COO	ICRISAT, 303 Bldg, Patancheru 5023224	91-040-30713222 karuppanchetty @cgiar.org

Kongu Engineering College	Prof. S. Balamurugan- Executive Director - TBI	Kongu Engineering College, Perundurai -638052, Erode, Tamil Nadu.	91- 4294 220562, 220171, Direct 226650 balamurugan@ kongu.ac.in
Advance Materials Technology Incubator	Mr. Sanjay Bharadwaj - Co-ordinator	International Advance Research Centre for Powder Metallurgy & New Materials RCI Road, Opp. Ballapur Village, Hyderabad - 500005	91-40-24457104-7
Center for Entre-preneurship - SPJIMR	Prof. M. Suresh Rao - Program Co-ordinator	S.P. Jain Institute of Management & Research, Munshi Nagar, Dadabhai Road, Andheri (West), Mumbai - 400 058.	+91-22-2623 7454/0396/ 2401 Ext: 211 msrao@spjimr.org www.spjimr.org/cen tre_entrepreneurship/ho me.as p

Source: http://indianwebstartups.com/Incubators.html

23 CORPORATE SOCIAL RESPONSIBILITY

Introduction, The Concept of Corporate Social Responsibility, Corporate Social Responsibility in India, Responsible Companies in the age of Globalization, Changing Views of Management's Responsibility, The Social Responsibility of Business involves Ethics, Arguments for Social Responsibility, Social Responsibilities Strategies, Business as Responsible Person, Why Business should assume Social Responsibility? Whatever is Legal is Ethical? Social Responsibilities of Business towards Different Groups, Indian Scene - Business as a Responsible Person, Business Ethic's Core Responsibilities of Entrepreneurial Performance, Social Responsibility - Modern View, Summing Up.

Introduction

As companies face themselves in the context of globalization, they are increasingly aware that Corporate Social Responsibility can be of direct economic value. Although the prime goal of a company is to generate profits, companies can at the same time contribute to social and environmental objectives by integrating corporate social responsibility as a strategic investment into their business strategy. Whilst so far Corporate Social Responsibility was mainly promoted by a number of multinational companies, it is now also becoming important to small national companies.

A major challenge for companies today is attracting and retaining skilled workers. There is not only an image gain for the companies using CSR, but it is also important for the employees. Within the company, socially responsible practices primarily involve employees and relate to issues such as investing in human capital, health and safety and managing change. While companies increasingly recognize their social responsibility, many of them have yet to adopt management practices that reflect it: company employees and managers need training in order to acquire the necessary skills and competence.

A number of companies with good social and environmental records indicate that CSR activities can result in a better performance and can generate more profits and growth. Research has shown that company CSR programs influence to an extensive degree consumer purchasing decisions, with many investors and employees also being swayed in their choice of companies.

The Concept of Corporate Social Responsibility

The concept of Corporate Social Responsibility was first mentioned 1953, in the publication *'Social Responsibilities of the Businessman'* by **William J. Bowen**. However, the term CSR became only popular in the 1990s, when the German Betapharm, a generic pharmaceutical company decided to implement CSR. The generic market is characterized by an interchangeability of products. In 1997, a halt in sales growth led the company to the realization that in the generic drugs market companies could not differentiate on price or quality. This was the prelude for the company to adopt CSR as an expression of the company's values and as a part of its corporate strategies. By using strategic and social commitment for families with chronically ill children, Betapharm took a strategic advantage.

The term "corporate social responsibility" came in to common use in the late 1960s and early 1970s, after many multinational corporations were formed. The term stakeholder, meaning those on whom an organization's activities have an impact, was used to describe corporate owners beyond shareholders as a result of an influential book by **R. Edward Freeman**, *'Strategic Management: A stakeholder Approach'* in 1984. Proponents argue that corporations make more long-term profits by operating with a perspective, while critics argue that CSR distracts from the economic role of businesses. Others argue CSR is merely window-dressing, or an attempt to pre-empt the role of governments as a watchdog over powerful multinational corporations.

Corporate social responsibility also called corporate conscience, corporate citizenship, social performance, or sustainable responsible business, is a form of corporate self-regulation integrated into a business model. CSR policy functions as a built-in, self-regulating mechanism whereby business monitors and ensures its active compliance with the spirit of the law, ethical standards, and international norms. The goal of CSR is to embrace responsibility for the company's actions and encourage a positive impact through its activities on the environment, consumers, employees, communities, stakeholders and all other members of the public sphere. Furthermore, CSR-focused businesses would proactively promote the public interest by encouraging community growth and development, and voluntarily eliminating practices that harm the public sphere, regardless of legality. CSR is the deliberate inclusion of public interest into corporate decision-making, which is the core business of the company or firm, and the honoring of a triple bottom line: people, planet, profit.

Corporate social responsibility is basically a concept whereby companies decide voluntarily to contribute to a better society and a cleaner environment. Corporate social responsibility is represented by the contributions undertaken by companies to society through its business activities and its social investment. This is also to connect the concept of sustainable development to the company's level. Over the last years an increasing number of companies worldwide started promoting their Corporate Social Responsibility strategies because the customers, the public and the investors expect them to act sustainable as well as responsible. In most cases CSR is a result of a variety of social, environmental and economic pressures.

Corporate Social Responsibility in India

In India there are an existent but small number of companies which practice CSR. This engagement of the Indian economy concentrates mainly on a few old family owned companies, and corporate giants such as the Tata and Birla group companies which have led the way in making corporate social responsibility an intrinsic part of their business plans. These companies have been deeply involved with social development initiatives in the communities surrounding their facilities. Jamshedpur, one of the prominent cities in the northeastern state of Bihar in India, is also known as Tata Nagar and stands out at a beacon for other companies to follow. Jamshedpur was carved out from the jungle a century ago. **TATA's** CSR activities in Jamshedpur include the provision of full health and education expenses for all employees and the management of schools and hospitals.

Inspite of having such life size successful examples, CSR in India is in a very nascent stage. In the informal sector of the Indian economy, which contributes to almost the half of the GNP and where approximately 93% of the Indian workforce is employed, the application of CSR is rare. On the contrary, the fight against poverty, the development of education, as well as the conservation of the environment are not existent in most of the Indian enterprises.

India has an advantage as far as labor is concerned. To some extent, business and capital go to those places where costs are less or standards are lower like the ones in India. But also in India, the demand for responsible and ethical goods is constantly increasing.

To guarantee the supply of responsible and ethical goods, it is especially important to implement a nationwide system of CSR standards.

Corporate philanthropy is not new in India as well and not clear whether they would change their established ways of giving. The $72 billion Tata Group sowed the seed of constructive philanthropy—from setting up an endowment fund to improve education in 1892, to building prominent educational institutes hospitals and performing art centre in the country. Similarly, for the Birla's, philanthropy dates back a hundred years. Birla social vision is integrated into business vision with focus area like education health care and family welfare and women empowerment processes the group spends approximately ₹ 200 crore annually on philanthropy and CSR. In addition, Birla was able to mobilize ₹ 100 crore from funds earmarked by the government towards inclusive growth in Birla's role as catalysts.

While there are more than 400 million people (40% of India's population) below the poverty line, India lags developed economics with philanthropic donations of 0.6% of the country's GDP. Indians gave away about $7.5billion to charity in 2010, compared with $300 billion contributed by the US in 2009.

Twenty-five per cent of the shareholding of Godrej Group holding company (Godrej and Boyce Manufacturing Co.) which owns a large part of the shares of all its companies is held for many decades by the Pirojsha Godrej foundation where the main philanthropy activity is aimed at education health care and environment.

As the number of Indian billionaires grows and their income streams swell and become steady, optimists believe there will be a natural growth in corporate philanthropy. In India philanthropy is more in bound in nature with NGOs and organizations doing philanthropic work going to corporate and individuals for help. According to **Rana Kapoor**, founder/managing director and CEO, YES Bank, responsible banking is deeply embedded within the DNA of the organization wherein it incorporates sustainability principles in its core business operations consistently keeping triple bottom line objectives-people, profit, planet at the forefront of doing business. On the other hand Ahmadabad-based pharma Zydus Cadila prefers volunteer-driven philanthropy rather than chequebook philanthropy. The company's Shiksha Shikshak Jagruti Abhiyan is a mentoring programme to empower teachers in rural communities in Gujarat.

More and more wealthy individuals in India are establishing foundation. The Bajaj trusts have amassed $150 million, and the Bharati Foundation, started by **Sunil Mittal**, has lightly more than $60 million, according to the Bain report. **Azim Premji** recently transferred shares (213 million) worth $2 billion to a trust and the dividends would fund philanthropic work in India. Similarly, Shiv Nadar put in several crores into his pet education project.

Responsible Companies in the Age of Globalization

In recent years CSR has become a fundamental business practice and has gained much attention from the management of large international companies. They understand that a strong CSR program is an essential element in achieving good business practices and effective leadership. Companies have explored that their impact on the economic, social and environmental sector directly affects their relationships with investors, employees and customers.

Corporate social responsibility has long been a hot topic globally. Some corporations have won acclaim and awards for CSR. Two of them were BP, oil giant, and Goldman Sachs, the big investment bank. CSR award-winners have typically engaged in green activism and philanthropy. British Petroleum changes its name to plain BP, and launched a highly successful image-building campaign, labeling itself" beyond Petroleum." This showed BP as a green activities', with a new logo of a green and yellow sun. The company boasted it was among the biggest producers of solar panels and wind power, but these accounted for barely 3% of its total business. "Beyond Petroleum" won two "Campaign of the Year" awards from PR Week, and a gold "Effie" award from the American Marketing Association. BP funded green causes and won green plaudits, brushing aside accusation of "green washing" by green peace. Goldman Sachs was the superstar of Wall Street. Its top executives rose to powerful political positions. Examples include **Robert Rubin**, **Bill Clinton's** treasury secretary; **Hank Paulson**, **Bush's** treasury secretary; **Neel Kashkari**, **Paulson's** bailout chief; **Reuben Jeffrey**, interim treasury investment officer; **Stephen Friedman**, head of the New York Fed; and **Jon Corzine,** former governor of New **Jersey**. **Thomson - Reuter's** columnist **Chrystia Freeland** has called CSR "a fetish encouraged by the philanthropies that feed off it, and funded by the corporate executives who find that it serves their bottom line." Consumers have been willing to pay more and buy more from companies with a CSR halo.

Philanthropy has become the flavor of the season with American billionaires Warren Buffett and Bill Gates visiting India. However the jury is out on how successful their initiative would be here with homegrown corporate giving divergent views on whether there is a need to emulate western concepts. But this has not changed the image that Indians are frugal when it comes to donations. The idea continues to stick to the country even after billion of dollars were put aside as donations by software czar **Azim premji** and telecom tycoon **Sunil Mittal** to set up charitable foundations. **Warren Buffett** has given away 99% of his wealth to charity and philanthropic activities. Nothing can be more powerful a message for corporate than this.

CSR is titled to aid an organization's mission as well as a guide to what the company stands for and will uphold to its consumers. Development business ethics is one of the forms of applied ethics that examines ethical principles and moral or ethical problems that can arise in a business environment. ISO 26000 is the recognized international standard for CSR (currently a Draft International Standard). Public sector organizations (the United Nations for example) adhere to the triple bottom line (TBL). It is widely accepted that CSR adheres to similar principles but with no formal act of legislation. The UN has developed the Principles for Responsible Investment as guidelines for investing entities.

Changing Views of Management's Responsibility

There have been changes in attitudes of managements in taking social responsibility in the past century. Let us examine this:

Phase I. Profit maximizing management: This derives strength from **Adam Smith's** "*Wealth of Nations*", entrepreneurs produce what people want and they want profit. They produce more for self- interest to earn more profit and benefit all. Thus, competition will bring down prices. "What is good for business is good for country". The classical economic doctrine of maximizing profit was against corporate social responsibility.

Phase II. Trusteeship management began with diffusion of corporate ownership as shareholders. So managers are not only to maximize profits, but also serve as trustees of employees, stockholders, suppliers, customers and public at large. They emphasized concern for the interest of others as well as one's own. The change in society's attitudes and expectations is reflected in the socio-economic model of business. This model views business as a sub-system of society.

Phase III. Quality-of-Life Management (QOL): The values of QOL management contrast with both the profit maximiser and the trustee manager. Now the essential equation becomes "what is good for society is good for our company". While accepting profit as essential, the QOL management would neither produce nor sell unsafe or shoddy goods. It also considers government as a partner in a joint effort to solve society's problems.

The Social Responsibility of Business Involves Ethics

The social responsibility of business involves ethics which must be reflected in the philosophy of business organization. To be effective, a sound ethics must be recognized by top management and reflected in the policies of the firm. Members should voluntarily accept it.

Right leadership, integrity, proficiency, commitment to social values of a manager can change the expected behavior of individuals.

Top management commitment, leadership, examples are crucial to corporate ethics/culture. This commitment is communicated in many ways such as–speeches, directives, company publications, policy statements and most important, actions. Top management should establish clear policies that encourage ethical behavior.

Management must assume responsibility for disciplining wrongdoers.

Companies should provide mechanism for 'whistle blowing' as a matter of policy. Any employee becomes aware of unethical behavior should be encouraged to report incident to his superior.

Management should give training/orientation programmes explaining their organization's code of ethics. By offering course in business ethics in MBA programmes helps in creating conscientious managers with a morally responsible approach to business.

Arguments for Social Responsibility

Some relations for business to discharge social responsibility are as under:

(1) ***Public expectations from business has changed:*** It is argued that business exists because it satisfies the needs of society. If business at any time fails to live up to society's expectations, it may become extinct.

(2) ***Society creates better environment for business:*** A firm which is more responsive to improvement of community quality of life will get better community in which to conduct business. Getting manpower will be easy, crime will be less.

(3) ***Public image is improved if firm supports social goals:*** It may gain more customers, better employees.

(4) Before government stretches its long arms, business should discharge its obligations to society. Otherwise society will force government to make laws/regulations.

(5) ***Balance of responsibility with power:*** Business has vast social power and it affects economy and social problems. So equal amount of social responsibility is required.

(6) Business has vast pool of resources (men, talents, money, functional and professional expertise, etc.) and is in better position to work for social goals.

(7) Other institutions have failed to handle social problems, so society is turning to business.

(8) ***Prevention is better than cure:*** If business delays dealing with social problems, it may have to deal with more serious social breakdowns, therefore, business has moral responsibility.

(9) ***Citizenship argument:*** Corporations are citizens having civic duties and responsibilities, corporations must discharge these voluntarily.

Social Responsibilities Strategies

Business responses to social responsibility tend to fall within four degrees/ categories.

(1) ***Social opposition:*** This view is taken by the businesses which feel they have no obligation to society in which they operate. When they are caught for any offence, they cover it up by denying it. For example: M.S. Shoes for price rigging of shares.

(2) ***Social obligation:*** Companies have firm belief that they have obligation to obey the laws. e.g. install safety equipment required by the law.

(3) ***Social response position:*** It is taken by some companies that meet their social obligation as laid by law, and they will go beyond the legal requirement, if benefits out-weigh the costs.

(4) ***Social contribution:*** It is the position taken by companies which believe that they have deep obligation to serve society. They are responsible citizens and are eager to contribute to the improvement of society.

Business as Responsible Person

Business plays a very significant role in economic, social, political and technological affairs. So business owes responsibilities to all segments of society.

Wealth of country is to a great extent controlled by business. This gives business and its executives "enormous power" to affect the lives of employees, consumers, shareholders, etc.

Business is a part of the total environment in which we live, being influenced by it, while being a force in influencing it. The relationship between business and its environment is one of mutual benefit. Both take from and give to various segments. Only through such a relationship can a business survive and prosper.

Modern business has acquired a sense of social responsibility to society in general and to its different segments in particular. The objective of business is to balance the conflicting claims of 'stakeholders'. Business is not confined to productive or commercial activities as its social concern, but it has to take into account social problems which arise due to its activity. Social and ethical considerations must equally concern the business.

Why Business should Assume Social Responsibility?

There are five broad reasons:

(1) **Responding to demands of society:** As business gets larger, the public takes more interest opinion in it, as it has greater impact on the community. Manager responds to public opinion so as to maintain public image of their company. If an organization does not respond, the society will either force it to do so through laws or society may no longer permit it to survive,. e.g. Safety of products etc. The original purpose of corporations was to serve the public good.

(2) **Longer run self-interest of business:** For example,

   (a) Concern for employees can harmonies with company's best interest.

   (b) Responsibilities to shareholders for attracting investment.

   (c) Avoiding environmental pollutions.

(3) **Moral justification:** Business now tends to participate in the development of better world.

(4) Ethical behavior and generation of profits for shareholders is not compatible.

(5) All stakeholders have a "stake" in companies because they can be harmed, if a company behaves unethically.

Government has enacted number of laws to check these practices and to bring in an element of ethics into business. Government will continue to intervene by enacting legislation and impose penalties for unethical practices.

Whatever is Legal is Ethical?

This is to judge the business activities exclusively from the point of view of law. No, this is inadequate view. For example, even though maximization of profit is one primary goal of an organization, but charging unfair prices or exploitation of workers is considered as unethical practices.

Some unethical practices in business are:

- Piracy of products and copyrights;
- Deceptive advertising;
- Bribery, payment of kickbacks, corruption, scandals;
- Employee theft;
- Sexual harassment;
- Discriminatory personal policies, favoritism in promotions, compensation, etc;
- Black-marketing;
- Production of unsafe products;
- Exploitation of environment by manufacturers;
- Giving confidential information/secrets to competitor by employees; and
- Under invoicing.

Such acts indirectly create moral stress and impair the ability of competent managers to act with total integrity. Improved managerial ethical decision making and moral performance can lead to both increased profitability and desirable organizational order.

Social Responsibilities of Business towards Different Groups

An entrepreneur cannot operate in isolation and cannot ignore its social obligations, besides of course, simultaneously ensuring its own existence. The interests of the society provide area of activity for business. The responsibilities and commitment of an entrepreneur towards various reactions of society for various interest groups can be divided under two broad categories:

(1) Internal interest groups.

(2) External interest groups.

Internal Interest Groups

(1) ***Investors:*** The first and foremost responsibility of an entrepreneur is towards its investors. The responsibilities include:

(i) To promote the interests of the shareholders.

(ii) Disclosure of financial informations.

(iii) A fair and regular return on investment in the form of dividends or interests. Fair return has to be more than bank rate and it should be reasonable.

(iv) Shareholders expect security of investment and share in capital appreciation as bonus shares.

(2) ***Workers and Employees:*** The entrepreneur owes its responsibility towards its workers and staff. As human resource is the most valuable asset for any organisation, they should be made to feel that they belong to the organisation. Employees and workers should be treated in such a way that they develop a 'sense of belonging' or a 'sense of oneness' with the organisation.

The traditional concept of "master-servant relationship" has to change the concept of "partnership" between labour and management.

The major areas of relationship are:

(a) ***Wages:*** These should be need-based and productivity-related.

(b) ***Salaries:*** Salaries for managerial personnel are to be linked to responsibilities. Ceiling on managerial remuneration by government to be adhered to. Besides it is to be seen there are not much disparities between wages of employees and salaries of managerial personnel.

(c) ***Relationship between employers and employees:*** There are various lapses on part of employees which include:

- Unsympathetic treatment to employees by supervisors.
- Favoritism in promotions, etc.
- Lack of communication between management and workers.
- Lack of appreciation of meritorious achievements and no condemnation of neglect and lethargy.
- Delay in settling grievances/disputes with employees.
- Lapses on part of employees, i.e. indiscipline in carrying out orders.
- Lack of desire by employees to improve efficiency.
- Role of politically inspired trade unions frequent strikes, gheraos, etc.

External Interest Groups

(1) ***Community (Society):*** The existence of any organisation depends on well wishes of the society. Hence, a entrepreneur has a lot of responsibility towards the community:

(i) Proper steps should be taken to prevent or minimize pollution and maintain ecological balance.
(ii) Adequate employment opportunities should be provided to the people.
(iii) Associate itself actively with community development programmes such as promotion of education, sports, medical facilities, etc.
(iv) Community is ultimate judges of business and its products. So it has to be ensured.

(2) ***Customers/Consumers:*** Customer is the king in the market and his satisfaction is of immense value to a successful entrepreneur. The responsibilities of an entrepreneur towards the customers include:

(i) Understanding consumer needs and to take necessary steps to satisfy these needs.
(ii) To supply proper information to the customers.
(iii) To assure good quality, unadulterated goods and services (ISI, Agmark).
(iv) To provide the required goods and services at reasonable prices.
(v) To offer improved and new products through technical and marketing research. There is no hoarding-concerning of products to raise prices.
(vi) After sales service is available.
(vii) Consumer associations are to be vigilant and to report falling of standards.

(3) ***Government:*** An entrepreneur cannot perform business activities properly without the protection of the government, who is also the best protector of social welfare. Following are the responsibilities of an entrepreneur towards the government:

(i) Paying correct and regular tax to the government.
(ii) Strictly abide the rules and regulation of the provisions of various laws and enactments.
(iii) Should not evade taxes and should not indulge in illegal and corrupt practices.
(iv) Not to purchase political support by unfair means.
(v) Not to corrupt public servants.
(vi) Avoid adulteration.
(vii) To maintain fair trade practices and avoid hoarding and concerning.

Indian Scene - Business as a Responsible Person

Indian socio-economic environment have lent an added significance to the concept of business as a "responsible person".

(1) Indian government has been committed to socialistic pattern of society, in which private interest is to be subordinated to national considerations.
(2) The Constitution of India provides for economic and social justices for all, welfare state, laws have been enacted for social justice.
(3) State financial institutions contribute to a great part of the financial needs of business.
(4) Emergence and development of professional management is wedded to the fulfillment of socio-economic objectives.
(5) There is growing public awareness and consciousness about the role of business in maintaining environmental protection and cleanliness.
(6) Growth of trade unions for protection of employees' interests.
(7) Emergence of consumer protection agencies/forums.

These factors contribute towards corporate social responsibility.

Many large enterprises in India have emphasized their social responsibility in their annual reports, e.g., TISCO, ITC, SAIL, BHEL, ONGC, etc., have developed neighborhood projects. The Sachar Committee (1978) appreciated that some enlightened business houses are contributing to solve problems of rural development, environment protection, control pollution and provision of clean water. They are recognizing social responsibility as development of corporate ethics.

It has to be realized that the future of business depends on its ability and willingness to respond to the changing expectations of society. Corporations must present themselves as being committed to social causes. A global company has to develop global sensitivity.

The corporations are now doing 'social audit', i.e., presenting additional objectives and comprehensive information about organization's social performance which reflect social responsibilities. Some areas covered in social audit are:

(a) ***Social benefits to the staff:*** Various facilities etc.
(b) ***Social benefits to the community:*** Local taxes paid to panchayats, municipality, environmental improvements, and generation of job potential.
(c) ***Social benefits to the public:*** Taxes paid and follow the duties towards government.

Business Ethic's Core Responsibilities of Entrepreneurial Performance

According to **Peter Pratley** (*The Essence of Business Ethics*), "it is important to define core moral responsibilities at a minimum level. By accepting an outspoken commitment to these responsibilities, TQM can gain a lot. The core moral responsibilities are three-fold.

First of all, the corporation is committed to its original and basic moral core responsibility: that is producing goods and services that are functional and safe for the individual consumer. On top of this perennial cornerstone of business, other core activities now have to be added.

The **second** moral commitment therefore concerns the larger environment: environmental core and reduction of resource depletion.

Finally, the third accepted responsibility refers to the quality of the corporation itself as a moral community. At a minimum level this implies the absence of certain abuses.

These three core moral responsibilities for business organizations aim at guaranteeing a minimum of moral excellence. They are linked with an idea of normative entrepreneurial performance and encapsulate what the public may at least expect from an entrepreneur committed to quality management.

These three entrepreneurial responsibilities also imply a redefinition of corporate objectives. It pushes the meaning of the famous separatist expression ‘mind your own businesses’ in quite opposite direction. Corporate mission statements that include these moral responsibilities enlarge the matters for which the public may hold business accountable for by insisting on safe and reliable customer relationships, environmental care and human working conditions.

The entrepreneur should gain this broader perspective as the corporation commits itself to wider human objectives, especially in relation to our common future.

Although industry will go through even more stringent reduction of employee numbers in the future, certain minimum standards, of working conditions should be agreed upon by all those committed to quality goods. This statement is moral appeal for legal means and voluntary covenants to enforce respect for minimum labour rights.

Social Responsibility - Modern View

Peter Drucker argued that management should assume social responsibility. It is thus important for management to consider the impact of every business policy and action upon society. It has to consider the actions are likely to promote the public good, to advance the basic beliefs of society, and to contribute to its stability, strength and harmony.

Drucker observed that managements to consider demands made by the society on the enterprise. It is for management to convert these demands from threats into opportunities with least damage to the enterprise. Here focus is on 'quality of product and customer service'.

'Now feeling (**Sandra Holmes** in her study of 540 Top Executives) is, in addition to making profit, business should help solve social problems whether or not business create these problems.

Summing Up

India has a history of philanthropic activities by individual corporate houses working in diverse fields sometimes not related to their business and has to act as an entity that is unique not only to the home town but also as a model for other countries as well, where an industry in a state has come together to implement CSR in the true sense of letter and spirit. CSR should really mean observing high standards' in the core business of corporations, in dealing with shareholders and clients and the communities they operate in. By all means let corporations also make green and philanthropic efforts.

Changing Views of Management's Responsibility

There have been changes in attitudes of managements in taking social responsibility in the past century. Let us examine this:

Phase I. Profit maximizing management

Phase II. Trusteeship management

Phase III. Quality-of-Life Management

The Social Responsibility of Business Involves Ethics

The social responsibility of business involves ethics which must be reflected in the philosophy of business organization. To be effective, a sound ethics must be recognized by top management and reflected in the policies of the firm. Members should voluntarily accept it. Right leadership, integrity, proficiency, commitment to social values of a manager can change the expected behavior of individuals. Top management commitment, leadership, examples are crucial to corporate ethics/culture. This commitment is communicated in many ways such as - speeches, directives, company publications, policy statements and most important, actions. Top management should establish clear policies that encourage ethical behavior.

Arguments for Social Responsibility

Some relations for business to discharge social responsibility are as under:

(i) Public Expectations from Business has changed.
(ii) Society creates better environment for business.
(iii) Public image is improved if firm supports social goals.
(iv) Before government stretches its long arms, business should discharge its obligations to society.
(v) Balance of responsibility with power.
(vi) Business has vast pool of resources (men, talents, money, functional and professional expertise, etc.) and is in better position to work for social goals.
(vii) Other institutions have failed to handle social problems, so society is turning to business.
(viii) Prevention is better than cure.
(ix) Citizenship argument.

Social Responsibilities Strategies

Business responses to social responsibility tend to fall within four degrees/ categories: Social opposition; Social obligation; Social response position; and Social contribution.

Business as Responsible Person

Business plays a very significant role in economic, social, political and technological affairs. So business owes responsibilities to all segments of society.

Business is a part of the total environment in which we live, being influenced by it, while being a force in influencing it. The relationship between business and its environment is one of mutual benefit. Both take from and give to various segments. Only through such a relationship can a business survive and prosper.

Why Business should Assume Social Responsibility?

There are five broad reasons: Responding to demands of society; Longer run self-interest of business; Moral justification; Ethical behavior and generation of profits for shareholders is not compatible; All stakeholders have a "stake" in companies because they can be harmed, if a company behaves unethically.

Whatever is Legal is Ethical?

This is to judge the business activities exclusively from the point of view of law.

Some unethical practices in business are:

- Piracy of products and copyrights;
- Deceptive advertising;
- Bribery, payment of kickbacks, corruption, scandals;
- Employee theft;
- Sexual harassment;
- Discriminatory personal policies, favoritism in promotions, compensation, etc;
- Black-marketing;
- Production of unsafe products;
- Exploitation of environment by manufacturers;
- Giving confidential information/secrets to competitor by employees; and
- Under invoicing.

Such acts indirectly create moral stress and impair the ability of competent managers to act with total integrity. Improved managerial ethical decision making and moral performance can lead to both increased profitability and desirable organizational order.

Social Responsibilities of Business towards Different Groups

An entrepreneur cannot operate in isolation and cannot ignore its social obligations, besides of course, simultaneously ensuring its own existence. The interests of the society provide area of activity for business. The responsibilities and commitment of an entrepreneur towards various reactions of society for various interest groups can be divided under two broad categories:

(1) Internal interest groups: Investors; Workers and Employees

(2) External interest groups: Community (Society); Customers/Consumers; Government

Indian Scene - Business as a Responsible Person

Indian socio-economic environment have lent an added significance to the concept of business as a "responsible person".

(1) Indian government has been committed to socialistic pattern of society, in which private interest is to be subordinated to national considerations.

(2) The Constitution of India provides for economic and social justices for all, welfare state, laws have been enacted for social justice.

(3) State financial institutions contribute to a great part of the financial needs of business.

(4) Emergence and development of professional management is wedded to the fulfillment of socio-economic objectives.

(5) There is growing public awareness and consciousness about the role of business in maintaining environmental protection and cleanliness.

(6) Growth of trade unions for protection of employees' interests.

(7) Emergence of consumer protection agencies/forums.

The corporations are now doing 'social audit', i.e. presenting additional objectives and comprehensive information about organization's social performance which reflect social responsibilities. Some areas covered in social audit are:

(a) ***Social benefits to the staff:*** Various facilities etc.

(b) ***Social benefits to the community:*** Local taxes paid to panchayats, municipality, environmental improvements, and generation of job potential.

(c) ***Social benefits to the public:*** Taxes paid and follow the duties towards government.

Business Ethic's Core Responsibilities of Entrepreneurial Performance

According to **Peter Pratley** (*The Essence of Business Ethics*), "it is important to define core moral responsibilities at a minimum level. By accepting an outspoken commitment to these responsibilities, TQM can gain a lot. The core moral responsibilities are three-fold.

First of all, the corporation is committed to its original and basic moral core responsibility; the second moral commitment; and finally, the third accepted responsibility.

Social Responsibility - Modern View

Drucker observed that managements to consider demands made by the society on the enterprise. It is for management to convert these demands from threats into opportunities with least damage to the enterprise. Here focus is on 'quality of product and customer service'. 'Now feeling (**Sandra Holmes** in her study of 540 Top Executives) is, in addition to making profit, business should help solve social problems whether or not business create these problems.

24 CONSUMER PROTECTION IN INDIA

Introduction, Growth of Market for Consumers, Development of the Consumer Movement, Consumer Protection in India, Provisions of the Consumer Law, Consumer Protection in Goa, Summing Up.

Introduction

The Consumer movement exercises considerable influence on the socio-economic environment of business. A strong consumer movement is the *sine qua non* of a healthy household sector in an economy.

India has an ancient history of consumer protection. Consumer protection was part of its ancient culture and formed the core of its administration. **Kautilya's** 'Arthasasthra' was the basic law of ancient India and it was strengthened with provisions to protect consumers. Sale of commodities was organized in such a way that general public was not put to any trouble.

If high profits put general public in trouble, then that trade activity was stopped immediately. For traders, profit limit was to be fixed. Even for services, timely response was prescribed for sculpturist, carpenter, tailor, washermen. Thus, for a washermen, it was said that he should return washed clothes in a given time period, i.e., light colored ones in five days, blue dark colored in 6 days and silken, woolen or embroidered in 7 days. Failing this they had to pay fine.

Growth of Market for Consumers

After Independence, a variety of consumer goods flooded Indian markets. The service industry also flourished as the economy progressed. The services like insurance, transport, electricity, housing, entertainment, finance and banking have been made available to the consumers. Well organized sectors of manufacturers and traders with better energy and markets have emerged affecting relationship between the traders and consumers with the help of media both electronic and print.

The advertisement of goods and services in television, newspapers, magazines have created great impact and influence on demand for the same by the consumers though there may be manufacturing defects or difficulties and shortages in the quality, quantity and the purity of the goods or there may be difference in the services rendered.

Thus, it became necessary to protect the consumers from the exploitation and to save them from adulterated and substandard goods and deficiency in services and to safeguard their interest.

In **1969, the Monopolies and Restrictive Trade Practices Act** was passed with the objective to prevent concentration of economic power and to control monopolistic and restrictive trade practices. The provision of the act proceeded on the assumption that if dealers, manufacturers or producers could be prevented from distorting competition, the consumers would get a fair deal. It may then put that the competitive market would provide the required protection to the consumers .but that was only partly true. However, this law did not curb the unfair trade practices of the traders. The unscrupulous manufactures and service providers benefitted as there was no comprehensive law and remedy against them

Most consumer could never hope to get compensation for any loss or suffering caused on account of defective goods or deficient services because seeking relief from a civil court not only involved a long wait for justice but also considerable expenditure on court fee and lawyers.

In course of time , there was greater recognition that consumers need to be protected not only from the effects of the restrictive trade practices but also from the practices which are resorted to by the trade and industry to misled or dupe the consumers.

Development of the Consumer Movement

The consumer movement against unfair trade practices gained momentum in the developed countries. The consumer groups demanded action against the traders and service providers for dealing in substandard goods and poor quality of service.

The first stage of movement was more representational in nature to make consumers aware of their rights through speeches and articles in newspapers and magazines and holding exhibitions. The second stage was direct action based on boycotting of goods, picketing and demonstration. However, direct action had its own limitations that led to the third stage of professionally managed consumer organizations. From educational activities and handling complaints, it ventured into areas involving lobbying, litigation and laboratory testing. This gave good results. Thus, for instance business sector has started taking notice and co-operating with the movement.

The Consumer Movement today is undergoing a silent revolution. The movement is bringing qualitative and quantitative changes in the lives of people. This has enabled the consumer association to organize themselves as an effective force to reckon with. But the path to reach this stage has not been easy. It has been a struggle against bad business which always put profit before fairness in transactions.

Consumer Protection in India

Following the consumer activist's pressure, the parliament enacted The Consumer Protection Act, 1986. It is significant to note that the act recognizes the role of the consumer organizations in assisting the consumer in securing justice through this nation-wide network of consumer disputes redressal agencies as envisaged under the Act.

The Consumer Protection Act, 1986, provide for better protection of the interest of the consumers. The law makes provisions for the establishment of the consumer council and other authorities in the settlement of consumer disputes It seeks to promote and protect the rights of the consumers such as protection against marketing of goods which are hazardous to life and property. The consumers are also given the right to be informed about the quality, quantity, potency, purity, standard and price of goods. Apart from this, the consumers have the right to seek redressal against unfair trade practices or exploitation of the consumers and right to consumer education. The object is also to provide speedy and simple redressal to consumer disputes at district and state level with National Commission at the helm at New Delhi.

Provisions of the Consumer Law

The Consumer Protection Act, seeks to promote and protect the rights of consumers. These rights include the right against the marketing of goods which are hazardous to life and property, the right to be informed about the quality, quantity, potency, purity, standard and price of goods to protect the consumers against unfair trade practices, The right to be assured wherever possible access to a variety of goods at competitive prices, The right to be heard and to be assured that consumers interest will receive due consideration at appropriate forum , the right to seek redressal against unfair trade practices or unscrupulous exploitation of consumers and the right to consumer education.

To widen the scope of securing justice, the law provides that apart from a consumer, any registered voluntary consumer association or the central Government or any state Government, one or more consumers, where there are numerous consumers having the same interest can file a complaint with the consumer forums.

The consumers can approach the court in case of an unfair trade practice or a restrictive trade practice has been adopted by any trader or service provider., the goods brought by him or agreed to be bought by him suffer from one or more defects, the services hired or availed of or agreed to be hired or availed of by him suffer from deficiency in any respect. The consumer can also take recourse to justice if he has been charge for the goods or services in excess of the price fixed.

The Act provides 3-tier quasi-judicial machinery at the national, state and district levels for redressing consumer grievance. *The National Consumer Disputes Redressal Commission at New Delhi was set up in the year 1988.* It has jurisdiction to handle the complaints in which the value of the goods and services exceeds ₹ 1 crore.

A comprehensive definition of the Consumer is provided under the law. *Consumer means a person who buys any goods for a consideration which has been paid or promised or partly paid and partly promised, or under any system of deferred payment.* The consumer includes any user of such goods. A person who obtains such goods for resale or for any commercial purpose is not a consumer. Consumer is entitled to file a complaint for defect in goods and deficiency in service.

More importantly, if the goods are purchased or services are availed by a person exclusively for the purpose of earning his livelihood then such purchase of goods or availing of services cannot be termed as commercial purpose.

Defect means any fault, imperfection or shortcoming in the quality, quantity, potency, purity or standard which is required to be maintained by or under any law for the time being in force under any contract, express or implied or as is claimed by the trader in any manner whatsoever in relation to any goods.

Deficiency means any fault, imperfection, shortcoming or inadequacy in the quality, nature and manner of performance which is required to be maintained by or under any law for the time being in force or has been undertaken to be performed by a person in pursuance of a contract or otherwise in relation to any service.

Service means service of any description which is made available to potential users and includes, but not limited to, the provision of facilities in connection with banking, financing insurance, transport, processing, supply of electrical or other energy, board or lodging or both, housing construction, entertainment, amusement or the purveying of news or other information, but does not include the rendering of any service free of charge or under a contract of personal service.

For ensuring compliance of the orders passed by the consumer courts, the law provides that Where a trader fails or omits to comply with any order made by the District Forum, the State Commission or the National Commission, such trader shall be punishable with imprisonment for a term which shall not be less than one month but which may extend to three years, or with fine which shall not be less than two thousands rupees but which may extend to ten thousand rupees, or with both.

Consumer Protection in Goa

The state government has notified Goa state consumer protection council, district consumer protection councils, consumer conciliation committee and consumer complaint cell after the CPA was enforced. This mechanism is constituted for promoting the interest of the consumer. There are a few voluntary consumer associations functioning in the state. Among these association, Goa civic and consumer action network is at the forefront of consumer awareness programme. Besides this, the government has also taken initiative of consumer awareness.

In the state of Goa there are three consumer forums for redressing the grievances of the consumers. *The Goa State Consumer Disputes Redressal Commission (SCDRC) at Panaji, the Consumer Disputes Redressal Forum (CDRF), North Goa and the Consumer Disputes Redressal Forum, South Goa.*

The SCDRC handles complaints against the opposite parties in which the value of the goods or the services rendered exceeds ₹ 20 lakh. The SCDRC also decided appeals filed against the orders passed by CDRF, North Goa and CDRF, South Goa. Apart from this, the SCDRC has provisional jurisdiction over both the forums in the districts.

As per the data compiled by the SCDRC, out of 2113 cases filed before it , since its inception in 1991, 2067 cases were disposed achieving a total disposal rate of 98 per cent by March 31, 2010. From 1991 to March31 200, the commission disposed of 1008 cases out of 1122 recording disposal of 89 per cent cases. The commission had sentenced five builders to imprisonment for at least three months for deficiency in service to the consumers during this period.

The CDRF, North Goa at Porvorim and CDRF, South Goa at Margao has jurisdiction to decide the disputes in which the value of the goods and services rendered does not exceeds ₹ 20 lakh.

Summing Up

The Consumer movement exercises considerable influence on the socio-economic environment of business. A strong consumer movement is the *sine qua non* of a healthy household sector in an economy.

India has an ancient history of consumer protection. Consumer protection was part of its ancient culture and formed the core of its administration. **Kautilya's** 'Arthasasthra' was the basic law of ancient India and it was strengthened with provisions to protect consumers. Sale of commodities was organized in such a way that general public was not put to any trouble.

Growth of Market for Consumers

After independence, a variety of consumer goods flooded Indian markets. The service industry also flourished as the economy progressed. The services like insurance, transport, electricity, housing, entertainment, finance and banking have been made available to the consumers. Well organized sectors of manufacturers and traders with better energy and markets have emerged affecting relationship between the traders and consumers with the help of media both electronic and print. The advertisement of goods and services in television, newspapers, magazines have created great impact and influence on demand for the same by the consumers though there may be manufacturing defects or difficulties and shortages in the quality, quantity and the purity of the goods or there may be difference in the services rendered. Thus, it became necessary to protect the consumers from the exploitation and to save them from adulterated and substandard goods and deficiency in services and to safeguard their interest. In 1969, the Monopolies and Restrictive Trade Practices Act was passed with the objective to prevent concentration of economic power and to control monopolistic and restrictive trade practices.

Development of the Consumer Movement

The Consumer Movement today is undergoing a silent revolution. The movement is bringing qualitative and quantitative changes in the lives of people. This has enabled the consumer association to organize themselves as an effective force to reckon with. But the path to reach this stage has not been easy. It has been a struggle against bad business which always put profit before fairness in transactions.

Consumer Protection in India

Following the consumer activist's pressure, the parliament enacted The Consumer Protection Act, 1986. **The Consumer Protection Act, 1986,** provides for better protection of the interest of the consumers. The law makes provisions for the establishment of the consumer council and other authorities in the settlement of consumer disputes. The consumers are also given the right to be informed about the quality, quantity, potency, purity, standard and price of goods. Apart from this, the consumers have the right to seek redressal against unfair trade practices or exploitation of the consumers and right to consumer education.

Provisions of the Consumer Law

The Consumer Protection Act seeks to promote and protect the rights of consumers. These rights include the right against the marketing of goods which are hazardous to life and property, the right to be informed about the quality, quantity , potency, purity, standard and price of goods to protect the consumers against unfair trade practices, The right to be assured wherever possible access to a variety of goods at competitive prices, The right to be heard and to be assured that consumers interest will receive due consideration at appropriate forum, the right to seek redressal against unfair trade practices or unscrupulous exploitation of consumers and the right to consumer education.

Consumer Protection in Goa

The state government has notified Goa state consumer protection council, district consumer protection councils, consumer conciliation committee and consumer complaint cell after the CPA was enforced. This mechanism is constituted for promoting the interest of the consumer. There are a few voluntary consumer associations functioning in the state. Among these association, Goa civic and consumer action network is at the forefront of consumer awareness programme. Besides this, the government has also taken initiative of consumer awareness.

In the state of Goa there are three consumer forums for redressing the grievances of the consumers. *The Goa State Consumer Disputes Redressal Commission (SCDRC) at Panaji, the Consumer Disputes Redressal Forum (CDRF), North Goa and the Consumer Disputes Redressal Forum, South Goa.*

B.Com. (Semester - V)
Examination, October 2009
Entrepreneurship Management — I

Duration: 2 hrs **Total marks: 80**

Instructions

(i) All questions are compulsory, however internal choice is available.
(ii) Answer sub-questions in question 1 and question 2 in not more than 100 word each.
(iii) Answer questions from question 3 to question 6 in not more than 400 word each.
(iv) Figure to the right indicates maximum marks to the questions/sub questions.
(v) Paper carries maximum of 80 marks.

1. Answer any four of the following: (4×4 = 16)
   (i) Origin and growth of entrepreneurship.
   (ii) Qualities of an entrepreneur. (any four)
   (iii) Sociological theory of entrepreneurship.
   (iv) Imitative entrepreneur.
   (v) Delphi technique.
   (vi) Concept of Intrapreneur.
2. Answer any four of the following: (4×4 = 16)
   (i) Importance of project report.
   (ii) Feasibility analysis.
   (iii) Project appraisal.
   (iv) Process need as a factor of purposeful innovation.
   (v) Role of incubation centres.
   (vi) Techno-economic analysis.
3. (a) Describe the skills required for entrepreneurship. 12

   OR

   (x) Explain the functions of an entrepreneur. 12
4. (a) Describe the role of entrepreneurship in economic development of our country. 12

   OR

   (x) Explain the various theories of entrepreneurship. 12
5. (a) Describe the steps involved in identification of a business opportunity. 12

   OR

   (x) Explain the contents of a project report. 12
6. (a) Explain the principles of purposeful innovation. 12

   OR

   (x) Explain the factors of purposeful innovation. 12

B.Com. (Semester - V)
Examination, April 2010
Entrepreneurship Management — I

Duration: 2 hrs **Total marks: 80**

Instructions

(i) All questions are compulsory, however internal choice is available.
(ii) Answer sub-questions in question 1 and question 2 in not more than 100 word each.
(iii) Answer questions from question 3 to question 6 in not more than 400 word each.
(iv) Figure to the right indicates maximum marks to the questions/sub questions.
(v) Paper carries maximum of 80 marks.

1. Write short notes on any four of the following: (4×4 = 16)
   (1) Explain any four skills of an entrepreneur.
   (2) Definition and concept of entrepreneurship.
   (3) Intrapreneurs.
   (4) Imitative entrepreneur.
   (5) Field survey techniques.
   (6) Sources of business opportunities.
2. Write short notes on any four of the following: (4×4 = 16)
   (1) Need for market research.
   (2) Project appraisal.
   (3) Entrepreneurial environment.
   (4) Delphi technique.
   (5) Role of incubation centres.
   (6) Break-even analysis.
3. (a) Explain any six qualities of an entrepreneur. 12

   OR

   (x) Explain any six functions of an entrepreneur. 12
4. (a) Comment on the role of an entrepreneur in economic development. 12

   OR

   (x) Explain any six types of entrepreneurs. 12
5. (a) What is SWOT analysis? Explain its significance for an entrepreneur. 12

   OR

   (x) Explain briefly the various elements of project formulation. 12
6. (a) What is Project Report? Explain briefly its general contents. 12

   OR

   (x) Explain the principles of purposeful innovation. 12

B.Com. (Semester - VI)
Examination, April 2010
Entrepreneurship Management — II

Duration: 2 hrs **Total marks: 80**

Instructions

(i) All questions are compulsory, however internal choice is available.
(ii) Answer sub-questions in question 1 and question 2 in not more than 100 word each.
(iii) Answer questions from question 3 to question 6 in not more than 400 word each.
(iv) Figure to the right indicates maximum marks to the questions/sub questions.
(v) Paper carries maximum of 80 marks.

1. Answer any four of the following: (4× 4 = 16)
   (i) What are the features of sole proprietorship?
   (ii) What is the procedure that entrepreneur has to follow in order to get power connection?
   (iii) Explain in brief the functions of Khadi and Village Industries Commission.
   (iv) What are the schemes that Goa Handicraft, Rural and Small-scale Industries Development Corporation offers?
   (v) Explain the seed capital assistance scheme.
   (vi) Explain the Prime Ministers Rozgar Yojana scheme.
2. Answer any four of the following: (4× 4 = 16)
   (i) What are the factors considered for selecting appropriate technology?
   (ii) Selecting an appropriate marketing channel depends on certain criteria. Explain.
   (iii) What are the internal causes of industrial sickness?
   (iv) What are the measures an entrepreneur should take to prevent industrial sickness?
   (v) What are the responsibilities of an entrepreneur towards environment protection?
   (vi) What are the responsibilities of an entrepreneur towards shareholders?
3. i. Explain in detail the registration procedure followed by small-scale units. 12

   OR

   ii. Explain in brief the steps taken by entrepreneurs to set-up a small-scale unit. 12
4. i. What is the role played by National Small Industries Corporation in entrepreneurship development? 12

   OR

   ii. Explain the functions of Economic Development Corporation in detail. 12
5. i. Explain the different external sources of recruitment. 12

   OR

   ii. Explain in brief the long and short-term sources of finance for entrepreneurs. 12
6. i. What is industrial sickness? What are the different symptoms of industrial sickness? 12

   OR

   ii. Explain in detail the incentives and subsidies offered by Government of Goa to entrepreneurs. 12

B.Com. (Semester - V)
Examination, October 2010
Entrepreneurship Management — I

Duration: 2 hrs **Total marks: 80**

Instructions

(i) All questions are compulsory, however internal choice is available.
(ii) Answer sub-questions in question 1 and question 2 in not more than 100 word each.
(iii) Answer questions from question 3 to question 6 in not more than 400 word each.
(iv) Figure to the right indicates maximum marks to the questions/sub questions.
(v) Paper carries maximum of 80 marks.

1. Answer any four of the following: (4× 4 = 16)
   (i) Concept of entrepreneur.
   (ii) Functions of an entrepreneur. (any four)
   (iii) Entrepreneur v/s Intrapreneur. (any four)
   (iv) Psychological theory of entrepreneurship.
   (v) Need for marketing research.
   (vi) Delphi technique.
2. Answer any four of the following: (4× 4 = 16)
   (i) Uses of break-even analysis.
   (ii) Role of incubation centres.
   (iii) Sources of business ideas.
   (iv) New knowledge as a factor of purposeful innovation.
   (v) Project appraisal.
   (vi) Field survey techniques.
3. (a) Explain the qualities that an entrepreneur requires to have. 12

   OR

   (b) Explain the skills of an entrepreneur. 12
4. (a) Explain any 6 types of entrepreneurs. 12

   OR

   (b) Describe the role of entrepreneurs in economic development. 12
5. (a) Explain the concept of SWOT analysis. 12

   OR

   (b) Explain the contents of a project report. 12
6. (a) Explain the different elements in project formulation. 12

   OR

   (b) Explain the principles of purposeful innovation. 12

B.Com. (Semester - VI)
Examination, October 2010
Entrepreneurship Management — II

Duration: 2 hrs **Total marks: 80**

Instructions

(i) All questions are compulsory, however internal choice is available.

(ii) Answer sub-questions in question 1 and question 2 in not more than 100 word each.

(iii) Answer questions from question 3 to question 6 in not more than 400 word each.

(iv) Figure to the right indicates maximum marks to the questions/sub questions.

(v) Paper carries maximum of 80 marks.

I. Answer any four of the following: (4× 4 = 16)

(i) Provisional registration of a SSI unit. (ii) Forms of ownership. (any one)

(iii) Role of district industry centre. (iv) Seed capital assistance.

(v) Duty exemption scheme. (vi) Need for incentives.

II. Answer any four of the following: (4× 4 = 16)

(i) Choice of marketing channel. (any four)

(ii) Importance of training and development. (any four)

(iii) Symptoms of industrial sickness. (any four)

(iv) Corrective measures by Banks and Government.

(v) Environmental concerns.

(vi) Argument for social responsibility.

III. (x) Discuss in brief the meaning, benefits and procedure for registration of a small-scale unit. 12

OR

III. (y) Explain the following steps relating to the setting up of a small industry. 12

(a) Selection of the product (b) Selection of site

(c) Designing capital structure

IV. (x) Write a brief note on the entrepreneurial development schemes of Goa Handicraft, Rural and Small-scale Industries Development Corporation and Economic Development Corporation. 12

OR

IV. (y) Explain the various schemes and incentives offered by the Government of Goa for entrepreneurship. 12

V. (x) What is meant by recruitment? Critically discuss the various sources of recruitment of employees. 12

OR

V. (y) "Working capital is the lifeblood of an enterprise". In the light of above statement, appreciate the importance of working capital for successful functioning of a small enterprise. 12

VI. (x) Define industrial sickness. State and explain the various causes of industrial sickness. 12

OR

VI. (y) Explain the concept of industrial sickness and discuss the various consequences of industrial sickness in India. 12

B.Com. (Semester - VI)
Examination, April/May 2011
Entrepreneurship Management — II

Duration: 2 hrs **Total marks: 80**

Instructions

(i) All questions are compulsory, however internal choice is available.
(ii) Answer sub-questions in question 1 and question 2 in not more than 100 word each.
(iii) Answer questions from question 3 to question 6 in not more than 400 word each.
(iv) Figure to the right indicates maximum marks to the questions/sub questions.
(v) Paper carries maximum of 80 marks.

1. Answer any four of the following: (4×4 = 16)
   (a) What are the features of Private Limited Company?
   (b) What is the procedure that entrepreneur has to follow before placing an order for machinery?
   (c) Explain in brief the role of National Alliance of Young Entrepreneurs.
   (d) What are the schemes that Economic Development Corporation offers?
   (e) What do you mean by incentives and subsidies?
   (f) Explain the Prime Minister's Rozgar Yojana Scheme.
2. Answer any four of the following: (4×4 = 16)
   (a) What are the problems faced by an entrepreneur while marketing industrial products?
   (b) State the different sources of fixed capital.
   (c) What are the internal causes of industrial sickness?
   (d) What are the effects of industrial sickness?
   (e) What are the responsibilities of an entrepreneur towards society?
   (f) What do you mean by "Environmental Impact Assessment"?
3. Explain the following steps relating to setting up of a small-scale industry: 12
   (a) Preliminary preparation of a project report. (b) Procurement and installation of machinery.
   (c) Recruitment and training of staff.

   OR

   How will you choose the most appropriate form of entrepreneurial organization for your business? 12
4. What is the role played by Entrepreneurship Development Institute of India in entrepreneurship development? 12

   OR

   Explain the functions of a State Financial Corporation. 12
5. What is Fixed Capital? Explain its significance in business enterprise. 12

   OR

   Explain the factors which need special thought while selecting a precise channel of distribution. 12
6. What is Industrial Sickness? Explain the different counteractive ways to prevent industrial sickness. 12

   OR

   Explain in detail the incentives and subsidies offered by Government of Goa to Entrepreneurs. 12

B.Com. (Semester - V)
Examination, April/May 2011
Entrepreneurship Management — I

Duration: 2 hrs **Total marks: 80**

Instructions

(i) All questions are compulsory, however internal choice is available.
(ii) Answer sub-questions in question 1 and question 2 in not more than 100 word each.
(iii) Answer questions from question 3 to question 6 in not more than 400 word each.
(iv) Figure to the right indicates maximum marks to the questions/sub questions.
(v) Paper carries maximum of 80 marks.

1. Write short notes on any four of the following: $(4\times4 = 16)$
   (a) Explain any four skills of an entrepreneur.
   (b) Integrated theory of entrepreneurship.
   (c) Intrapreneur.
   (d) Women entrepreneur.
   (e) Economic factors influencing entrepreneurship.
   (f) Market research.
2. Write short notes on any four of the following: $(4\times4 = 16)$
   (a) Unexpected success/failure as a factor of innovation.
   (b) Incubation centres.
   (c) Project appraisal.
   (d) Significance of project report.
   (e) Social cost benefit analysis.
   (f) Break-even analysis.
3. (a) Define entrepreneurship and explain any six functions of an entrepreneur. 12

   OR

   (b) "Success in entrepreneurship depends on certain coherent qualities". Comment. 12
4. (a) Elucidate the role of entrepreneurship in the upliftment of the economy. 12

   OR

   (b) Explain any six types of entrepreneurs. 12
5. (a) What is project formulation? Explain the various steps involved in the project formulation. 12

   OR

   (b) Comment on SWOT as a technique of identifying and analyzing a business opportunity by an entrepreneur. 12
6. (a) What is project report? Explain general contents to be embodied in a project report for its impressive presentation. 12

   OR

   (b) Explain the Peter Druckers views on the dos and don'ts in purposeful innovation. 12

B.Com. (Semester - V)
Examination, Oct/Nov. 2011
Entrepreneurship Management — I

Duration: 2 hrs **Total marks: 80**

Instructions

(i) All questions are compulsory, however internal choice is available.
(ii) Answer sub-questions in question 1 and question 2 in not more than 100 word each.
(iii) Answer questions from question 3 to question 6 in not more than 400 word each.
(iv) Figure to the right indicates maximum marks to the questions/sub questions.
(v) Paper carries maximum of 80 marks.

1. Write short notes on any four of the following: (4×4 = 16)
   (a) Explain Procuring and Mobilizing resources as a function of an Entrepreneur.
   (b) Intrapreneurs.
   (c) Economic Theory of Entrepreneurship.
   (d) Delphi Technique.
   (e) Importance of SWOT analysis of a Project Idea.
   (f) Explain any four qualities of an Entrepreneur.
2. Attempt any four of the following: (4×4 = 16)
   (a) Preliminary evaluation of a project idea.
   (b) Significance of a project report.
   (c) Social cost benefit analysis.
   (d) Need for innovation in entrepreneurship.
   (e) Role of entrepreneurial incubation centres.
   (f) Techno-economic analysis.
3. (a) Define Entrepreneurship and explain the skills required in entrepreneurship. 12

   OR

   (b) Explain the following theories on entrepreneurship. 12
   (i) Psychological theory.
   (ii) Integrated theory.
4. (a) Explain the various types of Entrepreneurs. 12

   OR

   (b) Explain briefly the Role of Entrepreneur in Economic Development.
5. (a) What is Market Survey? Explain the various techniques of Market Survey. 12

   OR

   (b) Explain briefly the various elements of Project Formulation.
6. (a) What is a Project Report? Explain the general contents of a Project Report. 12

   OR

   (b) What is purposeful innovation? Explain the principles of purposeful innovation suggested by Peter Drucker.

B.Com. (Semester - VI)
Examination, Oct/Nov. 2011
Entrepreneurship Management — II

Duration: 2 hrs **Total marks: 80**

Instructions

(i) All questions are compulsory, however internal choice is available.
(ii) Answer sub-questions in question 1 and question 2 in not more than 100 word each.
(iii) Answer questions from question 3 to question 6 in not more than 400 word each.
(iv) Figure to the right indicates maximum marks to the questions/sub questions.
(v) Paper carries maximum of 80 marks.

1. Write short notes on any four of the following: (4×4=16)
   (a) Provisional and Permannent Registration of a SSI Unit.
   (b) Role Small Industries Development Organisation.
   (c) Adverse effects of offering Incentives to Entrepreneurs.
   (d) Special incentives offered for I.T. sector in Goa.
   (e) Commercial Banks assistance to entrepreneurs.
   (f) Factors influencing choice of location and site of project.
2. Write short notes on any four of the following: (4×4=16)
   (a) Material Management.
   (b) Marketing problems faced by SSI Units.
   (c) Internal causes of industrial sickness.
   (d) Social responsibility of entrepreneurs towards employees.
   (e) Training and development of human resources in SSI units.
   (f) Fixed capital and Working capital.
3. (a) State and explain briefly the steps involved in setting up of a SSI unit. 12

   OR

   (b) Comment on the role and functions of Goa Industrial Development Corporation.
4. (a) Comment on the role and functions of Micro Small and Medium Enterprises Service Institute. 12

   OR

   (b) Explain the role of Government in promoting small scale industies in Goa.
5. (a) What is Inventory Control? Why it is required in SSI units? Explain the various methods of Inventory Control. 12

   OR

   (b) What is Human Resource Management? Explain the various sources of recruitment for a SSI unit.
6. (a) "Industrial sickness is an epidemic in the small scale sector" comment on the statement and explain the measures in tackling this problem. 12

   OR

   (b) Explain the social responsibilities of an entrepreneur towards customers and Society at large.

B.Com. (Semester - VI)
Examination, April 2012
ENTREPRENEURSHIP MANAGEMENT- II

Duration: 2 hrs **Total marks: 80**

Instructions

(i) All questions are compulsory, however internal choice is available.
(ii) Answer sub-questions in question 1 and question 2 in not more than 100 word each.
(iii) Answer questions from question 3 to question 6 in not more than 400 word each.
(iv) Figure to the right indicates maximum marks to the questions/sub questions.
(v) Paper carries maximum of 80 marks.

1. Answer any four of the following: (4×4=16)
   (a) Which are the different NOC's required for setting up of a small-scale industrial unit?
   (b) Explain the procedure to be followed by an entrepreneur to obtain a power connection.
   (c) Discuss the functions of National Small Industries Corporation Limited.
   (d) Explain in brief the role played by commercial banks.
   (e) Evaluate the tax benefits available for small-scale industries.
   (f) Discuss the Seed Capital Assistance Scheme.
2. Answer any four of the following: (4×4=16)
   (a) Evaluate the importance of purchase department in small scale units.
   (b) Explain the factors influencing choice of channels.
   (c) Discuss the symptoms of industrial sickness.
   (d) Comment on the impact of industrial sickness.
   (e) Evaluate the responsibilities of an entrepreneur towards his employees.
   (f) Comment on the responsibilities of an entrepreneur towards protecting the environment.
3. (a) Describe in detail any four forms of organization for an entrepreneur to undertake a business. 12

   OR

   (b) Explain in detail the registration procedure followed by small-scale units.
4. (a) Explain the functions of Goa Industrial Development Corporation. 12

   OR

   (b) Describe the role played by Khadi and Village Industrial Commission.
5. (a) What is Production Management? Describe the important factors which influence choice of technology. 12

   OR

   (b) What is Recruitment? Explain the various sources of recruitment.
6. (a) Explain in detail the incentives and subsidies offered by Central Government to an entrepreneur. 12

   OR

   (b) Explain the various causes and remedial measures to overcome industrial sickness.

B.Com. (Semester - V)
Examination, April 2012
ENTREPRENEURSHIP MANAGEMENT- I

Duration: 2 hrs **Total marks: 80**

Instructions

(i) All questions are compulsory, however internal choice is available.
(ii) Answer sub-questions in question 1 and question 2 in not more than 100 word each.
(iii) Answer questions from question 3 to question 6 in not more than 400 word each.
(iv) Figure to the right indicates maximum marks to the questions/sub questions.
(v) Paper carries maximum of 80 marks.

1. Attempt any four of the following: (4×4=16)
   (i) Need for market orientation for an entrepreneur.
   (ii) Integrated theory of entrepreneurship.
   (iii) Distinguish between desk research and field survey technique.
   (iv) Distinguish between entrepreneur and intrapreneur.
   (v) Need and importance of a market research.
   (vi) Skills required for an entrepreneur.
2. Attempt any four of the following: (4×4=16)
   i. Techno-economic analysis.
   ii. Social cost-benefit analysis.
   iii. Sources of business ideas.
   iv. Financial analysis.
   v. Entrepreneurial incubation centres.
   vi. Changes in demography as a factor of purposeful innovation.
3. (a) Define entrepreneurship and explain the Various types of entrepreneurs. 12

   OR

   (b) Explain briefly the various functions of an entrepreneur.
4. (a) Account for the growth of entrepreneurship in India and also highlight the role of entrepreneur in economic development. 12

   OR

   (b) Explain the various environmental factors which influence entrepreneurial growth
5. (a) "Project formulation involves objectives evaluation of various elements. Highlight these elements and suggest its significance in entrepreneurship. 12

   OR

   (b) What is market research? Explain the various techniques of market research.
6. (a) Explain briefly the guiding principles suggested by Peter Drucker for successful innovation. 12

   OR

   (b) What is a project report? What are the various purposes served by a systematic project report?

Model Question Paper Set I
B.Com. (Semester - V) Examination
ENTREPRENEURSHIP MANAGEMENT- I

Duration: 2 hrs **Total marks: 80**

Instructions

(i) All questions are compulsory, however internal choice is available.
(ii) Answer sub-questions in question 1 and question 2 in not more than 100 word each.
(iii) Answer questions from question 3 to question 6 in not more than 400 word each.
(iv) Figure to the right indicates maximum marks to the questions/sub questions.
(v) Paper carries maximum of 80 marks.

I. Write short notes on any four of the following: (4×4=16)
  (a) Any four functions of an entrepreneur.
  (b) Economic theory of entrepreneurship.
  (c) Entrepreneur v/s Intrapreneur.
  (d) Concept of an entrepreneur.
  (e) Explain any four qualities of an entrepreneur.
  (f) Product-oriented technique.

II. Write short notes on any four of the following: (4×4=16)
  (a) The characteristics of knowledge-based innovation.
  (b) Role of incubation centres.
  (c) Break-even analysis.
  (d) Attributes characterize projects.
  (e) SWOT Analysis.
  (f) Any four sources of ideas.

III. (a) Define entrepreneurship and explain any six skills of an entrepreneur. 12

OR

(b) Who is an entrepreneur? Briefly describe the evolution of entrepreneur definitions. 12

IV. (a) Elucidate role of entrepreneurs in the present milieu. 12

OR

(b) Explain the following: 12
  i. Innovative Entrepreneur.
  ii. Imitative entrepreneur.
  iii. Fabian entrepreneur.
  iv. Drone entrepreneur.

V. (a) What is Project Formulation? Explain the various elements of project formulation. 12

OR

(b) What is a Market Survey? Describe briefly the different techniques of market survey. 12

VI. (a) What is a Project Report? Elucidate the significance of project report. 12

OR

(b) Explain the briefly the seven sources for innovation opportunity. 12

Model Question Paper Set II
B.Com. (Semester - VI) Examination
ENTREPRENEURSHIP MANAGEMENT- II

Duration: 2 hrs **Total marks: 80**

Instructions

(i) All questions are compulsory, however internal choice is available.
(ii) Answer sub-questions in question 1 and question 2 in not more than 100 word each.
(iii) Answer questions from question 3 to question 6 in not more than 400 word each.
(iv) Figure to the right indicates maximum marks to the questions/sub questions.
(v) Paper carries maximum of 80 marks.

I. Answer any four of the following: (4×4=16)
 (i) Provisional and Permanent registration of a SSI unit.
 (ii) Write a note on Micro, Small and Medium enterprise in Goa.
 (iii) Narrate the role of Economic Development Corporation.
 (iv) Write a brief note on Goa Handicraft, Rural and Small-scale Industries Development Corporation.
 (v) What do you mean by the term "Subsidy" and "Incentive"?
 (vi) What are the needs for incentives?

II. Answer any four of the following: (4×4=16)
 (i) What are the Marketing Problems faced by SSI units? (any four)
 (ii) Write a brief note on Management of Working Capital.
 (iii) What are the Symptoms of industrial sickness? (any four)
 (iv) Write a brief note on Sick Industrial Companies Act.
 (v) "Environmental concern is the need of the hour" Elucidate
 (vi) State the reason why business should assume Social Responsibility.

III. (a) Discuss the factors determining a suitable form of business organization. 12

OR

(b) Explain briefly the steps involved in setting up of a new venture.

IV. (a) What are the roles played by District Rural Development Agency in entrepreneurship development? 12

OR

(b) Explain the functions of District Industrial Centre in detail.

V. (a) What is meant by distribution channels? Explain briefly the channels of distribution for industrial goods. 12

OR

(b) State and explain the factors influencing choice of technology for a business unit.

VI. (a) State and explain the external and internal causes of Industrial Sickness. 12

OR

(b) Explain in detail the schemes and incentives offered by the Government of Goa to inculcate entrepreneurship qualities.

Model Question Paper Set III
B.Com. (Semester - VI) Examination
ENTREPRENEURSHIP MANAGEMENT- II

Duration: 2 hrs **Total marks: 80**

Instructions

(i) All questions are compulsory, however internal choice is available.
(ii) Answer sub-questions in question 1 and question 2 in not more than 100 word each.
(iii) Answer questions from question 3 to question 6 in not more than 400 word each.
(iv) Figure to the right indicates maximum marks to the questions/sub questions.
(v) Paper carries maximum of 80 marks.

I. Answer any four of the following: (4×4=16)
(a) What are the benefits of registering a Business Unit?
(b) What are the factors influencing a suitable form of business organization? (any four)
(c) Narrate the role of Small Industries Development Bank of India.
(d) What are the schemes that Khadi and village Industries Commission offers?
(e) Write a brief note on Seed Capital Assistance.
(f) Explain the Chief Ministers Rozgar Yojana Scheme.

II Answer any four of the following: (4×4=16)
(a) What are the problems faced by an entrepreneur while marketing industrial products?
(b) Write a brief note on Management of Fixed Capital.
(c) What are the external causes of industrial sickness? (any four)
(d) What are the effects of industrial sickness? (any four)
(e) State the arguments for and against social responsibility.
(f) What do you mean by "Environmental Impact Assessment"?

III. (a) Critically examine the various forms of ownership available for setting up a new venture. 12

OR

(b) Explain briefly the steps involved in setting up of a new venture.

IV. (a) What is the role played by Goa Industrial Development Corporation? 12

OR

(b) What are functions of National Institute for Entrepreneurship and Small Business Development?

V. (a) What do you mean by Working Capital? Briefly narrate the sources of Working Capital Finance. 12

OR

(b) What is meant by recruitment? Briefly explain the importance of recruitment methods.

VI. (a) State and explain the Social Responsibility of Entrepreneurs towards various Stakeholders. 12

OR

(b) Explain the concept of industrial sickness and discuss the various remedial measures to overcome and avoid industrial sickness in India.

REFERENCE & READING SUGGESTED

Books

- Vasant, Desai, "*Dynamics of Entrepreneurial Development and Management*", Sixth Revised Edition Himalaya Publishing House, Mumbai, Delhi, Nagpur, 2001.
- Narender, K Chadha., "*Human Resource Management, Issued Case Studies and Experimental Exercises*, 2nd Revised Edition, Shri Sai Printographer educational publishers, New Delhi, 2002.
- C.B., Gupta, N.P.,Srinivasan., "*Entrepreneurial Development*", Reprint, Sultan Chand and Sons, New Delhi, 2008.
- Manmohan, Prasad, "*Management Concepts and Practices*, Third Revised Edition, Himalaya Publishing House Mumbai, Delhi, Nagpur, 2003.
- N.G. Kale, "*Principles and Practice of Marketing*" Vipul Prakashan, Bombay.
- Vijay, Dubey, "*Production Management*" King Books, Delhi, 2001-02.
- S.N. Maheshwari, "*Elements of Financial Management*" Fifth Revised and Enlarged edition, Sultan Chand and Sons, New Delhi, 1997.
- Mahesh V. Joshi, "*Towards Success, The Basic Elements of Entrepreneurship*", 1st edition, Abhyayan Publishers and distributors, Delhi, 2004.
- S.S. Khanka, "*Entrepreneurial Development*" First Edition, S. Chand and Company Ltd., New Delhi, 1999.
- Millier, Paul, "*Marketing the Unknown, Developing Market Strategies for Technical Innovations*", John Wiley and Sons, Ltd., 1999.
- Abbas H, Lokhandwala, Anwar, Shaikh, "*Business Entrepreneurship*" First edition, Shri D.K. Furia, Nirali Prakashan, October, 1999.
- S.A. Sherlekar, V.S., Sherlekar, "*Global Marketing Management*" Millennium edition, Himalaya Publishing House, Mumbai, Delhi, Nagpur, Bangalore, Hyderabad, 2000.
- S.K. Misra, V.K. Puri, "*Indian Economy – Its Development Experience*" twenty sixth edition, Himalaya Publishing House, Mumbai, New Delhi, Nagpur, Bangalore, Hyderabad, Chennai, Pune, Lucknow, Ahmadabad, Ernakulum 2008.
- Rajeev Roy, "*Entrepreneurship*", fourth impression, Published by Oxford University Press YMCA Library Building, Jai Singh Road, New Delhi 110001, 2010.
- Robert D. Hisrich, Michael P. Peters, Dean A Shepherd, "*Entrepreneurship*", Sixth edition, Tata McGraw-Hill Publishing Company Limited New Delhi, 2007.
- S. A. Chunawalla, "*Consumer Behaviour*", second revised edition, Himalaya Publishing House, Mumbai, New Delhi, Nagpur, Bangalore, Hyderabad, Chennai, Pune, Luck now, Ahmadabad, Ernakulum, 2005.
- Goa State industries association, a complete guide to industries and enterprises in Goa, 2008 edition.

ARTICLES/ GAZETTE/MAGAZINES/NEWSPAPERS

- D. Joel Edwinraj (2007 Annual issue) "Micro finance to rural poor through Self Help Groups", published by *Journal of Co-operative Management,* Vaikunth Mehta National Institute of Co-operative Management University Road, Pune.
- B. Tamilmani (2009) "Rural Women Micro entrepreneurs: An empirical study on their social profile, business aspects and economic impact", Published by The Icfai University, *Journal of Entrepreneurship Development;* Vol. VI No. 2.
- S. Mukherjee (2009) "Women entrepreneurship development: The catalytic role of NGOs" Published by The Icfai University, *Journal of Entrepreneurship Development;* Vol. VI No. 2.
- S. Abbasian &C. Bildt (2009)"Empowerment through entrepreneurship: a tool for integration among immigrant women", Published by The Icfai University, *Journal of Entrepreneurship Development.* Vol. VI No. 3 & 4 Sep & Dec.
- Pednekar A.P. (2010) "Women Empowerment through Entrepreneurship - A Case Study of Goa" 63rd Annual All India Commerce Conference organized by Faculty of Commerce Goa University.
- Pednekar A.P. (2011) "A Study of Self Help Groups as a Thriving Strategy and Achievable Loom to Empower Goan Women" in *"Entrepreneurship Business Review Bi-Annual Referred International Journal"* Vol 1 No 1 Published by Director Centre for ESBM, Maharshi Dayanand Saraswati University, Ajmer.
- Official Gazette, Govt. of Goa, Dept. of Finance, Revenue and expenditure Division, office of the Commissioner of Excise, Panaji – Goa, Series I No. 42.
- Edgar, Thorpe, Showick, Thorpe, the Pearson General Studies for the UPSC Civil Services Preliminary Examination, Manual 2007.
- Competition Refresher April 2006 "Special Economic Zones (SEZs) Act".
- *The Times of India*, Goa Friday, February 11, 2011, "plastic bags now come at a price".p.6
- *The Times of India*, Goa Tuesday, February 8, 2011, "Margao AC toilet finally gets NOC from *UHC"*. p.4
- *The Times of India*, Goa Tuesday, March 1st, 2011, "green light blinks for green cars gadgets". p.9
- *The Financial Express*, Goa Monday, February 14, 2011, "green norms make NYMEX, ice mull switch to diesel benchmark". p.16
- *The Times of India*, Goa, Thursday, March 24, 2011, "Giving away 99% of Wealth…there can't be a more powerful message".

WEBLIOGRAPHY

- www.in.reset.to/knowledge/corporate-social-responsibility-csr-%E2%80%93-societal-responsibility-companies?gclid=CNGQm66U-KcCFYZ66wod4nP0qg
- www.norwayemb.org.in/News_and_events/Business/CSR-in-India/
- www.icmrindia.org/casestudies/catalogue/Business%20Ethics/BECG093.htm
- www.orissadiary.com/ShowBussinessNews.asp?id=25446
- www.en.wikipedia.org/wiki/Corporate_social_responsibility
- www.entrepreneurship.org
- www.entrepreneur.com
- www.wikipedia.com